MUP ACADEMIC
DEFENCE STUDIES

Series editors
Dr Peter J. Dean and Associate Professor Brendan Taylor

The aim of this series is to publish outstanding works of research on strategy and warfare with a focus on Australia and the region. Books in the series take a broad approach to defence studies, examining war in its numerous forms, including military, strategic, political and historic aspects. The series focus is principally on the hard power elements of military studies, in particular the use or threatened use of armed force in international affairs. This includes the history of military operations across the spectrum of conflict, Asia's strategic transformation and strategic policy options for Australia and the region. Books in the series consist of either edited or single-author works that are academically rigorous and accessible to both academics and the interested general reader.

Dr **Peter J Dean** is a Fellow and Director of Studies at the Strategic and Defence Studies Centre, Australian National University, a managing editor of the journal *Security Challenges*, contributing editor for *Global War Studies* and the current Fulbright Fellow in Australia–United States Alliance Studies. Peter is the author/editor of numerous works on Australian military history and defence policy, including *The Architect of Victory* (2010) and *Australia 1942: In the Shadow of War* (2012).

Dr **Stephan Frühling** is a Senior Lecturer at the Strategic and Defence Studies Centre, Australian National University, and a managing editor of the journal *Security Challenges*. He is the author of *Defence Planning and Uncertainty* (2014) and *A History of Australian Defence Policy Since 1945* (2009).

Dr **Brendan Taylor** is Head of the Strategic and Defence Studies Centre, Australian National University. He is a specialist on great power strategic relations in the Asia–Pacific, economic sanctions and Asian security architecture. His work has featured in such leading academic journals as *International Affairs*, *Survival* and the *Australian Journal of International Affairs*. He is the author/editor of five books, including *Australia as an Asia–Pacific Regional Power* (2007) and *Sanctions as Grand Strategy* (2010).

Australia's Defence

Towards a New Era?

Edited by
Peter J Dean, Stephan Frühling,
Brendan Taylor

MELBOURNE
UNIVERSITY
PRESS

MELBOURNE UNIVERSITY PUBLISHING
An imprint of Melbourne University Publishing Limited
11-15 Argyle Place South, Carlton, Victoria 3053, Australia
mup-info@unimelb.edu.au
www.mup.com.au

First published 2014
Text © Peter J Dean, Stephan Frühling, Brendan Taylor 2014
Design and typography © Melbourne University Publishing Limited, 2014

Cover design by Phil Campbell Designs
Typeset by J & M Typesetting
Printed in Australia by OPUS Group

National Library of Australia Cataloguing-in-Publication entry

Dean, Peter, author.

Australia's defence: towards a new era?/Peter Dean, Brendan Taylor and Stephan Fruehling.

9780522866070 (paperback)

9780522866087 (ebook)

Includes bibliographical references.

National security—Australia—21st century.

Australia—Defenses.

Australia—Military policy—21st century.

Other Authors/Contributors:

Taylor, Brendon, author.

Fruehling, Stephan, author.

327.1700994

Contents

Maps, Charts, Graphs   vii

List of Acronyms   ix

Acknowledgements   xii

Contributors   xiii

Introduction   1
Brendan Taylor

Part I: The National Context

1   Politics and the Defence Debate   11
    Russell Trood

2   Australia as a Middle Power   37
    Andrew Carr

3   Public Attitudes to Defence   61
    Charles Miller

Part II: International Context

4   Australia and Northeast Asia   81
    Amy King

5   Australia, Indonesia and Southeast Asia   107
    John Blaxland

6   Australia and the South Pacific   140
    Joanne Wallis

Part III: Strategy

7   Defence Policymaking   165
    Paul Dibb

8   Australian Strategy and Strategic Policy   184
    Stephan Frühling

9 ANZUS: The 'Alliance' and its Future in Asia   206
   Peter J Dean

Part IV: Size and State of Our Defences

10 The Evolution of the ADF into a Joint Force   237
   James Goldrick

11 Funding Australian Defence   257
   Mark Thomson

12 Developing ADF Force Structure and Posture   283
   Richard Brabin-Smith

Appendix: ANZUS Treaty   305

Bibliography   309

Index   327

Maps, Charts, Graphs

Table 2.1: Comparison of Population, Economy, Defence
Spending and Armed Forces of Middle Power Countries   49

Figure 4.1: Australia's Trade with Japan, Korea, the United
States and Great Britain as a percentage of Australia's Total
Foreign Trade   85

Figure 5.1: Australia and the Region   109

Box 5.1: Agreement between the Republic of Indonesia and
Australia on the Framework for Security Cooperation
(commonly known as the Lombok Treaty)   114

Box 5.2: Five Powers Defence Arrangements   120

Figure 6.1: Map of the South Pacific Region   141

Figure 8.1: China's Anti-Access-Area Denial Ranges   199

Figure 10.1: Headquarters Joint Command Structure   242

Figure 11.1: Australian Defence Spending as a Share of GDP,
1901–2013   258

Figure 11.2: Australian Defence Personnel Numbers, 1950–2013   260

Figure 11.3: Recent and Prospective Defence Spending   264

Figure 11.4: Average US Navy Cost per Active Duty Vessel,
1951–2011   267

Figure 11.5: Comparative Australian and United States Defence
Spending, 1950–2012   270

Figure 11.6: Projected Number of Australians
Aged 18–26 Years   273

Figure 11.7: The Defence Organisation   276

Table 11.1: Growth in Command and Management Overheads   280
in Defence

List of Acronyms

AANZFTA	ASEAN Australia-New Zealand Free Trade Agreement
ABS	Australian Bureau of Statistics
ACSC	Australian Command and Staff College
ADC	Australian Defence College
ADF	Australian Defence Force
ADFA	Australian Defence Force Academy
ADFWC	Australian Defence Force Warfare Centre
ADIZ	Air Defence Identification Zone
ADMM-Plus	ASEAN Defence Ministers Meeting-Plus
AES	Australian Election Survey
AIF	Australian Imperial Force
AJASS	Australian Joint Anti-Submarine School
AJMWC	Australian Joint Maritime Warfare Centre
AMSA	Australian Maritime Safety Authority
ANZUS	Australian, New Zealand, United States Security Treaty
APC	Asia-Pacific Community
APEC	Asia-Pacific Economic Cooperation
ARF	ASEAN Regional Forum
ASEAN	Association of Southeast Asian Nations
ASEAN ISIS	ASEAN Institutes of Strategic and International Studies
ASPI	Australian Strategic Policy Institute
AST	Australian Theatre
ASW	anti-submarine warfare
AUSMIN	Australia United States Ministerial
AWD	Air Warfare Destroyers
BCOF	British Commonwealth Occupation Force
BPC	Border Protection Command
CAS	close air support
CDF	Chief of the Defence Force
CJOPS	Chief of Joint Operations
CSCA	Conference on Security and Cooperation for Asia
CSP	Commercial Support Program
DCP	Australia-Philippines Defence Cooperation Program
Defence	Department of Defence
DJFHQ	Deployable Joint Force Headquarters
DMO	Defence Materiel Organisation

DoA	Defence of Australia doctrine
DRP	Defence Reform Program
DSD	Defence Signals Directorate
DSTO	Defence Science and Technology Organisation
EEZ	exclusive economic zones
ESA	East Asia Summit
FBS	Fleet Battle Staff
FPDA	Five Power Defence Arrangements
HADR	humanitarian assistance and disaster relief
HQAST	Headquarters Australian Theatre
HQJOC	JOC Headquarters
ICNND	International Commission for Non-Proliferation and Disarmament
INTERFET	International Force for East Timor
JACIT	Joint Amphibious Capability Implementation Team
JCA	Joint Capability Authority
JCC	Joint Capability Coordination
JLC	Joint Logistics Command
JLG	Joint Logistics Group
JOC	Joint Operations Command
JOPC	Joint Offshore Protection Command
JP	Joint Project
JSF	Joint Strike Fighter
JSSC	Joint Services Staff College
JTF	Joint Task Forces
LHD	Landing Helicopter Dock
LPA	Landing Platform Amphibious
LSD	Landing Ship Dock
LSH	Landing Ship Heavy
MOD	British Ministry of Defence
NATO	North Atlantic Treaty Organization
NSA	National Security Adviser
NSCC	National Security Committee of Cabinet
OECD	Organisation for Economic Co-Operation and Development
RAAF	Royal Australian Air Force
RAMSI	Regional Assistance Mission to Solomon Islands
RCEP	Regional Comprehensive Economic Partnership

RIMPAC	Rim of the Pacific
SASR	Special Air Service Regiment
SDF	Japanese Self-Defence Forces
SEATO	South East Asian Treaty Organisation
SOFA	Status of Forces Agreement
SRP	Strategic Reform Program
TAFTA	Free Trade Agreement
TPP	Trans–Pacific Partnership
UKUSA	United Kingdom-United States of America Agreement 1947–48
UN	United Nations
UNAMET	United Nations Assistance Mission to East Timor
UNTAC	UN Transitional Authority in Cambodia
VCDF	Vice Chief of Defence Force
WGS	Wideband Global Satellite
WoT	War on Terror

Acknowledgements

A book of this kind always depends on the quality of the authors who have contributed their knowledge to the project. The breadth and depth of knowledge of these authors in this book, their commitment to their research areas and their support for getting this project into print has been splendid. For readers who are conversant with Australian strategic and defence policy many of these names will be familiar, but a few may well be new. The list of authors in this book represents an excellent combination of up and coming researchers as well as some of the most recognised and respected scholars of defence studies in Australia. New or well established, all of the authors have been a pleasure to work with. Many of the authors are colleagues at the Strategic and Defence Studies Centre at The Australian National University and we would like to pay tribute to their support and comradeship. We would also like to extend our great thanks to Russell Trood, Mark Thomson and James Goldrick for their contributions and enthusiastic support for the book.

Our thanks is extended to the support we have received from the cartography team at the College of Asia and the Pacific at the Australian National University (CartoGIS), in particular, Karina Pelling, for her outstanding production of the maps. Mark Thomson provided excellent data for the construction of charts and diagrams and kindly provided his permission to reproduce this material in the book. A great deal of work has gone into pulling all of the threads together to make this book possible. In order for this to happen, in the efficient and timely manner that it did, we owe a special thanks to our research assistant Olivia Cable. Olivia threw herself into her work, was fastidious in the preparation of the manuscript and showed great forbearance and patience. Finally the production of any book would not be possible without the work of a publisher. In this endeavour Melbourne University Publishing has also been an exemplary partner. We would especially like to thank Colette Vella, Cathryn Smith and Penelope White.

Peter J Dean, Stephan Frühling and Brendan Taylor
Canberra, 2014

Contributors

Dr John Blaxland is a senior fellow at the Strategic and Defence Studies Centre, Australian National University. His work focuses on military history, intelligence and security, and Asia-Pacific affairs. His latest book is entitled *The Australian Army From Whitlam to Howard* (2014). Earlier publications include *Strategic Cousins* (2006), *Revisiting Counterinsurgency* (2006), *Information-era Manoevre* (2007) and *Signals—Swift and Sure* (1999). He is also a co-convener of the course 'The Australian Intelligence Community: Its Evolution and Roles' at the ANU's Strategic and Defence Studies Centre.

Dr Richard Brabin-Smith AO is a Visiting Fellow at the Strategic and Defence Studies Centre, Australian National University, where he follows his interests in Australian and regional security. Before this, he had spent some thirty years in the Australian Department of Defence, where his positions included Chief Defence Scientist and Deputy Secretary for Strategic Policy. His recent publications include an essay on *Contingencies and Warning Time* in the SDSC's *Centre of Gravity* series, and with Emeritus Professor Paul Dibb, a paper on the subject of 'Australian Defence: Challenges for the New Government', published in *Security Challenges*.

Dr Andrew Carr is a Research Fellow at the Strategic and Defence Studies Centre, Australian National University. His work focuses on Australian foreign and defence policy, middle power theory and Asian security. He is the editor of *Australian Foreign Policy: Controversies and Debates* (2014) and *Asia-Pacific Security After the Pivot* (2014). He is currently writing a book on how Australia has influenced Southeast Asian security. Andrew is also the editor of the *Centre of Gravity Series*, and co-editor of the peer-reviewed journal *Security Challenges*. He is a frequent media commentator in both Australian and Southeast Asian press. Andrew previously worked as an associate editor for the Lowy Institute for International Policy and is a recipient of the Herbert Burton Medal from the University of Canberra.

Dr Peter J Dean is a Fellow and Director of Studies at the Strategic and Defence Studies Centre, Australian National University, and the current Fulbright Scholar in Australia-United States Alliance Studies. He is managing editor of the journal *Security Challenges*, contributing editor for the journal *Global War Studies* and editor of the Melbourne University Press Defence Studies series. Peter was a Research Associate at the United States Studies Centre, Sydney University (2011), and Visiting Fellow at Georgetown University, Washington DC (2011 & 2014). Peter is the author/editor of numerous works on Australian military operations and defence policy, including *The Architect of Victory* (2010), *Australia 1942: In the Shadow of War* (2012) and *Australia 1943: The Liberation of New Guinea* (2013).

Emeritus Professor Paul Dibb AM is a professor emeritus in the Strategic and Defence Studies Centre, Australian National University. He was Head of the Centre from 1991–2003. His previous positions include: deputy secretary at the Department of Defence, director of the Defence Intelligence Organisation and Head of the National Assessments Staff (National Intelligence Committee). He is the author of five books and four major reports to government, as well as more than 150 academic articles and monographs focusing on the security of the Asia-Pacific region, the Australia-US alliance and Australia's defence policy. He wrote the 1986 Review of Australia's Defence Capabilities (the 'Dibb report') and was the primary author of the 1987 Defence White Paper. He was made a member of the Order of Australia in 1989.

Dr Stephan Frühling is a Senior Lecturer at the Strategic and Defence Studies Centre, Australian National University, and a managing editor of the journal *Security Challenges*. He is the author of *Defence Planning and Uncertainty* (2014) and *A History of Australian Defence Policy Since 1945* (2009). He was the inaugural Director of Studies (acting) of the Australian National University's Master in Military Studies at the Australian Command and Staff College in 2012, and Deputy Director of Studies 2012-2013. In 2014 (after the completion of the chapter in this book) he was appointed by the Minister for Defence to the external panel of experts on the 2015 Defence White Paper.

Rear Admiral James Goldrick, AO, CSC, RAN (Ret) is a fellow at the Sea Power Centre, and the Lowy Institute for International Policy, and an adjunct professor at the Strategic and Defence Studies Centre at The Australian National University, as well as the University of New South Wales, Canberra. He commanded HMA Ships *Cessnock* and *Sydney* (twice), the multinational Maritime Interception Force in the Persian Gulf and the Australian Defence Force Academy. He led Australia's Border Protection Command and then the Australian Defence College. His books include *No Easy Answers: The Development of the Navies of India, Pakistan, Bangladesh and Sri Lanka* (1997) and *Navies of South-East Asia: A Comparative Study* (2013) with Jack McCaffrie.

Dr Amy King is a lecturer at the Strategic and Defence Studies Centre, Australian National University. She graduated with a PhD in International Relations from the University of Oxford in 2013, where she studied as a Rhodes Scholar. Amy's research focuses on China-Japan relations, Asia-Pacific security and the legacy of war, imperialism and late industrialisation in Asia. Amy is working on a book project that draws on recently declassified Chinese archives to examine China's Japan policy during the early Cold War. Her research has been published with the *East Asia Forum Quarterly*, *The China and Eurasia Forum Quarterly* and the Australian Strategic Policy Institute.

Dr Charles Miller is a lecturer at the Strategic and Defence Studies Centre, Australian National University. He received his PhD in political science at Duke University in May 2013. He is the author of the monograph *Endgame for the West in Afghanistan? Explaining the Decline in Support for the War in Afghanistan in the United States, Great Britain, Canada, Australia, France and Germany* (2010) published by the Strategic Studies Institute in the US Army War College. He is also the author of 'Prediction and its Discontents' (forthcoming) in the *Australian Journal of International Affairs*.

Dr Brendan Taylor is Head of the Strategic and Defence Studies Centre, Australian National University. He is a specialist on great power strategic relations in the Asia–Pacific, economic sanctions and Asian security architecture. His work has featured in such leading academic journals as *International Affairs*, *Survival* and the *Australian Journal of International Affairs*. He is the author or editor of five books, including *Australia as an Asia–Pacific Regional Power* (2007) and *Sanctions as Grand Strategy* (2010).

Dr Mark Thomson is a senior analyst at the Australian Strategic Policy Institute. Mark's research interests include strategy, defence economics and defence industry policy. In 2008 and 2009, Mark was a member of the ministerial advisory panel for the Defence White Paper.

Professor Russell Trood is Professor of International Relations at the School of Government and International Relations, Griffith University and an Adjunct Professor in the Defence and Security Program, US Studies Centre at the University of Sydney. From 2005–11 he was a Senator for Queensland in the Australian Parliament, serving a term as Chair of the Senate Committee on Foreign Affairs, Defence and Trade and as a member of the Parliamentary Joint Committee on Intelligence and Security, among other committees. From 2011–12, he was the Special Envoy of the Prime Minister of Australia for Eastern Europe. Professor Trood has lectured and published extensively on international relations, Australian foreign and defence policy and Asian security, including *The Emerging Global Order: Australian Foreign Policy in the 21st Century* (2008). Professor Trood's most recent work has focused on Japanese security policy; Australian foreign policy; the G20 Organisation; Australia's public diplomacy; and Australian defence policy.

Dr Joanne Wallis is a lecturer at the Strategic and Defence Studies Centre, Australian National University, where she convenes the 'Asia-Pacific Security' program. She graduated with a PhD in Politics and International Studies from the University of Cambridge in 2012. Her research on state-building in the South Pacific has been published in leading international journals and her first book, *Constitution-Making During State-Building*, will be published by Cambridge University Press in 2014. Joanne has also conducted research consultancies for Australian and international NGOs, and writes analyses for a leading global political risk advisory service.

Introduction by Brendan Taylor

When Professor TB Millar produced *Australia's Defence*—the book from which the current volume draws its inspiration—almost fifty years ago, it was literally the first of its kind. Very little if anything had been written on the subject, aside from a handful of official and unofficial histories of the two World Wars and the Korean War. Public debate on the subject of Australia's defence was next to non-existent. There were no think tanks or academic institutes dedicated to the study of the subject. It would take the foresight of Millar, and his boss and English derided namesake JDB Miller, to found the Strategic and Defence Studies Centre at the Australian National University in 1966, the year after *Australia's Defence* was published. As Millar has written elsewhere, Australia's defence at that time 'in the government's view, was not a matter for public inquiry or debate; the public should simply accept the Defence provisions which the Australian government, in its superior wisdom and knowledge, provided'.[1]

Half a century on, the scope of public debate on the subject of Australia's defence is radically different. Issues of defence policy are vigorously contested amongst leading defence intellectuals—many of whom have previously served in senior positions in the Australian government or the military—on the opinion pages of mainstream print media and across numerous blog sites.[2] Unlike in 1965, Australia is now home to some of the world's leading think tanks—such as the Australian Strategic Policy Institute (ASPI) and the Lowy Institute for International Policy—whose work focuses upon Australian defence issues and whose very existence, at least in the case of the former, was intended by the Australian government to facilitate a better informed public debate on issues of defence. Increasingly, issues of Australian defence are also garnering attention amongst a wider international audience.[3]

Yet despite the impressive growth in Australian public debate which has occurred during the fifty years since Millar penned *Australia's Defence*, there remains a surprising shortage of comprehensive studies dedicated to the subject as a whole. One exception is Ross Babbage's *A Coast Too Long*.[4] This book was a seminal contribution to a larger body of work developing the 'Defence of Australia' concept—including a number of edited volumes and academic working papers—which were produced during the 1970s and 1980s.[5] More broadly focused volumes addressing Australia's foreign policy, but which encompassed the subject of Australia's defence, were also published from this period and into the 1990s.[6]

As in Millar's day, official and unofficial histories addressing Australia's involvement in international conflicts have continued to be regularly produced,[7] yet book-length studies devoted explicitly to the subject of Australia's defence have been few and far between. By bringing together some of Australia's leading analysts and intellectuals to write on a broad spectrum of issues and challenges facing Australia's defence—in greater depth than shorter publication formats such as newspaper articles, blog posts and policy papers allow—the present volume seeks to go some way towards filling this gap.

As with Millar's book, the current volume is intended to be accessible to a wide audience. His target audience was the 'intelligent layman' (perhaps more appropriately termed the 'intelligent layperson' in contemporary parlance) and it is to this demographic that the current volume is also addressed. Following in Millar's footsteps, each of the chapters in this volume contains some historical background of pertinence to the subject that they are addressing. Their principal focus, however, is 'to deal with Australia's defence situation as it is today.'[8] In addition, this contemporary volume is also intended to be forward looking, unpacking a range of challenges—some new, some more enduring—that Australia's defence faces into the future.

The volume addresses the theme 'towards a new era'. This 'new era' that Australia's Department of Defence is currently entering is a challenging and multifaceted one. It is one where Australia's strategic position between a 'rising China' and a 'rebalancing America' is being hotly contested. It is an era where Australia's status as a 'middle power' and its capacity to maintain its longstanding military technological edge over other countries in its region will likely be tested, as Asia's giants (such as China and India) and other medium sized powers (such as Indonesia, South Korea and Vietnam) stand up. And it is the beginning of an era of new government for Australia, which will lead to the publication of a new Defence White Paper in 2015.

Drawing inspiration from Millar's approach, the current volume is divided into four parts. Part I examines the national context underpinning Australia's defence. In the first chapter of this section, Russell Trood examines the symbiotic relationship between policy and politics that has been such an enduring feature of Australia's defence. Trood provides a unique perspective on this relationship—and the institutions and processes which facilitate and, sometimes, inhibit it—based in part on his time as a Senator for Queensland and member of the Joint Committee on Foreign Affairs, Defence and Trade. In Chapter 2, Andrew Carr goes on to interrogate the concept of Australia as a 'middle power', which has formed, and continues to form, such an important part of Australia's defence identity and strategic culture. Yet rather than viewing the 'middle power' construct as an end its itself—as has traditionally been the case—Carr makes the case that Canberra would, instead, do well to see Australia's middle power status as a starting point to inform an overdue debate on Australia's defence into the future. In the final chapter of Part I, Charles Miller reviews the current state of Australian public opinion on foreign policy and defence issues. Miller points out that public opinion polling on defence issues is a relatively new phenomenon in Australia, as reflected by how little attention issues of public opinion received in Millar's 1965 book. Drawing from a number of modern-day polls, Miller surveys the current state of Australian public attitudes on a range of defence issues including threat perception, defence spending, support for operational commitments and casualty tolerance.

Part II of the current volume moves to examine another central driver of Australia's defence, its broader international context. This section focuses its attention upon three sub-regions of the Asia-Pacific (or what some Australian defence planners and commentators increasingly refer to as an emerging 'Indo-Pacific' strategic system). Northeast Asia, the first of these sub-regions, is examined by Amy King in Chapter 4 of this volume. In this chapter, King considers the interplay between economic and security factors which has traditionally shaped Australian policy towards this part of the world. King argues that some form of reconciliation between these two sets of factors will need to be sought in the period ahead as a largely unprecedented degree of tension and potential contradiction emerges between them. In Chapter 5 John Blaxland outlines Australia's defence engagement with Southeast Asia. As Blaxland observes, Southeast Asia is becoming more central in Australian defence thinking as Canberra conceives of its security prospects as lying not *against* Asia—as Millar and many of his contemporaries did—but rather *with* this increasingly dynamic and strategically central part of the world. In the final chapter of Part II Joanne Wallis considers Australia's engagement with the South Pacific. Wallis observes that the South Pacific has traditionally been regarded by Australian defence planners as an 'arc of instability' from, and through, which threats to Australia could emanate—or in Millar's terms, 'an exposed and vulnerable front door'.[9] While some of the threats which informed those perceptions remain—and while new South Pacific strategic challenges have also emerged—Wallis argues that Canberra should strive to see the South Pacific not as an 'arc of instability' but as an 'arc of opportunity' that can achieve more enduring stability with the help of appropriately calibrated Australian assistance.

The third part of the volume examines issues of 'strategy'. In a recent book on the subject, Lawrence Freedman defines strategy 'as being about maintaining a balance between ends, ways and means; about identifying objectives; and about the resources and methods available for meeting such objectives'.[10] This is the ground traversed by Paul Dibb in Chapter 7 and Stephan Frühling in Chapter 8 of the current volume as each reflects upon the various factors which have previously occasioned fundamental turning points in Australia's defence posture. They then move on to identify the contemporary strategic and financial challenges that will demand a fundamental change in direction of Australian defence policy. In the final chapter of Part III, Peter Dean examines Australia's alliance with the United States—a relationship described in the Australian government's January 2013 *National Security Strategy* as a 'pillar' of this country's strategic and security arrangements.[11] In his chapter, Dean reviews the remarkable adaptability of the Australia-US alliance and makes the case that, as the centre of gravity in international politics gradually shifts toward the Asia-Pacific region, the alliance is presently entering yet another key turning point in its history.

Part IV of the volume examines the size and state of Australia's defences. In Chapter 10, James Goldrick traces the evolution of the Australian military towards a more 'joint' force—defined as activities and operations where at least two of the services (Army, Navy, Air Force) participate. While significant progress has been made—including implementation of some of the recommendations that Millar made in his 1965 volume—Goldrick demonstrates that the Australian Defence Force's (ADF) journey towards jointery remains a work in progress, one whose success ultimately hinges critically on the provision of adequate budgetary resources and an ability to avoid sacrificing single service strengths and expertise.

Mark Thomson then goes on in Chapter 11 to explore two of the present constraints on the size and state of Australia's defences—the scale of the human and financial resources that Australia devotes to this task and the efficiency with which Australia uses those resources. His analysis of these issues bear a striking resemblance to the albeit much shorter analysis of budgetary issues contained in Millar's book. Consistent with Millar's assessments, Thomson concludes that Canberra currently has little choice other than to find more money, or to moderate Australia's ambitions for its defence policy and security into the future.

In the final chapter of Part IV, Richard Brabin-Smith concludes the volume by examining the considerations that should determine the shape of the ADF—its force structure and posture. Brabin-Smith begins by outlining some of the key principles which have guided force structure and posture decisions in recent decades. He considers some of the imminent challenges in this area, including determining the appropriate size and shape of Australia's future submarine force, questions surrounding the new Joint Strike Fighter (JSF) program and re-focusing the Australian Army closer to home after long and protracted 'expeditionary' operations in places like Iraq and Afghanistan. While Brabin-Smith does not predict radical change in the ADF away from its current high-end maritime focus— particularly given some of the natural advantages which Australia's relatively distant strategic geography bestows—he does call for the government to become even more open with the Australian people about Defence in an era when the balance between strategic ambition and budgetary realities is set to become increasingly vexed.

In closing, a few words seem in order here about what the current volume is not. First and foremost, it is not a work of advocacy. While, in keeping with the academic tradition, each of the contributors advances a range of arguments and suggestions, the views expressed herein are very much their own. *Australia's Defence: Towards a New Era?* does not portend to be an alternative policy document or government White Paper. That said, the editors and contributors alike are hopeful that the volume will be seen as a useful resource for those developing future White Papers and other relevant government policies; for the men and woman of the Australian defence organisation who are tasked with implementing those policies; and to the broader Australian public who—given the resource commitments involved—has an interest in Australia's security. For as the very last sentences of Millar's book observe: 'let us not be frightened to have a public discussion on Defence. It is the public, after all, which seeks and needs to be defended.'

Notes

1   TB Millar, 'Strategic Studies in a Changing World', in M Thatcher and D Ball (eds), *A National Asset: Essays Commemorating the 40th Anniversary of the Strategic and Defence Studies Centre (SDSC)*, no. 165, *Canberra Papers on Strategy and Defence*, Strategic and Defence Studies Centre, Australian National University, Canberra, 2006, p. 16.

2   See, for example, P Dibb, 'Why I Disagree with Hugh White on China's Rise', *The Australian*, 13 August 2012.

3   See, for example, J Thomas, Z Cooper and I Rehman, *Gateway to the Indo-Pacific: Australian Defense Strategy and the Future of the*

Australia-US Alliance, Center for Strategic and Budgetary Assessments, Washington DC, 2013.

4   R Babbage, *Rethinking Australia's Defence*, University of Queensland Press, St Lucia, 1980; and R Babbage, *A Coast Too Long: Defending Australia Beyond the 1990s*, Allen & Unwin, Sydney, 1990.

5   See, for example, R O'Neill (ed), *The Defence of Australia: Fundamental New Aspects*, Strategic and Defence Studies Centre, Australian National University, Canberra, 1976.

6   See, for example, Coral Bell (ed), *Agenda for the Eighties: Contexts of Australian Choices in Foreign and Defence Policy*, Australian National University Press, Canberra, 1980; Desmond Ball and Pauline Kerr, *Presumptive Engagement: Australia's Asia-Pacific Security Policy in the 1990s*, Allen & Unwin, Canberra, 1996.

7   See, for example, D Horner, *Australia and the New World Order: From Peacekeeping to Peace Enforcement: 1988–1991*, vol. 2, *The Official History of Australian Peacekeeping, Humanitarian and Post-Cold War Operations*, Cambridge University Press, Port Melbourne, 2011; and PJ Dean (ed), *Australia 1943: The Liberation of New Guinea*, Cambridge University Press, Port Melbourne, 2013.

8   TB Millar, *Australia's Defence*, Melbourne University Press, Carlton, 1965, p. 6.

9   ibid., p. 150.

10   L Freedman, *Strategy: A History*, Oxford University Press, New York, 2013, p. xi.

11   Commonwealth of Australia, *Strong and Secure: A Strategy for Australia's National Security*, Commonwealth of Australia, Canberra, 2013, p. vii. www.dpmc.gov.au/national_security/docs/national_security_strategy.pdf (viewed February 2014).

Part I:
The National Context

1

Politics and the Defence Debate

Russell Trood

It was no coincidence that in October 2013, the centenary of the arrival of the first ships of the Royal Australian Navy in Sydney was celebrated in such a public and spectacular way. With, among other things, an impressive international fleet review on Sydney Harbour, a dazzling fireworks display focused on the Opera House and a massive crowd of people in attendance, including royalty, it was a memorable occasion. That it was such a grand public event was not just a reflection of the Navy's (and the wider defence force's) pride in its history and achievements. It was yet another affirmation of the high esteem in which Australia's defence forces and the military, as an institution, are held in the collective Australian memory.

As the anniversary spectacularly underscored, the Australian Defence Force (ADF) does more than bear the burden of the nation's defence and the Department of Defence (Defence) is more than just a great department of state dedicated to providing it with the means to do so. Together, the men and women, both military and civilian, who comprise Australia's defence community, are the contemporary embodiment of an Australian heritage of military affairs that stretches back to well before Federation in 1901. The challenges associated with preparing for war, waging it and dealing with its aftermath are etched deeply into the Australian consciousness. So much so that the nation's history—its political values and even some of its social ideals—have been shaped significantly by conflict. As TB Millar remarked in his path-breaking 1965 study, *Australia's Defence*, we 'are a people that has been tempered by war, and for whom the memories of war have permeated the years of peace'.[1]

While the idea that war casts a long shadow over a society is a familiar theme in history, it almost always does so in unique and distinctive ways. Societies engage in war, adjust to its reality and deal with its often terrible consequences in ways that reflect the wider influences of their strategic culture. This chapter argues that strategic culture is a useful way to comprehend the complex array of factors and variables that underpin and help to explain the politics of Australia's defence and security policy. It contends further that the strategic questions which are in contest, the actors who raise and debate them, the public policy processes through which they are mediated and ultimately, the parameters of the policy choices that may or may not be acceptable to the Australian people are a function of these broad societal influences. While in the end it may be the policymakers in government—the politicians together with their civilian and military advisors—who take the decisions on matters such as strategic objectives, force structures, capability development and all the other elements of defence policy, they do so in an environment which is itself partly constitutive of those decisions.

In an effort to explore this broad terrain, the chapter begins with a brief discussion of the nature of strategic culture and the elements of Australia's military heritage that have helped to shape it. Part II deals with the governmental context of Australia's defence and more specifically, the constitutional and political principles which underpin it. Part III explores the importance of the parliament in defence policy and analyses the role of public opinion and interest group behaviour. In Part IV, the chapter looks inside the defence portfolio and focuses on the politics of decision making within the large and very complex organisation that is the Department of Defence. The last part of the chapter takes up a theme that resonated throughout Millar's 1965 book, namely the urgency for change. It may be that Australia's strategic circumstances are not as dangerous as Millar perceived them to be nearly half a century ago, but in the early part of the twenty-first century, the necessity of reform is no less evident. Accordingly, this part of the chapter takes up three future challenges: the development of a national security community, organisational change within the defence portfolio and improving the standards of accountability in defence.

Strategic culture and the Context of Australia's Defence

Strategic culture can be defined as a 'distinctive and lasting set of beliefs, values and habits regarding the threat and use of force, which have their roots in such fundamental influences as geographical setting, history and political culture'.[2] As David Kilcullen notes, inherent 'in the notion of strategic culture is the idea that a nation's enduring circumstances give rise to a distinctive manner of perceiving and using, national power, including military power'.[3] It follows that strategic cultures are rarely the same, and even among close allies, such as Australia and the United States, cultures can be very different from one another with potentially significant implications for alliance management. While strategic cultures are distinctive and change over time, their content is not always easy to define with any precision. Accordingly, Graeme Cheeseman contends that while Australia's strategic culture is characterised by a tendency to mimic 'important aspects of its powerful friends, it does contain its own nationalist and some internationalist strands'.[4] By contrast, Michael Evans has argued that it consists of four main features: the pervasive reality of Australia's geopolitical status in policy definition, the triumph of continental philosophy over island consciousness, the irrelevance of strategic theory to military practice and the tendency to fuse statecraft with strategy.[5] Then again, Kilcullen contends that 'policy decisions by successive Australian leaders indicate a strategic culture of forward engagement'.[6]

However Australia's strategic culture might be characterised, the important point for the purposes of this discussion is that strategic culture is not merely about Australia's way of war, its grand strategy or the content of higher defence policy. Inherent in the nature of strategic culture is the *way* policies are decided in relation to these matters. Strategic culture, in other words, is infused with traditions and ways of acting and behaving that shape policy *processes* as much as they contribute to policy *outcomes*. These processes inform decisions on defence budgets, capability planning, forces structures and much else in defence policy, as much as they do grand strategy.

Viewing strategic culture at least in part, through the lens of processes sharpens the focus on the politics of defence—to enjoin, as per Harold Lasswell, the who gets what, when, and how of defence policy. This in turn, draws attention to the numerous participants in defence debates, both inside and outside of government and the complex way they interact with each other. This is a dynamic arena of public policy. Defence issues rise and fall on the political agenda, debates are of significance or not depending on time and context and the actors who participate are active at some times, less engaged and influential on others. Nevertheless, it is the contention of this chapter that in Australia, defence policy is informed by the character of the nation's constitutional architecture and by a readily recognisable group of key actors who frequently, either directly or indirectly, interact with one another to create the political landscape of policymaking. The controversies of Australian defence policy are not just the preserve of the decision makers formally responsible for resolving them, they are an integral, if sometimes rather distant and arcane, part of much broader political discourse engaging key parts of the wider Australian community.

Before exploring this academic territory in detail, it is useful to recognise that Australian strategic culture and the politics which are reflected in and refracted through it, owes much to the way that Australians have, for well over a century, perceived realities of the international environment. Long before Britain's Australian colonies federated to establish the Commonwealth of Australia in 1901, issues of security and indeed on occasions, colonial survival itself, were often foremost on colonial government agendas. Throughout the nineteenth century, a succession of foreign threats, from among others, French, Russian and Chinese interests created anxiety, even panic, within Australia's small and widely dispersed communities and led to active preparations for defence including, in several colonies, the raising and training of colonial militias. Towards the end of the century some of these were offered to Britain to assist with the defence of Empire interests as far afield as the Sudan and South Africa. As the movement towards Federation gained momentum in the 1890s many Australians regarded the opportunity it offered for improved (national) defence as one of its most compelling arguments. Against this background it was perhaps hardly surprising that one of the most important obligations undertaken by the Commonwealth in the new Australian Constitution is to be found in Section 119, in the form of a responsibility to 'protect every State against invasion and, on the application of the Executive Government of the State, against domestic violence'.[7]

If anything, the dawning of the new, twentieth century, only served to strengthen the apprehensions of Australians about the threatening character of international affairs and their implications for the nation's prosperity and security. As the century unfolded, Australian governments not only committed military forces to fight in a succession of distant conflicts—at home they began to develop an elaborate infrastructure of defence, evolving all the means necessary to prepare for and prosecute war. This was not always a smooth, linear process, but rather one undertaken in fits and starts consonant with the perceived realities of the international environment and their convergence with domestic policy imperatives. In the evolution of this Australian tradition of arms, the landings at Gallipoli in April 1915 have a special resonance, but over nearly a hundred years campaigns in other conflicts and emergencies have contributed—the exertions of the World War II, Korea, Malaya, Vietnam, the Solomon Islands, East Timor, Iraq and Afghanistan to name but a few. This is an enduring legacy, one that, even as we have entered the twenty-first century, shapes contemporary strategic debates as it continues to form and evolve.

The Constitution and the Executive

If Millar is correct that this heritage has had a significant impact on Australian society, its reach has been no more profound than in the institutions and practices which have emerged around the formulation and implementation of our defence policy and the way that the art of politics so thoroughly infuses it. To begin, Australia's defence and the policymaking that surrounds it, reflects a unique set of constitutional arrangements. After Federation, the colonies transferred their defence powers to the Commonwealth as reflected in the protection obligation in section 119 of the Constitution. In other parts of the Constitution, this responsibility is reinforced by grants of power in relation to other matters—now broadly regarded as related to national security—including: the naval and military defence of the Commonwealth; external affairs; the influx of criminals; and immigration.[8] These, and other parts of the Constitution, now allow contemporary Australian governments to exercise power over a wide range of issues related to the national security of the state including: military defence, foreign affairs, intelligence, border protection, transnational crime, cyber security and international terrorism.

Another important element of Australia's constitutional design is that it not only envisages the Commonwealth to be the responsible level of government in relation to defence, it places that power in the hands of civilian authority consistent with the principles of responsible government. This reflects Australia's adoption of Westminster traditions of responsible government and is reinforced, if somewhat ambiguously, by section 68 of the Constitution which vests command of the nation's defence forces in the Governor General. This anticipates, however, that the power will always be exercised on the advice of the responsible minister, as made clear in section 8 of the *Defence Act 1903* which declares that the minister shall have general control and administration of the Defence Force and that powers vested under the act will be exercised in accordance with any directions of the minister.[9]

The Executive

Against the background of these firm constitutional principles, the day-to-day management and administration of Australian defence policy moves into the realm of Executive power and the politics that surround it. Central to this exercise of power are the ministers themselves. Typically, given the size and complexity of defence, the prime minister makes several appointments to the portfolio. In the second Gillard government (2010–13), responsibilities were divided between a senior (Cabinet) level minister, a minister for Defence Science and Personnel, a minister for Defence Materiel and a parliamentary secretary. In the Abbott government (elected in 2013), there is only a cabinet minister, Senator David Johnston, an assistant minister and a parliamentary secretary.

For all their power, most ministers have little or at best limited knowledge of defence matters prior to their appointment, though the appointment of Kim Beazley as minister for Defence in the Hawke government in 1985 was a notable exception. Holding office at the will of the standing prime minister, ministers invariably find themselves appointed for reasons other than talent—party political and factional balance, seniority and accommodation of state interests being most prominent among them. Regardless of the motivations, however, the regrettable record is that most occupants of the defence minister's office have served for a relatively short period of time.[10] Much the same can be said of Secretaries of Defence, of whom there has been a steady procession. In neither case has this been helpful to the stability of leadership in Defence or contributed to the continuity of policymaking.

Between 1983 and 2013 Australia had twelve defence ministers, an average occupancy of the office of 2.5 years, with the longest period of service being that of a Labor minister, Senator Robert Ray (1991–96, 5 years and 342 days) and the shortest, aside from the current incumbent, a Liberal, Peter Reith (2001) with a period of 300 days. Perhaps more telling is the fact that no defence minister in the last 20 years has ever gone onto serve in another senior cabinet position, though two—Kim Beazley (Labor) and Brendan Nelson (Liberal) did go on to serve as leaders of the opposition. Others have either resigned, often leaving the parliament, been removed by prime ministerial whim or lost office as a result of being defeated at an election. In Australia, the office of defence minister has rarely been occupied by an 'up and comer' keen to make a mark, but more generally by people at the end of their career. Whether this has served the interests of good public administration is perhaps an open question, but at the very least it underscores the high level demands of the office and the personal toll it takes on those who hold it. Experienced or otherwise, enjoying a long period of service or not, ministers bring different skills and talents to their office. Some prove highly competent, others considerably less so and are accident prone. Either way, the minister's competence is being tested constantly.

In the politics of defence, no relationship is more important to a defence minister than that which he or she shares with the prime minister. As ministries are in the prime minister's gift under Australia's Westminster traditions, retaining the confidence of the prime minister is critical to a minister's political fortunes. Generally Australia has been fortunate that over time and across many governments, both Coalition and Labor, this relationship has been cooperative and collaborative, lending a high measure of coherence to policymaking within the context of Executive government. Perhaps because of the complexities of the portfolio, prime ministers have been inclined to trust their ministers to 'get on with it', save for moments of acute controversy and/or crisis. Wartime government's aside, prime ministers have been less inclined to take an active, interfering role in defence issues, compared to say, foreign policy. There, every modern prime minister quickly finds on coming to office that foreign affairs is an arena of public policy not easily avoided.

Yet the relationship may well be changing. Two recent prime ministers—Howard (1996–2007) and Rudd (2007–10 and 2013) have shown more interventionist inclinations, reflecting their broad personal interest in security issues. Howard, for instance, undertook the single most significant reform of government decision-making in the area of defence in recent decades, by establishing the National Security Committee of Cabinet (NSCC) as the central clearing house for all policy decisions on national security. Howard also had a very direct personal involvement in a range of other defence and security issues during his tenure of office, including Australia's first and only activation of the provisions of the ANZUS alliance following the September 11 2001 terrorist attacks in the United States (see Chapter 9). This decision is one of many that serve to underscore the largely untrammelled power of the Executive in defence policymaking. Other examples can be found in Australia's interventions in Afghanistan, Iraq, East Timor and the Solomon Islands, and in the aftermath of the 2002 and 2004 Bali bombings, among others. Howard's strong personal interest in Australia's military heritage—for example he actively encouraged a greater national consciousness around the Gallipoli traditions—and the high tempo of overseas ADF deployments during his time in government, helped to define Howard as a 'defence prime minister'. This underscores the point that in Australia the personal preferences of office holders, most especially the prime minister, can significantly shape the parameters and politics of the defence debate.

Rudd's interests appeared to lay more with the foreign rather than the defence side of national security. Even so, his ideas on security in East Asia and a very active role in drafting his government's 2009 Defence White Paper, apparently to strengthen the sections on the challenges posed by China's rise, serve to highlight his abiding interest in the responsibilities of the portfolio. Whether this tendency towards the 'prime ministerialisation' of defence will continue under the Abbott government is difficult to say after less than a year in office. It was less noticeable during the Gillard government (2010–13) though even here, Gillard took a deep personal interest in enhancing the strength of Australia's alliance with the United States and could not escape ultimate custody of Australia's continuing participation in Afghanistan.

In the future, prime ministerial temperament and interest in defence matters will be an important variable in defining the role they assume, but no less than the extent to which defence issues force themselves onto the public policy agenda. In recent years this has occurred more often than most governments would have chosen had they the capacity to do so. Regardless of the origins of controversy in defence, it is an arena of public policy where new governments and ministers can anticipate, with some certainty, that the unpredictable will happen and create a situation requiring careful political management. At least in the early years of a government, these situations may well be less the result of policy decisions by incumbents than the consequence of legacies left by predecessors. Either way, in administering a large complex bureaucratic organisation such as Defence, failures of administration are almost certain to occur, the constant challenge for most ministers is to try and manage the consequences.

The Politics of the Policy Debate

In recent years, Defence has had to confront a large number of controversial issues, including: the operational shortcomings of the Collins submarines, the treatment of prisoners in war zones, frequent cost overruns in the acquisition of defence equipment from helicopters to air warfare destroyers to landing helicopter docks (LHDs), and the damaging fallout from the all too frequent revelations of systemic abuses of military justice in the ADF. No government can afford to not respond to such controversies when they emerge. The challenge for ministers is not just in having to rectify a serious policy failure or in the short term public relations challenge that may represent, but in the capacity of these events to undermine the long term respect, confidence and esteem in which Defence, and more particularly the men and women of the ADF, are held with the Australian community: persistent policy failure is corrosive of morale and confidence both inside and outside Defence.

While governments have to be nimble enough to confront unanticipated developments, most new ministers come to the role from a period of opposition with at least some form of policy platform. Even so, it is rare for Australian election campaigns to focus on defence policy, and for it ever to be a subject of intense partisan debate at the time—although the 1966 'Vietnam election' was an exception, as was the intense debate over conscription during World War I. Opposition policy platforms are often sketchy and devoid of detail, sometimes as part of a conscious electoral strategy, but no less regularly from the difficulty of summoning adequate resources for policy development. Once in office, governments are making increasing use of the previously mentioned NSCC to be the engine room of Executive policymaking and implementation in Defence. A notable exception, however, were the sometimes quixotic approaches to policy development of Prime Minister Rudd, who was widely viewed both inside and outside government as running an often dysfunctional policy process.[11]

The NSCC concentrates defence and security policy in the hands of a small group of ministers—usually the prime minister, deputy prime minister, defence and foreign affairs ministers and the attorney general with others attending as required. It deals with all of the most important policy matters, including at times, decisions to deploy the ADF overseas, senior defence appointments, approval of major equipment purchases and scrutiny of the defence capability plans. While the NSCC is an important innovation in the day-to-day routine of policymaking, for more strategically significant statements of policy, governments continue to prepare and publish defence white papers These were once documents that appeared only sparingly, in for example 1976, 1987 and 1994. In recent years however they have become more frequent with papers being published in 2000, 2009, again in 2013, with another now promised by the incoming Abbott government within the next 18 months. While significant changes in strategic circumstance, either at home or abroad, were once the primary drivers of white papers, the Gillard government's 2013 Defence White Paper, following so closely on the heels of Rudd's 2009 Defence White Paper, was widely criticised as serving no more compelling purpose other than positioning the government for the forthcoming 2013 election.[12] There can be costs associated with this kind of politicking, not least reduced rather than enhanced domestic policy credibility, serious disruption to the normal routines of policy development within Defence and the wider national security community and finally, confusion and misunderstandings abroad about Australian policy among friends and adversaries alike. None contribute to sound public policy.

To an extent, much the same might be said of the numerous enquiries and reviews to which Defence has been subject in the recent years. Over the last decade few departments of state have been so comprehensively reviewed as Defence. Thus, since 2003 and leaving aside parliamentary reviews, ADF boards of enquiry and Commonwealth audits, there have been over fifteen external reviews within the Defence portfolio covering a wide range of issues from Defence Procurement (2003) through to the Defence Force Posture Review (2012).[13] While these reviews often reflect either a measure of policy failure or an unrelated desire for substantive policy reform, the reality is that recent governments seem to have been inclined to take the review path as a political tool to manage internal controversies and challenges. Independent reviews certainly have their place in this connection, and can be important to restoring public confidence in areas where that may have been lost. But arguably, governments and Defence itself have become too dependent on them as a mechanism of governance and need to look closely at other ways to manage challenging internal issues.

Parliament, Interest Groups and Public Opinion

One approach would be to expand the role of the Commonwealth parliament in the management of Australia's defence. To many, government officials, politicians, security analysts and others this would involve a radical departure from existing practice. As we have seen, by constitutional fiat and custom, the reality in Australia is that political power in defence matters is overwhelmingly in the hands of the Executive arm of government. Parliament's task is essentially threefold: to provide one or more of Australia's political parties with a majority on the floor of the House of Representatives, which will enable it or them to form a government with a workable majority; ensuring the passage of any legislation relating to the management and conduct of Australia's defence, and to provide oversight, scrutiny and accountability of and within the defence portfolio largely through the mechanisms of parliamentary committees.

Parliament is the arena where defence most obviously enters the realm of partisan politics. During the early years of the Commonwealth at the start of the twentieth century, the configuration of Australia's electoral system and the structure of its political parties often made parliamentary majorities problematic and unstable. Since World War I however, with one or two notable exceptions (the early 1960s and most recently between 2010–13), the post World War II period has delivered more or less reliably stable governments with strong parliamentary majorities. This has enabled Australian governments to manage defence policy with a high degree of confidence that their policy agenda can be implemented. Thus, even in periods of considerable controversy, such as during Australia's decade long (1962–72) participation in the Vietnam War—and increasingly over the more recent involvement in Afghanistan—governments of the day have had the parliamentary power and authority to sustain sometimes unpopular policies.

Traditionally, Australia's political parties have adopted rather different approaches to the nation's defence. While several fringe parties on both the right and left of politics—the Democratic Labor Party and the Nuclear Disarmament Party, for example—have managed to secure election to parliament with radically different agendas on Australia's defence, among Australia's mainstream parties—the Liberals and the Nationals (the Coalition parties) on the right and Labor on the left—the spectrum of differences is much narrower. Generally, the Coalition parties are stronger on defence, typically advocating higher defence budgets and a stronger commitment to the Australia-US alliance, for example, than Labor—though in more recent years the differences appear to have narrowed. In opposition, Labor opposed the Howard government's strong support of US intervention in Iraq, but not its intervention in East Timor in 1999 or the Regional Assistance Mission to Solomon Islands (RAMSI) in 2003. After the Howard government's defeat in 2007, Labor's Rudd and then Gillard government continued Australia's commitment to Afghanistan, strongly supported the US-led campaign against al-Qaeda and international terrorism and foreshadowed significant increases in defence spending on new ADF capability, especially in air combat and maritime defence.

Whether this convergence in mainstream party opinion over defence is going to be a permanent part of Australia's political landscape remains to be seen. In the meantime, much of the day-to-day debate over defence policy tends to revolve around administrative competence and the best way to manage the defence capability and force structure changes required by Australia's transforming strategic environment. On this score, the outgoing Labor government received a considerable amount of criticism for its inability to match the budgetary means of defence to plausible strategic ends.[14] This is not a new theme in Australian defence. Indeed, over decades it has been a recurring debate. But in this new era, in a different and increasingly complex strategic environment, it reflects a profound challenge for Australian policymakers, one requiring the kind of innovative thinking that Millar hoped might be stimulated by his book of 1965. Yet, half a century on, there is reason to lament the poverty of strategic debate in Australia. Save for some notable contributions from some of Australia's most well regarded academics and think tanks, so far little has emerged from the political process to encourage confidence that the nation's policy choices are being fully reviewed and evaluated.

Yet for all the partisan differences over defence policy in Australia, it tends to be an area of public policy where the gulf between right and left is not always as great as it may seem. A political culture across all shades of Australian politics that reveres Australia's military history and traditions, holds the men and women serving in the ADF in high esteem, and tends to be cautious about playing too much politics with the sensitivities of national security, serves as a restraint on the potential excesses of political partisanship and debate. On the other hand, a party seeming to traduce any of these closely held values is fair political game. Thus, prior to the 2013 federal election a policy proposal from the then opposition to install a senior military officer as the head of a new command structure to police and manage Australia's border security (an idea said to be militarising an essentially civilian area of public policy) was widely criticised, including by Labor ministers and lobby groups such as the Australian Defence Association.[15] There is little evidence, however, that the public was excessively troubled by the plan, and following the election, the new Abbott government promptly implemented it.

One of the factors that constrains the role of parliament in the conduct of Australian defence policy and correspondingly enhances the power of the Executive is the absence of a frequent need for the passage of defence legislation. Periodically, special pieces of legislation are required to follow through on policy initiatives, such as the creation of an Australian Military Court and on occasions amendments are required to the *Defence Act 1903*, but governments are able to accomplish a great deal in defence by the passage of the annual appropriation or budget bills, which underwrite the portfolio's massive financial demands on the public purse. Most notable here is the absence of any constitutional requirement forcing a government to seek parliamentary approval for the deployment of Australian forces abroad. While controversial at different times in Australian history and although called for on occasions, governments, not surprisingly, have shown little interest in such a reform, making any change in this direction in future highly unlikely.

Further limiting parliamentary engagement on defence issues is the relatively modern practice of governments making less and less use of parliament as a forum for defence debates. Increasingly, policy statements are made outside the parliament, as was the case with the introduction of the 2013 Defence White Paper, which was launched in an aircraft hangar at Fairbairn airport amid an array of impressive defence weaponry and a large contingent of the media, military brass and civilian Defence officials.[16] The parliament's 2010 debate on Afghanistan was a rare moment when a government of the day thought to give parliamentarians an opportunity to discuss and dilate on a matter of wide interest to the public and important to the conduct of Australian defence policy. As defence analyst Peter Jennings has noted, the growing tendency to take the defence into the public domain and beyond the reach of parliament is troubling, for the disrespect it demonstrates to both parliament and parliamentarians, and the avoidance of parliamentary accountability, which is at the core of Australia's system of responsible government.[17]

Yet, not all is lost in this regard. Although parliamentary question time is a much-diminished institution of Executive accountability, parliament's role is, to an extent, preserved in an extensive system of parliamentary committees. While backbench committees and some individual parliamentarians may have a role in policy debates, these are the exception, as it is the committee system that stands out as the locus of political action. Although infrequent, any piece of defence legislation is almost certain to be scrutinised by at least one committee, usually from the Senate, before its passage into law. Beyond that however, other committees do important and valuable work. The Joint Standing Committee of Foreign Affairs Defence and Trade, for example, was established originally by resolution of the parliament in 1951. It not only has a specific responsibility to scrutinise the Annual Defence Report, but wide powers of investigation and enquiry though the issues it pursues need to be approved by the minister. In recent years, however, the committee has investigated a wide range of defence matters including the Middle East Area of Operations. A more recently established committee is the Parliamentary Joint Committee on Intelligence and Security, the only committee of the parliament requiring members to be approved by the prime minister. This committee's mandate is to scrutinise the work of Australia's intelligence community, including those agencies within defence—the Defence Intelligence Organisation, the Australian Signals Directorate and the Defence Imagery and Geospatial Organisation.

Of longer standing and arguably of more immediate significance are several senate committees. The Foreign Affairs, Defence and Trade Committee has developed an impressive record of parliamentary review in recent years through enquiries on issues such as naval shipbuilding (2006) and, perhaps most impressively, its long investigation into Australia's military justice system, which proposed a long list of reforms to the culture of abuse which had become widely established within Defence. Hardly less important is the Senate Estimates process, through which three times a year—February, June and October—in relation to defence, the Senate Foreign Affairs

Defence and Trade committee transforms itself in to a mechanism to investigate the operations of government through an examination of government budgetary allocations. The process requires the attendance before the committee of the most senior (and sometime more junior) management of defence, both military and civilian, to answer questions on virtually any issues relating to the conduct of the portfolio. If the process is benign in terms of matters it might discover (which is often the case), on occasions it can expose egregious failures of policy. Such outcomes can cost individuals, including ministers, their job—as occurred in 2009 when the incumbent defence minister, Joel Fitzgibbon, resigned his position following committee revelations relating to his conduct as a minister.

The value in these enquiry processes is that they permit detailed and sustained investigation of defence policy issues by the parliament to which the Executive arm of government is responsible. Generally, this demands the calling of submissions from agencies as well as interested members of the public, the taking of oral evidence and eventually the presentation to the parliament of a report made publically available. The process is educative of parliament and public alike, and imposes the discipline of accountability on the Executive. Often the power of this process is all the more significant for the fact that committees in this area of public policy, often manage to produce consensus reports with unanimous policy recommendations.

Interest Groups

In Australia, the political landscape of defence is densely populated by a wide array of individuals and interest groups which while not necessarily sharing a common philosophical outlook on defence, are at least united in their general desire to try and shape the public policy debate, and often the direction of defence policy. These groups can be categorised in several different ways, but a useful approach divides them into four. First, and perhaps the most recognisable, are the members of the defence and security policy community who are generally professionally engaged in the analysis of Australia's defence and foreign policy. This group includes think tanks with a specific interest in defence and foreign policy such as the ASPI, the Lowy

Institute for International Policy, the Kokoda Foundation and the Australian Defence Association. All have a wealth of analysts: for example, Peter Jennings from ASPI, who publishes actively and appears regularly in the media; retired defence force officers—among them Admiral Chris Barrie, and Generals Peter Leahy, Jim Molan and John Cantwell; and a wide range of academic commentators, generally with university affiliations and often from research centres such as the Strategic and Defence Studies Centre at the Australian National University. Most prominent among them are Professors Des Ball, Paul Dibb, Hugh White and Brendan Taylor. Beyond the defence specialists are a significant number of individuals from other academic disciplines whose work often tracks important defence debates.

A second interest group covers the specialist defence correspondents employed by Australia's media outlets—Paul Kelly, Brendan Nicholson, Greg Sheridan, John Kerin and Cameron Stewart among others who are well informed (and connected) and write regularly, and usually authoritatively, on defence issues.

Third, are the service veteran's groups, whose ranks are generally made up of those who at some stage have served in the defence forces and are now members of clubs and associations whose mandates can be wide, but are often focused on securing improved conditions and benefits for members. These include the Returned Services League, the Vietnam Veterans Association and the Submariners Association.

Finally, interest groups are completed by business and industry enterprises, often defence contractors who are either suppliers or hope to be suppliers of defence equipment to the defence forces. The industry sector in defence includes a large number of players ranging in size from the global corporations such as Boeing, Thales and Raytheon to a vast number of mainly small and medium Australian enterprises. It also includes state governments, many of which—South Australia perhaps most notably—actively promote their defence industries as a matter of state trade and investment policy.

The wide diversity of Australia's defence interest groups makes generalisations on their roles and activities something of a fraught exercise. Suffice to say, most have specific aims or objectives whether it is contributing to public education on defence, securing better benefits for veterans, gaining a specific defence supply contract, or something else. While they may on occasions act in consort with one another, the more important point is that they reflect aggregations of community interest around defence issues and to this extent operate across the government/public/private divide engaging governments, ministers, parliament and bureaucrats in a pluralist model of political engagement that reflects Australia's democratic institutions of governance.

One of the ways in which these interest group activities is important is that they contribute to the Australian public's perceptions of the value and competence of Australia's defence forces and the overall needs of Australia's defence, helping to shape the political environment of the defence debate. While public opinion in defence is explored more fully in Charles Miller's valuable contribution to this book, a few points need to be made here. The first is that historically speaking, the ADF has enjoyed a high level of community support, built on over a hundred years of dedicated service and sacrifice in war, but also through humanitarian service, peacekeeping activities and community involvement.

As Miller will show, this support has generally translated into a significant tolerance for relatively high levels of defence spending. One consequence is that defence debates in Australia often attract high profile public attention and sometimes controversy, as the 2011 revelations over sexual harassment among cadets at the Australian Defence Force Academy underscores. Second, this places all Australian governments and ministers on notice that the way they manage Australia's defence is under constant scrutiny and can be a factor in determining perceptions of a government's competence and capacity to govern effectively. Third, public opinion 'reaches' into the defence portfolio in significant ways. No minister can afford to be insensitive to the public relations consequences of their decisions and must always have a strategy to deal with the issues with which they may be grappling however routine they may seem. Finally, beyond the minister's office—inside the Department of Defence itself—public opinion is unlikely to be, and indeed, arguably should not be, a compelling factor in decision-making. It is a ministerial matter, but being at least aware of the way the decision may 'play out' in the public domain, is something that cannot be ignored within the politics of defence.

The Department of Defence

Public opinion is just one way in which politics penetrates the defence portfolio, and though important, is perhaps not the most significant manifestation of it. As noted earlier, a large and complex arena of government policy, such as defence, cannot easily avoid the daily reach of politics. Politics not only swirls around and sometimes engulfs the portfolio, it is a facet of decision making within the Department of Defence itself. This is an issue explored more fully by Paul Dibb in Chapter 7, but no discussion of the politics of defence would be complete without some treatment of the issue.

It is useful to note at the outset that had it not been for the implementation in 1976 of the 1973 Tange reforms, the inter agency politics of defence would be far more complex and fraught than they are today. TB Millar himself had some reservations about the likely impact of the Tange reforms which have proved prescient, but they have resulted in a much more integrated defence bureaucracy, doing away with separate service ministers and ministries and leaving Australia to this day with the 'diarchy' model of administration with a single minister and a secretary to oversee the civilian side of the department and a Chief of Defence Force heading up the military side.[18]

Although comprehensive, the Tange reforms did not remove the influence of political forces on the bureaucratic processes that are at the heart of policymaking in any large government agency. These forces may not be as intense as sometimes occurs in Washington or perhaps Whitehall, but in any organisation where the sum of its parts consists of many different organisational elements with sometimes significantly different cultures, having to mediate issues and problems through a labyrinth of complex standard operating procedures, debates over policy choices can sometimes become intense and bureaucratically debilitating. Regardless of the issue, every policy outcome in Defence generally needs to be negotiated through a complex system of organisational procedures, committees and levels of decision making. As policy options are raised, considered and either approved, rejected or set aside for further evaluation, the potential for bureaucratic tension and even conflict is omnipresent.

Fortunately, perhaps, much of this bureaucratic pulling and hauling takes place behind closed doors only rarely breaking into public view. Even so, over time, some of the pressure points for policy tension in Defence have become clear. One of the most serious potentially is that between the office of the minister and the organisation. In 2013 this was widely speculated to be the reason the relatively recently installed Secretary of the Department and distinguished former Special Air Service Regiment Commander, Duncan Lewis, suddenly quit his position to take up the position of Australia's representative to NATO and Ambassador to Belgium.[19] A less ambiguous example, though one subsequently mired in extensive controversy, occurred in 1999 when a previous secretary, Paul Barratt, was dismissed by Minister John Moore after a series of well publicised disagreements.

The second divide reflects a challenge faced by most defence organisations around the world, namely the differences in institutional culture between the civilian and military sides of Defence. Australia has a long history of effectively managing the tensions that can emerge as the 'suits and the uniforms' work in close proximity to one another. This cooperation has been especially effective on operational deployments such as RAMSI and in disaster relief such as the Bali Relief mission in 2002. Inside Defence however, where critical policy issues are at stake, collaboration can occasionally be more fraught as the practical operational experience of the military confronts the instincts of the civilian public service bureaucrat. [20]

Finally, there is a pressure point around service rivalries as the Army, Navy and Air Force all seek to preserve their operational capacities, policy influence and status often against the background of scarce budgetary resources. On occasions, fierce inter-service tensions can break out over new equipment purchases, as was the case during 1983 when the Navy fought hard, but eventually lost the battle, to secure an aircraft carrier replacement following the decommissioning of the carrier HMAS Melbourne. In a more contemporary setting, press accounts persist that inter-service rivalries are evident over the need for new generations of ground, maritime and air capability as Defence seeks to make significant budgetary savings.

In some defence establishments—that of the United States comes most obviously to mind—the tensions over policy issues can be severe and highly destructive of usually well-ordered decision making. In Australia, however, the political pulling and hauling that is a natural part of policymaking in all government agencies tends to be mitigated by a more cohesive organisational structure and the relatively small nature of the defence bureaucracy. The structural military/civilian diarchy reinforced by sometimes-close personal relationships, particularly among senior officials on both sides, often serves to encourage collaboration rather than conflict and where differences develop offer paths for conflict resolution. That said, the politics of bureaucracies is a natural part of defence policy formulation and reflects strains of the nation's strategic culture. There is order, rationality and a logic to the process, in terms of standard operating procedures—the two pass system for defence equipment acquisitions for example, but that does not preclude possibly furious debates over options and choices. If it is so that periods of budgetary constraint can serve to intensify some of these bureaucratic tensions, it may be that as Australia's defence budget comes under greater pressure in the coming years, the politics of decision inside the defence bureaucracy will also intensify significantly.

Future Challenges

The modern politics of Australian defence reflect the deep heritage of the nation's strategic culture adapted to an international environment of constant change and the shifting domestic imperatives of Australia's robust system of responsible government. There are patterns to the interaction of ideas, actors and events, but they are often more visible as part of a complex mosaic of behaviour than an orderly, entirely rational process of governance. This has been the heritage and despite governments' persistent and sometimes energetic efforts for reform, there is every reason to anticipate that these patterns will endure. Change will certainly occur and over time, the character of Australia's strategic culture will be affected, but for policymakers, the challenges inherent in the politics of Australia's defence are certain to be demanding and will cast a long shadow over their ambitions well into the next decades of the twenty-first century.

Against this background, Australia faces some enormous security challenges, many as Millar once again foresaw, in the changing nature of the regional security environment. But the domestic context of defence concentrates attention on the need for reform at home, where policymakers and the Australian community as a whole face some clear challenges.

A National Security Community

One involves the place of defence as an integral part of Australia's national security community and demands an answer to the growing pressures for greater cohesion in defence and security policymaking. These have been evident for some time, but have gained greater salience as a result of the increasingly interconnected globalised security environment where the threats to national security are now more diverse and may emanate not just from other states, but from a range of non-state actors using an increasingly sophisticated array of weapons.

On coming to office in 2007, the Rudd government addressed this issue, at least in part, by creating a more centralised national security office within the Prime Minister's Office, appointing Australia's first National Security Adviser (NSA) and publishing the nation's first National Security Statement in 2008. Since the first Rudd government's removal from office, this new national security establishment has been progressively downgraded, to the point where under the new Abbott government, the NSA position has been abolished and the bureaucratic infrastructure largely dismantled. This may prove to be a wise decision. On the other hand, at a time when several of Australia's close defence partners, including the United Kingdom and Japan have institutionalised a more centralised national security apparatus with the establishment of national security councils, there is good reason to consider whether the move is an appropriate response to the security challenges of the day and whether the creation of a more visible national security community may be necessary.

Organisational Reform in Defence

A second challenge is evident in the need for organisational reform in the Defence portfolio where persistent and repeated policy failures have exposed widespread shortcomings and weaknesses in the management of the department, eroded public confidence in the political and organisational leadership of defence and begun to undermine its historic and hard won reputation as one of the iconic and centrally important institutions of the Australian society.

As noted earlier in this chapter, there is a long list of readily recognisable reasons for the growth of these perceptions. It is equally evident that their solution does not lie in the employment of more public relations personnel to better explain the defence position. Defence needs internal reform to address effectively the areas of policy failure. This is an ambitious, long-term undertaking demanding significant changes in policymaking procedures. Potentially more challenging, however, is the need to change an organisational culture that has become too tolerant of poor management practices developed over decades and no longer sustainable in the challenging security environment of the contemporary era. Stripping away old, out-of-date values and practices and replacing them with more contemporary management ideals will not only be exacting task in an organisation as complex as defence, but one requiring creative leadership from the highest levels of today's political, civilian and military leaders.

Defence As An Accountable Institution

Finally, confronting the challenges of the future requires reforms to the way defence responds to the demands placed upon it as a publically accountable institution. While interests groups and the media have roles to play, constitutionally, the defence department is accountable for its decisions to the parliament through the authority of the minister. In recent years, however, policy failures have seen this arrangement under pressure and fraying at the edges, seemingly with the instinctive response to institute yet another review or enquiry, public or otherwise, by an individual or organisation outside defence.

Outside enquiries certainly have their place in government, indeed they can be immensely important as a foundation for change, but their frequency in relation to defence raises serious questions as to whether the existing mechanisms for defence accountability are adequate. A strengthened system of internal defence oversight flagging possible threats to sound policy development might help to address the problem, as might expanded ministerial oversight, something the Australian Defence Association has called for over a long period of time. While not mutually exclusive to either of these solutions, another route would be to increase parliamentary oversight and scrutiny. As noted earlier, this already takes place through an extensive array of parliamentary committees, but strengthening this system through expanded mandates and more regular scrutiny of key aspects of the defence portfolio would be valuable and timely reforms. More frequent ministerial statements to parliament together with more regular debates over key policy issues would also enhance accountability. Whatever is done, the widespread perception of a defence ministry being a law unto itself and largely beyond the reach of appropriate oversight and accountability mechanisms neither serves its interest nor those of the Australian public and justifies far greater attention that it has yet to receive.

Further Reading

Bonnor, Janelle, 'The Politics of Defence in Australia', no. 68, *Australian Defence Studies Centre working paper*, Australian Defence Studies Centre, Canberra, July 2001.

Jennings, Peter, 'The Politics of Defence White Papers', *Security Challenges*, vol. 9, no. 2, 2013, pp. 1–14. www.securitychallenges.org.au/ArticlePDFs/SC9-2Jennings.pdf.

Millar, Thomas Bruce, 'The Political-Military Relationship in Australia', in Ball, Desmond (ed), *Strategy and Defence: Australian Essays*, Allen & Unwin, Sydney, 1982, pp. 278–290.

Wilson, Isaiah and Forrest, James JF (eds), *Handbook of Defence Politics: International and Comparative Perspectives*, Electronic Book Text, United Kingdom, December 2008.

Woolner, Derek, 'Drowned by Politics: Australia's Challenges in Managing its Maritime Domain', *Security Challenges*, vol. 9, no. 3, pp. 63–90. www.securitychallenges.org.au/ArticlePDFs/SC9-3Woolner.pdf.

Notes

1   TB Millar, *Australia's Defence*, Melbourne University Press, Carlton, 1965, p. 10.

2   A Macmillan; K Booth; and R Trood, 'Strategic Culture', in K Booth and R Trood (eds), *Strategic Culture in the Asia-Pacific Region*, Macmillan Press, London, 1999, p. 8.

3   D J Kilcullen, 'Australian Statecraft: the Challenge of Aligning Policy with Strategic Culture', *Security Challenges*, vol. 3, no. 4, 2007, p. 47. www.securitychallenges.org.au/ArticlePDFs/vol3no4Kilcullen.pdf (viewed February 2014).

4   G Cheeseman, 'Australia: The White Experience of Fear and Dependence', in K Booth and R Trood (eds), *Strategic Culture in the Asia-Pacific Region*, 1999, p. 273.

5   M Evans, *The Tyranny of Dissonance: Australia's Strategic Culture and Way of War 1901–2005*, study paper 306, Land Warfare Studies Centre, Canberra, February 2005, p. 23.

6   D Kilcullen, 'Australian Statecraft: the Challenge of Aligning Policy with Strategic Culture', 2007, p. 50.

7   Commonwealth of Australia, *The Commonwealth of Australia Constitution Act*, Commonwealth of Australia, 1900. www.austlii.edu.au/au/legis/cth/consol_act/coaca430/ (viewed February 2014).

8   ibid., section 51 (vi); section 51 (xxix); section 51 (xxviii) and section 51 (xxvii) respectively.

9   These issues are well canvassed in M Thomson, *Serving Australia: Control and Administration of the Department of Defence*, no. 41, *APSI Special Report*, Australian Strategic Policy Institute, Canberra, June 2011, p. 9. www.aspi.org.au/publications/special-report-issue-41-serving-australia-control-and-administration-of-the-department-of-defence/5_28_33_PM_SR41_Serving-Australia.pdf (viewed February 2014).

10   Details are available at Wikipedia, 'Minister for Defence (Australia)', www.en.wikipedia.org/wiki/Minister_for_Defence_(Australia) (viewed February 2014).

11   See R Trood, 'Kevin Rudd's Foreign Policy Overshoot', *Quadrant*, vol. LIV, no. 11, November 2010. www.quadrant.org.au/magazine/2010/11/kevin-rudd-s-foreign-policy-overshoot/ (viewed February 2014).

12   See C Stewart, 'Defence White Paper Goes Down in Flames', *The Australian*, 4 May 2013.

13   Details can be found at the Department of Defence website: www.defence.gov.au/ips/reviews.htm.

14   See M Thomson and A Davies, 'Defence', in P Jennings et al., *Agenda for Change: Strategic Choices for the Next Government*, Australia Strategic Policy Institute, Canberra, August 2013, pp. 17–30. www.aspi.org.au/publications/agenda-for-change-strategic-choices-for-the-next-government/3_55_03_PM_Strategy_agenda_for_change.pdf (viewed February 2014).

15   See, for example, National Nine News, 'Opposition's Military-Led Refugee Plan Slammed', National Nine News, 25 July 2013. www.news.ninemsn.com.au/national/2013/07/25/05/56/coalition-boat-policy-to-involve-military (viewed February 2014).

16   For an account, see Stewart, 'Defence White Paper Goes Down in Flames', 2013.

17   Thomson and Davies in Jennings et al., *Agenda for Change: Strategic Choices for the Next Government*, 2013, p. 16.

18   For Tange's own account of the reforms see, A Tange in P Edwards (ed), *Defence Policy-Making: A Close Up View 1950–1980—A Personal Memoir*, no. 169, *Canberra Papers on Strategy and Defence*, Australian National University Press, 2006.

19   G Barker, 'Turmoil as Defence Chief Exits', *Australian Financial Review*, 17 September 2012; and G Dobell, 'Labor Loses Defence, and a Secretary', *The Interpreter*, Lowy Institute for International Policy, 17 September 2012. www.lowyinterpreter.org/post/2012/09/17/Labor-loses-Defence-as-well-as-a-Secretary.aspx (viewed February 2014).

20   In Tange's view, 'It is not derogatory to suggest also that the Service Officer's antennae are differently tuned from the antennae of public servants to recognising policy indications that come out of Ministers in various degrees of imprecision. And why not when the military profession has its hands full in mastering the military art as its raison d'etre?' See R Brabin-Smith, 'Defence and the Need for Independent Policy Analysis', *Security Challenges*, vol. 6, no. 2, 2010, p. 11. www.securitychallenges.org.au/ArticlePDFs/vol6no2BrabinSmith.pdf (viewed February 2014).

2
Australia as a Middle Power

Andrew Carr

In general terms, good strategy can be boiled down to connecting three things: the nation's ends, ways and means. It is 'about identifying objectives; and the resources and methods available for meeting such objectives'.[1] In Australia, most defence attention is rightly focused on the last two concerns: the ways and means of strategy. These are often the most difficult and least obvious. Yet thinking about the ends—namely the overall ambition of the nation's strategic policy—is also a vitally important task. Without regular consideration of the long term ends of national policy, it is easy to fritter away prosperity and miss opportunities. The friction of habit and tradition, especially in times of comfort, can be very damaging to good strategy.

Early in the twenty-first century, Australia's material capacity has never been greater. It enjoys both security and prosperity. Yet this strength is built upon a number of fundamental assumptions that are coming into question. Most important is whether the US-led order in Asia can continue, and Washington's will to defend it. The cause of this challenge to the US order is well known: rising powers are emerging at a time of intense economic, social, environmental and technological disruption. While the giants like China and India are presenting headaches for the United States, Australia is finding its own weight-class crowded, as Indonesia, Vietnam and South Korea push for status and threaten to compete for economic opportunities. How might Australia find its security in this new era? As TB Millar recognised, questions like this might end with a defence policy, but they do not begin there. Alongside *Australia's Defence*, Millar also wrote *Australia in Peace and War*, a grand sweeping narrative of Australian history that attempted to contextualise the defence choices Australia faced and explains how Australia found itself in these circumstances. Millar was pessimistic about Australia's external affairs. He worried that while Australia had at times been highly influential, it had been 'essentially a reactor rather than an actor on the world stage'.[2] Without an 'enemy at the gates' or over-riding ideology to arouse the passions of the Australian people, the nation would not seek influence or significance and thus risk its current good fortune.

This chapter follows Millar's lead in examining Australia's defence in the larger context of national policy, especially its diplomatic, economic and social aspects. Yet it takes a slightly more optimistic attitude. It shows how, through the use of the 'middle power' label, Australian governments have developed strategies to advance the national well-being. It is only now with the hindsight of our current position that we can appreciate the sheer radicalism and success of many Australian initiatives. Yet Millar's concern seems of more importance today than it has been at any time in the last thirty years. The successful achievement of Australia's basic security and prosperity has allowed the debate about the ends of national strategic policy to lapse. In the last decade we have seen a celebration of both pragmatism and activism as defining elements of government policy. However without a coherent national strategy, both approaches have essentially frittered away the good fortune of our times. This chapter argues that by taking Australia as a middle power as our starting point, a much needed debate on the ends of national strategic policy can occur, one that hopefully restores the role of strategy and long term thinking in Australian political life.

Is Australia a Middle Power?

For some analysts, the term middle power has outlived its usefulness. Its heydays were in the 1940s and early 1990s, associated with a soft and fuzzy insistence on multilateralism as the 'band aid' solution to every international problem.[3] Yet the term has had a resurgence amongst policymakers. In Australia the term returned to favour under the governments of Kevin Rudd (2007–2010, 2013) and Julia Gillard (2010–2013), while governments in South Korea, Indonesia, Mexico and Turkey amongst many others, have also embraced the concept. Middle powers are understood as 'states that can protect their core interests and initiate or lead a change in a specific aspect of the existing international order'.[4] That is, middle powers should not fear invasion by larger states, though nor can they impose their will on most states in the international arena either. Middle powers should be able to show global leadership and be influential in shaping their immediate region. Both of these tasks require not only an essential material capacity but also a will or desire to operate as a middle power, something that not all states have.

Identifying Australia as a middle power is a useful way to think about the ends towards which Australia's national power is used. It helps us to ask and think through questions such as can Australia defend itself? If so, against what type or size of an opponent? Can Australia undertake significant campaigns overseas (military or diplomatic)? How much coalition support (if not reliance) does Australia need to achieve its main security interests? In short, what sort of role do Australians see their country playing in the twenty-first century? This goes to the purposes towards which the nation's capabilities are developed and applied. According to Australia's 2013 Defence White Paper:

> Our most basic strategic interest remains the defence of Australia against direct armed attack … The scope of this strategic interest encompasses defence of attacks on continental Australia, our maritime territory, our offshore territories and the critical sea lanes in our approaches.[5]

On current statistics, Australia would seem to possess the capacity for protecting these interests, though the sea-lanes might prove a real challenge. For nearly thirty years official Australian government publications have identified Australia as one of the safest countries in the world.[6] Australia has the fifth largest military budget in Asia, accounting for 8 per cent of regional arms spending.[7] It is the thirteenth largest in global terms. Compared to the great powers of its region, Australia's military spending is about half that of Japan's and around one quarter of China's.[8] While troop numbers are comparatively small, Australia makes up for this by maintaining a 'capability edge' over most countries in Asia. Thanks to its alliance with the United States, Australia has access to world-class military equipment. It manages its forces with one of the most professional and well-regarded bureaucracies in the world. While it is impossible to 'war-game' every scenario—Australia's massive geography (sixth largest land mass in the world) presents numerous challenges for defending (as well attacking)—the judgement of Australia's 2009 Defence White Paper that 'Australia will most likely remain, by virtue of our geostrategic location, a secure country over the period to 2030' seems valid.[9]

Australia has also demonstrated a significant capacity to influence regional and global discussions. Australia has played a leadership role on diverse issues such as reducing trade barriers, chemical and nuclear non-proliferation, fighting communism in Asia, anti-apartheid, peacekeeping, protecting Antarctica, creating regional forums and aiding the negotiation of global agreements. Achieving an influence far beyond its latent material capacity, Australia's diplomatic significance in regional and global affairs has been a result of Australian leaders setting clear ends for Australian strategic policy and pursuing them vigorously.

Australia clearly possesses the capacity to be a middle power state, yet over the last decade or so the nation's willingness to remain an active middle power has begun to wane. Enjoying security and prosperity, national strategic policy has been reduced to a 'steady as she goes' mentality, punctuated by the occasional short lived thought bubble. In both military and diplomatic spheres, Australian governments—supported by the Australian public—have accepted an under-investment of time, planning, effort and resources. Australian leaders have become reticent to identify areas of leadership or to dedicate the necessary resources and attention to preserve, let alone extend Australia's significance on the regional and global stage. Yet middle power status is about more than just material capacity and a few good ideas. It requires the self-belief and will to act, which is starting to come into question in Australia. As the writer George Megalogenis noted in 2011:

> Australia is in an unusual position as the last rich society standing … The United States, Japan and Great Britain—nations we have variously looked up to, been terrorised by or relied upon—would kill for what we have achieved and for the opportunity that the Asian century offers us. Yet we share their lack of confidence in the future, although our problems are minuscule by comparison.[10]

In the 1980s *The Economist* magazine famously concluded that Australia is 'one of the best managers of adversity the world has seen and the worst managers of prosperity'.[11] Millar himself echoed these comments noting that the 'wit and will of the Australian people [is] so difficult to arouse, so formidable when aroused'.[12] Yet without a sensible debate about the ends of national strategic policy, Australia's capacity to be aroused to action, and to manage future adversity, is being called into question.

History of Australia's Middle Power Status

Australia's self-perception as a middle power has often been strongest in moments of greatest challenge. After World War II, British commitments of support could no longer be viewed through the lens of maternal protection. Britain clearly viewed Australia as another country freed of this embrace, Australia needed to decide what kind of country it wanted to be. The choice of a middle power label was useful as a starting point precisely because of what it did not say. It did not commit Australia to regional or global affairs, but offered both. It suggested a capacity to influence events in international politics, but did not insist upon it. Being a middle power was at once a bland description of the capacity of the country, and yet also an empty vessel into which the awakening nation of Australia could pour its hopes.

For the governments of John Curtin (1941–1945) and Ben Chifley (1945–1949), the middle power label helped organise their internationalist ambition for Australia. Along with devoting himself to winning the war against the Japanese, Curtin worked to rebuild the

British Commonwealth with the dominions, taking on a much larger role in directing Empire strategy.[13] Curtin and Chifley's Foreign Minister Herbert 'Doc' Evatt meanwhile saw the formation of the United Nations (UN) as key to Australia's security. At the UN's foundational conference in San Francisco in 1945, Evatt proclaimed Australia as a middle power, and a self-appointed champion of the small and middle sized states. So great was his influence on the formation of the UN that Evatt was made the first president of the UN General Assembly. Barrister Geoffrey Robertson has argued that 'it was not Gallipoli, actually, that first put Australia on the international map—it was the conduct of Evatt and his team at the UN'.[14] Yet the early aspirations of the UN as a forum for guaranteeing international security proved elusive with the onset of the Cold War, which divided much of the world into two major power blocs centered around the United States and the USSR.

In the 1950s and 1960s, the ends of Australian strategic policy were geared towards retaining British and American interest in Australia's region and contributing to the defeat of communism in Asia. The government invested in Australia's defence and diplomatic spheres. The Australian military was regularly sent into the region to address communist threats. This was known as a policy of 'forward defence' due to its focus on tackling the threat as early and as far from the Australian continent as possible. Domestic critics often regard Australian policy during this period—especially the decision to participate in the Vietnam War—as a low point in the independence of the country. Yet to those in government at the time, the Vietnam War in particular was a demonstration of Australia's importance. The Australian government had strongly encouraged Washington's participation in the conflict and Australia was quick to volunteer for involvement.[15] This was seen as a way of ensuring the US remained focused on Asia, a condition vital for Australia's sense of security. This small western outpost regularly and unashamedly offered advice and guidance to the great powers of the world. Australia's confidence was an inherited legacy of the British Empire, born of a sense that those living on the continent of Australia were separated only in geographic terms from their peers in the West. While the British economic pivot to Europe and military withdrawal behind the Suez Canal caused the occasional crisis of confidence,

Australian's rarely lost their sense of being a globally significant country.

By late 1960s and early 1970s, however the pressure for change was strong. The Cold War showed no sign of relenting, and two decades of struggle had exhausted many. The United Kingdom had formally relinquished its interest in Asia and was increasingly focused on Europe. This affected not only Australia's security, but increasingly Australia's access to UK markets. The United States likewise found itself in turmoil thanks to bubbling social changes and the consequences of the war in Vietnam. What was increasingly clear to the Australian people—especially leaders such as Harold Holt (1966–67) and Gough Whitlam (1972–1975)—was that the fundamental assumptions of Australia, as a British people who possessed of a primary industry economy, could no longer stand. The nation's strategic policy needed rethinking and again the term middle power was refashioned in service of this goal.

While the Cold War was still the predominant challenge facing Australia, new sources of economic growth were needed. As postcolonial governments emerged in Southeast Asia, Australia's immediate region could no longer be ignored. These changes were traumatic—they required pulling down the barriers to foreign competition and migration which had helped protect and shield Australia since Federation. Australians were divided on what their 'post-British' identity should be, and struggled to accept the growing need to find new markets in formerly hostile countries such as Indonesia and China. The governments of Whitlam (1972–1975) and Fraser (1975–83) differed on where those changes needed to be made and the centrality of the Cold War, but both recognised the need for a new era in Australian policy. Together they took the first steps towards two important changes in the nation's strategic policy: first to end the 'fortress Australia' mentality, in racial and economic barriers from Asia, and second to articulate a doctrine for defending Australia's continent in a self-reliant manner. The pursuit of these two goals lies at the heart of modern Australia's security and prosperity. At one level these were modest goals, seeking to maintain foundations such as the Australia-US alliance and Australia's Western identity in place. But the success of these goals sometimes obscures the sheer radicalism of this process of relocation and re-imagination of the nation.

The 1980s and early 1990s are perhaps the period in which Australia's self-identification as a middle power reached its zenith. Boyed by a clear strategic ambition, the Labor governments of Hawke (1983–1991) and Keating (1991–96)—especially their Foreign Ministers Bill Hayden and Gareth Evans and Defence Minister Kim Beazley—injected a profound new sense of optimism and self-confidence into the nature of Australian policy. These leaders helped usher in a belief that Australia was now capable of the independent defence of its territory, that it was an integral part of its region and a diplomatic force on the world stage. With the collapse of the USSR in 1991, a Labor government again dreamed of finding national security in multinational institutions. Yet by 1993–94 it was clear that these dreams were as elusive as they had been half a century before. Grand initiatives such as the Asia-Pacific Economic Cooperation (APEC) proved useful but not significant. The role of the United States in Asia and how Australia interacted with it was barely re-thought at the senior levels. Though Paul Keating famously announced he wanted to seek security 'in Asia not from it' his government undertook only small steps towards his goal through agreements with Indonesia and support for cooperative security on non-traditional threats.

By the mid-1990s the government had fallen out of favour and new parties emerged to rail against the pace of change. The Keating government was tossed from office. The new prime minister John Howard (1996–2007) took heed of this message and took a more cautious and reactive approach to foreign and defence policy. Howard did not see a need—philosophically or practically—to debate the cornerstones of Australia's strategic policy. He viewed strengthening the Australia-US alliance as an uncomplicated good, kept security relations with Asia in a low-key fashion and continued the push to liberalise Australia's trade with Asia. These were ideas Howard had encouraged while Treasurer under the Fraser government. As prime minister, Howard would work to ensure they were locked into place but would go no further.

In 1999 Howard reluctantly sent Australian troops into East Timor to lead a UN mission to stabilise the country. This was a notable success that gained Australia regional and global respect. The intervention in East Timor and the 2001 terrorist attacks in the

US—triggering the War on Terror—led to an all too brief debate around a new strategic ambition for Australia. In an intense period from late 2001 to 2004, the Howard government began to conceive of Australia as having a form of regional responsibility for tackling insecurity and instability in the Pacific and Southeast Asia. During this period it led the fight against terrorism in Southeast Asia, in particular helping regional countries identify and tackle threats and strengthen regional counter-proliferation. It also undertook the Regional Assistance Mission to Solomon Islands (RAMSI) (see Chapter 6) and worked to address non-traditional challenges like irregular migration by creating the Bali Process. Yet the success of these efforts and onslaught of criticism when trying to articulate this role[16] saw the government revert to complacency about the long-term sources of Australia's security and prosperity. This suited the philosophical approach of the Howard government, which doubted the capacity of government to set and achieve long-term ambitions. Moreover, the government worried that such idealism too often interfered with the task they had been elected to achieve: a pragmatic advancement of the national interest.

Despite a booming economy and the War on Terror the Howard government's expansion of the Australian Defence Forces (ADF) was comparatively minor and ad-hoc. The Australian military has maintained roughly the same force structure it has had for over half a century. The Howard government focused on equipment and forces that could easily fit into US-led coalitions (such as the US-made M1A1 Abrams tanks and Special Forces troops). While there was an indulgence of funding for the military, there was no larger purpose to the spending or even effort to keep up with regional growth. The Howard government largely resisted changes to the essential character of the Australia-US alliance. American encouragement to adopt a responsibility for Southeast Asian security was flirted with and quickly dropped, while Australian support for US commitments overseas was in many ways half-hearted. Offering strong rhetorical support for the wars in Afghanistan and Iraq, the government insisted Australia's troop deployments were small in number and largely operated in comparatively safer regions of these countries.[17] Howard wanted to strengthen the Australia-US alliance, but keep it within the same rough parameters it had been for the past few decades. Meanwhile Australia's diplomatic presence overseas shrunk to one of the lowest in the developed world over the term of the Howard government.[18] Most of the burgeoning government revenue—thanks to a once in a lifetime economic boom driven by China's demand for raw materials—was returned to the Australian public in the form of taxation cuts and increased social spending.[19]

Where Howard was unwilling to identify a clear strategic policy for Australia, the Rudd and Gillard governments were keen but unable to. Both leaders kept trying to play the same middle power tune of the Hawke and Keating's governments, but kept hitting the wrong notes. At first, the 2007 election of Kevin Rudd seemed to herald a return to Australian activism and the new prime minister spoke of wanting to inject this into Australian foreign policy and contribute to the big strategic questions of his time, in particular the rise of China and the challenge of global warming.[20] Yet this ambition was not matched by innovation in rhetoric or tactics. Rudd had a tendency to simply repeat the formula of the Hawke and Keating governments in his descriptions of Australia as a middle power, sometimes adding the words 'creative' before it to dress it up.[21] The result was hollow rhetoric—as befitted much of Rudd's thinking about these issues.

The two big proposals for leadership that Rudd championed were to repeat the model of the Hawke government by creating a new institution—the Asia Pacific Community (APC)—and the Keating government with a new non-proliferation experts panel, the International Commission for Non-Proliferation and Disarmament (ICNND). Both re-runs were neither a tragedy nor farce, but merely uninspired. Both addressed important problems, but lacked the 'quick and thoughtful diplomatic footwork'[22] of their predecessors. Rudd even tasked the same diplomatic advocate, Richard Woolcott, as Hawke had nearly thirty years before. Rudd was right to recognise that the region lacked a forum where the United States, China and the interested smaller countries such as Australia could convene to discuss security issues. What he failed to appreciate was that thirty years on from Hawke's initiative, the Asia-Pacific faced institutional fatigue. The region has half a dozen major forums and conducts well over 1000 multilateral meetings per year. To add another giant new institution—especially one announced in an unclear and contradictory fashion—was always going to be an unlikely proposal.

Beyond the lack of fresh thinking, there was also a problem of sustained effort. The ICNND had real merit and was well timed with the election of a new US president who was committed to non-proliferation. Yet by the time the panel had finished their report, Rudd had moved on. When he was invited by US President Obama to speak to his report at the 2010 Nuclear Security Summit in Washington DC (the biggest meeting of international leaders on nuclear issues in history), he declined, citing the need to address domestic health reform in Australia.[23] Rudd was also closely involved in the writing of the 2009 Defence White Paper. While outlining a vision of a major upgrade in the Australian military (albeit without a clear strategy), it quickly suffered from a lack of support. Rudd's 2009 Defence White Paper was official policy for a mere nine days before domestic budget pressures led the government to cut, delay and defer its plans. Neither the Australian public nor Rudd's successor as prime minister, Julia Gillard, seemed overly concerned. Indeed Gillard undertook further cuts to the Defence Budget during her term. She also tried to copy her ALP predecessors by emulating the Hawke government's 1989 report *Australia and the Northeast Asian Ascendency* with her own *Australia in the Asian Century* White Paper. Like Rudd's APC idea, this also sunk without a trace upon release.

The failure here was not just one individual leader. Indeed, Rudd in particular should be commended for doing far more than any contemporary prime minister. He encouraged Australia to be bold, engaged in world affairs and assert its claim for middle power status. Yet over the last decade, while Australia's material capacity has boomed, the nation's focus has turned inwards. Australian politicians have had little choice but to follow this trend. For most countries, a period of strong economic growth would encourage them to become more confident of their place in the world. Australia by contrast has sought a retreat. As discussed in Chapter 3 of this book, public support for defence spending has declined, while polls consistently show that the first priority Australians expect of their foreign minister is 'protecting the jobs of Australian workers'.[24]

Contributing to this worrying turn of events is the absence of a common sense about the ends towards which Australian strategic policy should be aimed. Enjoying security and prosperity, things were allowed to just drift along. While the Howard government flirted with but never saw the need for a vision, the Rudd and Gillard governments thought the political achievements from the 1980s could be copied and pasted into the current era. The lack of a twenty-first century inspired vision for Australia's role in the world is telling. If this is not addressed in coming years, Australia will struggle to keep its alliance with the US an active partnership instead of mere insurance. Consequently, Canberra will find its voice less relevant and less heard in the region. By examining how other similar sized countries are pursuing their national interests, we can begin to see more clearly some possible ambitions for Australian strategic policy.

Present: End of the Middle Power Era?

One regular and valid criticism of the term 'middle power' in international politics is that it is seemed to refer to a select group of self-chosen Western countries (such as Australia and Canada) who helped support the global order established by the United States. While these middle powers had different views from the United States on a range of issues, they were working within the same world view and international framework. As critics such as Eduand Jordaan rightly noted, it was highly convenient that middle power behaviour, self-described as 'good international citizenship', also served the national interests of both the middle power states and their great power protector.[25]

In the last few decades, a number of non-Western states such as South Korea, Turkey, South Africa and Indonesia have begun identifying as middle powers. Scholars have also re-thought the term, keen to restore the focus on 'power' and states 'in the middle' and in the process restoring its use in debates over how national size and capacity shape outcomes in international politics. Before looking at how Australia compares to other middle power countries there are two important caveats to consider. First, state power and capacity is not automatically transferrable across issues or areas. By simply looking at statistics (instead of whether a country has the means for defence or influence) there is a tendency to 'average out' middle power countries. Second, which countries Australia is compared with can also significantly change how its capacity is understood.

Table 2.1: Comparison of Population, Economy, Defence Spending and Armed Forces of Middle Power Countries

2012	Australia	Argentina	Brazil	Canada	Indonesia	Israel	Mexico	Singapore	South Korea	Turkey
Population	22 015 576	42 192 494	199 321 413	34 300 083	248 645 008	7 590 758	114 975 406	5 353 494	48 860 500	79 749 461
Number of troops	79 700	104 350	2 053 500	101 450	1 076 500	641 500	417 100	504 100	8 159 500	1 041 500
Defence budget (US$ billion)	24.20	4.26	35.30	18.40	7.74	16.30	5.11	12.30	33tr	17.00
GDP US$ billion	1540.00	474.81	2430.00	1770.00	894.85	246.78	1160.00	267.94	1150.00	783.10

Source: International Institute for Strategic Studies, The Military Balance 2013, vol. 113, no.1, International Institute for Strategic Studies, London, 2013.

Australia accounts for 94 per cent of all military spending in the South Pacific region, making it a virtual regional hegemon. In the wider East Asia region, however, it accounts for only 8 per cent. While these figures do not invalidate the benefits of comparisons, they do highlight the need for caution.

The ideal middle power country would be one with the alliance influence of an Israel, the global character reference of a Sweden, the security of Canada and the regional significance of a Brazil. Of course, not all these roles are possible for a single country. The ultimate feature of middle power strategy is that it involves trade-offs. Directed carefully, these states can have a significant role in regional and global affairs. Used without caution, the country will be a weak 'jack-of-all trades', stretched too thin across too much ground and without significance or respect anywhere. The previous table helps show the general capacity of a range of middle power states.

Beyond the mere numbers, we can also look towards the actions and attitudes of these countries to see which are seeking influence and examine plausible roles for Australia. Brazil in South America and Turkey in the Middle East have both been seeking to develop their middle power position into one of regional leadership. This has been achieved by promoting ideas of regional identity and organisation that place them at the centre of affairs. Brazil is building economic and security links as part of a push for stronger Latin American regionalism. However economic challenges at home alongside headaches from dealing with more tempestuous neighbours who want a more radical approach (most notably Venezuela) have restricted Brazil's efforts to speak on behalf of the region and gain global significance. Turkey has also sought to develop its claim to regional leadership in the Middle East, focusing on common Islamic values. But like Brazil, economic and social problems at home and difficulty selling this vision to its neighbours have curtailed some of the enthusiasm for this approach. Is this applicable for Australia? Given the cultural difference between Australia and Southeast Asia and the acknowledged role of Indonesia as the region's de-facto leader, the approach of Brazil and Turkey would seem unlikely. Still, Australia has proven its capacity to encourage Indonesian leadership through regional initiatives—for example upgrading APEC in 1992 and the Bali Process in 2001.

Another challenging option is the approach taken by Israel and North Korea. Two very different middle power countries, yet both have been very successful at extracting significant resources and support from major powers. The downside to Israel and North Korea's approach is that both are controversial, even isolated figures, in regional and international affairs. Australians might look enviously at the way Israel has developed a solid domestic constituency in the United States which helps it shape the alliance to favour the smaller power, but it is Israel's besieged situation which sustains this influence. This is not a plausible or attractive approach for Australia. Likewise, going 'off the reservation' so-to-speak by following North Korea would only serve to cause economic and social harm to Australia. Still, these states show that small does not mean irrelevant or subservient in world affairs.

Some countries see the difficulty and challenge that claiming this label brings and they simply forgo the status. After all, mid-sized nation-states do not need to be incessantly activist, nor insert themselves into the predicaments facing great powers. Many states, regardless of their latent capacity, find that they can secure enough of their national interests by merely seizing opportunities rather than creating new conditions for change. Indonesia presents a good example of this approach. A country which has long had one of the largest populations and regional authority, it has spent much of the past few decades looking inwards. During the Cold War Jakarta willingly allowed itself to be 'constrained' within the Association of Southeast Asian Nations (ASEAN) and rejected participating in an alliance with either of the major power-blocs. Since then it has pursued a policy of 'a thousand friends, zero enemies', with a focus on its internal domestic and economic challenges. The Asian Financial Crisis in the late 1990s and establishment of a democratic order reinforced the appeal of this inward strategy. In more recent years however Indonesia's focus has begun to move beyond its borders. It has shown a new willingness to cooperate and lead on regional affairs and assert its voice on key issues. Indonesia is now beginning to see itself as a middle power with significance in the Asia-Pacific and beyond.

Another country starting to identify as a middle power is South Korea, which has sought to achieve a global influence in the early years of the twenty-first century. Wedged between an expanding

China, a more assertive Japan and the ever-unpredictable North Korea, Seoul could be forgiven for focusing on domestic concerns. In spite of, or indeed perhaps because of these challenges, South Korea has become one of the most active users of the middle power concept and participant in forums aimed at solving regional and global challenges. A recent example of their leadership was pushing the creation of a new middle power bloc in mid-2013 involving South Korea, Mexico, Indonesia, Turkey and Australia (MIKTA). The member states announced the grouping by stating that:

> Amid this rapidly changing global situation and environment, efforts only by big powers and other particular countries are not enough to select and address global issues that influence the entire international community. The launch of a new mechanism among middle-power countries, which have a certain level of political and economic status and capabilities, as well as the willingness to contribute to creating a new world order, is expected to help resolve issues facing the international community and maintain world peace.[26]

While this survey is brief and incomplete, it demonstrates the wide range of approaches available to middle power states. It also highlights the paucity of recent Australian efforts in this area. Since the mid-1990s Canberra has kept its military and diplomatic orientation essentially static, even as the region before it is substantially changing. This is not due to any single party, government or leader. It is a lethargy that has been encouraged by the comfortable conditions and appreciated by the Australian public. New ideas have been rare and usually abandoned in the face of even slight criticism. To overcome this, and find ways to escape the growing prediction of relative economic[27] and strategic decline[28] it is necessary for a renewed discussion by Australians about the ends of the nation's strategic policy.

Future: What role for Australia?

Being a middle power has never been as practically straightforward for Australia, yet more intellectually difficult than it is today. Australia has spent much of the last decade—if not longer—squandering its prosperity and drifting along in its strategy. Tough choices will need to be considered as China looks to challenge the US role in Asia, as Indonesia expands its authority and as the underlying norms, institutions and structures of the region shift. Even within the Australia-US alliance, there are changing expectations that Canberra has, for now, rebuffed, but it will not always be able to do so.

This chapter concludes by outlining five possible 'ends' for Australian strategic policy, based around the idea of Australia as a middle power. These proposals are less direct policy suggestions than attempts to push to more logical extremes the various and often contradictory threads that make up Australia's mixed-bag approach to strategic policy. Once an ambition has been chosen, then strategies, capabilities and policies can be devised around it. Of course, this needs to be an ongoing process, as the feasibility of strategies, availability of capabilities and the political temperate of the Australian community are taken in account. But the discussion and establishment of overarching ambitions is primary. Australia's defence requires far more than just efficient management of our available ways and means.

1. Sustain the Status Quo

The first option is to explicitly commit Australia to preserving the US-led Asia-Pacific regional order for as long as possible. This is effectively what Australia's current policy amounts to, though Australians have found it preferable not to say so publicly. American leadership and hegemony in the Asia-Pacific since 1945 has served Australia very well and the US alliance remains the most popular policy in Australia's foreign and defence policy toolbox. Such an approach would envisage a middle power role much like we have been undertaking, though with a more deliberate effort to encourage other states to cooperate with the United States, sustain Washington's interest and capacity in the region, and provide an interoperable force which could be applied when and where the United States needs Australia to act. This policy would be relatively uncomplicated in the short to medium term. It would enjoy strong public support and suit some of the recent developments in Australia's force posture, doctrine and capabilities. It would also be a role which many of Australia's regional allies and key partners (such as Japan, South Korea, Thailand and Singapore) would appreciate Australia playing.

The challenges to this position as a middle power enforcer of the current order would be both material and ideational. The 2013 Defence White Paper places 'contributing to military contingencies in the Indo-Pacific' (with a focus on Southeast Asia) as a third order task. But to sustain the US-led status quo long term this may become a 'non-negotiable' challenge for Australia. There would be no escaping the 'deputy sheriff' label this time around, though sustaining it long term will prove challenging, especially if the costs of doing so continue to rise. Finally should the United States decide the present order in Asia is not worth sustaining and decide to withdraw, Australia could end up exposed and out of step with the region. Before venturing down this role of 'same but more', as the current trend in Australia's strategic policy seems to imply, other approaches are worth also considering.

2. Collective Security in Asia

An alternative to sustaining the US-led order in Asia would be the integration of Australia's security with its Southeast Asian neighbours. Australia has already worked extensively with Southeast Asian countries to address non-traditional security issues such as terrorism, drug smuggling and irregular migration. Transferring this cooperation into the conventional security sphere presents real challenges but it is not inconceivable. Australia would need to dedicate its forces to defend and protect Southeast Asia. In turn the logic of geography, especially the Indonesian archipelago, would replace the US as the umbrella which helps Australia weather any future conflicts in Asia.

Of course, Indonesia might not be keen on playing this role. Any move to formal security relations with Australia would compromise their long standing non-alignment ideals while complicating Jakarta's leadership role in ASEAN. An even larger challenge would be convincing the Australian public of this approach. Australia may have 'found home' in Asia, but it is still a long way from being willing to entrust its security to the neighbours. It would probably take an event as cataclysmic as an American retreat from Asia to push Australia into a true collective security approach to the region. Australia would also have to invest in a larger defence force, especially naval to ensure it could meaningfully contribute to the region's security. And the Australian people would also have to be willing to deploy that force to resolve issues that might not be of immediate national interest—such as helping protect mainland Asian states from internal or regional conflicts.

3. A True Defence of Australia

Should regional security be too difficult and supporting US engagement no longer viable, Australia's historical record offers another option: updating and fully implementing the Defence of Australia (DoA) concept. This set of ideas from the 1970s and 1980s developed a strategy for Australia to coherently think about providing some measure of self-reliance in defending the continent. The DoA concept provides an intellectual framework, which could enable the Australian government to shape Australia's defence policy. This path would require not only a substantial increase in the defence budget but also reignite some highly contentious debates including whether to develop an Australian nuclear weapon program and the size and capabilities of the ADF, including for example the establishment of a continental missile defence system or armed drones and robotics.

Australia would also need to clearly identify the specific types of threats faced, perhaps including specific nations, so as to ensure efficient defence planning. Publicly identifying these threats could come at a cost to Australia's regional relationships and would also present domestic political challenges. The 'defence of Australia' path would likely only have appeal in a far more hostile region, where the potential for cooperation was low. It would also be difficult to balance this approach with regional cooperation to protect trade routes and provide assistance to other nations through stabilisation operations and military led humanitarian aid and relief.

4. A Major Power

Australia's middle power status is to some degree self-imposed by one fact alone: its small population. With the sixth largest landmass, Australia covers an area equal to much of the United States or Western Europe, yet has less than 10 per cent of their populations. In global terms Australians make up one third of 1 per cent of the world's population. This is partly a condition of low rainfall, which contributes to the dryness of the continent and other environmental challenges. But

Australians have also been very reluctant to grow, even though the country already produces enough food to feed 60 million people.[29] With good management and emerging technologies in agriculture and energy it could expand far beyond that. If the population grew rapidly Australia could come to have the economy and defence force of a major power. As the former Minister for Foreign Affairs Alexander Downer has noted, the term middle power can be viewed as a way of downplaying Australia's significance and suggest a country 'helplessly wedged between big and small powers with very little role to play'.[30] When thinking about Australia as a 'middle power' the term should not be allowed to become a ceiling to Australia's ambitions. Australia is just as well placed as any country in the world to take advantage of the economic opportunities in Asia and play a major role in shaping the region's security and governance. As noted earlier, what is most lacking most is a sense of purpose for such a role and willingness to consider and bear some of the initial costs. When Kevin Rudd announced his support for a 'big Australia' of 36 million, achieved by no more than the existing population growth, he was howled down. Until the willingness to even remain a middle power can be re-asserted, any dreams of being a major regional player beyond that will remain enticing but necessarily idle thoughts.

5. Road to Wellington

Finally, instead of striving to stay a middle power Australian leaders could seek security through obscurity. As defence white papers have echoed for the last thirty years, Australia is one of the safest countries on earth. The threats it faces are largely non-traditional and small scale. Australia could well take the 'road to Wellington' by emulating New Zealand and drastically reducing the defence force. It would be a decision that a middle power role was simply too expensive and difficult for Australia to maintain. This path would inevitably weaken the Australia-US alliance, and perhaps even lead to its termination. Washington might still be willing to help protect Australia in a future regional conflict, but the flow of regional support would be curtailed. In the meantime the country would have between 20–50 billion extra dollars every year to spend on health, education, industry or return to the population as taxation cuts. National leaders could stay focused on Australian domestic affairs, which may be appropriate for the general public sentiment in Australia in the early twenty-first century. The new era may well see Australia as a small power.

Conclusion: Towards a new era

Australia faces a new era in its foreign and defence policies. No longer does it fear the tyranny of distance. Instead it enjoys a proximity to prosperity alongside a booming Asia. As North Atlantic economies slumped during the 2008 Global Financial Crisis, Australia's powered on, thanks largely to growth in Australia's trade with Asia. Asian countries now account for 69 per cent of Australia's exports and 50 per cent of its imports (including four of Australia's top six import and export markets).[31] Today, Australia has the twelfth-largest economy in the world, making its material claim to be a middle power straightforward. It is secure and respected. These outcomes were not achieved by luck, but through the decision of a series of leaders to think about the long term ends of Australian strategic policy.

What role and ambitions Australia will set for itself in the next fifty years is yet to be made clear. Australian leaders have largely indulged in the prosperity and security of the last decade or so, and not undertaken a serious effort to think clearly about what role Australia can play to ensure its future security and prosperity. At a time when there is no direct existential threat to Australia's sovereignty, this approach is understandable, but it must rank as a missed opportunity. As the regional strategic environment changes, hard choices for Australia will be required. Will Canberra put its faith in sustaining the status quo or undertake the highly difficult approach of transferring its key security relationships into Southeast Asia? Will Australia seek to retreat to defending its territory and demur from a dangerous region or even seek a regional authority beyond a 'mere' middle power?

Much of what ensures Australia's defence are pragmatic, cautious choices about how to allocate scarce resources. But efficiency is not an end in itself. Thinking strategically also requires thinking about the goals towards which Australian leaders can devote their nation's energy and focus. As they have in the past, Australians can today use the middle power label to usefully guide discussion of the aims of national strategic policy and fashion a new approach, appropriate for the twenty-first century. Australia has enjoyed a long era of security, prosperity and comfort in the Asia-Pacific region. This situation cannot be taken for granted or assumed to endure long term. Australia's defence depends upon developing new ambitions towards which the nation can pursue in this new era.

Further Reading

Evans, Gareth and Grant, Bruce, *Australia's Foreign Relations: In the World of the 1990s*, Melbourne University Press, Melbourne, 1995.

Rear Admiral Hill, JR, *Maritime Strategy for Medium Powers*, Croom Helm, Sydney, 1986.

Keating, Paul, *Engagement: Australia Faces the Asia-Pacific*, Pan MacMillan, Sydney, 2000.

Millar, TB, *Australia in War and Peace: External Relations Since 1788*, Australian National University Press, Canberra, 1991.

Wesley, Michael, *The Howard Paradox: Australian Diplomacy in Asia 1996– 2006*, ABC Books, Sydney, 2007.

Notes

1   L Freedman, *Strategy: A History*, Oxford University Press, New York, 2013, p. xi.

2   TB Millar, *Australia in Peace and War*, 2nd edn., Maxwell Macmillan Publishing, Sydney, 1991, p. 2.

3   M Wesley, *There Goes the Neighbourhood: Australia and the Rise of Asia*, University of New South Wales Press, Sydney, 2011, p. 169.

4   A Carr, 'Is Australia a Middle Power? A Systemic Impact Approach', *Australian Journal of International Affairs*, vol. 68, no. 1, 2014, pp. 1–15.

5   Commonwealth of Australia, *2013 Defence White Paper*, Commonwealth of Australia, Canberra, 2013. www.defence.gov.au/whitepaper2013/docs/WP_2013_web.pdf (viewed December 2013).

6   P Dibb, *Review of Australia's Defence Capabilities: Report for the Minister of Defence*, Commonwealth of Australia, Canberra, 1986, p. 1. www.defence.gov.au/oscdf/se/publications/defreview/1986/Review-of-Australias-Defence-Capabilities-1986_Part1.pdf (viewed December 2013).

7   International Institute for Strategic Studies, *The Military Balance 2013*, vol. 113, no. 1, *The Military Balance*, International Institute for Strategic Studies, London, 2013, p. 249.

8   ibid., pp. 279–286.

9   Commonwealth of Australia, *Defending Australia in the Asia Pacific Century: Force 2030*, Commonwealth of Australia, Canberra, 2009, p. 49. www.defence.gov.au/whitepaper2009/docs/defence_white_paper_2009.pdf (viewed December 2013).

10   G Megalogenis, 'The Book of Paul: Lessons in Leadership and Paul Keating', *The Monthly*, Sydney, 2011.

11   Quoted by Minister for Communications M Turnbull, speech launching *Dog Days: Australia After the Boom* by Ross Garnaut, National Press Club,

Canberra, 15 November 2013. www.malcolmturnbull.com.au/media/breathing-life-back-into-australias-reform-era-launch-of-ross-garnauts-dog (viewed December 2013).

12   TB Millar, *Australia in Peace and War*, 1991, p. 391.

13   J Curran, *Curtin's Empire*, Cambridge University Press, New York, 2011, p. 95.

14   G Robertson, *The Statute of Liberty: How Australians Can Take Back Their Rights*, Vintage, Sydney, 2009, pp. 30–31.

15   D McLean, 'From British Colony to American Satellite? Australia and the USA During the Cold War', *Australian Journal of Politics and History*, vol. 52, no. 1, 2006, p. 77.

16   While there was some talk of a 'Howard Doctrine', a rhetorical misstep by the prime minister—failing to refute the suggestion Australia was acting as a 'sort of deputy sheriff'—led to strong criticism within Australia and Asia. Stung by the controversy and without the desire to pursue a fundamental shift in the nation's approach, the Howard government soon pulled back in its ambitions. See P Kelly, *The March of Patriots: The Struggle for Modern Australia*, Melbourne University Press, Carlton, 2009, p. 515.

17   Australian Special Forces are an obvious exception to this.

18   A Shearer and A Oliver, *Diplomatic Disrepair: Rebuilding Australia's International Policy Infrastructure*, Lowy Institute for International Policy, Sydney, 2011. www.lowyinstitute.org/files/pubfiles/Oliver_and_Shearer%2C_Diplomatic_disrepair_Web.pdf (viewed December 2013).

19   R Garnaut, *Dog Days: Australia After the Boom*, Redback, Melbourne, 2013, p. 7.

20   K Rudd, 'The Rise of the Asia Pacific and the Role of Creative Middle Power Diplomacy', speech to the Professor Bernt Seminar Series, Oslo University, Oslo, 19 May 2011. www.foreignminister.gov.au/speeches/2011/kr_sp_110519.html (viewed January 2014).

21   ibid.

22   G Evans and B Grant, *Australia's Foreign Relations: In the World of the 1990s*, Melbourne University Press, Carlton, 1995, p. 347.

23   N Stuart, *Rudd's Way: November 2007–June 2010*, Scribe Publications, Melbourne, 2010, p. 130.

24   F Hanson, *Australia and the World: Public Opinion and Foreign Policy*, Lowy Institute for International Policy, Sydney, 2011, p. 3. www.lowyinstitute.org/files/pubfiles/Lowy_Poll_2011_WEB.pdf (viewed December 2013).

25   E Jordaan, 'The Concept of a Middle Power in International Relations: Distinguishing Between Emerging and Traditional Middle Powers', *Politikon: South African Journal of Political Studies*, vol. 30, no. 1, 2003, pp. 166–167.

26   Ministry of Foreign Affairs, Republic of Korea, 'Launch of MIKTA: A Mechanism for Cooperation Between Key Middle-Power Countries', Ministry of Foreign Affairs, Republic of Korea, Seoul, 2013. www.mofa.go.kr/webmodule/htsboard/template/read/engreadboard.jsp?boardid=3

02&typeID=12&tableName=TYPE_ENGLISH&seqno=312809 (viewed December 2013).

27   R Garnaut, *Dog Days*, 2013.

28   H White, 'What Indonesia's Rise Means for Australia', *The Monthly*, June 2013. www.themonthly.com.au/issue/2013/june/1370181600/hugh-white/what-indonesia-s-rise-means-australia (viewed December 2013).

29   Prime Minister's Science, Engineering and Innovation Council, *Australia and Food Security in a Changing World*, Commonwealth of Australia, Canberra, 2010, p. 1. www.chiefscientist.gov.au/wp-content/uploads/FoodSecurity_web.pdf (viewed December 2013).

30   A Downer, 'Much More Than a Middle Power', speech to the Young Liberals Convention, Liberal Party of Australia, Canberra, 8 January 1996.

31   Department of Foreign Affairs and Trade, *Composition of Trade 2012–13*, Commonwealth of Australia, Canberra, 2013, p. 5.

3

Public Attitudes to Defence

Charles Miller

In the final sentence of the original *Australia's Defence*, TB Millar exhorted: 'Let us not be frightened to have a public discussion on defence. It is the public, after all, which seeks and needs to be defended.'[1] In spite of this, an examination of the original 1965 text reveals very little discussion of public opinion on defence. There is a brief reference to the low prestige of army officers relative to other professions. Millar also draws a distinction between the Chinese autocracy and Australia where foreign policies are 'subject to public scrutiny and debate'. But what is the state of this public debate today?

Millar is correct to note that in a democratic country like Australia, government policy *ought* to follow as closely as possible the will of the people. Of course, that is not always how it works out. It is quite possible for governments to continue with policies long after they have forfeited majority support and still be re-elected—the war in Afghanistan has not enjoyed the support of a majority of voters in any North Atlantic Treaty Organization (NATO) country since 2010 and yet many nations still maintain troops there.[2] As this fact serves to demonstrate, political leaders have more apparent slack in terms of foreign and defence policy than they do in domestic policy. Issues such as education, healthcare and taxation have an immediate and noticeable impact on the lives of most Australians.

Consequently, Australian voters are more likely to go to the trouble to inform themselves about these issues and to vote according to the parties' performance and policies on them. In foreign policy and especially when it comes to national security, by contrast, the impact of policy is very remote from the everyday lives of the vast majority of Australians. This means that most Australians have less ability to judge whether foreign policy is 'working' for them or not and less incentive to punish leaders in the event that it is not. Add to this the perception—not always warranted—that Australia enjoys a high degree of bipartisan consensus on foreign policy and Australian leaders are believed to have much more leeway in the conduct of foreign than of domestic policy. Indeed, in the Lowy Institute for International Policy's 'Australia and the World' 2010 poll, 69 per cent of respondents agreed that the Australian government 'pays too little attention to the opinions of people like (myself)'.[3]

Yet this is not the whole truth. Leaders who defy the will of the majority on foreign policy for too long on an issue which has become particularly salient, or who fail spectacularly in the international realm, can pave the way for dramatic electoral reversals. The reason why, for instance, the President of the United States is Barack Obama and not Hillary Clinton or John McCain is almost certainly related to Obama's timely opposition to the ill-fated war in Iraq. Australia does not offer quite such a spectacular example of the power of foreign policy issues to shape the domestic political land-scape, although some analysts do credit the shift in the electoral fortunes first toward the Liberals and then toward Labor in the 1960s and 1970s to the changing climate of opinion on the Vietnam War.[4] This goes to show the importance of understanding the relationship between public opinion and foreign policy—not only where the public stands on various issues, but what the key drivers of these views are.

Of all the countries in the world, American public opinion on global affairs is the most studied. This is understandable. For one thing, the United States remains the world's most powerful country in military and economic terms and so the views of the average American arguably matter far more for the rest of the world than the views of the average citizen of any other country. Moreover, US universities, think tanks, pollsters and media organisations have very deep pockets. The techniques and theories used to understand public opinion and foreign policy are therefore almost all of US origin.

Nonetheless, for a middle power, Australian public opinion on foreign policy is relatively well studied. When an issue such as the war in Afghanistan crops up in the news, Australian media organisations carry out sporadic polling which allows us to track the course of Australian opinion to a reasonable degree. Even more valuably, the Lowy Institute's Poll (Lowy poll) and the Australian National University's Australian Election Survey (AES) allow us to see what Australians think about the world around them consistently and over the long haul. Moreover, Australia has gone some way in following US researchers' lead and understanding *why* Australians think the way they do about foreign policy and not just *what* they think.

This chapter will proceed by summarising the current state of knowledge of Australian public opinion on five of the most important issues in Australian strategic and defence policy. These are: views on potential external adversaries/threats; views on defence spending; views on allies; support for conflicts/casualty tolerance; and the public opinion of the Australian Defence Force. The chapter will then summarise the main findings. Essentially, it concludes that Australians want to keep defence spending where it is, are pro-American, highly respectful of the ADF, relaxed about the overall security situation (though surprisingly suspicious of their Indonesian neighbours) and are casualty sensitive, though not casualty phobic.

1. External Adversaries/Threats to Australia

In broad terms, the picture which emerges over the last forty years of research on Australian public opinion is of a gradually declining perception of an external security threat. In 1975, the AES began asking Australians whether they thought a given list of countries posed a security threat to Australia—Russia, China, Indonesia, Japan and Vietnam. Approximately half of Australians consistently believed that at least one of these countries was a 'very likely' security threat to Australia. In 1981, this proportion peaked at 63 per cent following the 1979–1989 Soviet invasion of Afghanistan. Since the end of the Cold War, however, this proportion has dropped to one third.[5]

Of these specific countries, some interesting patterns have emerged. For instance, in 1967, 31 per cent of Australians viewed China as a security threat compared to 7 per cent for Indonesia. By 2007, this pattern had reversed itself almost entirely—28 per cent viewed Indonesia as a threat, while only 10 per cent viewed China in the same way. The 2013 Lowy poll revealed precisely the same pattern—54 per cent believed Indonesia to be a likely or very likely security threat to Australia. Yet only 41 per cent of respondents believed that China was likely to be a security threat to Australia in the next twenty years.[6]

The end of the Vietnam War and China's economic transformation may account for the reversal in Australian perceptions of China. The Indonesian pattern—whereby an increasing number of Australians have come to view it as a security threat—is particularly surprising however. First, because Australian elites no longer appear to believe Indonesia is a serious security threat.[7] Second, because proponents of the 'democratic peace theory' might have expected Indonesia's democratisation to have drastically reduced Australian perceptions of an Indonesian security threat.[8] Further polling may in fact provide something of a resolution to this conundrum. For one thing, only a minority of Australians believe that Indonesia is actually a democracy, despite its political transition.[9] It could therefore be surmised that Indonesia's democratisation has reduced the prospects of conflict with Australia, but only through its effect on Australia's better informed elite. This could in turn suggest an important caveat to the democratic peace proposition.

An alternative explanation for the Australian public's continued fear of Indonesia (but not China) could be that Indonesia is a majority Muslim country and China is not (Islam having replaced communism, since the end of the Cold War and especially since the 11 September 2001 terrorist attacks, as the ideological concern). In the 2013 Lowy poll, for instance, the proportion believing Indonesia to be a security threat was exactly the same as that believing it to be a 'dangerous source of Islamic terrorism'.[10] Indonesia's greater proximity to Australia cannot explain the China-Indonesia pattern, as this was also true in 1967.

Among other countries, Russia was once viewed as a threat by 40 per cent of respondents to the AES.[11] By 2000, this had dropped to

5 per cent, after which Russia was dropped from the list. Of potential security threats about which Australians were asked,[12] small minorities of Australians also continue to view Japan as a potential security threat. In the years since the question was first asked, however, on only two occasions have more than 10 per cent of respondents taken this view. In 2004, 6 per cent of Australian respondents believed the United States to be a security threat. Whether this means they believed the US would actually attack Australia, or whether they simply meant that the United States' recklessness might embroil Australia in unnecessary conflicts is of course debatable. Nonetheless, it does reflect unease amongst many Australians at the direction which US foreign policy took under the George W Bush Administration.[13]

The Lowy poll also reveals that Australians are now more concerned about 'non-traditional' security threats than about the danger posed by any one particular foreign state.[14] In 2006 and 2008, respondents were asked what they believed to be 'critical threats' to Australia's vital interests. The top two concerns in 2008 and top three concerns in 2006 were all non-traditional threats, with global warming placing first in 2006 and water shortages in 2008.[15] Of the 'traditional', state-on-state concerns, only nuclear proliferation and energy supply disruptions (assuming one can class these as 'state-on-state' concerns) were mentioned by a majority of respondents— 62 per cent in 2008, 70 per cent in 2006 for nuclear proliferation and 58 per cent and 51 per cent respectively for energy disruptions.[16] The rise of China was mentioned by only 34 per cent in 2006 and 25 per cent in 2008; China-Taiwan tensions by 31 per cent in 2006 and 33 per cent in 2008; and tensions on the Korean peninsula by 26 per cent in 2006 and 34 per cent in 2008.

By contrast, global warming and terrorism were mentioned as critical threats by majorities in both 2006 and 2008—68 and 66 per cent; and 73 and 66 per cent respectively. The majority of respondents also mentioned disease and Islamic fundamentalism as critical threats in 2006, though both came in at just under 50 per cent in 2008. However, some non-traditional threats did not rank especially high— 'immigration' was mentioned as a threat by only 33 per cent and 31 per cent of respondents respectively, while 'state failure' in Australia's own region concerned only 28 per cent of respondents in 2006 and 31 per cent in 2008.[17]

Overall, although non-traditional security threats are replacing traditional concerns for the Australian public, they are not generating an overall feeling of insecurity. In fact, according to the 2013 Lowy poll, an overwhelming proportion—91 per cent of Australians—feel either 'secure' or 'very secure'.[18] This stands in an interesting contrast to the United States, where a recent report highlights that a majority of respondents believe that the rise of non-traditional security threats—such as terrorism—has made the world an even more dangerous place than it was in the Cold War.[19] Australians clearly disagree.

2. Defence Spending

As Andrew Davies of the Australian Strategic Policy Institute (ASPI) points out, the number of Australians expressing a strong view either way over the issue of defence spending has declined over time, as the perception of a security threat to Australia has also shrunk. In other words, the issue of defence spending neither excites nor polarises Australians quite as much as it did during the Cold War.

On the one hand, rallying support for increased defence spending would be difficult. On the other, there is no groundswell of support for cuts to defence either. Defence expert Mark Thomson has been running polls every few years since 1987 on whether Australians support increasing defence spending, keeping it the same or reducing it. Unsurprisingly, support for increased spending rose in the aftermath of the 11 September 2001 and 2002 Bali terrorist attacks rose to over 60 per cent. With the absence of any further major terrorist attacks on Australians in the last few years, however, support for defence spending has fallen again, though only to the levels seen in the late 1980s. By contrast, even in 2010, only fractionally more than 10 per cent of Australians supported cutting defence expenditure. The 2013 Lowy poll confirms the same picture—47 per cent of respondents believed Australia spends 'about the right' amount on defence, 38 per cent would like Australia to spend more and only 12 per cent believe Australia should spend less.[20] What drives public opinion on defence spending?

As the bump in support for increased defence spending after the 11 September 2001 terrorist attacks shows, highly salient incidents are a clear driver. Whether great power competition is also a factor is more debatable. The level of support for increased defence spending as measured by AES barely changed with the end of the Cold War. However, the AES's polls showed a marked increase in support for defence spending following the Soviet invasion of Afghanistan in 1980—the period when Australians felt the most under threat.[21] Contrary to ASPI, the AES poll showed a marked decline in support for increased defence spending following the end of the Cold War. Similarly, the 2013 Lowy poll showed 68 per cent support for increased defence spending when it was framed in the context of the rise of Asia, 30 per cent higher than when it was not framed in this manner.[22]

In terms of factors that might reduce support for defence spending, it is intriguing that the Global Financial Crisis appears to have had little effect. Although Australia has been less severely hit by the crisis than most developed countries, with falling tax revenues and increased demands on the welfare budget, one might still have expected some demand for defence retrenchment after 2008. Instead, the proportion of respondents in favour of lower defence spending actually fell between 2007 and 2010 and only now in 2013 has returned to 12 per cent.

A potential explanation for the lack of support for cutting defence expenditure lies in the framing of previous defence spending questions.[23] Usually, polls conducted by the Lowy Institute, the AES or ASPI simply ask whether respondents support defence spending without pointing out that a dollar spent on defence is a dollar not spent on something else, returned to Australian taxpayers in the form of tax cuts or deducted from the national debt. In other words, the apparent levels of support for defence spending shown by the polls above could simply be another way of measuring whether Australians think defence is doing a good job and not what they think the Federal Government should spend money on, in preference to something else. This remains both an interesting avenue for future research and a possibly useful rhetorical strategy for leaders intent on defence retrenchment.

3. Key Allies

Despite the small minority of Australians who in 2004 believed that the United States posed a security risk to Australia, Australian public opinion is traditionally pro-American. However, this does not translate into uncritical support for US actions. Moreover, as with most US allies, Australian opinion towards the United States tends to be warmer under a Democratic than Republican administration: if Australia were the 'fifty-first state', it would be a deep shade of blue.[24]

The AES has asked two principal questions tapping into Australian opinion towards the United States for over twenty years. The first relates to the importance respondents attach to the Australia, New Zealand, United States Security Treaty (ANZUS). The lowest proportion of respondents who claimed that ANZUS was 'very important' was just under 40 per cent in 1993. This was shortly after the Cold War when Australians' perceptions of an external security threat were very low. Conversely, the proportion answering 'very important' was highest just after 11 September 2011, at almost 60 per cent. Although the proportion of Australians who say the ANZUS alliance is 'very important' has now dropped to just under 50 per cent, this proportion has never been lower than the proportion of respondents who say that the alliance is 'not very important', which peaked in 1993 at 20 per cent.[25]

The second question is whether respondents' trust that the United States would come to Australia's defence if it were threatened by a foreign power? Here, the figure for a 'very great' deal of confidence has usually been much higher than the figure for 'little' confidence. Only in 1993 and 2000—in the immediate aftermath of the East Timor crisis—has the figure for 'little confidence' been higher than the figure for 'very great' confidence.[26]

The Lowy poll asks a greater variety of questions about the Australia-US alliance, allowing a closer examination of the nuances in the relationship. The Lowy poll also asks about the importance of the American alliance, but phrases it in terms of the 'alliance with the USA', not ANZUS. This may account for the fact that the Lowy poll produces an even higher level of support for the US alliance than the AES equivalent—the lowest proportion of respondents ever recorded answering that the US alliance was 'fairly' or 'very' important to Australia was 63 per cent in 2011.[27] Generally, the proportion is over 70 per cent. In 2013 it reached 73 per cent.[28]

Similarly, the 2013 Lowy poll revealed that 48 per cent of Australians believed that the relationship with the United States was the most important which Australia has, versus only 37 per cent who believed the most important relationship was with China.[29]

Also heartening from the point of view of supporters of the Australia-US alliance is the proportion of respondents who trust the US to 'act responsibly' in global affairs. This proportion increased significantly following the election of Barack Obama. In 2009, Obama's international 'honeymoon' period, it stood at 83 per cent. However, even under George W Bush's Administration, a clear majority of Australians trusted the United States—60 per cent in 2006.[30]

However, there are a number of caveats to the overall picture of Australians as being broadly pro-American. First, the warmth of the Australia-US relationship varies as a function of the party which holds the White House. Australians favoured Barack Obama over Mitt Romney by a margin of 8 to 1 in 2012—similar to most European countries and higher than Obama's actual winning margin in any US state.[31]

Second, positive feelings towards the United States are higher in the older generation than in the younger. 69 per cent of Australians over sixty said that the Australia-US alliance is 'very important' in 2013, whereas only 48 per cent of those under sixty agreed.[32] This leaves open the possibility that Australia's generally positive attitude toward the United States will decline with the passage of time. An alternative perspective is that this simply reflects a general tendency of individuals to acquire more conservative views as they get older, so that today's 'America-sceptics' will prove to be tomorrow's 'America-philes'.

Third, Australian voters in general, not just younger ones, already believe that the United States exerts too much influence over Australian foreign policy. Even in 2009 under the Obama Administration, 50 per cent of respondents to the Lowy poll expressed this view. Under the Bush Administration, in 2008, the figure had been as high as 65 per cent.[33]

Fourth, support for the United States under a variety of circumstances is highly conditional. For instance, in 2013, 51 per cent of Australians were 'opposed to Australia supporting the US in a hypothetical military action against the Iranian nuclear program', only 38 per cent were in 'favour of supporting the US in a conflict between

China and Japan' and a majority believed that 'Australia should only support the US in a conflict with the authorisation of the United Nations'.[34]

Finally, the Lowy poll's 'thermometer' question—asking respondents how warm they feel towards various countries—has always shown on average a positive rating of the United States. The lowest the United States has ever scored is 60 'degrees' in 2007, but the US consistently ranks lower than a number of other Australian partners.[35] The United States scored 70 degrees out of a possible 100 in 2013, tied with Germany for second place but behind the United Kingdom at 77 degrees.[36] In previous years, the US trailed New Zealand in 2012, New Zealand and the United Kingdom in 2011, New Zealand, Canada, France and Singapore in 2010, New Zealand, Canada and Germany in 2009, the UK, France, Singapore and Japan in 2008, New Zealand, the UK, Singapore and Japan in 2007, and the UK, Singapore and Japan in 2006. In short, Australians are pro-American, but they are not uncritically pro-American, feel closer to other countries (especially those from the Commonwealth) and may become less pro-American over time.

A final word is in order about Japan, which current Australian Prime Minister Tony Abbott has referred to as 'Australia's closest friend in Asia'. It is clear from the data that this does reflect a genuinely positive image of Japan amongst Australians. On the Lowy poll's thermometer, Japan generally scores a little lower than the likes of the United Kingdom, and prior to 2011 outpolled the United States. Japan's thermometer score has never fallen below 60 degrees. On the 'trust' question, similar or greater proportions of Australians trust the Japanese to 'do the right thing' in global affairs as the Americans. In 2009, the figure stood at 81 per cent,[37] relative to 68 per cent in 2008[38] and 73 per cent in 2006.[39] Wartime scars are rapidly fading.

4. Support for Conflicts/Casualty Tolerance

At the time of writing, Australia had suffered forty casualties in Afghanistan and Australian public opinion has turned against the war.[40] On the face of it, it would appear that casualties have been driving the fall in support for Australian participation in Afghanistan. However, a close examination of the trends in support cast doubt on this simplistic explanation. For one thing, the first Australian polls to show majority opposition to the war were conducted when Australia had suffered only five casualties. Indeed, according to one poll, support had dropped to just 38 per cent by April 2009, by which time Australia had suffered ten casualties.[41] These were similar to levels of support in countries such as Britain whose forces had suffered much higher casualties.[42]

These statistics might suggest that Australians are casualty sensitive relative to other participating countries. However, while Australian casualties have more than quadrupled since April 2009, public support for the war has fluctuated but generally remained at the same levels as 2009. Indeed, the occasional poll was still showing majority support for the war as late as October 2010, by which time Australia had suffered over twenty casualties.[43]

Polling for the ADF carried out by the AES in the early 2000s suggests that Australians are far more likely to tolerate casualties in the defence of Australia directly (such as missions to prevent the entry of drugs or illegal immigrants into Australia, or stabilisation missions in Australia's immediate neighbourhood) than in wars fought on behalf of allies far from Australia or on United Nations (UN) peacekeeping missions.[44]

Two things remain to be seen. Firstly, is Australian public opinion on conflicts responsive to 'partisan cues' like its American counterpart? Secondly, are Australians, like Americans, more swayed by a mission's prospects for success than by the casualties incurred in it?

It is widely assumed that Australian foreign policy is marked by a high degree of bipartisan consensus. However, Australian political parties, like their American counterparts, were divided over the Vietnam and Iraq Wars. They could conceivably also divide over future conflicts too. It is therefore rather interesting to see whether bipartisan consensus would have an impact on Australian casualty tolerance, as it has been shown to do in the American case.

One key difference between Australia and the United States is that the United States has far more influence on the overall outcome of a war than any of its allies, including Australia. In fact, it is doubtful whether any single American ally would or could make the difference between the success or failure of an allied mission. This brings with it the temptation for any American ally to 'free-ride' on the American contribution to overall success.[45] American allies therefore often participate in America's wars in order to remain on good terms with the United States as much as for the overall goal of the allied mission, which they typically cannot affect alone. In the case of Afghanistan, for instance, success for the United States means establishing a functioning government which denies al-Qaeda access to the country. For Australia, however, the goal is arguably different. Although in public Australian leaders will proclaim that Australia's goal is the same, the reality is quite different. 2000 Australian soldiers do not make the difference between the success and failure of the overall allied mission in Afghanistan the way 100 000 Americans do. To the extent that the Australian public recognises this, prospects for success may have a very different meaning for them than they do for Americans.

5. The Public's Opinion of the Australian Defence Force

Public attitudes toward the ADF are probably the most straightforward of all the issues under consideration in this chapter. The ADF is highly respected not only in comparison with other Australian institutions, but also in comparison with the militaries of most other developed democracies.

The World Values Survey is the most comprehensive attempt to measure comparative public opinion across countries at relatively regular intervals. Questions are phrased identically across over fifty countries in order to ensure comparability. One of the major issues covered by the survey is confidence in the armed forces.

On this score, the ADF is one of the most trusted militaries in the developed world. In fact, adding together the proportion of respondents expressing either a 'great deal' or 'quite a lot' of confidence in the military, the ADF scores even higher than the US military. 25.8 per cent of Australians have a 'great deal' and 57.9 per cent have 'quite a lot' of confidence in the armed forces for a total of 84.7 per cent, compared to 34.7 per cent and 47.7 per cent in the US, for a total of 82.4 per cent. Moreover, a slightly higher proportion of Australian than American respondents answered that they would be supportive of their children pursuing a career in the military—68 per cent versus 51 per cent respectively.[46]

The rest of the 'Anglosphere' exhibited somewhat lower levels of confidence in the military. Overall confidence in the armed forces was at 78.6 per cent in the United Kingdom, 72 per cent in Canada and 72.5 per cent in New Zealand. Lower still were the continental European countries. Of these, confidence in the armed forces was highest in France at 68.3 per cent and lowest in the Netherlands at 46.2 per cent, with Spain at 53.2 per cent and Germany just over 50 per cent. In short, the ADF is one of the most respected militaries in its home society.[47]

A Pretty Prudent Public?

Pushing back against the view of the American people as ignorant and ill-informed on foreign policy, Bruce Jentleson coined the term the 'pretty prudent public' to describe American attitudes to the use of force overseas. The picture presented here is similarly one of a pretty prudent Australian public. This does not mean to say that most Australians would be able to name the President of Indonesia or China's current average growth rate. Yet the bigger picture is that Australian voters have a coherent view of world affairs which is not especially out of kilter with expert opinion.

Australians recognise that the post-Cold War world is actually very stable. They are not particularly concerned about security threats from regional powers, with the surprising exception of Indonesia. They believe that 'non-traditional' security threats such as terrorism and climate change are more likely to preoccupy policy-makers in future relative to older concerns. In light of this, they believe the current level of defence spending to be correct—there is no majority for either increasing or cutting it. Whether this is indeed an appropriate level of spending for the threat environment the majority believe Australia faces is an open question. However, as Ian McAllister has noted, explicitly framing defence spending in the context of trade-offs against other areas of government spending (or increased taxes and deficits) might produce larger numbers in favour of cuts.[48]

Australians are also pro-American, but not reflexively so. Australians trust the United States to 'do the right thing' in international affairs and believe the Australia-US alliance to be very important. The United States consistently garners positive feelings—something which was true even in the years of the George W Bush Administration—which Australians judged very negatively. Perhaps as a legacy of these years, however, there is a great deal of scepticism in Australia about helping the United States in a number of contexts in future—whether it be in a military confrontation with China on the side of Japan or against an Iranian nuclear weapons program—especially if this were to contravene international law. Australians are also very positive about Japan, suggesting that the legacy of distrust created by World War II has dissipated in a way not quite so true in many other parts of the Asia-Pacific. Finally, even though the Commonwealth is decreasing in importance in Australia's foreign policy, Commonwealth countries such as the United Kingdom and New Zealand retain higher levels of popularity amongst Australians than any other countries.

Australians are sensitive to casualties, but to argue that they are casualty phobic would be to misread the trajectory of recent conflicts. It is true that public support for the war in Afghanistan fell rapidly with the first few Australian casualties. However, a near quadrupling of Australian casualties subsequently had very little clear effect on support for the mission. This suggests that Australia may follow the same pattern as that identified in the United States—a minority of the public are casualty phobic and will desert a mission after only a few deaths, but some proportion will remain solid in spite of a large number of casualties while others are prepared to tolerate losses as long as they are convinced that the mission will succeed. As in the United States, moreover, the impact of casualties is contingent on other factors that are to a greater extent within policymakers' control. For example, Australians will be more prepared to tolerate casualties, it would seem, in operations directly related to Australia's national interest than in interventions outside Australia's region—especially UN peacekeeping operations. At the same time, the legality of the mission is also an important consideration—conflicts waged without the imprimatur of the UN are likely to lose support when the ADF starts taking casualties more quickly than conflicts which have UN backing. Finally, on a bright note for the ADF, the men and women of Australia's armed forces can take pride in the fact that they have more backing from their home society than almost any other military in the developed world.

Further Reading

McAllister, Ian, *Public Opinion in Australia Towards Defence, Security and Terrorism*, no. 16, *APSI Special Report*, Australian Strategic Policy Institute, Canberra 2008. www.aspi.org.au/publications/special-report-issue-16-public-opinion-in-australia-towards-defence,-security-and-terrorism/SR16_Public_opinion.pdf.

Oliver, Alex, *Australia and the World: Public Opinion and Foreign Policy*, Lowy Institute for International Policy, Sydney, 2013. www.lowyinstitute.org/files/lowypoll2013_web_1.pdf.

McAllister, Ian, *The Australian Voter: 50 Years of Change*, University of New South Wales Press, Sydney, 2011.

Gelpi, Christopher, Feaver, Peter D, and Reifler, Jason, *Paying the Human Costs of War: American Public Opinion and Casualties in Military Conflicts*, Princeton University Press, Princeton, New Jersey, 2010.

Palazzo, Albert, 'No Casualties Please, We're Soldiers', *Australian Army Journal*, vol. 5, no. 3, 2008, pp. 65–79.

Notes

1   TB Millar, *Australia's Defence*, Melbourne University Press, Carlton, 1965, p. 167.

2   C Miller, 'Endgame for the West in Afghanistan? Explaining the Decline in Support for the War in Afghanistan in the United States, Great Britain, Canada, Australia, France and Germany', Strategic Studies Institute, Carlisle, PA, 2010. www.strategicstudiesinstitute.army.mil/pdffiles/pub994.pdf (viewed November 2014).

3   F Hanson, *Australia and the World: Public Opinion and Foreign Policy*, Lowy Institute for International Policy, Sydney, 2010, p. 23. www.lowyinstitute.cachefly.net/files/pubfiles/LowyPoll_2010_LR_Final.pdf (viewed February 2014).

4   P King (ed), *Australia's Vietnam: Australia in the Second Indo-China War*, Allen & Unwin, Sydney, 1983.

5   I McAllister, *Public Opinion in Australia Towards Defence, Security and Terrorism*, no. 16, *APSI Special Report*, Australian Strategic Policy Institute, Canberra 2008. www.aspi.org.au/publications/special-report-issue-16-public-opinion-in-australia-towards-defence,-security-and-terrorism/SR16_Public_opinion.pdf (viewed February 2014).

6   The apparent difference between the AES and the Lowy Institute's poll on threat perceptions of China is probably accounted for by the wording—individuals who believe China is *not* a security threat now but could be, for instance, in fifteen years would be obliged by the AES's wording to answer 'no', by Lowy's to answer 'yes'. A Oliver, *Australia and the World: Public Opinion and Foreign Policy*, Lowy Institute for International Policy, Sydney, 2013. www.lowyinstitute.org/files/lowypoll2013_web_1.pdf (viewed February 2014); and I McAllister and J Clark, *Trends in Australian Political Opinion: Results from the Australian Election Study 1987–2007*, Australian Election Study, 2008, p. 35. www.assda.anu.edu.au/aestrends.pdf (viewed February 2014).

7   H White, *A Focused Force: Australia's Defence Priorities in the Asian Century*, Lowy Institute for International Policy, Sydney, 2009.

8   MW Doyle, 'Kant, Liberal Legacies, and Foreign Affairs', *Philosophy and Public Affairs*, vol. 12, no. 3, 1983.

9   A Oliver, *Australia and the World: Public Opinion and Foreign Policy*, 2013, p. 13.

10 ibid.

11 I McAllister, *Public Opinion in Australia Towards Defence, Security and Terrorism*, 2008, p. 11.

12 ibid.

13 ibid., p. 27.

14 I Cook, *Australia, Indonesia and the World: Public Opinion and Foreign Policy*, Lowy Institute for International Policy, Sydney, 2006. www.lowyinstitute.org/files/pubfiles/Lowy_Institute_Poll_2006.pdf (viewed February 2014); A Gyngell, *Australia and the World: Public Opinion and Foreign Policy*, Lowy Institute for International Policy, Sydney, 2007. www.lowyinstitute.org/files/pubfiles/Lowy_Poll_2007_LR.pdf (viewed February 2014); F Hanson, *Australia and the World: Public Opinion and Foreign Policy*, Lowy Institute of International Policy, Sydney, 2008. www.lowyinstitute.org/files/pubfiles/Lowy_Poll08_Web1.pdf (viewed February 2014); F Hanson, *Australia and the World: Public Opinion and Foreign Policy*, Lowy Institute for International Policy, Sydney, 2009. www.lowyinstitute.org/files/pubfiles/Lowy_Poll_09.pdf (viewed February 2014); F Hanson, *Australia in the World: Public Opinion and Foreign Policy*, Lowy Institute for International Policy, Sydney, 2010. www.lowyinstitute.cachefly.net/files/pubfiles/LowyPoll_2010_LR_Final.pdf (viewed February 2014); F Hanson, *Australia and the World: Public Opinion and Foreign Policy*, Lowy Institute for International Policy, 2011. www.lowyinstitute.org/files/pubfiles/Lowy_Poll_2011_WEB.pdf (viewed February 2014); F Hanson, *Australia in the World: Public Opinion and Foreign Policy*, Lowy Institute for International Policy, Sydney, 2012. www.lowyinstitute.org/files/lowy_poll_2012_web3.pdf (viewed February 2014); A Oliver, *Australia in the World: Public Opinion and Foreign Policy*, 2013.

15 Hanson, *Australia in the World: Public Opinion and Foreign Policy*, 2008.

16 See *Australia in the World: Public Opinion and Foreign Policy*, Lowy Institute for International Policy, from 2006–2013.

17 Hanson, *Australia and the World: Public Opinion and Foreign Policy*, 2008.

18 Oliver, *Australia and the World: Public Opinion and Foreign Policy*, 2013.

19 B Valentino, 'Poll Responses by Party ID', YouGov, Dartmouth College. www.dartmouth.edu/~benv/files/poll%20responses%20by%20party%20ID.pdf (viewed February 2014).

20 Oliver, *Australia and the World: Public Opinion and Foreign Policy*, 2013, p. 22.

21 McAllister and Clark, *Trends in Australian Political Opinion: Results from the Australian Election Study 1987–2007*, 2008, p. 35.

22 Oliver, *Australia and the World: Public Opinion and Foreign Policy*, 2013, p. 12.

23　The lowest proportion of respondents who saw the ANZUS alliance as 'very important' dropped to 20 per cent in 1993. See McAllister, *Public Opinion in Australia Towards Defence, Security and Terrorism*, 2008, p. 16.

24　'Blue states' represent a Democrat majority, and a 'red state' represents a Republican majority. Between 1980 and 2000, political mapmakers coined states as red or blue to make a distinction between the two parties. See, for example, P Farhi, 'Elephants Are Red, Donkeys Are Blue', *Washington Post*, 2 November 2004.

25　McAllister, *Public Opinion in Australia Towards Defence, Security and Terrorism*, 2008, p. 110.

26　ibid., p. 15.

27　Hanson, *Australia and the World: Public Opinion and Foreign Policy*, 2011, p. 9.

28　Oliver, *Australia and the World: Public Opinion and Foreign Policy*, 2013, p. 7.

29　ibid., p. 5.

30　Hanson, *Australia in the World: Public Opinion and Foreign Policy*, 2009, p. 8.

31　Hanson, *Australia in the World: Public Opinion and Foreign Policy*, 2012, p. 10.

32　Oliver, *Australia in the World: Public Opinion and Foreign Policy*, 2013, p. 7.

33　Hanson, *Australia in the World: Public Opinion and Foreign Policy*, 2009, p. 4.

34　Oliver, *Australia in the World: Public Opinion and Foreign Policy*, 2013, p. 8.

35　Hanson, *Australia in the World: Public Opinion and Foreign Policy*, 2007, p. 6.

36　Oliver, *Australia in the World: Public Opinion and Foreign Policy*, 2013, p. 15.

37　Hanson, *Australia in the World: Public Opinion and Foreign Policy*, 2009, p. 7.

38　Hanson, *Australia in the World: Public Opinion and Foreign Policy*, 2008, p. 8.

39　Hanson, *Australia in the World: Public Opinion and Foreign Policy*, 2006, p. 8.

40　iCasualties, 'Coalition Casualties: Operation Enduring Freedom', http:// icasualties.org/OEF/index.aspx (viewed November 2014); Commonwealth of Australia, 'Battle Casualties in Afghanistan', Commonwealth of Australia. www.defence.gov.au/operations/afghanistan/personnel.asp (viewed April 2014).

41　Miller, 'Endgame for the West in Afghanistan? Explaining the Decline in Support for the War in Afghanistan in the United States, Great Britain, Canada, Australia, France and Germany', 2010.

42　ibid.

43　iCasualties, 'Coalition Casualties: Operation Enduring Freedom'. www. icasualties.org/OEF/index.aspx (viewed November 2014).

44　I McAllister, *Public Opinion Towards Defence and Foreign Affairs: Results from the ANU Poll*, report no. 4, Research School of Social Sciences, Australian National University, 4 April 2009. https://lyceum.anu.edu.au/

wp-content/blogs/3/uploads//ANU%20Poll%20Defence%20
Report%201.pdf (viewed April 2014).

45 M Olson and R Zeckhauser, *An Economic Theory of Alliances*, RAND,
Santa Monica, CA, 1966.

46 World Values Survey Association, 'World Values Survey 2005–2008 Wave',
World Values Survey Association, 2005–2008. www.wvsevsdb.com/wvs/
WVSAnalize.jsp (viewed April 2014).

47 ibid.

48 McAllister, *Public Opinion in Australia Towards Defence, Security and
Terrorism*, 2008, p. 9.

Part II:
International Context

4

Australia and Northeast Asia

Amy King

In the opening pages of *Australia's Defence*, TB Millar put forward a bleak view of Northeast Asia:

> From that time [when the Japanese attacked Pearl Harbour] in 1941 we have been conscious of a direct or indirect threat from Asia. It came first from the Japanese, and the image of a threat or potential threat from Japan lingered long after the collapse of Japan's fighting strength in August 1945. The 'Japanese menace' was replaced, after the victory of the Communist forces in China in late 1949, and following the start of the Korean War in June 1950, by a 'Communist menace', not easily defined but apparently a single threat, subtle and powerful.[1]

Millar's depiction of Northeast Asia in 1965 is, in many ways, unsurprising. War with Japan was still a fresh memory for many in Australia, and Communist China was providing military and political support for wars of 'national liberation' in North and Southeast Asia. Yet Millar's depiction of Northeast Asia stands in stark contrast to the reality of Australia's economic ties to the region. In 1969, just four years after the publication of Millar's *Australia's Defence*, Japan would replace Great Britain as Australia's leading trade partner.

Since the end of World War II, Australia's economic and security policies towards Northeast Asia have moved along different tracks. At times, such as in the immediate postwar decades, this has produced a divergent view of the region. At other times, Australia's economic and strategic planners have converged, or have at least been spared choosing between the economic and security dimensions of Australia's national interest. This chapter explores how Australia's policy community has envisioned the opportunities and threats from Northeast Asia since the publication of TB Millar's book almost half a century ago. It examines the relative weight attached to economic and security issues in Australian policy towards the region, paying particular attention to how Australia has managed its relationships with Northeast Asia's two 'great powers'—China and Japan. While the China-Taiwan relationship and the security of the Korean peninsula also have a major impact on the Northeast Asian security environment, it is China and Japan—and the relationship between them in Northeast Asia—that have shaped Australia's strategic outlook and its economic interests more than any other factor. In recent years, Australians have observed how Northeast Asia's—and particularly China's—economic ascendancy has begun to disrupt the US-led strategic order upon which Australia has relied for its physical security and economic prosperity.[2] Northeast Asia remains more important to Australia's economic prosperity than any other region, but the region is now home to a range of pressing security challenges that cannot be ignored. Australia's future policy towards Northeast Asia must reconcile Northeast Asia's economic opportunities with the region's security tensions.

The Postwar Decades: Two Roads Diverge

Australian fears of the spread of Chinese-backed communism in the 1950s and 1960s help to explain Australia's active involvement in 'virtually every significant military confrontation in postwar Asia': from the Korean War, to the Malayan Emergency, to the wars in Indochina and Vietnam.[3] Even where conflicts posed no direct threat to Australia's security, such as the Sino-Indian border war of 1962, the Australian government contributed £2 million in arms and ammunition to the Indian side. The governments of the day justified Australia's involvement in these conflicts as part of the wider US-led strategy designed to contain Communist China.[4]

Australia's anxieties were not limited to China. Long after the end of World War II, both the Australian Labor Party and the Liberal-Country Party retained a deep anxiety about Japan's military future. Indeed, concerns about the possibility of Japanese rearmament led Australia's then minister of External Affairs, Percy Spender, to demand a security commitment from the United States against any future Japanese threat.[5] The United States, under President Truman, was willing to reassure Australia, and in 1951 signed the Australia, New Zealand, United States Security Treaty (ANZUS), as well as a separate security treaty with Japan that was designed to give the United States 'complete control over any rearmament plans Japan may adopt'.[6] Yet although these security treaties brought Australia and Japan together as US allies in the Cold War struggle against the Soviet Union, Australia's defence planners were at best ambivalent and at worst deeply suspicious of Japan throughout the 1960s and 1970s. Australia's 1972 *Australian Defence Review* made almost no mention of Japan, save for describing Japan as a likely 'prodigious economic power, whatever she may decide should be her level of military power'.[7] Similarly, Australia's 1976 Defence White Paper stated flatly that 'Japan appears most unlikely to change its longstanding policy of limiting its military development' and did not encourage a more active regional security role for Japan.[8]

Yet Australia's defence policy towards Japan in the 1950s, 1960s and 1970s was moving at a very different pace from that of its economic policy. In 1955, Japan's economy embarked on a period of high-speed growth, and by the 'golden sixties' the Japanese economy was growing at an average rate of 10.7 per cent per year.[9] Japan was thus well on its way to becoming the technological and industrial powerhouse that would prompt the publication of bestseller titles such as *Japan as Number One*.[10] Hungry for resources and raw materials, Japan turned to the Australian market. In 1957, amidst significant postwar animosity towards Japan within the Australian community, the two countries concluded a bilateral trade agreement.[11] Elsewhere in Northeast Asia, the economies of Taiwan and South Korea were also growing at a rapid rate and by the end of the

1970s, East Asian countries would be buying almost half of Australia's total exports.[12]

Personality and bureaucratic influence go a long way towards explaining this divergence in Australia's security and economic policy towards Japan. In spite of the paucity of attention given to Japan in Australian strategic documents from the 1960s and 1970s, Japan actually commanded a significant amount of policy attention during these decades. On the heels of Japan becoming Australia's leading trade partner in 1969, the Liberal-Country Coalition government established an inter-departmental committee (IDC) on Japan. This was the first time in Australia's history that the government brought together the heads of the departments of Foreign Affairs, the Treasury, Defence and Trade to examine and manage Australia's relationship with another country.[13] Though intended to integrate a broad range of policy views, the IDC in fact reflected deep discord about Japan within Canberra. The Department of Trade, and particularly its long-time minister, Sir John 'Black Jack' McEwen, was an early champion of closer economic relations with Japan and had been instrumental in ushering in the 1957 trade agreement with Japan.[14] Yet the minister for Foreign Affairs, William McMahon, sought to use the newly created IDC as a way of constraining McEwen's power and limiting Australia's engagement with Japan. This discord resulted in a deeply ambivalent set of policies towards Japan. The IDC sought to build 'the closest possible' economic and diplomatic relationship with Japan, while simultaneously discouraging 'the view that the rearmament of Japan should be speeded up or that Japan should play a direct security role in South-east Asia'. In fact, the IDC went so far as to endorse the view that Australia could serve as the 'counterbalance to Japanese influence' in the region.[15] Straddling this divide was, of course, impossible. A later Royal Commission would ultimately criticise the committee for its failed attempts to 'paper over differences in the search for a fragile consensus'.[16]

In the three decades after the end of World War II, Australia's economic policy towards Northeast Asia was moving in a completely different direction to its security policy. Australia's economic community recognised the rich opportunities that lay in trade with Northeast Asia, but the defence and foreign policy communities

Figure 4.1: Australia's Trade with Japan, Korea, the United States and Great Britain as a Percentage of Australia's Total Foreign Trade

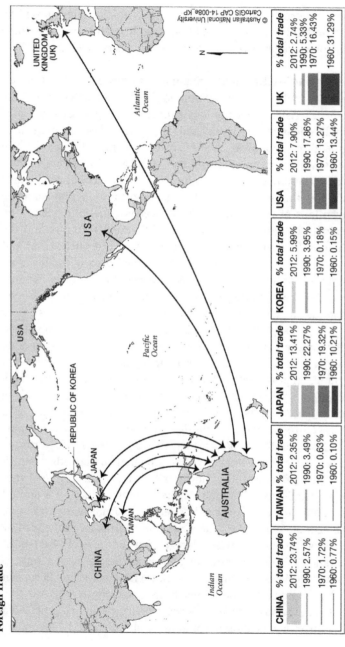

Source: International Monetary Fund, 'Direction of Trade Statistics'. www.elibrary-data.imf.org/ (viewed December 2013).

Map: CartoGIS, College of Asia and the Pacific, Australian National University, 2014.

placed far greater emphasis on the security challenges posed by Japan and Communist China. Straddling this divide would become an ongoing challenge for Australian policymakers (see Figure 4.1).

The Hawke-Keating Years: Security as Economic Prosperity

The 1980s and 1990s saw a dramatic shift in Australia's view of the Northeast Asian security environment. In previous decades Australia's defence community had viewed Northeast Asia as a source of great threat, but as we shall see below, defence white papers and other strategic planning documents published in the early 1990s indicate that the defence community joined the economic planners in viewing the region as a source of opportunity. These changing conceptions of the Northeast Asian security environment can be explained, in part, by the collapse of the Soviet Empire and the ending of the Cold War in 1989–91. The threat of nuclear war and Cold War-inspired conflicts in Asia seemed greatly reduced. Yet Australia's shifting view of Northeast Asia was also due to the fact that during the Hawke-Keating years Australia's national security interests were recast in predominantly economic terms.

In 1989, Australian economist Ross Garnaut was commissioned by the Hawke government to prepare a report on the economic growth and structural changes taking place in Northeast Asia. Garnaut's report, entitled *Australia and the Northeast Asian Ascendancy*, observed the stunning economic growth rates taking place in Northeast Asia. Noting that the region had emerged 'as a major centre of world economic activity', the Garnaut report reminded Australia's political leaders that export trade with Northeast Asia was more complementary than any of Australia's other important trading relationships. However, the report also argued that unless Australia tore down the 'defensive' protectionist walls around its economy, the country would not enjoy the fruits of the Northeast Asian economic miracle.[17] The economic reforms recommended by the Garnaut report formed an integral part of the wider East Asian orientation of the Hawke-Keating government. This was a government that believed that Australia's future lay not with its European past, but instead would be defined by its geography in Asia.[18]

As in previous decades, this was a policy vision first articulated by the Australian economic community and dictated by Australia's economic interests. Yet unlike previous decades, this recognition of Northeast Asia as a source of opportunity did not stop with Australia's economic policymaking community, but spilled over into the defence and foreign policy spheres as well. Instead of a divergence in Australia's economic and security policy towards Northeast Asia, by the early 1990s the Australian defence community redefined security to explicitly consider these economic concerns. Australia's 1993 Strategic Review encapsulated this new conception of security, and the prominent role of Northeast Asia in achieving that security:

> Australia's future lies with the Asia-Pacific region. In the economic sphere, Japan has long been our largest trading partner. More than half of our total exports go to East and South-East Asia ... The future of North-East Asia is an important factor in Australia's strategic outlook. We have important national interests in this sub-region. The policies and relationships of the major powers of North-East Asia will heavily influence, or even determine, the strategic environment of our nearer region. Five of Australia's ten most important trading partners are in North-East Asia.[19]

This was a profoundly different view to that of previous decades. Instead of seeing Northeast Asia as a source of great threat to Australia, Australia's terms of trade were now dictating an external policy that was based on the view that Australia's security and prosperity could be found in Northeast Asia. This was no more obvious than when, on his first visit abroad as Australian prime minister, Paul Keating noted 'rather pointedly' that Japan took three times as many Australian exports as the United States.[20] Coral Bell, one of Australia's leading strategic studies scholars, argued that Keating's comments not only implied that Japan might be more important to Australia than the US, but also signified for the first time in Australia's history that our main economic partner (Japan) was not the same as our main security partner (the United States).[21] Bell went on to suggest that the Hawke-Keating era was a 'long slow process of redefinitions', 'from a time when security considerations were dominant ... to a time when economic concerns were dominant'.[22] Others went even further, advocating that Australia's security interests be entirely redefined to reflect the importance of the Northeast Asian economy to Australia. In 1991, Alan Dupont wrote that the traditional definition of security—based on military threats alone—was a flawed conception. Trading nations such as Australia had no choice but to take 'a more integrated and holistic approach to security policy' that explicitly recognised the centrality of the trade, investment and people-to-people links that connect Australia and the countries of Northeast Asia.[23]

The view that economic factors were intimately connected to strategic concerns was also reflected in Australian defence policy documents published in the early 1990s. For instance, *Defending Australia*, the 1994 Defence White Paper, devoted two whole pages to the relationship between economics and security. It noted that economic growth allowed countries to devote greater resources to military spending, to develop more technologically sophisticated military capabilities and that the rise of economies such as China would reshape the Asian balance of power. As such, it argued that Australia's defence community could not afford to ignore the future strategic effects of economic growth taking place in Asia.[24] These policy documents also acknowledged that economic tensions between countries could contribute to political and security tensions. The 1993 Strategic Review cited concerns that growing economic disputes between the United States and Japan over macroeconomic imbalances threatened to harm the US-Japan security alliance.[25] Ultimately, however, the view remained a positive one. The 1993 Strategic Review struck an optimistic note, arguing that 'the likelihood that economic tensions and divergent growth patterns will spill over into military confrontation is not high' and that 'sound Asia-Pacific economic relationships will provide foundations for security relationships'.[26]

To be sure, this more optimistic view of Northeast Asia as a source of prosperity and opportunity did not hide the fact that the region faced a range of pressing security challenges between 1988 and 1996. In 1988 China sank three Vietnamese ships in the South China Sea; in 1993–94, North Korea withdrew from the Nuclear Non-Proliferation Treaty and the United States came within hours of conducting air strikes against North Korea's known nuclear facilities; and the 1995–96 Taiwan Straits Crisis brought the United States and

China closer to direct military conflict than at any other point since the Vietnam War.[27] Yet on the whole, Australia viewed the Northeast Asian security environment as a benign one. Despite profound concerns about China's future military behaviour, domestic political system, and abuse of human rights—highlighted by the Tiananmen Square massacre in June 1989—Australian strategic documents from the 1980s and 1990s reflected a view that China was now a very different country to the China of the Mao years. Australia's 1993 Strategic Review and 1994 Defence White Paper were hopeful that China could be peacefully engaged through new institutions such as the Asia-Pacific Economic Cooperation (APEC) process and the ASEAN Regional Forum (ARF).

Similarly, Australian views of Japan no longer displayed the same ambivalence about Japan's military future as they had in previous decades. By the late 1980s, Japan was unquestionably a major global economic power with significant economic ties to Australia. During the Hawke-Keating years, Japan imported between one-quarter and one-third of Australia's food, iron ore, minerals and other exports (see Table 1). Furthermore, despite its constitutional constraints on the use of force, Japan had the largest defence budget and most sophisticated military force in Asia.[28] In contrast to earlier decades, Australia began to strengthen bilateral defence ties with Japan and encouraged Japan's greater participation in regional security efforts. In 1989 and 1990, the Hawke government dispatched senior Australian defence officials, including the Chief of the Defence Force General Peter Gration and the Deputy Secretary of Defence Paul Dibb, on visits to Tokyo to discuss the two countries' shared security interests in Asia and the establishment of practical defence cooperation.[29] This practical cooperation was demonstrated when in 1992–1993, the Japanese Self-Defence Force (JSDF) participated in its first international peacekeeping operation, the Australian-commanded United Nations Transitional Authority in Cambodia. Following this, Australia supported Japan's greater international peacekeeping role and its bid for permanent membership of the UN Security Council.[30] Throughout the late 1980s and early 1990s, the two countries also worked closely together in developing new regional economic and security institutions such as APEC and the ARF. Australia's closer security cooperation with Japan did not always develop smoothly however. There was still some unease—particularly within the Liberal-National Coalition—of Japan's future regional security role. Furthermore, Japan was often reluctant to support Australian proposals for greater cooperation because it feared that regional security institutions—such as the ARF or the Australian proposal for a Conference on Security and Cooperation for Asia (CSCA)—might erode the basis for the US security commitment to Japan.[31]

The Hawke-Keating years witnessed a fundamental shift in Australia's view of the Northeast Asian security environment. For the first time in Australia's postwar history, Canberra recognised the reality of Northeast Asia's economic ascendancy and its strategic as well as economic significance to Australia. At the same time, the security environment seemed like a benign one. The Cold War had ended, economic growth in Northeast Asia had not resulted in Japan's resurgence as a threatening military power and Communist China appeared to be on the cusp of an important transition towards economic, if not political, liberalisation. All this made it possible to argue, as Paul Dibb did in his 1986 *Review of Australia's Defence Capabilities*, that 'Australia faces no identifiable direct military threat and there is every prospect that our favourable security circumstances will continue'.[32] This sense of optimism would last beyond the period of the Hawke-Keating government and into the Howard years, as we shall see below. Ultimately, however, the strategic shifts brought about by Northeast Asia's economic ascendancy would undermine much of this optimism within the Australian defence community.

The Howard Years: Having One's Cake and Eating It Too

Australia's close engagement with Northeast Asia continued during John Howard's tenure as prime minister from 1996 to 2007. This was unexpected. Howard came to power more determined to strengthen the Australia-US alliance than to continue the 'Asian identity' debates popularised by Paul Keating. However, as Michael Wesley puts it, the 'paradox' of the Howard years was that despite predictions that Howard would destroy Australia's relationships with Asia, Howard in fact pulled off the remarkable achievement of simultaneously strengthening Australia's relationships with the United States, China and Japan.[33]

Howard transformed Australia's security relationship with Japan. While earlier Australian initiatives to expand bilateral defence cooperation had often been constrained by Japan's own hesitancy, Howard was able to capitalise on a Japan that was now looking for ways to enhance its regional security role. In 1995, the United States released a new strategy for East Asia—the so-called 'Nye report'[34]—which reaffirmed the importance of US security alliances in the region. The US-Japan alliance had become increasingly strained over US charges that Japan was free-riding on the alliance and failing to open its markets to US exports or provide a meaningful contribution to regional security.[35] The Nye report argued that the United States and Japan could not allow economic tensions to poison the broader US-Japan security relationship. The report and subsequent new US-Japan defence guidelines signed in 1997 laid out a more expansive role for Japan particularly in providing logistical support for US forces operating in the region.[36] This new direction in the US-Japan alliance coincided neatly with the Howard government's own interests in encouraging the United States to remain engaged in Asia and for Japan to play a less restrictive security role. During Howard's tenure, Australia, Japan and the United States thus expanded their trilateral security cooperation, and in March 2006 Australia welcomed the United States and Japan to Sydney for the first formal Trilateral Security Dialogue. The following year, the Howard government reportedly tried to negotiate a formal security alliance with Japan, but the Japanese government refrained, arguing that Japan's pacifist constitution made it legally and politically difficult for Japan to enter into a collective security agreement with Australia.[37] What resulted instead was a joint declaration on security cooperation between Australia and Japan and a commitment to holding regular '2+2' meetings of Australian and Japanese foreign and defence ministers. The two countries were careful to stop short of including military cooperation within the joint declaration, which would have strayed too close to an alliance-type arrangement, and instead called for practical cooperation on a host of non-traditional security issues such as law enforcement, border security, maritime security and humanitarian assistance.[38] The terrorist attacks of 11 September 2001 provided a further catalyst for Japan to look for ways to make a more meaningful security commitment. Unwilling to face the same criticism from the United States for contributing only 'chequebook diplomacy' as it had during the first Gulf War (1990–91), the Japanese government made incremental legislative changes throughout the early 2000s that allowed the JSDF to be dispatched first to the Indian Ocean and then to Iraq in 2004. Yet Japanese troops were still constitutionally prohibited from playing a combat role abroad, and this provided Australia with another opportunity to step up its practical security cooperation with Japan. Between 2004 and 2006, Australian forces provided security cover to Japanese SDF engineers working in a humanitarian capacity in Samawah, Iraq.[39]

Amidst this expanding security cooperation with Japan and the United States, Australia also reached out to China. The Howard government initiated free trade agreement talks with China, became a stronger supporter of China's entry into the WTO, avoided publicly criticising Chinese human rights abuses and in 1999 hosted the first visit by a Chinese head of state to Australia.[40] Howard's success in simultaneously strengthening ties with both the United States and China was symbolically demonstrated when he invited Chinese President Hu Jintao and US President George W Bush to address the Australian Parliament on successive days in October 2003. Of course, as Michael Wesley argues, the times suited Howard. During Howard's tenure, Australia could enjoy the immense prosperity brought about by China's economic growth and its increasing demand for Australian raw materials without having to be overly concerned about how China's rise would affect Asia's regional security environment. From 1997 onwards, China stepped up its efforts to engage with the region's multilateral institutions, announced a 'new security concept' that sought to reassure neighbours about China's peaceful intentions, and worked hard to cooperate with its smaller Southeast Asian neighbours.[41] Furthermore, the events of 11 September 2001 meant that the world—and in particular the United States—was focused more on responding to international terrorism (with China as a partner), than on the strategic implications of China's meteoric rise.[42] While we should not underestimate Howard's successes in Northeast Asia, Howard was spared from having to choose between the economic and security dimensions of Australia's national interest. On occasions, there was some evidence that economic policy had gotten ahead of security policy, such as in August 2004 when then foreign minister Downer informed a journalist in China that Australia's obligations to the United States under the ANZUS Treaty would not necessarily commit Australia to being involved in a conflict between China and the United States over Taiwan.[43] Yet on balance, the economic and security dimensions of Australian policy towards Northeast Asia appeared to be working in harmony.

The Rudd-Gillard Years: Dr Jekyll and Mr Hyde

By the end of the first decade of the twenty-first century, cracks were beginning to appear in the foundations of Australia's policy towards Northeast Asia. During the Hawke-Keating years, Australia's views of the Northeast Asian security environment gave prominence to economic factors and played down the threat of traditional security challenges. Similarly, the Howard government could enjoy the fruits of Northeast Asia's economic prosperity while facing few major security challenges from Northeast Asia. However, in the wake of the 2007–2008 Global Financial Crisis (GFC), it appeared that Northeast Asia's security environment was deteriorating. The impact of the GFC led many commentators to argue that the world was witnessing the decline of the United States and the rise of an economically resilient and more assertive China. Whatever the merits of this zero-sum view of the world, it was difficult to dispute the many regional security crises that rocked North and Southeast Asia between 2009 and 2013: China's harassment of the US surveillance ship the USNS *Impeccable* in the South China Sea in 2009; skirmishes between Chinese, Philippine and Vietnamese vessels around the Spratly and Paracel Islands; worsening political relations between Japan and South Korea over the disputed Dokdo/Takeshima islands; North Korea's sinking of the South Korean naval vessel *Cheonan* and its bombing of Yeongpeong Island in 2010; and the China-India border dispute in 2013. Perhaps most worrying of all was the prospect of a military clash between Northeast Asia's two great powers, China and Japan, over disputed islands in the East China Sea. Yet amidst these regional security tensions, the economic fundamentals of Australia's relationship with Northeast Asia could not be ignored. Between 2000 and

2012, Australia's combined trade with Japan and China grew to around one-third of Australia's total trade. While it was China's demand for Australian commodities that commanded most attention, the mature industrial economies of Japan, South Korea and Taiwan were also increasingly important markets for Australian raw materials, agriculture, education and tourism.[44] (See Figure 4.1.)

This combination of anxiety about the Northeast Asian security environment and optimism about Northeast Asia's economic future led Evan Feigenbaum and Robert Manning to argue that the region was now divided into 'two Asias':

> There is 'Economic Asia', the Dr Jekyll—a dynamic, integrated Asia with 53 per cent of its trade now being conducted within the region itself, and a US$19 trillion regional economy that has become an engine of global growth. And then there is 'Security Asia', the veritable Mr Hyde—a dysfunctional region of mistrustful powers, prone to nationalism and irredentism, escalating their territorial disputes over tiny rocks and shoals, and arming for conflict.[45]

These two very different conceptions of Northeast Asia were once again reflected in the seemingly incompatible views of Australia's economic and security policy communities. Between 2009 and 2013, the Rudd and Gillard governments published three major White Papers in relatively quick succession. The first—the Rudd government's 2009 Defence White Paper—painted a pessimistic picture of the region. That White Paper acknowledged that Asia's regional order was 'being transformed as economic changes start to bring about changes in the distribution of strategic power',[46] and that '[s]tability in any multipolar global order will most likely result from economic interdependence and pragmatic political cooperation among the major powers'.[47] However, the 2009 Defence White Paper also warned darkly that 'it was by no means certain' that economic interdependence would prevent conflict between states, and that 'there are likely to be tensions between the major powers of the region'.[48] Conversely, just three years later, the Gillard government's 2012

Australia in the Asian Century White Paper characterised Northeast Asia and the broader region in far more optimistic terms, largely because of the opportunities offered by economic growth. The 2012 *Asian Century* White Paper did acknowledge that strategic shifts had occurred as a result of Asia's economic growth, but overwhelmingly concentrated on how Australia could prosper from being 'in the right place at the right time—in the Asian region in the Asian century'.[49]

This divergence between the optimism of the economists and the pessimism of the strategists is, perhaps, unsurprising. As Mark Thomson of the Australian Strategic Policy Institute (ASPI) recently put it:

> The core goal of public policy is very simple; we desire more good things and less bad things. Economists and strategists largely sit on opposite sides of this dichotomy. Economists seek to arrange society so that we can have more good things than would otherwise be the case. In contrast, strategists try to mitigate the risk of a particularly nasty class of bad things by reducing their likelihood and consequence.[50]

Fortunately, we have moved on from the post-war decades of the 1950s, 1960s and 1970s when Australia's economists and strategists started from completely different positions when formulating policy towards Northeast Asia. Since the late 1980s, Australian policy-makers have, on the whole, recognised that Northeast Asia's economic ascendancy has the potential to shape both Australia's economic and security environment. Though they tend to place different emphasis on whether it is peace that leads to prosperity, or prosperity that leads to peace, the economists and strategists are now at least cognisant of each other's approach. Reflecting this, the Gillard government's 2013 Defence White Paper noted the need for an integrated approach to defence, economic and foreign policy that would simultaneously 'build sustainable security and prosperity'.[51] Yet while the Gillard government's articulation that Australian policy must try to pursue both security and economic prosperity is encouraging, it is not yet clear that Australia has the policy or institutional frameworks to do so.

Towards a New Era in Northeast Asia?

Australia's future relationships with Northeast Asia's two great powers—China and Japan—contain major challenges for the Australian policy community. Managing them both at once, in a way that meets our economic and security interests, will be especially difficult.

Australia's future security environment and economic prosperity will be shaped more by China than by any other state. Much energy has and should be spent on trying to quantify China's future economic size, the scale of its military capabilities and the extent to which domestic challenges will disrupt straight-line projections of Chinese growth. But the more important question is how China will use its growing power. Trying to predict the answer to that question is fraught with risk, given the lack of transparency surrounding Chinese policymaking and the many voices within China offering and influencing different future alternatives.[52] But two things stand out. First, China's more 'assertive' behaviour over the last three to five years has undermined much of the good work that Beijing had accomplished since the late 1990s. Second, there are small signs that the Xi Jinping government is beginning to understand this and is trying to play a more active role in shaping and centralising control over some of the more conflict-prone aspects of Chinese external policy. For example, in September 2012, just two months before coming to power as General Secretary of the Chinese Communist Party, Xi Jinping was put in charge of the office dealing with the Senkaku/Diaoyu territorial dispute between China and Japan. The fact that Xi, as incoming General Secretary and President of China, was put in charge of this issue likely reflects the importance of the Senkaku/Diaoyu dispute to the Chinese leadership, and its need for high-level management. Furthermore, in March 2013, Beijing decided to consolidate bureaucratic control over the multiple maritime agencies involved in patrolling the East and South China Seas under a single State Oceanic Administration. It is hoped this will reduce some of the bureaucratic competition between these Chinese agencies that has inadvertently contributed to security incidents with other claimant states in the South China Sea.[53] Finally, at the Third Plenum in November 2013, a meeting of the Chinese Central Committee where major new reforms have traditionally been announced, the Xi government announced that China would establish a new National Security Commission.

Though it is still too soon to tell what role the National Security Commission will serve and the extent to which it will actually deal with external security challenges (such as territorial and maritime disputes in the East and South China Seas), official documents, media analysis and interviews with Chinese researchers indicate that the core goal of the Commission is to avoid the 'stove-piping' that has afflicted Chinese policymaking in the past by centralising and better coordinating policy decisions.[54] As Linda Jakobson has argued, the lack of attention paid to foreign and security policy challenges by China's senior leadership is a 'recipe for disaster' for China and its neighbours.[55] Greater coordination on foreign and security policy matters does not necessarily imply that we will see a less 'assertive' China, but it will hopefully lessen the risk that China's behaviour will be dangerously reactive.

While China will affect Australia's economic prosperity and security environment more than any other state, it is the relationship with Japan that will serve as a bellwether of how Australian policy-makers view the Northeast Asian security environment and the challenge posed by China's rise. During the Howard years, the Australian government stepped up its cooperation with Japan on non-traditional security issues, established trilateral and quadrilateral dialogues with Japan, the United States and India, and elevated the bilateral relationship to a security partnership. The Rudd and Gillard governments then 'quietly but substantially expanded' Australia's security cooperation with Japan, despite public perceptions that the Australia-Japan relationship had been downgraded as a result of tensions over Japanese whaling and Rudd's greater focus on China.[56]

Since coming to power in September 2013, the Abbott government has endorsed even stronger security ties with Japan. On 9 October 2013 on the sidelines of the East Asia Summit (EAS), Prime Minister Tony Abbott told Japanese Prime Minister Shinzo Abe in front of a media audience that '[a]s far as I'm concerned, Japan is Australia's best friend in Asia and we want to keep it a very strong friendship'.[57] Dispelling any perception that Abbott's statement simply reflected the ebullience of a new prime minister, in October 2013 at the Kokoda Foundation Annual Dinner in Canberra, Minister for Defence David Johnston repeated the statement in front of the US and Japanese Ambassadors to Australia. Minister Johnston described Japan as 'a great trading nation and customer' of Australia and as a country with whom we 'share values and strategic interests'. Furthermore, reflecting similar language to that of the Howard era, Johnston closed his speech stating that:

> Australia looks forward to Japan making a greater contribution to security in our region and beyond—including through our respective alliances and friendship with the United States. We seek to support Japan's plan to work towards a more normal defence posture to help it play that greater role ... We recognise that our defence capabilities are [complementary]. Australia and Japan, as allies of the United States, have mutually supportive roles to play in the security of the region.[58]

At face value none of this seems particularly controversial. Australia and Japan are both allies of the United States, and since the Hawke-Keating years Australia has tried to encourage a more active regional security role for Japan. Yet the problem is, as Hugh White has argued, in Asia's changing strategic environment, a closer Australia-Japan security relationship has implications for Australia's relationship with China.[59]

While Australia and Japan share a number of common security interests, our geography, history and domestic political environment means that we do not always share the same vision of China. Australia periodically faced this problem during the Howard years, when certain Japanese leaders took a harder line on China than their Australian counterparts. For instance, Japanese prime minister Junichiro Koizumi was willing to tolerate high levels of political animosity in the China-Japan relationship over issues such as his visits to the Yasukuni Shrine, while Yuriko Koike, who served as defence minister during Shinzo Abe's first stint as prime minister, was a long standing supporter of Taiwan and favoured a strategy of containment against China.[60] Ultimately, however, Japan and China managed their bilateral relationship during the Howard years without allowing political spats to spill over into the security sphere, and Australia was spared from having to make a difficult decision about where its allegiances lay.

However, Australia may not always be spared such a decision. In 2010 Japan arrested the captain of a Chinese fishing boat after it rammed a Japanese coast guard ship in contested waters around the Senkaku/Diaoyu islands. In 2012, Japan then purchased three of the islands in the Senkaku/Diaoyu chain from their private Japanese owner in order to prevent them from being sold to the right-wing mayor of Tokyo. Amidst these headline-grabbing events, China has dramatically increased its surveillance by coast guard and law enforcement vessels of the waters around the islands, and the People's Liberation Army Navy has held exercises in the East China Sea, very close to Japanese territory. The large number of ships and aircraft now traversing the waters and airspace around these islands—combined with the absence of a legal or normative framework for dealing with such incidents, and China's demonstrated willingness to allow its ships and aircraft to sail or fly dangerously close to foreign vessels—has dramatically increased the risk of an accidental collision.

Tensions escalated further in November 2013 when Beijing announced the introduction of an Air Defence Identification Zone (ADIZ) over airspace that overlaps with Japan's own ADIZ, and includes the territorial airspace over the Senkaku/Diaoyu islands. In the past, Australian governments have elected not to take sides in this bilateral dispute between China and Japan and have instead called on both sides to resolve the dispute peacefully, and in accordance with international law. However, in its first few months in power, the Abbott government has taken a different approach. Following China's announcement of the ADIZ, the Australian government called in the Chinese Ambassador to express Australia's concerns and to request an explanation from China about this 'sudden' move.[61] In explaining Australia's position, Prime Minister Abbott stated that '[w]e are a strong ally of the US, we are a strong ally of Japan, we have a very strong view that international disputes should be settled peacefully'.[62] Prime ministerial sound bites aside, Australia is not an ally of Japan and Australians must seriously consider whether we wish to become one. Australia and Japan share a number of security interests and a closer strategic relationship may offer great benefits to Australia. But the key question is whether Canberra would be willing to come to Japan's aid in a contingency involving China? In 2007, the Howard government reportedly answered 'yes' to this question. But Northeast Asia's strategic environment has changed since the Howard years. Whether Australians are really prepared to enter an alliance with Japan is a question that still merits much greater discussion and debate within the Australian community. Otherwise Australia risks sleepwalking into a situation that may have devastating implications for Australia's economic and security interests.[63]

At the same time, Australia must not forget that the region's economic prosperity is tied to a healthy economic relationship between China and Japan. The China-Japan bilateral trade relationship is the third largest in the world. An even more significant aspect of the China-Japan economic relationship is the role the two countries play in regional and global supply-chain networks. Two-thirds of the goods that China imports from Japan are the technology, capital or input parts that are used to produce the goods that China exports to the world.[64] This means that the China-Japan economic relationship is relatively immune from political or security disputes. Although there was a slight downturn in China-Japan trade following Japan's 2012 purchase of three islands in the Senkaku/Diaoyu chain, bilateral economic ties have not been disrupted as much as one might expect because the Chinese government could not freeze Japanese trade or investment without jeopardising China's own economic growth.[65] One important sign of the resilience of this economic relationship is that in 2012, a Japanese survey found that 98 per cent of Japanese multinational companies had no intention of reducing their investment in China in the next two years.[66] While we cannot afford to overlook the challenging security tensions that exist in this relationship, it would be foolish to assume that China and Japan will willingly abandon a relationship upon which both economies are so dependent.

What are the options for Australia's future policy towards Northeast Asia? There is a risk that Australia could return to the postwar decades of the 1950s, 1960s and 1970s when economic and security policy diverged and there was only a fragile consensus in Australian policy towards Northeast Asia. But we must avoid this temptation. Australia will face more policy challenges like that posed in 2013 when Communications Minister Malcolm Turnbull and Trade Minister Andrew Robb parted company with Attorney-General George Brandis and the broader national security community over the role that Chinese telecommunications firm Huawei would play in the Australian National Broadband Network.[67] As Chinese firms expand their investment, Australia must ensure that its economic planners are talking to its security ones. Yet reconceptualising security in purely economic terms—the approach taken during the Hawke-Keating years—would be a similarly flawed approach. Northeast Asia faces a range of pressing security challenges and so far economic interdependence and Asia's multilateral institutions have been unable to fully transform the interests or constrain the behaviour of Asia's great powers.[68] Equally, while Howard's emphasis on separately building strong bilateral relationships with each of China, Japan and the United States was successful, China's jostling for position and the escalation of tensions between China and Japan means that Australia can no longer assume that the bilateral relationship with China will be immune from developments in the Australia-Japan relationship, and vice-versa.

Australia requires a new approach that better integrates these economic and security demands. This does not require choosing between our economic and security needs but rather recognising that both are intimately connected. Fortunately, we are not the only state in the region grappling with these issues. Most states in the Asia-Pacific region, including the United States, count China as a major—if not the major—trading partner. We should learn more from our neighbours about how they integrate the economic and security imperatives in their policy. Of these states, Australia must pay particularly close attention to how policymakers and the business communities in China and Japan envision their relative economic and security interests, and the implications of this for Australia. Two recent studies by James Reilly of the University of Sydney and Mark Thomson of ASPI are an important first step in this direction.[69] Furthermore, we need to ensure that Australia's economists and strategists are talking to one another about how regional trade policies—such as the Trans-Pacific Partnership (TPP) and the ASEAN-led Regional Comprehensive Economic Partnership

(RCEP)—will affect security dynamics in the region. Finally, Australia should encourage the United States to better explain the United States' 'rebalance' towards Asia, the United States' own economic and security interests in the region and the role it envisages for allies such as Australia. In 1995 the United States released its East Asia Strategy Report which became a major blueprint for US economic and security policy towards the region. It is time for another such document.

Further Reading

Bell, Coral, *Dependent Ally: A Study in Australian Foreign Policy*, 3rd edn., Allen & Unwin, Sydney 1993.

Dupont, Alan, *Australia's Security Interests in Northeast Asia*, Strategic and Defence Studies Centre, Australian National University, Canberra, 1991.

Garnaut, Ross, *Australia and the Northeast Asian Ascendancy: Report to the Prime Minister and the Minister for Foreign Affairs and Trade*, Commonwealth of Australia, Canberra, 1989.

Tow, William T and Trood, Russell, *Power Shift: Challenges for Australia in Northeast Asia*, Australian Strategic Policy Institute, Canberra, 2004.

Wesley, Michael, *The Howard Paradox: Australian Diplomacy in Asia 1996–2006*, ABC Books, Sydney, 2007.

White, Hugh, *The China Choice: Why America Should Share Power*, Black Inc., Collingwood, 2013.

Notes

1   TB Millar, *Australia's Defence*, Melbourne University Press, Carlton, 1965, pp. 1–2.

2   See, for example H White, 'Power Shift: Australia's Future Between Washington and Beijing', *Quarterly Essay*, vol. 39, September 2010; H White, *The China Choice: Why America Should Share Power*, Black Inc., Collingwood, 2012.

3   JB Welfield, 'Australia and Japan in the Cold War', in P Drysdale and H Kitaoji (eds), *Japan and Australia: Two Societies and Their Interaction*, Australian National University Press, Canberra, 1981, p. 401

4   ibid.

5   DW Mabon, 'Elusive Agreements: The Pacific Pact Proposals of 1949–1951', *Pacific Historical Review*, vol. 57, no. 2, 1988, pp. 163–164.

6   Notes on Conversation among Ambassador Dulles, Australian and New Zealand Ministers for External Affairs, 16 February 1951, in VD Cha, 'Powerplay: Origins of the US Alliance System in Asia', *International Security*, vol. 34, no. 3, 2009/2010, p. 185.

7   'The Review sought to inform the public of the nature and extent of Australia's defence capabilities, the foreseeable or contingent roles of the ADF, the environments in which these could be envisaged, and the resources involved in sustaining them. It also aimed to define Australia's

interests and outline defence policy to protect them.' Department of Defence, *Australian Defence Review*, Commonwealth of Australia, Canberra, 1972, p. 9. www.defence.gov.au/oscdf/se/publications/defreview/1972/Australian-Defence-Review-1972.pdf (viewed January 2014).

8 Commonwealth of Australia, *Australian Defence*, Canberra, November 1976, p. 4. www.defence.gov.au/oscdf/se/publications/wpaper/1976.pdf (viewed January 2014).

9 C Johnson, *MITI and the Japanese Miracle: The Growth of Industrial Policy, 1925–1975*, Stanford University Press, Stanford, 1982, p. 237.

10 EF Vogel, *Japan as Number One: Lessons for America*, Harvard University Press, Cambridge, MA, 1979.

11 P Drysdale, 'Australia and Japan in the Pacific and World Economy', in Drysdale and Kitaoji (eds), *Japan and Australia: Two Societies and their Interaction*, 1981, p. 421.

12 C Bell, *Dependent Ally: A Study in Australian Foreign Policy*, 3rd edn., Allen & Unwin, Sydney 1993, p. 169.

13 Welfield, 'Australia and Japan in the Cold War', 1981, p. 404; T Matthews and GS Reid, 'The Australian Bureaucracy and the Making of Foreign Policy', in Drysdale and Kitaoji (eds), *Japan and Australia: Two Societies and their Interaction*, 1981, p. 308.

14 Department of Foreign Affairs and Trade, '222 Agreement on Commerce Between the Commonwealth of Australia and Japan: Published Letters and Agreed Minutes', Historical Publications, Commonwealth of Australia, Canberra, 1957. www.info.dfat.gov.au/info/historical/HistDocs.nsf/(LookupVolNoNumber)/20~222 (viewed December 2013).

15 Matthews and Reid, 'The Australian Bureaucracy and the Making of Foreign Policy', p. 321.

16 ibid., p. 323.

17 R Garnaut, *Australia and the Northeast Asian Ascendancy: Report to the Prime Minister and the Minister for Foreign Affairs and Trade*, Commonwealth of Australia, Canberra, 1989.

18 P Keating, 'Asia-Australia Institute Address', Sydney, 7 April 1992, in M Ryan (ed), *Advancing Australia: The Speeches of Paul Keating, Prime Minister*, Big Picture Publications, Sydney, 1995, pp. 187–196.

19 Commonwealth of Australia, *Strategic Review 1993*, Canberra, 1993, pp. 2, 9. www.defence.gov.au/oscdf/se/publications/stratreview/1993/1993.pdf (viewed January 2014).

20 Bell, *Dependent Ally*, 1993, p. 169.

21 ibid., pp. 169–173.

22 ibid., p. 173.

23 A Dupont, *Australia's Security Interests in Northeast Asia*, Strategic and Defence Studies Centre, Australian National University, Canberra, 1991, p. xi.

24 Commonwealth of Australia, *Defending Australia*, Canberra, 1994, pp. 9–10. www.defence.gov.au/oscdf/se/publications/wpaper/1994.pdf (viewed January 2014).

25   Commonwealth of Australia, *Strategic Review 1993*, 1993, p. 6.

26   ibid.

27   On the 1993–94 North Korean nuclear crisis, see JS Wit et al., *Going Critical: The First North Korean Nuclear Crisis*, Brookings Institution Press, Washington DC, 2004. Note also that the highest point of tension in the 1995–96 Taiwan Straits Crisis came in March 1996, shortly after the Australian Federal election which brought the Liberal-National Party Coalition into power as the new government of Australia.

28   A Dupont, *Australia's Security Interests in Northeast Asia*, 1991, pp. 22–23. (Not including the United States or Soviet Union.)

29   ibid., pp. 16–19.

30   Y Sato, 'Japan-Australia Security Cooperation: Jointly Cultivating the Trust of the Community', *Asian Affairs: An American Review*, vol. 35, no. 3, 2008, p. 154.

31   A Dupont, *Australia's Security Interests in Northeast Asia*, 1991, pp. 19–21.

32   P Dibb, *Review of Australia's Defence Capabilities: Report for the Minister of Defence*, Commonwealth of Australia, Canberra, 1986, p. 1. www. defence.gov.au/oscdf/se/publications/defreview/1986/Review-of-Australias-Defence-Capabilities-1986_Part1.pdf (viewed April 2014).

33   M Wesley, *The Howard Paradox: Australian Diplomacy in Asia 1996–2006*, ABC Books, Sydney, 2007.

34   Named after its lead author, Joseph Nye, former US Assistant Secretary of Defense for International Security Affairs. See Office of the Secretary for Defence, *United States Security Strategy for the East Asia-Pacific Region*, United States Department of Defense, Washington DC, 1995.

35   This problem had also been acknowledged in Commonwealth of Australia, *1993 Strategic Review*, 1993, p. 6.

36   Office of the Secretary for Defence, *United States Security Strategy for the East Asia-Pacific Region*, United States Department of Defense, Washington DC, 1995, pp. 25–26; Ministry of Foreign Affairs of Japan, 'The Guidelines for Japan-US Defense Cooperation', Ministry of Foreign Affairs of Japan, Tokyo, 1997. www.mofa.go.jp/mofaj/area/usa/hosho/kyoryoku.html (viewed January 2013).

37   G Sheridan, 'Tokyo Rejects Security Treaty', *The Australian*, 12 March 2007. www.news.com.au/national/tokyo-rejects-security-treaty/story-e6frfkp9-1111113136781 (viewed January 2014).

38   Ministry of Foreign Affairs of Japan, 'Japan-Australia Joint Declaration on Security Cooperation', Ministry of Foreign Affairs of Japan, Tokyo, 13 March 2007. www.mofa.go.jp/region/asia-paci/australia/joint0703.html (viewed December 2013).

39   Sato, 'Japan-Australia Security Cooperation', 2008, p. 157.

40   A Downer, 'Australia and China—Partners for Progress', speech by the Minister for Foreign Affairs and Trade, China Oration of the Australia-China Business Council, Sydney, 1999. www.foreignminister.gov.au/speeches/1999/991125_aust_china.html (viewed December 2013).

41   D Shambaugh, 'China Engages Asia: Reshaping the Regional Order', *International Security*, vol. 29, no. 3, 2004/2005, pp. 64–99.

42 Wesley, *The Howard Paradox*, 2007, pp. 125–130.

43 Sato, 'Japan-Australia Security Cooperation', 2008, p. 165.

44 It should be noted that while China and Japan are Australia's two top trading partners, Australia's top three investment partners are the United States, United Kingdom and Japan. Commonwealth of Australia, *Australia in the Asian Century*, Canberra, 2012, Chapters 2–3. www.asiaeducation. edu.au/verve/_resources/australia-in-the-asian-century-white-paper.pdf (viewed January 2014).

45 EA Feigenbaum and RA Manning, 'A Tale of Two Asias', *Foreign Policy*, 31 October 2012. www.foreignpolicy.com/articles/2012/10/30/a_tale_of_ two_asias (viewed November 2013).

46 Commonwealth of Australia, *Defending Australia in the Asia Pacific Century: Force 2030*, Canberra, 2009, p. 49. www.defence.gov.au/ whitepaper2009/docs/defence_white_paper_2009.pdf (viewed January 2014).

47 ibid., p. 32.

48 ibid., pp. 32–33.

49 Commonwealth of Australia, *Australia in the Asian Century*, 2012, p. 1.

50 M Thomson, 'Economists and Strategists', *The Strategist*, Australian Strategic Policy Institute, 29 April 2013. www.aspistrategist.org.au/ economists-and-strategists/ (viewed November 2013).

51 Commonwealth of Australia, *Defence White Paper 2013*, Canberra, 2013, p. 7. www.defence.gov.au/whitepaper2013/docs/WP_2013_web.pdf (viewed January 2014).

52 L Jakobson and D Knox, *New Foreign Policy Actors in China*, no. 26, *SIPRI Policy Paper*, Stockholm International Peace Research Institute, 2010. www.books.sipri.org/files/PP/SIPRIPP26.pdf (viewed January 2014).

53 International Crisis Group, 'Stirring up the South China Sea (I)', no. 223, *Asia Report*, International Crisis Group, 2012, pp. 8–19. www.crisisgroup. org/~/media/Files/asia/north-east-asia/223-stirring-up-the-south-china-sea-i.pdf (viewed January 2014).

54 J Wuthnow, 'Decoding China's New "National Security Commission"', Center for Naval Analyses, Alexandria, 2013. www.cna.org/sites/default/ files/research/CPP-2013-U-006465-Final.pdf (viewed January 2014).

55 L Jakobson, 'China's Foreign Policy Dilemma', *Lowy Institute Analysis*, Lowy Institute for International Policy, Sydney, 2013, p. 1. www. lowyinstitute.org/files/jakobson_chinas_foreign_policy_dilemma_web3_ use_this.pdf (viewed January 2014).

56 H White, 'An Australia-Japan Alliance?', Centre of Gravity Series, Strategic and Defence Studies Centre, Australian National University, Canberra, 2012, p. 2. www.ips.cap.anu.edu.au/sites/default/files/COG4_White.pdf (viewed January 2014).

57 AAP, 'Tony Abbott reaches out to Australia's 'best friend in Asia', Japan', *The Australian*, 10 October 2013. www.theaustralian.com.au/national-affairs/policy/tony-abbott-reaches-out-to-australias-best-friend-in-asia-japan/story-fn59nm2j-1226736508726 (viewed March 2014).

58   D Johnston, 'Minister for Defence—Kokoda Foundation Annual Dinner—
      Rydges Hotel Canberra', speech to the Kokoda Foundation Annual
      Dinner, Canberra, 31 October 2013. www.minister.defence.gov.
      au/2013/10/31/minister-for-defence-kokoda-foundation-annual-
      dinner-rydges-hotel-canberra/ (viewed November 2013).
59   White, 'An Australia-Japan Alliance?', 2012.
60   A King, *Resignation of Japanese Defence Minister Fumio Kyuma:
      Implications for Australia*, no. 10, *ASPI Policy Analysis*, Australian
      Strategic Policy Institute, Canberra, 23 July 2007. www.aspi.org.au/
      publications/resignation-of-japanese-defence-minister,-fumio-kyuma-
      implications-for-australia-by-amy-king/Policy_analysis10.pdf (viewed
      January 2014).
61   Minister for Foreign Affairs the Hon. J Bishop, 'China's Announcement of
      an Air-Defence Identification Zone over the East China Sea', Minister for
      Foreign Affairs, Media Release, Department of Foreign Affairs and Trade,
      Commonwealth of Australia, 26 November 2013. www.foreignminister.
      gov.au/releases/2013/jb_mr_131126a.html (viewed December 2013).
62   P Hartcher, 'China Vents its Anger at Australia's Stand on Airspace Rights',
      Sydney Morning Herald, 3 December 2013.
63   C Clark, *The Sleepwalkers: How Europe Went to War in 1914*, Penguin
      Books, London, 2013. For more on Australia's regional alliance
      obligations under the ANZUS Treaty, see Peter Dean's analysis of ANZUS
      in Chapter 9 of this book.
64   R Katz, 'Limits to Chinese Economic Leverage, Economic Fallout from
      Senkakus, Part 2', *The Oriental Economist*, 11 February 2013, p. 2.
65   R Katz, 'Mutual Assured Production: Why Trade Will Limit Conflict
      Between China and Japan', *Foreign Affairs*, July/August, 2013, p. 19. www.
      foreignaffairs.com/articles/139451/richard-katz/mutual-assured-
      production (viewed January 2014).
66   R Katz, 'Chinese-Based Assemblers Need Japanese Parts', *The Oriental
      Economist*, 19 February 2013, p. 2.
67   C Joye, 'NBN Ban on Huawei Stays: Brandis', *Australian Financial Review*,
      29 October 2013.
68   E Goh, 'Institutions and the Great Power Bargain in East Asia: ASEAN's
      Limited "Brokerage" Role', *International Relations of the Asia Pacific*, vol.
      11, 2011, pp. 373–401.
69   J Reilly, 'China's Economic Statecraft: Turning Wealth Into Power', Lowy
      Institute for International Policy, Sydney, November 2013. wwww.
      lowyinstitute.org/files/reilly_chinas_economic_statecraft_web.pdf
      (viewed January 2014); M Thomson, *Trade, Investment and Australia's
      National Security ... Or How I Learned to Stop Worrying and Love Chinese
      Money*, no. 56, *ASPI Strategic Insights*, Australian Strategic Policy Institute,
      Canberra, 18 April 2012. www.aspi.org.au/publications/strategic-
      insights-56-trade,-investment-and-australias-national-security...or-
      how-i-learned-to-stop-worrying-and-love-chinese-money/SI56_Trade_
      investment_security.pdf (viewed January 2014).

5
Australia, Indonesia and Southeast Asia

John Blaxland

For much of its history, Australia has sought to bolster its defence and security arrangements from Asia rather than with Asia. When TB Millar first penned *Australia's Defence*, Australia had not yet abandoned the 'White Australia' policy that sought to exclude migrants from Asia. By the end of the first decade in the twenty-first century, Australia had become a much more ethnically-diverse and multicultural society than he could have envisaged, drawing in large numbers of migrants from across Southeast Asia and beyond. That diversity has been paralleled by a different approach to regional engagement on security affairs as well.

While in recent years much of Australia's trade and security preoccupations have been concerned largely with the Northeast Asian states of China, Japan and Korea, it is the countries to Australia's immediate north in Southeast Asia—primarily Indonesia—that have a direct bearing on Australia's national security. Apart from Indonesia, the countries of Southeast Asia have tended not to feature prominently in Australians' consciousness. In fact, their enduring significance to the future security of Australia is often underappreciated.

The Association of Southeast Asian Nations

The ten-nation grouping of the Association of Southeast Asian Nations (ASEAN) has a population of about 600 million, with English as the common language of commerce and diplomacy. ASEAN was established in 1967 and Australia was its first dialogue partner in political, economic and practical cooperation—including in defence and security matters—and has remained a longstanding partner ever since. Yet ASEAN has not been seen as a cohesive body politic like the European Union.

Building such strength has proven challenging in the face of the region's diversity. ASEAN includes small and large states with people of many races, religions and historical legacies. It is, effectively, a multicultural grouping of nations with many enduring interests in common with Australia, but until recently, has had little incentive for greater collective action.[1]

Australia has been a great beneficiary of the waves of migration from Southeast Asia. Those in Australia who are born or descended from Vietnam are estimated at nearly 180 000, and those from Thailand at about 150 000. Conversely, in countries like Thailand for instance, the alumni of Australian universities and colleges are plentiful and strong, with frequent reunions and strong feelings of affinity towards Australia. Bilateral education links with Southeast Asian countries stretch back sixty years since the founding of the Colombo Plan in 1951. Today, Australia is a leading provider of higher education for several Southeast Asian nations with a considerable number of graduates of Australian universities in senior and powerful positions across the region, an outcome that provides Australia with unprecedented levels of personal, professional and diplomatic access.

Former ASEAN Secretary General, Dr Surin Pitsuwan, at a speech at the launch of the Southeast Asia Institute at the Australian National University in 2012 declared 'now Australia has found Southeast Asia, it is in our best interest to continue to focus on cooperation, support and involvement in that region'.[2] To be fair, Australia has for some time already 'found' Southeast Asia. This is most visibly demonstrated by Australia's membership of a range of ASEAN-centric international bodies such as the East Asian Summit (EAS), the ASEAN Regional Forum (ARF), the ASEAN Defence Ministers Meeting-Plus

Figure 5.1: Australia and the Region

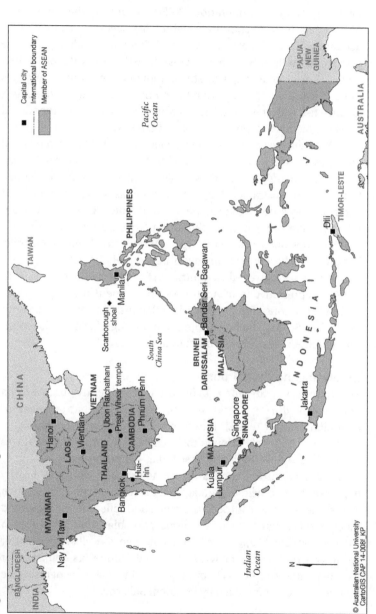

Source: CartoGIS, College of Asia and the Pacific, Australian National University, 2014.

(ADMM-Plus), as well as other regional groupings such as the Asia-Pacific Economic Cooperation (APEC) forum. At the same time, ASEAN has been broadminded about its security arrangements, accommodating the Philippines' and Thailand's military alliance arrangements and Singapore's close logistic ties with the United States as well as a range of still nominally communist countries under the one roof. Their flexibility on this point suggest Australia's alliance ties with the United States would not be problematic should it seek to be more closely integrated with ASEAN.

Australia has demonstrated its good intentions through regional engagement which has earned considerable goodwill across ASEAN. Today, despite only limited direct financial investment from Australia to the region, Australia is largely recognised as being more nuanced and culturally attuned than in the past and more regionally savvy and relevant than other non-neighbouring Organisation for Economic Co-Operation and Development (OECD) countries. In effect, Australia has proved to be a natural and enduring partner of ASEAN.

When aggregated, the countries of Southeast Asia, embodied in ASEAN, represent one of Australia's pre-eminent trading partners and its most consequential security relationships beyond that with the United States. The most prominent and significant of the countries of ASEAN, of course, is Indonesia.

Indonesia and East Timor

The Indonesian archipelago featured prominently for Australia particularly during World War II. Following Japan's defeat of Australian and British Empire forces in Malaya and Singapore in February 1942, it was through the archipelago—primarily what was then called the Netherlands East Indies—that the Japanese forces advanced, capturing thousands of Australians who had hastily deployed there to help defend against the Japanese onslaught. Then as the tide of the war turned, Australian and Allied troops reclaimed much of this territory by force of arms, particularly in the territory of what is now called Papua, the island of Borneo, as well as Timor. After World War II, Australia actively supported Indonesia's demands for its independence to be acknowledged and formally recognised the Indonesian government led by President Sukarno.

However with the onset of the Cold War, Sukarno proved more sympathetic to the communists and established close relations with the USSR and China and acquired Soviet military equipment and weapons. From the late 1950s Indonesia pushed for the handover of the remaining territory held by the Dutch in Irian Jaya. Australia initially sided with the Dutch, hoping they would stay longer and consider an amalgamation of territories with those of Papua and New Guinea—then under Australian administration—but covert Indonesian special forces operations in Irian Jaya made the Dutch position untenable. It soon became evident that the Dutch would not remain and, being eager to avoid having Indonesia fall completely into the Soviet Union's orbit as well as wanting to build closer ties to exploit economic opportunities, the United States backed the Indonesian plan for annexation of Papua.

Sukarno also objected to the establishment of Malaysia and launched a period of armed 'Confrontation' from late 1963 until 1966. United States officials made it clear to their Australian counterparts that placating Indonesia over Papua was more important to them than backing Australia. In addition they stated that the Confrontation over the Federation of Malaysia was a concern for Britain and Australia more so than the United States. This had a sobering effect on Australian defence policy makers who came to realise the limits of their influence in Washington and how important Indonesia was to the United States as part of the Cold War manoeuvrings between superpowers.[3]

The strategic equation changed dramatically following the crushing of the Communist Party of Indonesia in 1965 and the subsequent replacement of Sukarno with Suharto—an army general who maintained a purportedly non-aligned stance for his country while in fact being pro-West—as evident through a notable preference for military exchanges with and equipment purchases from the United States.[4] Largely as a result of Soeharto's ties with the United States and the removal of the country's internal communist threat, Indonesia was transformed in Australia's security consciousness from being a potential threat to a prospective security partner. Furthermore, with the Netherlands no longer in contention for control of the territory of Papua and the United States' clear support for Indonesia's position,

Australia raised no objections to the United Nations (UN)-supervised Act of Free Choice in Papua in 1969, which saw 1026 hand-picked indigenous representatives vote in favour of incorporation into Indonesia.

With the prospect of independence for East Timor following Portugal's dismantling of the remnants of its empire in 1974, Indonesia worried about what might emerge from the apparent political vacuum. Suharto looked unfavourably at East Timor's most powerful pro-independence groups which were seen to have communist sympathies. He faced what appeared to be a stark choice: intervene and annex the small territory, or accept the prospect of a potentially Marxist state on Indonesia's doorstep. Gough Whitlam, the Australian Labor prime minister from 1973–75, sympathised with Suharto's dilemma and offered tacit support for Indonesian intervention. But Indonesia's heavy-handed invasion and the death of five Australian journalists reporting from the border town of Balibo derailed Australia's efforts for maintaining a sympathetic stance and soured bilateral relations for decades.

Eventually under the prime ministership of Paul Keating (1991–96), and after years of low-key military and diplomatic engagement to build mutual trust and understanding, a security treaty between Australia and Indonesia was negotiated (in secret) and signed in 1996.[5] The treaty was enacted shortly before the onset of the Asian Financial crisis of 1997—a crisis which led Indonesia to experience massive unrest and successive changes of government. Suharto was forced to resign and his technocratic deputy, Habibie, took over in May 1998. In the meantime the internal security situation in East Timor continued to fester and in late 1998 Australian Prime Minister John Howard wrote to Habibie calling for a fresh approach to the situation there. Howard was not to know that his letter would trigger such a strong reaction. Rather than looking to assuage concerns, Habibie precipitated change by calling for a referendum on the fate of the territory of East Timor.[6]

After protracted negotiations, the unarmed United Nations Assistance Mission to East Timor (UNAMET) was deployed in mid-1999 to supervise the referendum, despite the presence of armed and angry 'pro-integration' militia groups aligned with the Indonesian military. At the ballot in early September the people of East Timor voted overwhelmingly in favour of not opting for integration—a vote which implied a strong desire for independence. The militias unleashed a wave of violence which triggered calls for an international intervention force to deploy into East Timor.

The International Force for East Timor (INTERFET)—as the mission came to be known—was headed by Australian Army Major General Peter Cosgrove. But the mission would not have been possible without Indonesian consent and the active participation of other ASEAN partners. Thailand was the first ASEAN country to agree to participate alongside Australia, offering a battalion-sized force and a deputy force commander, Major General Songkitti Jaggabatra. This arrangement highlighted the little-known significance of the countries of ASEAN to Australia's security and represented a significant return on decades of investment in the bilateral relationship with Thailand through Australia's Defence Cooperation Program and earlier ties through the Southeast Asia Treaty Organisation (SEATO) that was in effect during the early-to-mid years of the Cold War (from 1954–76).[7]

The bilateral security agreement between Australia and Indonesia was effectively torn up as a result of INTERFET. At first it seemed bilateral relations would take decades to return to their previous levels of cordial and relatively close engagement. But events in Bali and Jakarta in 2002 and 2005 changed that. Foreign trained and inspired terrorist bombings in the tourist resort area of Bali and repeated bombings in Jakarta (at an international hotel and in front of the Australia Embassy) provided an extraordinary opportunity for Australia to lend a hand in the immediate recovery and in tracking down the perpetrators. For Indonesia to accept this offer was a sign of genuine goodwill.

Relations continued to improve in the years immediately after. The Indian Ocean tsunami in December 2004 prompted Australia to offer immediate aid and assistance for the recovery operations in Aceh province on the island of Sumatra that lasted well into 2005. This combination of natural and man-made disasters had the unexpected effect of bringing Australia and Indonesia closer together than ever before. The Lombok Treaty of mutual security cooperation, signed in 2006, was made possible by these series of events.[8] But for Indonesia, this security pact was as much about receiving an assurance from Australia that the role it played in East Timor would not be repeated in Papua and the Lombok Treaty reaffirmed that Australia would not interfere in the internal affairs of Indonesia[9] (see Box 5.1).

Box 5.1: Agreement between the Republic of Indonesia and Australia on the Framework for Security Cooperation (commonly known as the Lombok Treaty)

The key articles which the Government of the Republic of Indonesia and the Government of Australia (hereinafter referred to as the 'Parties') have agreed to are as follows:

Article I

The main objectives of this Agreement are:

1. to provide a framework for deepening and expanding bilateral cooperation and exchanges as well as to intensify cooperation and consultation between the Parties in areas of mutual interest and concern on matters affecting their common security as well as their respective national security

2. to establish a bilateral consultative mechanism with a view to encouraging & intensive dialogue, exchanges and implementation of co-operative activities as well as strengthening institutional relationships pursuant to this Agreement.

Article II

In their relations with one another, the Parties shall be guided by the following fundamental principles, consistent with the Charter of the United Nations:

1. Equality, mutual benefit and recognition of enduring interests each Party has in the stability, security and prosperity of the other

2. Mutual respect and support for the sovereignty, territorial integrity, national unity and political independence of each other, and also non-interference in the internal affairs of one another

3. The Parties, consistent with their respective domestic laws and international obligations, shall not in any manner support or participate in activities by any person or entity which constitutes

a threat to the stability, sovereignty or territorial integrity of the other Party, including by those who seek to use its territory for encouraging or committing such activities, including separatism, in the territory of the other Party

4. The Parties undertake, consistent with the Charter of the United Nations, to settle any disputes that might arise between them by peaceful means in such a manner that international peace, security and justice are not endangered

5. The Parties shall refrain from the threat or use of force against the territorial integrity or political independence of the other, in accordance with the UN Charter

6. Nothing in this Agreement shall affect in any way the existing rights and obligations of either Party under international law.

Article III

The scope of cooperation of this Agreement shall include:

- Defence Cooperation
- Law Enforcement Cooperation
- Counter-terrorism Cooperation
- Intelligence Cooperation
- Maritime Security
- Aviation Safety and Security
- Proliferation of Weapons of Mass Destruction
- Emergency Cooperation
- Community Understanding and People-to-People Cooperation.

Article VIII

Disputes arising in relation to the interpretation or implementation of this Agreement shall be settled amicably by mutual consultation or negotiation between the Parties.

Since the signing of the Lombok Treaty a number of stresses in 2012–2014, associated with 'beef, boats and spies', have buffeted the relationship.[10] Issues such as the short-notice cancellation of the live cattle trade, people smuggling and the political campaign to 'stop the boats' carrying refugees to Australia from Indonesia, and the security and intelligence leaks in 2013 created their own tensions in the bilateral relationship. These, in turn, have demanded close attention and intensive management to avoid unduly affecting ties.

In seeking to address the conundrum of irregular boat arrivals—an issue of greater priority for Australia than for Indonesia—Australia has drawn extensively on the networks that have developed through diplomatic, defence, police, customs and other links with Indonesia. As Australia looks to address these and other regional security concerns more holistically and effectively, and as Indonesia becomes more prosperous and powerful, Australia's efforts to enhance its relationship with Indonesia have become all the more important. At the same time, Indonesia remains proudly non-aligned, eager to avoid formal alliance arrangements with another power.

The Lombok Treaty paved the way for enhanced bilateral security arrangements between Australia and Indonesia. Notwithstanding the security crisis experienced in 2013 and 2014, significant bilateral security ties endure. While temporarily 'on ice', a wide range of activities have enduring significance for both countries. These include high-level defence and foreign ministers talks and chiefs of defence talks; bilateral naval, air and land exercises; student exchanges; scholarships; alumni associations; collaborative arrangements with customs, quarantine, federal police, trade bodies and educational institutions; and the '2+2' meetings between Australian and Indonesian defence and foreign ministers; a key annual forum to maintain bilateral engagement.[11]

Today Indonesia is more economically vibrant and politically dynamic than ever before, and bilateral ties are as important as ever. As Australia seeks to bolster trade ties through regional economic partnerships, innovative ways are called for to boost trade, cultural and security ties in order to broaden and deepen the bilateral relationship. In terms of Defence cooperation, a number of measures have been taken. As Australia's new amphibious ships become operational, additional opportunities to engage in collaborative training and development and humanitarian assistance activities throughout the archipelago may present themselves as being of mutual benefit to the Australian and Indonesian defence forces. These opportunities should be firmly grasped by Australia and Indonesia alike.

Despite the growing importance of Indonesia to Australia (and apparent declining importance of Australia to Indonesia) there is little public awareness or understanding of the depth and breadth of the ties between Indonesia and Australia today. For policy insiders, the strength and utility of these ties suggests there may also be benefits in considering whether existing arrangements could be the basis for wider initiatives in cooperation: for instance by seeking to extend these arrangements to include some other close Australian security partners such as Malaysia, Singapore and New Zealand as well as other interested and contiguous ASEAN partner countries.

Some in Australia look with concern at the situation in Papua and see the potential for what, in broad terms, could be described as a repeat of the scenario which unfolded in East Timor in 1999. This is at best a remote possibility as it is a position not supported by the major political parties in Australia and only gains support amongst fringe, but sometimes vocal activist groups. It would be a grave mistake if Australian policy was to be led towards such thinking. While some may criticise how Papua came to be incorporated into Indonesia in 1969, it remains an internationally recognised part of this archipelagic nation. As a result of decades of transmigration, particularly from Java, the population mix in Papua today is not exclusively Papuan and the majority are understood to identify themselves unequivocally with the Indonesian state. Beyond this, there are a number of signs, including stated government policy, that Indonesia is eager to address the human rights and separatist concerns of Papuans to keep the matter as a domestic issue, even considering special autonomy measures to placate local and international concerns. In addition, unlike with East Timor, there is no strongly organised internal resistance force and virtually no strong and active indigenous political body advocating for anything more than incremental internal reform. Nonetheless, there remains a risk that a heavy-handed response by security forces to actions by militant separatist could weigh heavily on bilateral relations. Australia has sought to invest in the bilateral relationship with Indonesia for mutual benefit. To further such mutual benefit, the best approach Australia can take is to continue to advocate politely but consistently for justice and respect for the human rights of the indigenous people of Papua.[12]

As Australia considers ways to enhance security engagement with Indonesia, it needs to be mindful of a number of factors. First, Indonesia is one of the world's largest nations with a proud and long tradition of seeing itself as non-aligned. As a result, engagement needs to be couched in a way that allays concerns of any security ties being portrayed as an alliance. Second, it remains a significant regional power not just because of is population size and geographic spread, but because it sits astride the arteries connecting the Indian and Pacific Oceans. Third, Indonesia sees China as having the potential to be a threat but has sought to avoid saying so publicly. In effect much of its defence posture remains oriented inwards, focused on maintaining national cohesion; perceptions of threats outlined in the 2008 Indonesian Defence White Paper are primarily internal, terrorism and separatism.[13] Where it considers external security concerns its orientation is overwhelmingly towards the north rather than the south, towards Australia. The concerns to the north spring in part from the contestation over the South China Sea: with China's 'nine-dash line' representing a considerable intrusion into Indonesia's Exclusive Economic Zone (EEZ) surrounding Natuna Islands, which jut out into the South China Sea between East and West Malaysia.

Indonesia has a long shopping list of preferred military hardware capabilities which it aspires to acquire, including the recent controversial purchase of modern main battle tanks from Germany and attack helicopters from the United States. In part, this spending is intended to restore the confidence of the military after the post Suharto slowdown in military preferential treatment. There is a broad recognition by Indonesian authorities of the need to rebuild the Indonesian National Armed Forces (*Tentara Nasional Indonesia*, or TNI) as a more professional force, but there is considerable inertia. The TNI has an overly wide variety of weapons systems deployed in small batches, with inadequate training, limited logistic support, few spare parts and a number of distracting, but enduring domestic security and economic priorities. Combined, these circumstances present the TNI with almost insurmountable challenges on the path to increased professionalism.[14]

Indonesia's northern orientation and internal security reform augurs well for United States Marine Corps personnel, who rotate through Darwin for six month deployments during the dry months. The wet and hot summer months preclude training opportunities in

Australia's north for virtually half of each year, pointing to the practicality of sending the Marines home to their US bases for the Northern Territory's wet season. Protestations in 2012 by Indonesia's foreign minister, Marty Natalegawa, over Australia's apparent failure to consult with Indonesia before making the decision and the announcement over the US Marines pointed to areas of significant apparent unease. But President Susilo Bambang Yudhoyono allayed concerns and effectively endorsed the US Marine presence. Indeed, Indonesian military practitioners have few if any qualms and welcome the opportunity to train closely with the US Marines and even engage in trilateral training activities alongside US and Australian forces.

Beyond the utility of the Marines' collocation alongside the Australian forces in Darwin, the United States understands the importance of engaging with the Indonesian military for the American efforts towards a 'rebalance' in the Pacific. In fact, the US-Indonesia security relationship is significant in its own right, independent of Australia's ties with Indonesia and the United States. Conversely, Australian access in Southeast Asia is bolstered by its relationship with the United States, being a preferred Status of Forces Agreement (SOFA) partner for many Southeast Asian countries after the United States. In addition, Australia's close intelligence ties with the other 'five eyes' countries (US, UK, Canada and New Zealand) have tended to be seen by partner countries in the region as advantageous. Having a close US security partner like Australia nearby has helped to generate positive spin-off effects for the forces of those countries that engage closely with Australia.

Malaysia, Singapore and the Five Power Defence Arrangements

Beyond Indonesia, Australia's second-most important strategic relationship in Southeast Asia is its participation alongside Malaysia and Singapore (as well as New Zealand and Britain) in the Five Power Defence Arrangements (FPDA). The FPDA came into force in 1971 as a loose consultative arrangement after Confrontation with Indonesia and the announcement in 1968 by Britain's Labour government that it would withdraw its military forces from 'east of Suez' by 1971.

Box 5.2: Five Power Defence Arrangements

Communique issued at the conclusion of the Five Power Ministerial Meeting on the External Defence of Malaysia and Singapore, London, 15–16 April 1971:

1. Ministers of the Governments of Australia, New Zealand, Singapore and the United Kingdom met in London on the 15th and 16th April 1971, in order to consider matters of common interest to all five Governments relating to the external defence of Malaysia and Singapore.

2. The Ministers of the five governments affirmed, as the basic principles of their discussions, their continuing determination to work together for peace and stability, their respect for the sovereignty, political independence and territorial integrity of all countries, and their belief in the settlement of all international disputes by peaceful means in accordance with principles of the United Nations Charter.

3. In the context of their Governments' determination to continue to co-operate closely in defence arrangements which are based on the need to regard the defence of Malaysia and Singapore as indivisible, the Ministers noted with gratification the development of the defence capability of Malaysia and Singapore, to which the other three Governments had given assistance, and the decisions of the Governments of Australia, New Zealand and the United Kingdom, which had been welcomed by the other two Governments, to continue to station forces there after the end of 1971.

4. In discussing the contribution which each of the five Governments would make to defence arrangements in Malaysia and Singapore, the Ministers noted the view of the United Kingdom Government that the nature of its commitment under the Anglo-Malaysian Defence Agreement required review and that that Agreement should be replaced by new political arrangements. They declared that their Governments would continue to co-operate, in accordance with their respective policies, in the field of defence after the termination of the Agreement on 1st November 1971.

5. The Ministers also declared, in relation to the external defence of Malaysia and Singapore, that in the event of any form of armed attack externally organised or supported or the threat of such attack against Malaysia or Singapore, their Governments would immediately consult together for the purpose of deciding what measures should be taken jointly or separately in relation to such attack or threat

6. The Ministers reviewed the progress made regarding the establishment of the new defence arrangements. In particular:
   - They welcomed the practical steps being taken to establish the Integrated Air [later Area] Defence System for Malaysia and Singapore on 1st September 1971.
   - They agreed to establish an Air Defence Council, comprising one senior representative of each of the five nations, to be responsible for the functioning of the Integrated Air Defence System, and to provide direction to the Commander of the Integrated Air Defence System on matters affecting the organisation, training and development and operational readiness of the System.
   - They noted the progress made by the Five Power Naval Advisory Working Group.
   - They decided to set up a Joint Consultative Council to provide a forum for regular consultation at the senior official level on matters relating to the defence arrangements.

   Ministers also noted that further discussion would take place between Governments on the practical arrangements required for the accommodation and facilities for the ANZUK forces to be stationed in the area. They looked forward to the early and successful conclusion of these discussions as an essential basis for the completion of plans for the new defence arrangements.

7. The Ministers agreed that from time to time it might be appropriate for them to discuss their common interests. It would also be open to any of the participating Governments to request at any times, a meeting to review these defence arrangements.

Source: 'Five Power Defence Arrangements', Level Four, Hedley Bull Centre, Australian National University, Canberra.

Australia's military engagement with Malaysia and Singapore stretches back to the years prior to World War II. During that period Australia placed great emphasis on Britain's 'Singapore Strategy' of building up an apparently impregnable island fortress as a security guarantee for Britain's Empire in the so-called 'Far East' against anticipated Japanese aggression. This was backed up with the commitment of the bulk of the 8th Division to the fateful defence of Singapore in 1941 and early 1942. In the immediate post war years Britain reasserted itself in the region, but during the 1960s it started to withdraw from East of Suez and Malaysia and Singapore gained independence. As a result Australia's direct engagement in the security arrangements for these two countries became more prominent.

The FPDA was initially conceived as a transitional agreement to provide for the defence of Malaysia and Singapore until these new states could fend for themselves. Over the past forty years, however, the FPDA has moved beyond its initial preoccupation with the air defence of the Malaysian peninsula and Singapore to area defence and the scope of its remit has expanded to include combined and joint exercises. In recent years the FPDA has addressed asymmetric threats, maritime security issues and humanitarian assistance and disaster relief (HADR). In sum, the FPDA has proven remarkably resilient surviving the end of the Cold War and the rapprochement with Indonesia after Confrontation in the mid-1960s to become 'the quiet achiever' in the region, even after the difficulties imposed by the East Timor intervention in 1999. The end result is that the FPDA has continued contributing to regional security, providing Australia with unparalleled access to and training opportunities with Malaysia and Singapore.[15] No longer does Malaysia or Singapore have cause for deep concerns about Indonesia's intentions. But to Indonesians the FPDA still evokes memories of the past. Senior Indonesian officials understand that the FPDA emerged from the wake of Indonesian Confrontation with Malaysia. Not surprisingly, therefore, while the purpose and nature of the FPDA has evolved, Indonesia is not interested in joining.

In addition to the FPDA, Australia has extensive bilateral security ties with Malaysia and Singapore that date back to the mid to late 1950s, before the period of the Malayan Emergency and the Indonesian Confrontation in the mid-1960s. As a primary security role, Australia maintained air, land and naval forces in Singapore and Malaysia as part of the British Commonwealth Far Eastern Strategic Reserve, until the British presence diminished and the UK-dominated arrangements altered in the lead up to the establishment of the FPDA.

Since then, Australia has scaled back its air force presence from a squadron of Mirage III, and subsequently FA/18 Hornet, fighter aircraft at the Royal Australian Air Force (RAAF) controlled airbase at Butterworth, Malaysia to rotational flights into and out of the same airbase now operated by the Royal Malaysian Air Force (RMAF). The FPDA's Integrated Air Defence System (IADS) was modified after the end of the Cold War to become the Integrated Area Defence System, covering maritime and land components as well. Rotational ship visits continue but on a reduced basis, primarily coinciding with major annual FPDA exercises. Operation Gateway—the maritime surveillance operation using the RAAF's P3C Orion aircraft and conducted in conjunction with the RMAF—has made a significant contribution to the region's maritime safety and security, particularly in the Indian Ocean and the approaches to the Malacca Strait. At the same time it has facilitated close collaboration between the RMAF and RAAF, thus bolstering bilateral ties.

For the Australian Army during much of the Cold War, its contribution tended to revolve around an infantry battalion on rotation as part of the 28th Commonwealth Brigade supported with various other attached elements. This was scaled back after the Vietnam War to a rotational rifle company based at Butterworth. During the 'lean years' of low operational tempo after Vietnam, the three-month rotation to Butterworth was a highlight for many soldiers otherwise exposed only to rotational training activities around one of the Army's main bases in Townsville, Brisbane and Sydney, and from the early-to-mid 1990s, Darwin as well. Exercising in Singapore and Malaysia provided excellent opportunities for jungle warfare training as well as the chance for soldiers to have a significant cross-cultural experience in Southeast Asia. Exercises included a range of air, land and maritime activities. In 2012 for instance, Exercise 'Bersama Shield' involved the deployment of twelve RAAF aircraft, two RAN vessels and twenty personnel to work in the exercise headquarters deploying in Malaysia, the South China Sea and Singapore.[16] Another exercise, 'Suman Protector', was a command post exercise held at Singapore's

Changi Command and Control Centre and involving the planning of conventional operations at the combined joint task force level, including a HADR scenario. Exercises involving the land, air and maritime forces of the Singaporean, UK, Malaysian, Australian and New Zealand (SUMAN) armed forces have proceeded on an annual basis, taking various forms like this for over forty years.[17] The legacy of such activities is a wide range of multilateral formal and informal ties between the armed services of these five countries.

Bilateral Relationships with Other ASEAN Members

Whereas Indonesia is the single most important country in ASEAN for Australia, and the FPDA represents the closest and most intense defence cooperation relationship, Australia also has long and deep defence relationships with a range of other ASEAN members.

Thailand

As prisoners of war in the early 1940s, Australian soldiers had undergone a deeply traumatic experience working for the Japanese in constructing the infamous Thai-Burma railway. A decade later, Australia contributed several military personnel to the establishment of the SEATO Headquarters in Thailand's capital, Bangkok. From 1962–68 the RAAF deployed two squadrons of F-86 Sabre fighter aircraft to Ubon in Thailand's Northeast. Initially, this was in response to fears over the future of neighbouring Laos. The RAAF's ties with the Royal Thai Air Force (RTAF) have been strong and deep ever since and today bilateral air exercises between the RAAF and RTAF offer highly valued and realistic training, providing ongoing validation for the utility of bilateral defence ties. Other land, naval, peacekeeping and Special Forces exercises are conducted routinely alongside the Royal Thai Armed Forces (RTArF) both in Australia and in Thailand.

The first Thai graduate of Australian Army Staff College in 1959, Saiyud Kerdphol retired after having become the Supreme Commander of the RTArF and having led the successful counter-insurgency campaign against the Communist Party of Thailand in the 1980s. Thailand's Crown Prince Vajiralonkorn studied at Duntroon and underwent Special Forces training with Australia's Special Air Service Regiment (SASR). Today the Thai alumni of Australian staff colleges, the ADF Academy and various other military courses number in the many hundreds. Thailand's willingness to contribute forces in Australia's hour of need in East Timor in September 1999 points to the remarkable utility and significance of investing in the bilateral military ties between Thailand and Australia. The strength of the bilateral relationship stretches beyond the security sector to trade and investment as well as tourism. As noted above the Thai-Australia Free Trade Agreement (TAFTA) came into effect in 2005 and since then bilateral trade has more than doubled.[18] In addition, over 730 000 Australians visited Thailand in 2012.[19]

Philippines

Australian defence ties with the Philippines stretch back to the latter stages of World War II, when over 4000 Australians fought alongside US and Philippine forces to liberate their nation. Particularly since the end of the Cold War and the significant reduction in US forces based there following the closure of Subic Bay Naval Base and Clark Air Force Base, the Australia-Philippines Defence Cooperation Program (DCP) grew significantly. The DCP's focus has been primarily on counter-terrorism, maritime security and assistance to the Philippines Defence Reform Program. A Status of Forces Agreement was signed in May 2007 in order to provide a more comprehensive legal framework to support ADF and Philippines personnel engaged in Defence Cooperation activities in their respective countries. The Defence Cooperation Scholarship Program has seen students from the Armed Forces of The Philippines attend a wide range of courses in Australia, including undergraduate study at ADFA, mid-level and senior-level career courses at the Australian Defence College and sponsored postgraduate education. Over several years, the ADF undertook annual counter-hijack training in the Philippines, much like the kind of training undertaken with other regional countries like Thailand.[20]

In a similar vein to Thailand, the Philippines committed troops in support of the Australian led intervention into East Timor in 1999. As was the case for Thailand, this move reflected a strong and favourable disposition towards Australia. In recent years, Australia has sought to assist the Armed Forces of the Philippines offering riverine craft to support their ability to maintain sovereignty and control over fractious parts of southern Mindanao, the Filipino territory adjacent to the island of Borneo. Australia, however, has avoided playing a partisan role in the Philippines dispute with China over parts of the South China Sea claimed by both countries. Filipino vessels have been shut out of the South China Sea's Scarborough Shoal in recent years, raising the level of concern amongst senior Armed Forces of The Philippines commanders. But Australia has studiously avoided taking sides in the dispute. Like the United States, Australia is eager to avoid the entanglement that would ensue from an undue promise of support over such contentious claims.

Cambodia

Across on the other side of the South China Sea, Australia has had diplomatic relations with Cambodia for over sixty years. Under Prince Norodom Sihanouk, Cambodia broke off diplomatic relations with the United States in 1965 as it aligned itself more with North Vietnam and China. From 1965–70, Australia's diplomatic mission remained open. From 1970 the US-backed General Lon Nol was in power and he was eventually overthrown by Pol Pot and the Khmer Rouge in April 1975. The invasion of Cambodia in 1979 by Vietnamese forces saw the Khmer Rouge flee westwards and seek shelter on the Thai-Cambodian border. It was not until the end of the Cold War at the start of the 1990s that the impasse between competing Cambodian factions could be resolved. Australia played a prominent role in finding that resolution through the United Nations with Australia's activist foreign minister, Gareth Evans, brokering a peace agreement that would see an interim UN authority oversee elections. The force commander for the UN Transitional Authority in Cambodia (UNTAC) was Australian Lieutenant General John Sanderson. Australia played a prominent role because the matter concerned a neighbouring Southeast Asian state with which Australia had had extensive engagement for decades. Australia provided communications personnel, Blackhawk helicopters and crew and staff officers to work on the UNTAC Headquarters in Phnom Penh with Sanderson. Afterwards Australia participated with development projects and support of the Cambodian Mine Action Centre. But eventually, Cambodia's Prime Minister, Hun Sen, asserted himself extra-constitutionally. Since then Australia has played a diminished role in the development of the country, particularly as China has asserted itself and extended its influence in the Kingdom of Cambodia.

Vietnam

Relations with erstwhile Cold War enemy, Vietnam, have been transformed in recent years. Formal bilateral defence relations were established in February 1998 and the Defence Attaché Office at the Australian Embassy in Hanoi opened in 1999 under Colonel Gary Hogan. Vietnam reciprocated, establishing its first Defence Attaché in Canberra in September 2000.

Since then the bilateral defence relationship has grown considerably and now includes activities ranging from regular naval visits to Vietnam; training of Vietnamese military officers in Australia under the Defence Cooperation Program; and visits between Australian and Vietnamese senior Defence officials. At the inaugural ADMM-Plus meeting held in Hanoi in October 2010, Australia and Vietnam signed a Memorandum of Understanding on Defence Cooperation.[21] Subsequently, in August 2012, Vietnam and Australia agreed to further enhance defence relations through a range of bilateral defence initiatives, including the establishment of an Annual Defence Ministers' Dialogue, with the first one held in Canberra in March 2013.[22] Australia and Vietnam also have held a senior officials-level bilateral Regional Security Dialogue since 1998. This was upgraded in February 2012, when the inaugural Joint Foreign Affairs/Defence Australia-Vietnam Strategic Dialogue was held in Canberra at deputy-secretary/vice-minister level. Australia and Vietnam also conduct annual Australia-Vietnam Defence Cooperation Senior Officials' talks.[23] In addition to the Defence cooperation, the Australian Federal Police maintains Law Enforcement Liaison Offices in Hanoi and Ho Chi Minh City, much as is the case in Australia's other Southeast Asian embassies.[24]

Laos

Laos retreated into virtual isolation following the Communist victory in Indo-China in 1975 and only slowly emerged following the end of the Cold War. Today, Australia has a modest defence relationship with Laos, aimed at assisting the Lao Defence Force to engage more broadly in the region. Activities are focused primarily on English language assistance and training in Australia.[25]

Myanmar

After independence, Australia maintained defence relations with (then named) Burma and assisted with the training of the Burmese Armed Forces for a period in the 1950s. With the accession to power of General Ne Win and the adoption of the 'Burmese Road to Socialism' ideology in the early 1960s, Australian advisers were pulled out. They would remain away for virtually half a century, with a limited and (from the late 1980s) only occasional military attaché presence in the interim. But with the significant changes inside Burma (renamed Myanmar in 1989) following the adoption of a new constitution in 2011 and general elections for the majority of parliamentarians, a new permanently based Defence Attaché was established in early 2014. Initial defence engagement remained modest as scoping work was undertaken to consider appropriate additional engagement opportunities.

Brunei

Australia's modest defence relationship with Brunei has centred on Special Forces training and exercises. Other activities have included working level dialogues, senior visits, biennial land exercises and regular assistance in developing the air capability of the Royal Brunei Armed Forces.[26]

Regional Fora

Beyond the bilateral issues, Australia has a vested interest in working alongside ASEAN countries in fostering regional trade ties and in encouraging a strengthening of regional security and stability mechanisms that are associated with various international fora that have emerged since the end of the Cold War. The first such forum to emerge was the Asia-Pacific Economic Cooperation Forum (APEC). Established in 1989, its primary purpose is to facilitate economic growth and prosperity in the region, with the vision of creating a seamless regional economy. APEC pursues these objectives through trade and investment liberalisation, business facilitation and economic and technical cooperation. But at times of crisis, APEC has also facilitated significant advances in the security sector on the margins of its proceedings. For instance in 1999, the APEC forum in Auckland facilitated in-person discussions between US President Bill

Clinton, Australian Prime Minister John Howard and Indonesian President Habibie. With the emergence of competing economy-related regional bodies, APEC's pre-eminent place in the pantheon of regional groupings has lost its lustre. It retains some relevance however and with an apparent reluctance to close down such groups, looks set to continue in the medium term, even though its agenda items increasingly are also addressed in other forums.

The East Asia Summit (EAS) is a regional leaders' forum for strategic dialogue and cooperation between the ten member states of ASEAN and the countries of Australia, China, India, Japan, New Zealand, the Republic of Korea, the United States and Russia; cumulatively representing about 55 per cent of the world's population and global gross domestic product. The EAS provides a useful opportunity for leaders to engage in frank, open discussions on the issues that matter to East Asia and to set the direction for practical regional cooperation. In particular, the Summit has facilitated significant discussions on strategic, political and economic issues including maritime security; regional economic integration; global health and pandemics; the environment; education; people trafficking and natural disaster mitigation.[27]

The ASEAN Regional Forum (ARF) is yet another international grouping, but this one draws together twenty-seventy countries which have a stake in the security of the Asia Pacific region. Established in 1994 with Australia as a founding member, it includes the participants in the EAS as well as Canada, India, the European Union, Papua New Guinea, Mongolia, North Korea, East Timor, Bangladesh and Sri Lanka. The Department of Foreign Affairs and Trade has responsibility for Australia's ARF policy, in consultation with the Department of Defence and other agencies. The expanded ARF grouping provides a unique forum for security dialogue in Asia covering a wide range of topics. These range from disaster relief to counter-terrorism, transnational crime, non-proliferation and disarmament and most recently, cyber-confidence building measures. The ARF is characterised by consensus decision making—a constraint which makes for glacial progress on many issues.

Debate continues as to whether the ARF is able to achieve very much. But the fact that these countries meet at all facilitates cooperative measures to enhance peace and security in the region. To date the ARF has made only modest gains but it has helped build a sense of strategic community, which is widely recognised as making the effort worthwhile. In 2009 the first ARF field exercise, located in the Philippines, focused on disaster relief. The second was held in Manado, Indonesia in 2011 and a third one, in Hua Hin, Thailand in 2013. Apart from field exercises, where Australia has been an active participant, inter-sessional working-group meetings and senior officials meetings provide the venue for attempts to make progress on these wide-ranging security issues.[28]

Beyond the ARF and EAS (official, first-track institutions), second-track institutions (non-official institutions including the Council for Security Cooperation in the Asia Pacific (CSCAP) and the ASEAN Institutes of Strategic and International Studies (ASEAN ISIS))—have helped generate ideas and inputs for ARF deliberation. These 'second-track' institutions, involving academics and security officials, conduct seminars on regional security issues. These meetings often are held back-to-back with the main ARF meetings.[29]

The ASEAN Defence Ministers Meeting-Plus (ADMM-Plus) brings together defence ministers from the ten ASEAN countries and eight partner countries: China, Japan, the Republic of Korea, India, the United States, Russia, Australia and New Zealand. The ADMM-Plus is critical in building trust around the ASEAN region, particularly as it facilitates taking the issue beyond foreign ministries to extend it into the defence and security domain. The ADMM-Plus facilitates defence ministers and senior officials and expert working groups exchanging views on regional and international security challenges. Unlike the ARF, Australia's engagement in the ADMM-Plus arrangement is led by the Department of Defence rather than the Department of Foreign Affairs and Trade. Topics that have featured since its inception in 2010 include humanitarian assistance and disaster relief (HADR), maritime security, military medicine, counterterrorism and peacekeeping. Discussion on these topics also has led to a range of related field exercises involving the armed forces of member countries. In 2013, expert working groups on humanitarian mine action and the disposal of explosive remnants of war were created as well and Australia has supported these activities.[30]

The Asia-Europe Meeting (ASEM) was first established in 1996 and has since expanded into an inter-regional forum that includes not just the twenty-seven European Union (EU) member nations and the 10 member states of ASEAN, but it also includes a range of other East Asian and European countries including China, Japan, the Republic of Korea, India, Mongolia, Pakistan, Russia, Australia and New Zealand. These biennial senior level meetings foster cross-pollination on a range of political, economic and socio-cultural and educational matters. The ASEAN states recognise the major differences with the EU but see merit in dwelling on the parallels between these two supra-national bodies and the lessons and experiences they can share. As a first world country identified with its European roots and now closely tied in with the Asian region, Australia has a significant stake in the ASEM deliberations.

Critics contend that these various forums are more 'talkfests' than action meetings. In a region lacking a central organising body such as the EU or North Atlantic Treaty Organization (NATO), however, a multi-layered approach to regional security engagement and confidence building offers better prospects than would be the case in their absence. Lacking a common language, culture, history, legal framework or political system, the countries of East Asia continue to value the utility of these meetings, using English as the *lingua franca*.

The Countries of ASEAN and Relations with China

Concerns over the security of the South China Sea have featured prominently in recent years, particularly as China has asserted its 'nine–dash line' claim of virtually all the waters of the South China Sea. In 2002, China and ASEAN agreed on a declaration that would lead to a code of conduct between rival claimants operating in the South China Sea. For a decade, however, negotiations to finalise a code of conducted stalled, with China preferring to deal bilaterally rather than multilaterally (through ASEAN-related forums) with rival claimants. China's stance appears to discount the rival claims of Malaysia, Brunei, the Philippines and Vietnam. While Indonesia has no territory claimed by China, China's 'nine-dash line' also encroaches on some of Indonesia's exclusive economic zone (EEZ) around the Natuna Islands north east of Singapore and China has been assertive in exercising its claims there through strong-arm 'maritime law enforcement' tactics involving armed confrontations with fishing vessels in the contested EEZs.[31] Australia is not a claimant and has no direct interest in the affairs of the competing claimants of the South China Sea. But Australia has a vested interest in seeing the region to its north emerge as stable, secure and as unaffected by security instability as possible in order to foster its trade through the South China Sea and with the rival contiguous claimants.

China has repeatedly emphasised that ASEAN should remain in the driver's seat of the numerous regional international forums. At the same time, ASEAN has been grappling with the issue of how to engage with a more assertive China without having to 'kowtow' unduly and lose economic and political leverage in the process. The reduction of obstacles in the way of ASEAN unity and the greater imperative for strength in numbers in the face of a much larger, assertive and economically powerful neighbour suggests that the future of ASEAN may well be one of greater strength through greater unity. But there are some obstacles along the way with a marked divide between those with competing claims over the South China Sea—including Vietnam, the Philippines, Malaysia, Brunei and even Indonesia (when including the Natuna Islands EEZ). States with no such claims are the mainland Southeast Asian states of Thailand, Laos, Cambodia and Myanmar.

The different and at times competing views of how to manage security affairs in the South China Sea and elsewhere points to the importance for Australia of not only remaining engaged with ASEAN but of actively participating with the regional grouping. In so doing, Australia can help provide a useful differing perspective, offer 'good offices' facilities to trusted neighbours and provide advocacy on issues others might be reluctant to speak out about for fear of upsetting regional protocols.

Regional Trade Ties

Australia's security strategy is linked to its economic fortunes and regional trade ties are an integral part of that equation. Today Australia is more invested and connected through a maze of networks across East Asia and those economic ties cannot be completely separated from Australia's security partnerships and regional security priorities. The most pronounced trade ties are with the countries of Northeast Asia, but when aggregated, the more proximate Southeast

Asian states feature prominently as well. For this reason, a quick scan at regional trade ties helps put security ties in context.

In addition to bilateral trade deals, like the Thai-Australia Free Trade Agreement (TAFTA) signed between prime ministers Thaksin Shinawatra and John Howard in 2005, Australia has continued to cultivate a range of additional economic ties. One of the most significant such ties is through the ASEAN-Australia-New Zealand Free Trade Agreement (AANZFTA), which came into effect in January 2010 and is the largest Free Trade Agreement that Australia has ever signed. AANZFTA is intended to bind low tariffs and over time, eliminate tariffs on between 90 and 100 per cent of tariff lines, covering 96 per cent of current Australian exports to the region. Beyond these arrangements there are additional ones under negotiation which reflect different visions for future intra-regional trade. One is the US-backed Trans-Pacific Partnership (TPP), which includes Japan and the United States but excludes China and India. The other is the ASEAN-centric Regional Comprehensive Economic Partnership (RCEP) which includes Japan, China and India but excludes the United States. Reflecting its efforts to balance multi-faceted relationships, Australia is a party to both sets of negotiations.[32]

With trade barriers coming down in the region, AANZFTA is expected to deliver new opportunities across the board for Australian exporters and investors. AANZFTA also is expected to create greater certainty for Australian investors in the region with access to international arbitration extended to the whole region.[33]

Future Australian Regional Engagement

As the Afghanistan commitment winds down, the ADF must refocus on bolstering security and stability in Australia's inner arc. Although Australia's 'arc of instability' can be seen as an 'arc of opportunity',[34] geo-strategic concerns point to heightened risks of conflict and environmental crises in the Indo-Pacific. Increased uncertainty suggests conflict could be sparked at short notice, potentially drawing in Australia in support of international norms and regional security partners. So a variety of war fighting skills and capabilities need to be maintained by the ADF at a relatively high level.[35]

While the threat of near-term conflict in the Indo-Pacific is greater than for many years, there also remain significant prospects of environmental catastrophe requiring military intervention. The ADF therefore must prepare for short-notice HADR related tasks. As it happens, ever since the Indian Ocean tsunami in 2004, ASEAN and its regional partners including Australia have recognised the remarkable utility of HADR-related multilateral military engagement. Such engagement helps prepare forces for likely contingencies, while also building trust, understanding and mutual respect. In the face of constrained funding, enhancing regional security and stability through HADR-related exercises and planning activities needs to become a top priority.

Australia should closely engage its Southeast Asian neighbours. Without question ASEAN and the individual countries that make up this grouping will be of enduring significance to Australia's strategic calculus. Due to proximity and its size, Indonesia will remain the most significant neighbour and bilateral trade and security partner. But as experience in INTERFET has demonstrated, there is enduring utility in remaining closely engaged with other ASEAN member states as well. The investment in the relationship provides a range of mutual benefits. The FPDA helps facilitate a wide range of annual air, sea and land exercises that help build trust and a common understanding of military proficiency that can be called on in an emergency, such as the search for the missing Malaysian Airlines plane. Where possible, Thailand and the Philippines also should be included, aligned with scheduled FPDA events. Even Myanmar should be engaged to encourage consolidation and extension of reform initiatives and to bolster ASEAN's role. Much of this could be done alongside Australia's principal ally, the United States. But the most important country for Australia to engage with in Southeast Asia is unquestionably Indonesia.

Australia's security is intimately linked with that of Indonesia, so the relationship needs careful management, attuned to the different cultural predispositions and respectful of their mores and their proud and independent heritage. This points to the need for the ADF to enhance its level of cultural awareness and regional language skills. With modern technology and methods, much of this can be done economically on a distributed basis. 'Manis' in Indonesian means sweet, and there is a clear case for Malaysia, Australia, New Zealand, Indonesia and Singapore (MANIS) to work together to sweeten regional security co-operation. A MANIS regional security co-operation forum could address a range of security priorities of mutual concern. There is a pressing need for some creative regional diplomacy to help bring such an arrangement into effect.

The most challenging security question faced by Australian and Southeast Asian security and defence planners is how to manage the rise of China and the so-called US rebalance in Asia. While there has been some debate about this in Australia, the overwhelming emphasis has been on bolstering security ties with the United States and her allies in East Asia while seeking to foster constructive ties and evoke a positive response from China. Interestingly, China's People's Liberation Army, with its navy and air force, has only participated peripherally so far in the kinds of military exercises that Australia has conducted routinely and intimately with the aforementioned security partners. Perhaps the time has come for China to become more active in such activities, and to feature more prominently on the East Asian international scene.

In the light of the MH370 aircraft disaster in the southern Indian Ocean, a surprising opportunity for collaboration emerged with no notice. Much akin to the recovery efforts after the Indian Ocean tsunami of 2004, the loss of Flight MH370 appears to have triggered unprecedented cooperation and collaboration between the air forces of regional powers. There appears to be momentum to capitalise on this event and foster additional activities that may bolster trust and mutual understanding and, perhaps, at the same time, reduce the prospect of uncertainty and misunderstanding across the region.

A sober reflection on the geostrategic realities should be the main determinant for funding. With so many contingencies to be prepared for, Australia still needs to maintain a balanced joint force adaptable to a wide range of possible eventualities, with sufficient air, sea and ground forces to respond to the challenges expected in modern conflict. A visionary, comprehensive and co-ordinated regional engagement plan is needed to mitigate some of the security and environmental concerns now faced. With so many challenges, Australia, as a middle power, must rise above its small power pretensions, and work to build the regional stability in Southeast Asia on which its future security will depend.

Further Reading

Ball, Desmond, and Pauline Kerr (eds), *Presumptive Engagement: Australia's Asia-Pacific Security Policy in the 1990s*, Allen & Unwin, Sydney, 1996.

Edwards, Peter, *Crises and Commitments: The Politics and Diplomacy of Australia's Involvement in Southeast Asian Conflicts 1948–1965*, Allen & Unwin, Sydney, 1992.

Goldsworthy, David (ed), *Facing North: A Century of Australian Engagement with Asia*, vol. 1, vol. 2, Melbourne University Press, Carlton, 2001, 2003.

Osborne, Milton, *Southeast Asia: An Introductory History*, 11th edn., Allen & Unwin, Sydney, 2013.

Storey, Ian, Ralf Emmers and Daljit Singh (eds), *Five Power Defence Arrangements at Forty*, ISEAS Publishing, Singapore, 2011.

Roberts, Christopher B, *ASEAN Regionalism: Cooperation, Values and Institutionalisation*, Routledge, Oxford, 2012.

Notes

1   C Roberts, *ASEAN Regionalism: Co-operation, Values and Institutionalisation*, Routledge, Oxford, 2012.

2   S Pitsuwan, opening address of the Australian National University's Southeast Asia Institute, Australian National University, Canberra, 24 October 2012.

3   One of the best books on the foreign policy implications of the Indonesian annexation of Papua and Confrontation for Australia remains G Pemberton, *All The Way: Australia's Road to Vietnam*, Allen & Unwin, Sydney, 1987.

4   President Sukarno was one of the founding leaders of the Non-Aligned Movement, a body established during the Cold War by developing Asian, African and Latin-American countries advocating a middle path between the competing Cold War groupings: the US-aligned West countries and the Communist countries of the Eastern Bloc.

5   For background information on the Treaty, see G Brown, F Frost and S Sherlock, 'The Australian-Indonesian Security Agreement—Issues and Implications', *Research Paper 25: 1995–1996*, Commonwealth of Australia, Canberra, 1995. www.aph.gov.au/About_Parliament/Parliamentary_ Departments/Parliamentary_Library/pubs/rp/RP9596/96rp25 (viewed January 2014).

6   I Henry provides an excellent overview of the policy deliberations in the lead-up to INTERFET in 'Playing Second Fiddle on the Road to INTERFET: Australia's East Timor Policy Throughout 1999', *Security Challenges*, vol. 9, no 1, 2013, pp. 87–111. www.securitychallenges.org.au/ ArticlePDFs/SC9-1Henry.pdf (viewed January 2014).

7   The author was a participant in INTERFET.

8   Department of Foreign Affairs and Trade, 'Agreement Between the Republic of Indonesia and Australia in the Framework for Security Cooperation', Commonwealth of Australia, Canberra, 2006. www.dfat.gov. au/geo/indonesia/ind-aus-sec06.html (viewed December 2013).

9   Australia's military involvement in Southeast Asia during this period is covered in J Blaxland, *The Australian Army from Whitlam to Howard*, Cambridge University Press, Melbourne, 2014.

10 J Blaxland, 'Beef, Boats and Spies: Australia's Brash Treatment of Indonesia', Australian Broadcasting Corporation, 21 November 2013. www.abc.net.au/news/2013-11-21/beef-boats-and-spies-australias-brash-treatment-of/5109520 (viewed December 2013).

11 B Carr, 'Australia Indonesia Inaugural 2+2 Dialogue', Department of Foreign Affairs and Trade, Commonwealth of Australia, 15 March 2012. www.foreignminister.gov.au/releases/2012/bc_mr_120315.html (viewed December 2013).

12 G Hogan, 'Indonesia: Signs of New Thinking on Papua', *The Interpreter*, Lowy Institute for International Policy, Sydney, 1 March 2013. www.lowyinterpreter.org/post/2013/03/01/Indonesia-Signs-of-new-thinking-on-Papua.aspx (viewed January 2014); G Hogan, 'Is Papua the Next East Timor? Part II', *The Strategist*, Australian Strategic Policy Institute, Sydney, 13 May 2013. www.aspistrategist.org.au/is-papua-the-next-east-timor-part-ii/ (viewed January 2014).

13 B Schreer, *Moving Beyond Ambitions? Indonesia's Military Modernisation*, APSI Strategy Paper, Australian Strategic Policy Institute, Canberra, November 2013, p. 15.

14 ibid., p. 24.

15 CA Thayer, 'The Five Power Defence Arrangements: The Quiet Achiever', *Security Challenges*, vol. 3, no. 1, 2007, pp. 79–96. www.securitychallenges.org.au/ArticlePDFs/vol3no1Thayer.pdf (viewed October 2013).

16 Department of Defence, 'Exercise Bersama Shield 2012—Partners In Peace Enhance Regional Security', Defence Media Release, Commonwealth of Australia, Canberra, 24 April 2012. www.news.defence.gov.au/2012/04/24/exercise-bersama-shield-2012-partners-in-peace-enhance-regional-security/ (viewed January 2014).

17 CA Thayer, 'The Five Power Defence Arrangements: The Quiet Achiever', 2007.

18 Department of Foreign Affairs and Trade, 'Thailand-Australia Free Trade Agreement'. www.dfat.gov.au/fta/tafta/ (viewed October 2014).

19 Department of Foreign Affairs and Trade, 'Thailand: Smart Traveller'. www.smartraveller.gov.au/zw-cgi/view/Advice/Thailand (viewed October 2014).

20 B Nelson, 'Australia and Philippines Strengthen Defence Ties', Defence Media Release, Commonwealth of Australia, Canberra, 31 May 2007. www.defence.gov.au/minister/49tpl.cfm?CurrentId=6724 (viewed October 2013).

21 S Smith, 'Australia and Vietnam Deepen Defence Cooperation', Defence Media Release, Commonwealth of Australia, Canberra, 11 October 2010. www.defence.gov.au/minister/105tpl.cfm?CurrentId=10924 (viewed December 2013).

22 S Smith, 'Minister for Defence—Inaugural Australia-Vietnam Defence Ministers Meeting', Defence Media Release, Commonwealth of Australia,

Canberra, 19 March 2013. www.minister.defence.gov.au/2013/03/19/
minister-for-defence-inaugural-australia-vietnam-defence-ministers-
meeting/ (viewed December 2013).

23 S Smith, 'Minister for Defence Stephen Smith—Minister for Defence
Completes Visit to Vietnam', Defence Media Release, Commonwealth of
Australia, Canberra, 31 August 2012. www.minister.defence.gov.
au/2012/08/31/minister-for-defence-stephen-smith-minister-for-
defence-completes-visit-to-vietnam/ (viewed December 2013).

24 Department of Foreign Affairs and Trade, 'Vietnam Country Brief', www.
dfat.gov.au/geo/vietnam/vietnam_brief.html (viewed December 2013).

25 Joint Standing Committee on Foreign Affairs, Defence and Trade, *Inquiry
Into Australia's Relations with ASEAN*, Commonwealth of Australia,
Canberra, 2009.

26 ibid.

27 Department of Foreign Affairs and Trade, 'The East Asia Summit'. www.
dfat.gov.au/asean/eas/ (viewed December 2013).

28 Department of Foreign Affairs and Trade 'ASEAN Regional Forum (ARF)'.
www.dfat.gov.au/arf/ (viewed December 2013).

29 The Department of Foreign Affairs and Trade and Department of Defence
support the activities of the Australian Member Committee of the
Council for Security Cooperation in the Asia Pacific (AUS-CSCAP).

30 S Smith, 'Minister for Defence—Minister For Defence Attends Second
ASEAN Defence Minister's Meeting-Plus in Brunei', Defence Media
Release, Commonwealth of Australia, Canberra, 29 August 2013. www.
minister.defence.gov.au/2013/08/29/minister-for-defence-minister-for-
defence-attends-second-asean-defence-ministers-meeting-plus-in-
brunei/ (viewed October 2013).

31 S Bentley, 'Implications of Recent Incidents for China's Claims and
Strategic Intent in the South China Sea (Part 2)', *The Strategist*, Australian
Strategic Policy Institute, 28 November 2013. www.aspistrategist.org.au/
implications-of-recent-incidents-for-chinas-claims-and-strategic-intent-
in-the-south-china-sea-part-2/ (viewed December 2013); *Jakarta Globe*,
'Indonesia's Military Flexes Muscle as S. China Sea Dispute Looms',
Jakarta Globe, 13 March 2014. www.thejakartaglobe.com/news/
indonesia-military-flexes-muscle-s-china-sea-dispute-looms/ (viewed
April 2014).

32 Department of Foreign Affairs and Trade, 'Regional Comprehensive
Economic Partnership Negotiations'. www.dfat.gov.au/fta/rcep/; and
Department of Foreign Affairs and Trade, 'Trans-Pacific Partnership
Agreement Negotiations'. www.dfat.gov.au/fta/tpp/.

33 Australian Trade Commission, 'The ASEAN-Australia-New Zealand Free
Trade Agreement (AANZFTA)'. www.austrade.gov.au/AANZFTA (viewed
October 2013).

34 J Wallis, 'The Pacific: From "Arc of Instability" to "Arc of Responsibility"
and Then to "Arc of Opportunity"?', *Security Challenges*, vol. 8, no. 4, 2012,
pp. 1–12. www.securitychallenges.org.au/ArticlePages/vol8no4Wallis.
html (viewed December 2013).

35   J Blaxland, 'Refocusing the Australian Army', *Security Challenges*, vol. 7, no. 2, 2011, pp. 47–54. www.securitychallenges.org.au/ArticlePages/vol7no2Blaxland.html (viewed December 2013); and J Blaxland 'All Aboard: ADF and Regional Defence Diplomacy', in *A New Flank: Fresh Perspectives for the Next Defence White Paper*, Centre of Gravity Series, Strategic and Defence Studies Centre, Australian National University, Canberra, April 2013. www.ips.cap.anu.edu.au/sdsc/cog/COG6_NewFlank_WEB.pdf (viewed December 2013).

6

Australia and the South Pacific

Joanne Wallis

Paul Dibb has argued that 'geography is the key to a sound defence strategy and one of the most important factors driving military posture and force structure'.[1] If one looks at Australia's strategic geography, it becomes clear why the South Pacific region, which lies in close proximity to the north and east of Australia, is of vital importance to its defence. The South Pacific consists of twenty-nine island states and territories, comprising thousands of individual islands. The region reaches over 30 million square kilometres, 98 per cent of which is ocean, through which cross the air and sea approaches that link Australia to vital trading and defence partners in North America and Northeast Asia. Moreover, while there is presently no external power that is likely to use the region to launch a direct attack on Australia, the Japanese advance during World War II graphically illustrated Australia's vulnerability to this scenario. Indeed, writing in 1965, TB Millar reflected that 'if the whole island [of Papua New Guinea] were to sink under the sea, the net result for Australia in terms of military strategy would be a gain. It is an exposed and vulnerable front door'.[2]

The South Pacific can be broken up into three geographic and cultural areas (see Figure 6.1). The first area is Melanesia, which

Figure 6.1: Map of the South Pacific Region

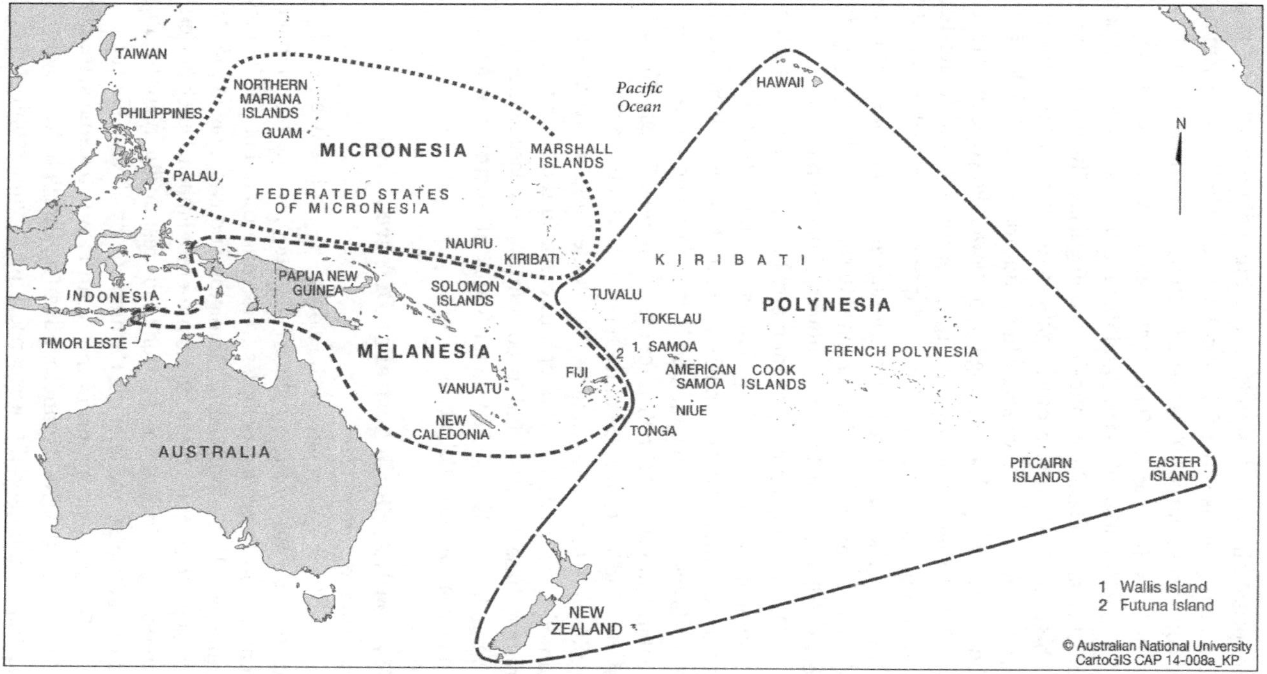

Source: CartoGIS, College of Asia and the Pacific, Australian National University, 2014.

comprises the arc of islands to the immediate north and east of Australia. There is some debate concerning whether East Timor can be considered part of Melanesia, given its similarities to other states in the area. In general, Melanesian states have comparatively large populations and land masses and rich natural resources. Melanesian societies are generally ethnically and linguistically diverse and tend to be organised around quite egalitarian sociopolitical structures. The second area is Polynesia, which comprises the triangle of states above New Zealand, stretching up to Hawaii. Polynesian islands are small and their societies tend to be ethnically and linguistically homogenous and organised around quite hierarchical sociopolitical structures. The third area is Micronesia, which comprises the band of islands to the north of Melanesia. Micronesian islands tend to be very small, and socially homogenous and hierarchical.

Due to geographical location and historical factors, such as its colonial history in Papua New Guinea, and inherited British interests in the Solomon Islands, Vanuatu and Fiji, Australia's focus has been on Melanesia. New Zealand and France focus on Polynesia, as New Zealand inherited British interests in Samoa, Tonga, Niue, Cook Islands and Tokelau and France retains control of French Polynesia, Wallis and Futuna, as well as New Caledonia in Melanesia. The United States maintains strategic interests in the Micronesia, via its military base in Guam and its constitutional relationships with the Marshall Islands and Federated States of Micronesia; as well as American Samoa in Polynesia.

The South Pacific in Australian Defence Policy
Prior to independence
The strategic geography of the South Pacific has been evident to Australian leaders since before Federation. In the late nineteenth century the Australian colonies were concerned that hostile powers could establish a foothold in the region and encouraged the United Kingdom to colonise territories to pre-empt French, Dutch or German interest. After Federation, Australia took responsibility for the British colony of Papua, and later the German colony of New Guinea.

The strategic import of the South Pacific became stark during World War II. The Japanese advance through the region was Australia's 'moment of truth' concerning its vulnerability to security threats from or through the South Pacific.[3] Despite this, once the region returned to colonial control Australian defence planners gave it little attention. The exception was the territory of Papua and New Guinea which, as the 1959 *Strategic Basis of Australian Defence Policy* reveals, preoccupied Australia given the possibility of a limited war against Indonesia over the territory.[4]

After defence policy shifted to the concept of the Defence of Australia (DoA), the region beyond Papua and New Guinea continued to play little role in defence planning. However, the 1973 *Strategic Basis* did include a separate section on the region, and while it concluded that no state could directly threaten Australia, it identified Papua New Guinea as being of abiding strategic significance because of its importance to Australia's military and trade lines of communication.

Post-independence

Australian defence planners began to focus on the region from the mid-1970s, when most South Pacific states gained their independence. Australia's first Defence White Paper in 1976 represented the first time that the region had been publicly identified as the area of Australia's primary strategic concern.[5] Australia adopted a policy of 'strategic denial' to attempt to exclude external powers from gaining influence—a risk that was heightened by US and Soviet Cold War interest.[6] Australia accordingly provided South Pacific states with generous aid and defence assistance under the Defence Cooperation Program, both to advance their development and to establish an Australian military presence. Australia also remained concerned that it might be called upon in the event of conflict over the border between Indonesia and (the now independent) Papua New Guinea, which was acknowledged in both the 1975 and 1976 *Strategic Basis*. In this regard, the 1976 *Strategic Basis* also addressed the Indonesian invasion of East Timor in December 1975. It argued that Australia's defence interests would be served by East Timor's incorporation into Indonesia, which was seen as preferable to the formation of a weak state which might be open to external interference.

As defence planners began to refocus on Australia's strategic geography during the 1980s, the South Pacific continued to gain prominence. In the 1986 *Review of Australia's Defence Capabilities*, also known as the 'Dibb-Review', the region was identified as the 'area from or through which a military threat to Australia could most easily be posed'.[7] That sentiment was repeated in the 1987 Defence White Paper, which stated that the region was the 'most likely route through which any major assault could be launched against Australia', as it lies across important trade routes and approaches to Australia's east coast.[8] Despite this, the Dibb-Review was conservative in its recommendations for the capability that Australia would require to operate in the region. It concluded that the Landing Ship Heavy (LSH) HMAS *Tobruk*, along with the supply ship HMAS *Jervis Bay*, were 'sufficient to support any modest deployments of ground forces or other equipment that could not be handled by aircraft or land transport'.[9]

Declining stability in the region

Although Australian defence planning focused more sharply on the South Pacific during the late 1970s and 1980s, Australia chose to assume that Pacific states were functioning well and required minimal involvement in their political and economic affairs. This assumption was shaken by the Santo Rebellion in pre-independence Vanuatu in 1980. It was shattered when Fiji experienced its first two coups in 1987, a self-determination conflict began in the Bougainville region of Papua New Guinea in 1989, and several other South Pacific states were weakened by political, economic, environmental and law and order challenges. Subsequently, Australia began to acknowledge that it was likely to be drawn into internal crises in the region. It also began to realise that the 1987 Defence White Paper's conservative approach to Australia's capability needs in the region was unsustainable. After the first Fiji coup in May 1987, a plan to rescue the deposed Fijian prime minister Timoci Bavadra had to be abandoned after it was recognised that 'Australia simply could not have deployed a land force into the South Pacific safely and effectively if there was any prospect of onshore opposition to such a move'.[10]

The limits of Australia's capability in the South Pacific became more prescient in light of the acknowledgement in the 1989 *Australia's Strategic Planning in the 1990s* document that the Australian Defence Force (ADF) was likely to be involved more in the region, including in the evacuation of citizens and disaster relief.[11] As a result, the 1991 Force Structure Review identified that, although Australia would likely need to 'respond to regional requests', it had 'no single vessel capable of operating a number of helicopters simultaneously',[12] a vital capability given the South Pacific's geography.

Accordingly, it was decided that the roll on/roll off support ship HMAS *Jervis Bay* would be replaced with a dedicated training and helicopter support ship. However, after the government baulked at the expense, it instead opted to acquire two surplus United States Navy *Newport* Class 8 500 tonne Landing Platform Amphibious (LPA) ships. These ships were refitted and became the HMAS *Kanimbla* and *Manoora*.

With the exception of the continuing Bougainville conflict, the situation in the South Pacific calmed during the early 1990s. Consequently, the 1994 Defence White Paper focused on Papua New Guinea, which it described as Australia's 'most substantial' defence relationship in the region.[13] The relationship had been enhanced by the 1987 *Joint Declaration of Principles*, which committed the two states to consult to decide what response should be made if an external armed attack was threatened against either country.[14] As this Joint Declaration related only to external attack it did not oblige Australia to respond to the Bougainville conflict, and beyond providing military training and assistance to the Papua New Guinea Defence Force (PNGDF), Australia decided against direct military intervention.

The 'arc of instability'

As the Bougainville conflict wore on it threatened to destabilise Papua New Guinea. In light of Papua New Guinea's strategic import to Australia, in the mid-1990s there was increasing pressure on the Australian government to respond. The necessity of taking action was exacerbated by the Sandline crisis in 1997, in which the Papua New Guinea government's decision to engage mercenaries to attempt to reopen Bougainville's Panguna mine further threatened to destabilise the state.[15] Consequently, from 1997 Australia cooperated with New Zealand to facilitate peace talks, and provided unarmed observers to monitor a truce, and later peace, agreement between the Bougainville parties and the Papua New Guinea government.

Australia's willingness to engage in ending the Bougainville conflict signalled a new phase of broader engagement with the South Pacific. This engagement was motivated by the deteriorating stability of the region in the late 1990s, which saw frequent changes of government, constitutional crises, coups (and attempted coups), instability within militaries and police forces, tension over resource exploitation and distribution, rising crime, declining government service delivery, corruption and poor standards of governance. These factors generated a perception that the region, particularly Melanesia, was an 'arc of instability' composed of weak and failing states.[16] To some extent the region's challenges arose because arbitrary European colonial borders had forced populations to live together within states they would not necessarily have chosen were they given the right to self-determination. These challenges were also partly attributable to a degree of incompatibility between local sociopolitical practices and the institutions of the Weberian rational-legal state, and to the low level of economic development in most states. As Sinclair Dinnen argues, 'weak' South Pacific states were often not properly built in the first place.[17]

Despite its apparent willingness to engage, Australia did little in response to the 1998 conflict that broke out in the Solomon Islands, beyond helping to negotiate the Townsville Peace Agreement in October 2000, and contributing to a small International Peace Monitoring Team from November 2001 to June 2002. However, Australia took more direct action when it decided to lead the United Nations Security Council mandated International Force for East Timor (INTERFET) in September 1999. INTERFET's role was to restore security after the violence that had followed the announcement that the Timorese people had voted to end the Indonesian occupation and become independent. The Royal Australian Navy (RAN) ships HMAS *Kanimbla* and *Manoora* had not entered service at the time, but the ADF was fortunate to secure Dili harbour and its wharf and crane before they could be damaged by the retreating Indonesian military or their supporting militia. Consequently, the ADF was able to rapidly build force ashore, and to successfully secure and stabilise the territory. Therefore, INTERFET's mission highlighted 'not only the potential requirement for amphibious operations, but also the stark lack of capability the ADF had at the time'.[18]

Written in the immediate aftermath of the INTERFET deployment, the 2000 Defence White Paper explicitly stated that ameliorating 'challenges to the stability and cohesion of neighbouring countries' in the South Pacific was one of Australia's core strategic challenges and one of the ADF's key tasks.[19] The 2000 Defence White Paper also clearly reaffirmed Australia's security commitments to Papua New Guinea under the *Joint Declaration of Principles* and articulated what Hugh White describes as 'in effect, a unilateral security guarantee by Australia to the islands of the South Pacific',[20] when it stated that '[w]e would be very likely to provide substantial support in the unlikely event that any country in the Southwest Pacific faced substantial external aggression'.[21]

With this undertaking in mind, the 2000 Defence White Paper committed the government to purchasing two new amphibious vessels to replace the HMAS *Tobruk*, *Kanimbla* and *Manoora* and to assist its capability to conduct stabilisation operations in the South Pacific. The 2000 Defence White Paper recognised that the main requirements for RAN force structure that arose from this focus were 'a capability to patrol South Pacific waters, and for amphibious lift'.[22] Consequently, the 2003 Defence Capability Review noted the importance of 'the ability to safely deploy, lodge and sustain Australian forces offshore'.[23] By the time of the 2004 Defence Capability Plan, the size of the two ships had doubled to 27 500 tonne Landing Helicopter Dock (LHD) ships, to become operational in 2014 and 2016.[24]

New interventionism

The 2000 Defence White Paper's increased focus on the South Pacific proved prescient, as the early 2000s signalled the start of an era of 'new interventionism' by Australia in the region.[25] Several factors might explain this new interventionism. The 11 September 2001 terrorist attacks had changed the way in which weak states were perceived. Instead of primarily posing a risk to their inhabitants, it was now argued that they could act as incubators for transnational crime and terrorism.[26] Coupled with this, the end of the Cold War had created space for the emergence of the concept of humanitarian intervention,[27] justified by the 'responsibility to protect'.[28] Australia had also become more concerned about the vulnerability of weak South Pacific states to external influence; a risk highlighted in the 1994 Defence White Paper,[29] the 1997 Strategic Policy Report[30] and the 2000 Defence White Paper.[31] While Australia already had an extensive development assistance program, the 'new' aspect of Australia's policy was that it adopted a 'whole-of-government' approach to strengthening 'weak' South Pacific states, which inserted police officers and public servants directly into South Pacific police forces and government departments to operate as employees of those agencies, rather than as technical advisers or consultants.

Most significantly, in July 2003 Australia led the Regional Assistance Mission to Solomon Islands (RAMSI), with the approval of the Pacific Islands Forum under its 2000 *Biketawa Declaration*. RAMSI was invited by the Solomon Islands' government and has been described as a 'cooperative intervention', as it did not involve the violation of state sovereignty.[32] RAMSI initially consisted of over 330 police offers and 1880 military personnel from Australia, New Zealand, Papua New Guinea, Tonga and Fiji; although the majority came from Australia. Phase I of the operation was designed to restore law and order, while Phase II was to assist the recovery of the institutions of governance and the economy. In its early stages RAMSI managed to restore security, implement a gun amnesty, arrest militia leaders and clean-up the police force. RAMSI was well received by many Solomon Islanders, who consistently expressed their belief that the security situation improved after its arrival.[33]

As RAMSI achieved initial successes, in February 2004 Australia embarked on the bilateral Enhanced Cooperation Program (ECP) in Papua New Guinea. The ECP involved the insertion of 230 Australian police advisers into the Papua New Guinea Police Force and Australian public servants seconded into government agencies. Like RAMSI, the ECP attracted relatively widespread public support in Papua New Guinea. However, it was resented by certain political leaders and Australia had to withdraw its police in May 2005, after the constitutionality of arrangements that gave Australian police immunity was successfully challenged. This left Papua New Guinea with forty-four advisers who continued to work in treasury, finance, planning, transport, customs and law and justice.

The controversy surrounding the ECP signalled emerging questions about Australia's new interventionism, including whether it was managing to strengthen 'weak' states and to achieve sustainable gains.[34] These questions became louder in April 2006, when rioters destroyed much of the Solomon Islands' capital after the national election, and an increased ADF deployment was required to restore stability. They reached a crescendo in late April and early May 2006, when a major security crisis broke out in East Timor and at the Timorese government's request, Australia led an International Stabilisation Force to restore security. This Force represented the first deployment of the RAN's Amphibious Readiness Group, which had been formed by HMAS *Tobruk*, *Kanimbla* and *Manoora*. This was crucial to the mission, as the Dili harbour facilities were not secured. The combination of two crises in the region in a short space of time led to the government's August 2006 decision to increase the Army by two battalions, with then prime minister Howard justifying the increase on the basis that 'Australia has, and is seen to have, a leadership role in contributing to security and stability in our region'.[35]

The exception to Australia's new interventionism was Fiji, which experienced a civilian coup in May 2000 and then a military coup in December 2006. In the lead-up to the 2006 coup Fijian prime minister Laisenia Qarase called Australian prime minister John Howard and asked for support. Howard declined, in large part because Fiji had a very well trained and effective military—not least due to training and support it had received from Australia. Instead, after the coup Australia deployed the Amphibious Readiness Group off Fiji to provide permissive evacuation of Australian citizens, although ultimately this was not needed. Australia's broader response focused on diplomatic means, including 'smart' sanctions against the Fijian military regime.

The 2009 Defence White Paper continued the focus on Australia's strategic geography and again identified the 'security, stability and cohesion of our immediate neighbourhood' as Australia's second most important strategic priority, behind the defence of Australia against armed attack.[36] It was written after a change of government, which shifted Australia's approach to the South Pacific from one of 'new interventionism' to one of 'partnership and engagement'. This shift was signalled in the *Port Moresby Declaration*,[37] delivered by prime minister Kevin Rudd on 6 March 2008. The Declaration claimed to signal that the government wanted a 'new era of cooperation' with South Pacific states that respected their independence and work with them 'on the basis of partnership, mutual respect and mutual responsibility'.[38]

Reflecting the new era of partnership and engagement, Australia entered into the bilateral *Pacific Partnerships for Development*[39] with South Pacific states to tackle the causes of instability by seeking to improve education, healthcare, infrastructure, youth unemployment, microfinance, governance and security. In 2008 the ECP was also renamed the *Strongim Gavman* (Strong Government) Program, which provided for greater consultation with Papua New Guinea and new arrangements to enable Australian police to serve as advisers. The exception to Australia's new era of partnership and engagement was again Fiji. The Australian government continued to impose sanctions and supported the suspension of Fiji from the Pacific Islands Forum and the Commonwealth in 2009. However, tentative moves towards engagement were evident in July 2012, when Australia and New Zealand announced that they would restore full diplomatic relations with Fiji.

Contemporary Issues

The 2013 Defence White Paper continued to identify that the 'security, stability and cohesion' of the South Pacific sits only behind a 'secure Australia' in the hierarchy of Australia's strategic interests.[40] It also echoed earlier defence white papers when it stated that, while the principal task of the ADF is to 'deter and defeat attacks on Australia', its second priority is to 'contribute to stability and security in the South Pacific and Timor-Leste'.[41] In 2013 the ADF drew down from East Timor and the Solomon Islands reflecting improved stability in both states. Despite this, the 2013 Defence White Paper identifies that the region continues to face 'major challenges', in the form of population growth, high unemployment, ineffective governance, crime, violence and the effects of climate change.[42] These concerns were echoed in the Gillard government's 2013 National Security Strategy, in which it identified the continued security risk posed by 'probable ongoing low-level instability in Australia's region'.[43]

The most likely sources of instability are in Melanesia. Although the ADF has drawn down, RAMSI remains in the Solomon Islands as a police and civilian mission. RAMSI has improved law and order and (re)built the government's capacity to collect revenues and to deliver (limited) public services and encouraged economic development. However, it has been less successful in the long term, and much more difficult, task of dealing with the deeper social, political, economic and institutional causes of instability. Complicating future plans to withdraw RAMSI is the suggestion that Solomon Islanders lack confidence in their government and perceive that continuing stability depends on RAMSI's presence. This suggests that Australia will remain involved in the Solomon Islands well into the future and it is not unforeseeable that the ADF may again be deployed, particularly if the causes of instability rise to the surface.

Although the ADF has drawdown from East Timor, the stability of that country is fragile. The Timorese government has engaged in a program of significant public spending on cash payment schemes and infrastructure programs that have effectively 'bought peace' in the period since the 2006 security crisis. However, almost all of the government's spending is funded by its oil and gas revenues, which some forecasts predict will run out by 2025. Whether stability will endure after that period will depend on whether the government is able to generate sufficient economic development and resolve some of the underlying causes of tension. As it is uncertain whether the government will be able to do this, it is not unforeseeable that Australia may again be called upon to restore stability in East Timor.

Similarly, although Papua New Guinea has experienced considerable economic growth, it remains at risk of instability, particularly once large revenues from its massive liquefied natural gas project begin to flow and potentially exacerbate existing government corruption and patronage. As Papua New Guinea experiences crime, inter-group fighting and declining government service delivery, it is not unforeseeable that a serious breakdown in law and order may occur. Australia could be obliged to respond with a prolonged stabilisation mission, although whether this would be politically or practically feasible is questionable. Another challenging situation might arise in the highly unlikely event of conflict along Papua New Guinea's border with Indonesia, most likely caused by Indonesian incursions in pursuit of residents of its Papua province seeking either asylum or temporary shelter in Papua New Guinea. Under the *Joint Declaration of Principles*, Australia may be obliged to assist Papua New Guinea in such a conflict, which would place Australia in direct military opposition to Indonesia—something it was desperate to avoid when it led INTERFET, given how this could amplify into a larger conflict. If it involved Australian incursions into Papua, such a response might also test Australia's commitment to respect Indonesia's sovereignty under the 2006 Lombok Treaty.[44]

Australia could find the need to intervene in Papua New Guinea in the event of conflict arising from the upcoming referendum on Bougainville's future political status (a key element of the 2001 Bougainville Peace Agreement), which is scheduled to take place between 2015 and 2020. Given changed international attitudes towards humanitarian intervention, it is unlikely that Australia will repeat the hands-off approach that it took in 1989 in the event of a serious recurrence of conflict. Australia's response will be determined by the nature of the conflict. As long as Bougainville remains part of Papua New Guinea, Australia would most likely seek approval from the Papua New Guinea government before any intervention. If the conflict is between pro-independence and pro-integration Bougainvilleans, the Papua New Guinea government may allow Australia to intervene, given that any intervention by the PNGDF would probably escalate the conflict. If the conflict is between Bougainvilleans and Papua New Guinea, in the event that Papua New Guinea refuses to hold the referendum (perhaps on the grounds that weapons disposal is incomplete), or in the event that a majority of Bougainvilleans vote for independence but the result is not ratified by the Papua New Guinea parliament, Australia could be faced with having to either forcibly intervene and damage its relationship with its strategically-important neighbour, or do nothing and allow a grave humanitarian crisis to potentially develop on its doorstep.

Before the Bougainville referendum occurs Australia may face a challenge in relation to New Caledonia's referendum on its political future, scheduled to be held between 2014 and 2018. It is unclear whether the referendum will be held, given that it has already been delayed once. If it is held, the outcome is also unclear, given that only 45 per cent of the total population are indigenous *Kanaks*, which suggests that they are unlikely to achieve a majority vote in favour of independence. In the event that the referendum is again delayed, or is held and the vote is in favour of continued integration in France, it is possible that pro-independence groups may resort to violence. France maintains a sizable military deployment in New Caledonia and could probably deploy more forces to quell unrest. Although it is unlikely, it is possible that Australia may be called upon under the 1992 France, Australia and New Zealand (FRANZ) Agreement, the 2006 Defence Cooperation and Status of Forces Agreement and the 2012 Strategic Partnership[45] to provide assistance.

2014 is also scheduled to bring the return to democracy in Fiji, which has made a new constitution and announced that democratic elections will be held. While Australia would welcome a return to democracy in Fiji, the potential legitimacy of the new constitution and its capacity to create stability in Fiji may be undermined by political and social restrictions imposed by the regime. More broadly, corruption remains rife, there is little transparency in government affairs, economic growth is stagnating and poverty is on the rise. Therefore, Australia could be faced with a difficult decision regarding how it will relate to a democratic—but potentially illegitimate Fiji—and how it would respond if questions arising from the conduct of the elections give rise to conflict. Australia would have a clear obligation to seek to evacuate Australian citizens in Fiji, but it is unclear what obligation it would feel in relation to a humanitarian emergency amongst the Fijian people.

Therefore, although the South Pacific is going through a phase of relative stability, Australia is not entering a 'new era' in its relations with the region. Instead, there are several contemporary issues that are likely to continue to challenge this, which suggests that Australia has to find new ways to seek to promote enduring stability. Although INTERFET and RAMSI have illustrated that Australia is good at restoring security, the risk of ongoing instability in the Solomon Islands, East Timor and Papua New Guinea suggests that Australia has not been particularly effective at dealing with the underlying causes of conflict, which generally include political, economic, societal, cultural, gender, demographic, environmental and historical dimensions. The solutions to these causes of conflict are complex and their multidimensional character suggests that they will require a whole-of-government response. During its lifetime RAMSI has developed these characteristics, but as it has had difficulty dealing with the deep-seated causes of conflict in the Solomon Islands. This suggests that more work needs to be done in this regard.

The likelihood that Australia will be engaged in more stabilisation missions, as well as evacuating Australian citizens from regional trouble spots or responding to humanitarian and natural disasters, suggests that Australia needs a sufficient amphibious capability and other joint maritime capabilities, to operate in the region. Accordingly, the 2013 Defence White Paper emphasised the role of amphibious capability as a 'central plank of our ability to conduct security and stabilisation missions' and of our 'cooperation and engagement activities in the South Pacific and Timor-Leste, including bilateral or multilateral exercises with regional security forces'.[46] Peter Dean has argued that this capability will 'play a key part in humanitarian assistance, evacuation and peacekeeping efforts' in the region.[47] As the HMAS *Kanimbla* and *Manoora* have been decommissioned, the acquisition of the two LHDs, due to be commissioned in 2014 and 2016, will be a 'game changer for any future contingencies the ADF may face in the [South] Pacific', alongside the recently-acquired Bay Class Landing Ship Dock (LSD), HMAS *Choules*.[48]

Future Directions, Challenges and Opportunities

Although Australia faces an array of contemporary issues that are likely to necessitate its future involvement in the South Pacific, Australia's capacity to exert its influence in the region is declining. This is evident in its relationship with Papua New Guinea. As Papua New Guinea's population and economy continue to grow, it is likely to take a more active role in the region, to be less susceptible to Australian influence and potentially to be more open to the influence of other external powers.

It is also evident in its relationship with Fiji. As noted, after the 2006 military coup Australia attempted to isolate Fiji. The Fijian regime responded by adopting a 'look north' policy, whereby it explicitly sought a closer relationship with China. Fiji has also sought to enhance the role of the sub-regional Melanesian Spearhead Group, an inter-governmental organisation of Melanesian states from which Australia and New Zealand are excluded. This has undermined the influence of the Pacific Islands Forum, which is the main multilateral grouping through which Australia and New Zealand exercise influence in the region. With Chinese support, Fiji actively promoted the creation of the Group's Secretariat and the building of its headquarters in Vanuatu. Moreover, Australia's loss of influence over Fiji means that it has also lost ground in the South Pacific's most important transport, communications and economic hub. Fiji is also home to most regional organisations and most offices of international organisations within the region. This suggests that Australia urgently needs to rethink its approach to Fiji. It may be opportune for Australia to apply its policy of partnership and engagement to its future relationship with Fiji in order to regain influence both in Fiji and in the broader region.

The need for Australia to regain influence in the South Pacific is enhanced by the increased presence of external powers. Indeed, the 2013 Defence White Paper acknowledged that 'attitudes to our role are changing' in the region, as 'the growing reach of Asian nations opens up a wider range of external players for our neighbours to partner with'.[49] China is the most active external power and has invested heavily in aid and diplomacy. Australia's concern that a potentially hostile power could establish a military base in the region from which to challenge our control of our air and sea approaches or project force against us was identified as a risk in both the 2009 and 2013 Defence White Papers.

Although presently unlikely that China would seek to do either of these things, as China gains influence in the South Pacific this raises the risk of great power competition. While China's Assistant Minister of Foreign Affairs Cui Tiankai declared in 2012 that China is 'here in this region not to seek any particular influence, still less dominance',[50] in 2011 United States Secretary of State Hillary Clinton admitted her concern that '[w]e are in a competition with China … China is in there [in Papua New Guinea] every day in every way trying to figure out how it's going to come in behind us, come in under us'.[51] The United States has accordingly resumed a more active diplomatic and development role in the region and announced its intention to increase its military presence in Guam. Given how marginal the region is to the broader international strategic environment there is only a minimal a risk that China and the United States could engage in zero-sum competition for military influence in the region. If this did occur, Australia would be faced with a difficult choice between its major economic partner and its major defence partner. It is more likely that China and the United States will merely seek to gain economic and diplomatic influence with South Pacific states.

A more pressing future challenge for Australia is how to deal with the effects of climate change in the South Pacific, particularly in the form of the increased frequency and magnitude of natural disasters and rising sea levels. The South Pacific is already highly susceptible to natural disasters, to which Australia is frequently called to respond, and the commissioning of the new LHDs should improve our already well-developed capacity to do so. However, the challenge of rising sea levels is new. Many islands, particularly in Polynesia and Micronesia, are only a few metres above sea level and several have already become uninhabitable, resulting in the displacement of their occupants. To date, the number of people affected has been relatively small, but if the effects of climate change continue to worsen, these numbers will increase. It is not unforeseeable that, if these numbers stretch into the tens of thousands, the people affected will be unable to be resettled within their home states, which could result in a tide of climate refugees to surrounding developed states, particularly Australia and New Zealand. Depending on how the Australian government decides to respond to potentially large numbers of displaced people in the region, this may raise significant maritime security challenges.

Australia also faces a number of other maritime security challenges arising within and from the South Pacific, including irregular maritime arrivals such as: people seeking asylum; terrorism, including the protection remote offshore oil and gas installations; transnational crime, smuggling and piracy; bio-security risks; illegal exploitation of natural resources, including illegal fishing; and pollution of its maritime environment. At present twelve Commonwealth agencies have responsibility for Australia's maritime security. The involvement of so many agencies raises questions about logistics, efficiency and coordination and has led to proposals for Australia to create a coast guard to consolidate maritime security functions. This proposal has not gained traction, but if maritime security challenges escalate, it may be something that Australia has to take more seriously.

Australia has also been active in promoting the maritime security of South Pacific states. Their exclusive economic zones (EEZs) cover 35 million square kilometres and include approximately 70 per cent of the world's catch of tuna. If they could harness the full value of the tuna caught in their EEZs this would constitute a significant source of revenue, which would probably reduce their dependence on development assistance, much of it from Australia. However, vessels from China, Taiwan and Japan, and even the European Union and Latin America, fish in the EEZs of most South Pacific states. These distant-water fishing nations and vessels registered in them often breach their licence agreements and under-report their catchments. There is also significant corruption in the management and governance of fisheries, in terms of granting fishing licences and access agreements and in the monitoring and inspection of fishing vessels.

Australia provides significant funding to the Forum Fisheries Agency and the Secretariat of the South Pacific Community to deal with these issues. Australia also coordinates aerial maritime surveillance support in partnership with the United States, New Zealand and France through the regular Quadrilateral Defence Coordinating Group talks. Australia's most significant contribution has been the Pacific Patrol Boat Program, which has involved Australia donating boats to South Pacific states and then providing them with technical and operational support. Increased operating costs and budgetary constraints have resulted in the boats falling short of their potential capacity and there have been claims that rising fuel costs and a lack of ownership by South Pacific states have made the program too expensive to sustain. However, the Program has increased the maritime security of South Pacific states, including increasing their fisheries revenue. The Program has also played an important role in Australia's humanitarian and disaster response capability and has given Australia a strategic presence in the region. The Program will be replaced by the Pacific Maritime Security Program in 2018 as the first of the donated boats reach the end of their life. Although still being designed, according to the 2013 Defence White Paper this new Program will involve the replacement of the existing boats.[52]

Reflecting Australia's new approach of partnership and engagement, at the inaugural South Pacific Defence Ministers meeting in May 2013 the Australian Defence Minister undertook to consult South Pacific states regarding their views of this new Program.[53]

Writing in 1965 TB Millar cautioned that if Papua New Guinea was in 'hostile hands' it would 'make attacks on our east coast much easier—Port Moresby, after all, is closer to Sydney than Darwin is'.[54] Australia's strategic geography has not changed since that time. This chapter has described several challenges that the South Pacific is likely to face to its future security and stability, in which Australia may need to engage in what Paul Dibb has described as 'conflicts of necessity'.[55] However, if Australia is able to assist South Pacific states to achieve enduring stability we could see Australia's relations with the region enter a new era. The region might come to be viewed as an 'arc of opportunity', which could provide Australia with a security screen,[56] that would, in the words of Millar, act as a 'restraint upon a hostile power',[57] something that may become increasingly vital should the power structure of the broader Asia-Pacific region become more threatening.

Further Reading

Dibb, Paul, 'The Importance of the Inner Arc to Australian Defence Policy and Planning', *Security Challenges*, vol. 8, no. 4, 2012, pp. 13–31. www.securitychallenges.org.au/ArticlePDFs/Vol8No4Dibb.pdf.

Dinnen, Sinclair and McLeod, Abby, 'The Quest for Integration: Australian Approaches to Security and Development in the Pacific Islands', *Security Challenges*, vol. 4, no. 2, 2008, pp. 23–43. www.securitychallenges.org.au/ArticlePDFs/vol4no2DinnenandMcLeod.pdf.

Dobell, Graeme, 'The "Arc of Instability": History of an Idea', in Huisken, Ron and Thatcher, Meredith (eds), *History as Policy: Framing the Debate on the Future of Australia's Defence Policy*, Australian National University Press, Canberra, 2007.

Hegarty, David and Powles, Anna, 'South Pacific Security', in Ayson, Robert and Ball, Desmond (eds), *Strategy and Security in the Asia-Pacific*, Allen & Unwin, Sydney, 2007, pp. 257–269.

'Security in the Pacific Arc: Special Issue', *Security Challenges*, vol. 8, no. 4, 2012, pp. 1–116. www.securitychallenges.org.au/TOCs/vol8no4.html.

White, Hugh, 'Australia-South Pacific', in Brendan Taylor (ed), *Australia as an Asia Pacific Regional Power: Friendship in Flux?*, Routledge, Abingdon, 2007, pp. 117–128.

Notes

1   P Dibb, 'The Importance of the Inner Arc to Australian Defence Policy and Planning', *Security Challenges*, vol. 8, no. 4, 2012, p. 1. www. securitychallenges.org.au/ArticlePDFs/Vol8No4Dibb.pdf (February 2014)

2   TB Millar, *Australia's Defence*, Melbourne University Press, Carlton, 1965, p. 150.

3   G Dobell, 'The "Arc of Instability": History of an Idea', in R Huisken and M Thatcher (eds), *History as Policy: Framing the Debate on the Future of Australia's Defence Policy*, Australian National University Press, Canberra, 2004, pp. 85–104.

4   *Strategic Basis* papers between 1953–75 are reproduced in S Frühling (ed), *A History of Australian Strategic Policy Since 1945*, Commonwealth of Australia, Canberra, 2009, pp. 167–542.

5   Commonwealth of Australia, *Australian Defence*, Commonwealth of Australia, Canberra, 1976, p. 6. www.defence.gov.au/oscdf/se/ publications/wpaper/1976.pdf (viewed January 2014).

6   D Hegarty and A Powles, 'South Pacific Security', in Robert Ayson and Desmond Ball (eds), *Strategy and Security in the Asia-Pacific*, Allen & Unwin, Sydney, 2007, p. 258.

7   P Dibb, *Review of Australia's Defence Capabilities: Report for the Minister of Defence*, Commonwealth of Australia, Canberra, 1986, p. 4. www. defence.gov.au/oscdf/se/publications/defreview/1986/Review-of-Australias-Defence-Capabilities-1986_Part1.pdf (viewed January 2014).

8   Commonwealth of Australia, *The Defence of Australia*, Commonwealth of Australia, Canberra, 1987, p. 15. www.defence.gov.au/oscdf/se/ publications/wpaper/1987.pdf (viewed January 2014).

9   Dibb, *Review of Australia's Defence Capabilities*, 1986 p. 145.

10 J Blaxland, 'Game-Changer in the Pacific: Surprising Options Open Up With The New Multi-Purpose Maritime Capability', *Security Challenges*, vol. 9, no. 3, 2013, p. 35. www.securitychallenges.org.au/ArticlePDFs/ SC9-3Blaxland.pdf (viewed January 2013).

11 Department of Defence, *Australia's Strategic Planning in the 1990s*, Commonwealth of Australia, Canberra, 1989. www.defence.gov.au/ OSCDF/se/publications/Australias-Strategic-Planning-1990s.pdf (viewed January 2013).

12 Department of Defence, *Force Structure Review*, Commonwealth of Australia, Canberra, 1991, p. 28. www.defence.gov.au/oscdf/se/ publications/ForceStructureReview1991_opt.pdf (viewed January 2014).

13 Commonwealth of Australia, *Defending Australia*, Canberra, Commonwealth of Australia, 1994, p. 92. www.defence.gov.au/OSCDF/se/ publications/wpaper/1994.pdf (viewed January 2014).

14 Department of Foreign Affairs and Trade, 'Joint Declaration of Principles Guiding Relations Between Australia and Papua New Guinea', 1987, as amended by exchange of letters in 1992, Commonwealth of Australia, Canberra. www.dfat.gov.au/geo/png/jdpgr_aust_png.html (viewed November 2013).

15 S Dinnen, R May and AJ. Regan, *Challenging the State: The Sandline Affair in Papua New Guinea*, Research School of Pacific and Asian Studies, Australian National University, Canberra, 1997; S Dorney, *The Sandline Affair*, ABC Books, Sydney, 1998.

16 P Dibb, DD Hale and P Prince, 'Asia's Insecurity', *Survival*, vol. 41, no. 3, 1999, p. 18.

17 S Dinnen, 'The Trouble with Melanesia', in I Molloy (ed), *In the Eye of the Cyclone: Issues in Pacific Security*, University of the Sunshine Coast, Sippy Downs, 2004, pp. 67–75.

18 P Dean, 'Amphibious Warfare and the Australian Defence Force', McMullen Naval History Symposium, United States Naval Academy, Annapolis, 20 September 2013.

19 Commonwealth of Australia, *Defence 2000: Our Future Defence Force*, Commonwealth of Australia, Canberra, 2000, p. x. www.defence.gov.au/publications/wpaper2000.pdf (viewed 28 January 2014).

20 H White, 'Australia-South Pacific', in Brendan Taylor (ed), *Australia as an Asia Pacific Regional Power: Friendship in Flux?*, Routledge, Abingdon, 2007, p. 121.

21 Commonwealth of Australia, *Defence 2000: Our Future Defence Force*, 2000, p. 44.

22 S Frühling, 'Golden Window of Opportunity: A New Maritime Strategy and Force Structure for the Australian Navy', *Security Challenges*, vol. 4, no. 2, 2008, p. 89. www.securitychallenges.org.au/ArticlePDFs/vol4no2Fruehling.pdf (viewed January 2014).

23 Department of Defence, *Defence Capability Review: Statement of Findings*, Defence Media Release, Commonwealth of Australia, Canberra, 142/01, 7 November 2003. www.defence.gov.au/minister/13tpl.cfm?CurrentId=3252 (viewed November 2013).

24 Department of Defence, *Defence Capability Plan 2004–2014*, Commonwealth of Australia, Canberra, 2004, p. 68.

25 S Dinnen, *Lending a Fist? Australia's New Interventionism in the South Pacific*, State, Society and Governance in Melanesia Discussion Paper 2004/5, State, Society and Governance in Melanesia conference, Australian National University, Canberra, 2004. www.digitalcollections. anu.edu.au/bitstream/1885/42136/2/04_05_dp_dinnen.pdf (viewed January 2014).

26 E Wainwright, *Our Failing Neighbour: Australia and the Future of the Solomon Islands*, Australian Strategic Policy Institute, Canberra, 2003. www.digitalcollections.anu.edu.au/bitstream/1885/41686/3/solomons. pdf (viewed January 2014).

27 United Nations General Assembly, *A More Secure World: Our Shared Responsibility*, Report of the High-Level Panel on Threats, Challenges and Change, UN Doc. A/59/565; *In Larger Freedom: Towards Development, Security and Human Rights For All*, Report of the Secretary-General, UNGA 59th session, 21 March 2005, UN Doc. A/59/2005. www.un.org/en/peacebuilding/pdf/historical/hlp_more_secure_world.pdf (viewed January 2014).

28   International Commission on Intervention and State Sovereignty, *The Responsibility to Protect: Report of the International Commission on Intervention and State Sovereignty*, International Commission on Intervention and State Sovereignty, New York, 2001. www.responsibilitytoprotect.org/ICISS%20Report.pdf (viewed November 2013).

29   Commonwealth of Australia, *Defending Australia*, 1994, p. 92.

30   Department of Defence, *Australia's Strategic Policy*, Commonwealth of Australia, Canberra, 1997, p. 13. www.defence.gov.au/minister/sr97/SR97.pdf (viewed January 2014).

31   Commonwealth of Australia, *Defence 2000: Our Future Defence Force*, 2000, pp. 30–31.

32   G Fry and TT Kabutaulaka, *Intervention and State-Building in the Pacific: The Legitimacy of 'Cooperative Intervention'*, Manchester University Press, Manchester, 2008.

33   Regional Assistance Mission to Solomon Islands, *People's Survey*, ANU Edge and The University of The South Pacific. www.ramsi.org/solomon-islands/peoples-survey.html (viewed November 2013).

34   Fry and Kabutaulaka, *Intervention and State-Building in the Pacific*, 2008.

35   John Howard, 'A Stronger Army: Two More Battalions', Press Release, Department of Prime Minister and Cabinet, Canberra, 24 August 2006.

36   Commonwealth of Australia, *Defending Australia in the Asia Pacific Century: Force 2030*, Commonwealth of Australia, Canberra, 2009, p. 12. www.defence.gov.au/whitepaper2009/docs/defence_white_paper_2009.pdf (viewed January 2014).

37   Department of Foreign Affairs and Trade, 'Port Moresby Declaration', Commonwealth of Australia, Canberra, 2013. www.aid.dfat.gov.au/countries/pacific/Pages/Port-Moresby-Declaration.aspx (viewed January 2014).

38   ibid.

39   Department of Foreign Affairs and Trade, 'Pacific Partnerships for Development', Commonwealth of Australia, Canberra, 2008. www.aid.dfat.gov.au/countries/pacific/partnership/Pages/default.aspx (viewed January 2014).

40   Commonwealth of Australia, *Defence White Paper 2013*, Commonwealth of Australia, Canberra, 2013, pp. 24–25. www.defence.gov.au/whitepaper2013/docs/WP_2013_web.pdf (viewed January 2014).

41   ibid., pp. 30–31.

42   ibid., p. 15.

43   Commonwealth of Australia, *Strong and Secure: A Strategy for Australia's National Security*, Commonwealth of Australia, Canberra, 2013. www.dpmc.gov.au/national_security/docs/national_security_strategy.pdf (viewed January 2014).

44   Department of Foreign Affairs and Trade, 'Agreement Between the Republic of Indonesia and Australia on the Framework for Security Cooperation', 2006. www.dfat.gov.au/geo/indonesia/ind-aus-sec06.html (viewed January 2014).

45   Department of Foreign Affairs and Trade, 'Joint Statement of Strategic Partnership between Australia and France', 2012. www.dfat.gov.au/geo/france/joint_statement.html (viewed November 2013).

46   Commonwealth of Australia, *Defence White Paper 2013*, 2013, p. 62–3.

47   PJ Dean, 'Amphibious Warfare and the Australian Defence Force', 20 September 2013.

48   Blaxland, 'Game-Changer in the Pacific: Surprising Options Open Up with the New Multi-Purpose Maritime Capability', 2013, p. 37.

49   Commonwealth of Australia, *Defence White Paper 2013*, 2013, p. 15.

50   Quoted in D Flitton, 'Clinton Stresses US Role in Pacific Security', *Sydney Morning Herald*, 1 September 2012. www.smh.com.au/world/clinton-stresses-us-role-in-pacific-security-20120901-256sh.html (viewed January 2013).

51   Quoted in A Quinn, 'Clinton Says China Seeks to Outflank Exxon in Papua New Guinea', Reuters, 2 March 2011. www.reuters.com/article/2011/03/02/us-china-usa-clinton-idUSTRE7215UV20110302 (viewed January 2014).

52   Commonwealth of Australia, *Defence White Paper 2013*, 2013, p. 64.

53   Department of Defence, 'South Pacific Defence Ministers Meeting Joint Communique', Commonwealth of Australia, Canberra, 2 May 2013. www.minister.defence.gov.au/files/2013/05/South-Pacific-Defence-Ministers-Meeting-Joint-Communique2.pdf (viewed November 2014).

54   Millar, *Australia's Defence*, 1965, p. 150.

55   Dibb, 'The Importance of the Inner Arc to Australian Defence Policy and Planning', 2012, p. 15.

56   J Wallis, 'The Pacific: From "Arc of Instability" to "Arc of Responsibility" and Then to "Arc of Opportunity?", *Security Challenges*, vol. 8, no. 4, 2012, pp. 1–12. www.securitychallenges.org.au/ArticlePDFs/Vol8No4Wallis.pdf (viewed January 2014).

57   Millar, *Australia's Defence*, 1965, p. 150.

Part III:
Strategy

7

Defence Policymaking

Paul Dibb

'There is great need for an informed general public attitude to defence. There is also urgent need for more and better quality thinking at the highest level.'[1]

Defence policymaking is a complex and challenging process. From the outside it often seems to be perceived as arcane and unfathomable. Certainly, it is more of an art form than a science: it involves high-level policy judgements on an intricate mixture of intelligence inputs, strategic policy priorities, force structure decisions and spending a lot of money. Although in some areas quantitative analysis can be used (for example, when it comes to assessing military technology and the characteristics of weapon systems) it can never be a substitute for professional advice. In the absence of a clear and imminent military threat, defence policymaking is all about risk management and hedging against an uncertain future.

In democracies, it is the elected government that decides what sort of defence policy a country should have, and it is the politicians who decide whether a country uses armed force or not. Politicians have the responsibility to determine how much money can be allocated to a country's defence compared with competing claims from education, health and social welfare. Economic resources are limited and choices between competing government objectives are unavoidable. Money is not a free good and judging how much is enough is the eternal conundrum of formulating sound defence policy. A former secretary for Defence Sir Arthur Tange once said 'strategy without money is not strategy'. This is a crucial matter that too often receives little attention in the academic literature.

Sir Arthur Tange also observed that a map of one's own country is the most fundamental of all defence documentation. However, it is still conspicuously missing in force structure arguments coming from the single services, as well as some so-called expert commentators. The abiding nature of Australia's continental geography and its maritime surrounds should be an iron discipline in determining force structure priorities and Australian Defence Force (ADF) dispositions. Moreover, Australia's location in the Asia-Pacific region—or what is now often being termed the Indo-Pacific—increasingly determines Australia's strategic future as countries such as China and India rise to power. But it has only been in the last thirty years or so that intellectually rigorous policies have been developed for the independent defence of Australia and how to focus on the region as a primary strategic concern.

This chapter begins by briefly examining the historical background to defence policymaking in Australia and what factors have determined fundamental turning points in shaping Australia's defence posture. The main body of the chapter firstly turns to an analysis of the contemporary strategic and financial challenges facing Australia and then secondly looks into why this will demand fundamental changes in the future direction of defence policy. The basic theme is that the ever-present requirement for a defence policy maker is to understand that no policy stands alone: it has to be formulated in the political and economic context of the time.

Historical Changes in Australia's Defence Policy

Understanding that Australia has a long history of being deeply concerned about the security of this sparsely populated continent, is a useful starting point when addressing the current challenges of Australian defence policymaking. Geographical isolation and the tyranny of distance have influenced almost every facet of Australian life. This is not the place to pursue a detailed analysis of Australia's strategic history. It is, however, to note that unlike other continental-sized countries with small populations—such as Canada—Australia has long held deep-seated concerns about its security. True, those concerns have ebbed and flowed. In the nineteenth century it was France and Russia who were variously perceived as threatening and in the twentieth century it was Germany and Japan. None of these worries resulted in an invasion of Australia or occupation of its metropolitan territory, although in the case of Japan the public fear of occupation in 1942 was real. In both centuries, Australia has depended upon a great power ally to defend itself—namely Great Britain and then the United States. Australia's defence policy was essentially a derivative of governments' reluctance to think realistically about national security.

After World War II, Australia turned to a concept called 'forward defence', which was aimed at containing the threat from communism far from its shores in the Malayan Emergency, the Korean War, the Indonesia Confrontation and the Vietnam War.[2] Throughout this period from the 1950s to the 1970s, there was a strong belief that Australia could not defend itself without allies, and that if force were left unchecked anywhere in Asia, it would become a threat to Australia. In particular, there was a strident view that the spread of international communism could eventually overwhelm the country. The domino theory predicted that should the forces of communism prevail in Asia—and Vietnam come under the heel of Communist China—Malaysia would then be in danger of being outflanked. Thailand, Burma and Indonesia were then thought to become the next direct objects of further communist expansion. This paranoia culminated in April 1975 when South Vietnam fell to the North Vietnamese communists and America's costly military commitment in Indochina was defeated. Australian troops had been stationed in Asia since 1941, including a force in Vietnam for seven years (1965–72). Australia had considerable experience of war in the region, but none of it contemplated fighting an enemy on Australia's own soil.

The Forward Defence era was over and by the mid-1970s defence policymakers turned their minds for the first time in Australia's history to the concept of defence of the continent. After Vietnam, a broad national consensus had emerged that Australia and its maritime approaches should be defended primarily from the continent. The 1976 Defence White Paper, *Australian Defence*, was the first public document to talk about defence self-reliance and having a force that should have a substantial capability for independent operations.[3] It stated quite clearly that Australia no longer based its defence policy on the expectation that its Navy, Army or Air Force would be sent abroad to fight as part of another nation's larger force. It went on to argue that any future military operations were much more likely to be in the neighbourhood than in some distant or forward theatre, and that Australia's armed services would be conducting joint operations together as the Australian Defence Force. The 1976 Defence White Paper made it clear that Australia should avoid development of defence capabilities that were not relevant to its own requirements.

These were quite revolutionary concepts at the time, even though they were in part a belated reaction to the requirement of the so-called Nixon or Guam doctrine of 1969: that America's allies must accept primary responsibility for their own defence short of a major power attack. In fact, the 1976 Defence White Paper was advancing novel concepts such as self-reliance that the ADF increasingly found difficult to swallow. The Liberal government of the time pretended this concept did not refer to Australia and the succeeding Whitlam Labor government believed Australia faced no foreseeable threat for the next 15 years. In the meantime, a lot of detailed studies were undertaken within the Department of Defence (Defence) into concepts for the defence of Australia with a focus on the continent and its maritime surrounds. Some signals were clear: the nature of Australia's physical environment demanded that maritime capabilities occupy a prominent place in defence. This, however, went very much against the grain of the entrenched history of Australian military culture—which traditionally had given prominence to the Army. Land forces had predominated in every conflict Australia had been involved in for over ninety years. Moreover, the ADF simply had had no experience whatsoever in operating as a joint force.

The 1986 'Review of Australia's Defence Capabilities' and 1987 Defence White Paper

All this resulted in precious little progress until a young and highly intelligent minister for Defence, Kim Beazley, decided that something quite radical had to be done. He decided to appoint an independent person to undertake a fundamental review of Australia's defence capabilities. The author of this chapter was appointed to that position in January 1985 and delivered a classified report to the minister in March 1986 with the public version being released in June of that year. The problem was that eight years after the 1976 Defence White Paper, progress had been glacially slow. There was no agreement on basic defence policy judgments, such as the level of threat Australia could credibly face, or force structure priorities. To make matters much worse, the then Secretary of the Department of Defence and the Chief of the Defence Force (CDF)[4] proved unable to bring the warring civilian and military factions to some sort of workable compromise. Beazley was determined to bring about a resolution.

The adversarial relationship that existed between the Department and the ADF was deeply entrenched. The so-called 1986 Dibb Review proposed a way forward that gave priority to establishing an agreed national defence strategy and a clear hierarchy of military capability requirements for the defence of Australia. It also made recommendations about the basing of military forces in the north of Australia and the command and control arrangements required for managing conflict there. The central theme of the Dibb Review was that Australia is a defensible continent and that with some important reordering of priorities, the nation could provide for its own defence.[5]

The secretary and the CDF jointly agreed to most, but not all recommendations from the 1986 Dibb Review. The minister instructed Defence to write the 1987 Defence White Paper, *The Defence of Australia.*[6] Naturally, the ensuing Defence White Paper had a broader remit than the *Review*: for example, it went into much more detail on science and technology, defence industry and defence personnel. It rejected the strategy of denial proposed in the *Review*, which the Chiefs of Staff Committee deemed to be too defensive and instead proposed a strategy called 'defence in depth'. In practice, there was little difference between how the critical priorities for force development were presented in the 1987 Defence White Paper and in the *Review*. As this Defence White Paper said, the *Review*'s main recommendations for developing a self-reliant force structure formed the basis of the 1987 Defence White Paper and the government's defence policy. At long last, a clear definition of Australia's real defence needs in an era of self-reliance was established, as was the comprehensive approach needed to implement this policy.

As with practically all defence white papers, however, the problem came with finding the money necessary to support what was an ambitious forward defence program, which promised to allocate in the order of 2.6–3 per cent of Gross Domestic Product (GDP) on defence and financial guidance over the five years from 1987–92 of 3 per cent annual growth (see Figure 11.1). However, Australia's economic conditions rapidly worsened and the new minister for Defence, Senator Robert Ray, commissioned the secretary and CDF to prepare a Force Structure Review to ensure that defence planning for the 1990s took proper account of the likely resource environment.

In the four years since the 1987 Defence White Paper the real growth in defence outlays had averaged 0 per cent, and not the 3 per cent of the government's endorsed financial guidance. If the defence budget continued at this level, only about three-quarters of the White Paper program could be funded over the coming decade. If there were real reductions of minus 1 per cent per annum across the decade, advice was that less than half of the 1987 White Paper could be funded.[7]

The 1991 Force Structure Review warned the minister that it was important to avoid over-committing to unrealistic targets and savings expectations. It proposed personnel reductions, including those from defence efficiency measures and the new Commercial Support Program (CSP) amounting to almost 10 500 regular ADF personnel and over 3 800 defence civilians over the coming decade.[8] These reductions were supposed to be substantially offset by the introduction of some 4 100 'ready reserves' and the replacement of almost 4000 'service personnel' with contractor support primarily in the logistics, support and training functions.[9] These proposals were consistent with an assumption of no real financial growth over the decade. In effect, this is what occurred with defence expenditure falling from 2.3 per cent of GDP in 1991 to under 2 per cent of GDP in 1994 where it has remained ever since. The late 1980s and 1990s were lean years for defence and, in real terms, the defence budget was higher in 1985–86 ($14.5 billion) than it was 11 years later in 1996–97 ($13.7 billion).[10] The bottom line was that the 1987 Defence White Paper did not deliver on its promised program because of serious deterioration in Australia's domestic economic circumstances.

Contemporary Issues and the Crisis Facing Defence

What is the relevance of all this to Australia's contemporary situation? The challenges currently being experienced in the defence arena echo those that Australia had in the late 1980s and early 1990s. As in the late 1980s, Australia now has to focus strategically on its own region after over a decade fighting a distant war. This will demand of the ADF a challenging change of direction from a preoccupation with distant expeditionary operations to giving priority to the defence of Australia and the immediate neighbourhood, just as it had to do after the Vietnam War. In addition, Australia now finds itself in seriously straitened economic times like those defence planning faced in the 1990s. If future taxation revenues continue to be squeezed and government expenditure on health and social welfare remain on an upward trajectory, then it is likely that the defence budget will come under the sorts of pressures seen in the 1990s. This has serious implications for Australia's future force structure and its modernisation.

The two main policy challenges and choices facing defence now are how to shift Australia's strategic priority from Afghanistan to the region of primary strategic concern to the north—which is primarily a maritime theatre of operations—and how to manage the defence portfolio in a period of fiscal austerity where defence resources will continue to be constrained. It will be far from easy to manage these two contending policy pressures. Hence, Australia's strategic geography must return to its proper place in defence planning, and the financial outlook demands a rethink of its defence priorities.[11]

As was the case after the Vietnam War, Australia must not fall into the trap of losing its sense of strategic direction. Overreaching abroad and weaknesses closer to home are always a danger for middle powers. This applies particularly to Australia with its historical proclivity to prefer overseas expeditionary operations over the defence of the continent and the region. In the post-Afghanistan era, Australia's geography requires a maritime strategy for deterring and defeating attacks against Australia and contributing to the security of the immediate neighbourhood and within limits, the wider region. This requires the ability to generate a joint force able to operate in a maritime environment that extends from the eastern Indian Ocean to the mid-South Pacific and from Southeast Asia (including the South China Sea) to the Southern Ocean and Antarctic territories. This amounts to almost 20 per cent of the earth's surface, which is a challenging operational task for a defence force of less than 60 000.

The Enduring Importance of Geography for Australia's Defence

Australia must seek to optimise the significant advantages to be gained from the strategic depth provided by the geography of the continent. Compared with many other nations in the region, Australia should be grateful for the security that comes from its strategic geography. Australia's military strategy should emphasise the importance of the maritime domain to controlling the extensive sea and air approaches to the continent, particularly its vulnerable northern approaches. Although the Howard government's 2000 Defence White Paper talked about Australia needing a fundamentally maritime strategy, it failed to provide much detail and was overtaken by events in Iraq and Afghanistan for the next decade. And therein lies a problem: because of the preoccupation with expeditionary operations in distant theatres, Australian governments have run down some of the most crucial capabilities necessary to support a maritime strategy. These include antisubmarine warfare, mine hunting and minesweeping, electronic warfare and maritime surveillance and detection. Moreover, Australian defence bases and facilities in the north and northwest of the continent cannot sustain high tempo military operations. This is a problem that if left unaddressed, will be compounded as new ships and aircraft are introduced into the force. These deficiencies require urgent rectification.

Defence needs to refocus on the highly demanding nature of military operations in an archipelagic environment. This means refamiliarising the ADF with what is involved in operating in the seas of Southeast Asia and the South Pacific. Operating on and under the sea in the relatively confined waterways to Australia's north in particular will mean that avoiding detection and acquiring targeting data will be demanding. The technical specifications of sonars and radars will require optimisation for potential military operations in the archipelago—as will the capacity to detect and track targets in a theatre of operations where it will be easier for the opposition to conceal itself. All this points to the need to reinstitute those capabilities that have run down: intelligence, surveillance and reconnaissance capabilities, and targeting and network analysis must now be prioritised for the region's unique operating environment—not those of the Middle East.

There are three geographical areas that require the attention of the ADF. First, it needs to reacquaint itself with the north and northwest of the continent and its maritime approaches. The 2012 *Force Posture Review*, conducted by two former Secretaries for Defence, found that some northern bases have inadequate logistics support and infrastructure and lack basic protection.[12] The Abbott government has said it will consider the need for a greater presence of military forces in northern Australia, especially in resource-rich areas with little or no current military presence. If Australia is to protect its extensive maritime territory and strategically significant offshore territories and economic resources, more attention will need to be given to the adequacy of air, naval and land bases, as well as access to commercial infrastructure. Defence will also now need to pay more attention to the Indian Ocean approaches to Western Australia, which will increasingly feature in Australia's defence planning and its maritime strategy.

The second area of strategic focus is the immediate neighbourhood where Australia has important interests and responsibilities. The security and stability of the immediate neighbourhood—shared with Papua New Guinea, East Timor and the small island states of the South Pacific—are interests where Australia has a central strategic role. It is a part of the world where, if requested, Australian forces must be able to intervene. The drawing down of Australia's troop presence in East Timor and the Solomon Islands after more than 10 years does not spell an end to the requirements in the South Pacific for humanitarian and disaster relief, capacity building and governance, potential peacekeeping operations and military intervention (see Chapter 6). It is not too difficult to contemplate some demanding contingencies for the ADF in this part of the world. For example, a major breakdown in law and order in Papua New Guinea and the requirement to evacuate large numbers of Australian citizens would be an extremely demanding contingency requiring a service protected evacuation.

There is an important role here for Australia's new amphibious capabilities based on the two 27 000 tonne large amphibious ships (Landing Helicopter Docks, or LHDs). These will present a serious challenge to both the Army and Navy. They will be the largest ships ever operated by the ADF and will represent a step change in the way Australia deploys its land forces and their supporting systems in amphibious operations. The initial focus should be on security, stabilisation, humanitarian assistance and disaster relief tasks. These LHDs will be able to operate much further afield than the South Pacific but if they are to undertake high-intensity operations, it will take a great deal of the ADF's key military assets to protect them. The demands of such operations would risk the ADF becoming a one-shot Defence Force—something that must be avoided especially if the potential operational gain is not worth the strategic risk.

The third area of strategic focus is Southeast Asia, which as already mentioned, includes its seas and straits, including the South China Sea. The security of Southeast Asia is an enduring strategic interest because of its proximity to Australia's northern approaches and crucial shipping lanes. Southeast Asia is the fulcrum point between the Indian Ocean and the Pacific in what some observers are inclined to see as a single strategic entity called the Indo-Pacific. However, this geopolitical definition is too embracing in terms of what is a feasible defence focus for a small defence force like Australia's. It is the eastern Indian Ocean and the seas of Southeast Asia that should be a priority concern for force structure planning. The priority Australia gives to Southeast Asia should include being able to help Southeast Asian partners to meet external challenges, particularly given the uncertainties surrounding the strategic transformation of the wider region. This means Australia should be prepared to make substantial military contributions if necessary. In this context, Australia needs to give much more thought to the sort of ADF joint force that might be appropriate to credible Southeast Asian contingencies, as well as to how the ADF might operate in closer partnership with Southeast Asian countries as they become more militarily capable over time.

Australia will also have a modest capability to contribute to high-intensity conventional conflict in Northeast Asia. That is not, however, a part of the world where Australia can make a real military difference. Even so, meeting alliance commitments to the United States might involve niche contributions by some of the high-technology assets acquired for Australia's own force structure purposes that would also be relevant to Northeast Asian contingencies. A useful contribution in the event of high-intensity conventional war in Northeast Asia would be to 'a distant blockade', which would be a more proximate military operation for Australia in Southeast Asian waters.

The 2013 Defence White Paper observes that Australia's national prosperity is underpinned by its ability to trade through Indo-Pacific maritime routes and that the ADF needs to be prepared to play a role in keeping these sea-lanes secure.[13] It would be wrong to interpret this to mean that Navy will be required to defend sea-lanes all the way to the North Pacific or the western Indian Ocean. Rather, defence force efforts should concentrate on operations and focal areas closer to home, including the protection of trade vital to the economy and war effort.

All of this means that the Abbott government needs to focus on what is affordable and credible militarily within the ADF. In the event of high-intensity conventional combat operations in the region, Australia would always need to hold sufficient forces to defend the nation. Australia's military resources are limited and the first call upon them must be in respect of national security tasks. It should be a fundamental tenet of Australia's strategic policy that the scale of contributions will be determined by national interests and the limits of ADF capacity.

Defence in Times of Austerity

The outlook for the world economy is in many ways the biggest contemporary strategic uncertainty facing Australia. Until recently, Australia has not been affected significantly by the economic damage done to the United States and much of Europe where many nations are facing at least a decade of poor economic growth. For Australia, the economic outlook has dramatically changed: the resources boom is slowing, government revenues have taken a big structural hit, economic growth is well below trend and the Federal government's budget faces long-run structural deficits. Something serious has to be done about cutting government expenditure. Yet the government continues to load the budget with future debt. The outlook is made worse by the fact that Australia has an ageing population, which will impose rapidly increasing health and aged-care costs on the budget. Australia's economy will have to make some painful adjustments before serious and sustainable economic growth will resume. This means that public finances will be held under a tight rein for several years, perhaps for the foreseeable future.[14]

The outlook for the defence budget is therefore one of continuing austerity (see Figure 11.3), both because of government commitment to return to conditions of budget surplus as soon as practicable—most likely taking several years—and because of the other pressures on government expenditure already mentioned, as well as the rising demands of education and infrastructure development. There is a good case to spend more on defence as soon as practicable, given that its 1.6 per cent share of GDP is clearly unable to finance current military ambitions. However, there is nothing magic about a particular percentage of GDP. What matters more is the relationship between Australia's strategic outlook, realistic assessments of risk and prudent hedging against the need to use military force. The fact is that the region has been at peace now for almost forty years and there is a low likelihood of war between the major powers. The reasons for this are twofold: the fear of the use of nuclear weapons will remain a huge deterrent and the world is now so interconnected economically and technologically that there would be no winners in a major war.

Even so, miscalculation and misjudgement short of major war are a risk, as they have been throughout history. In the Asia-Pacific region, there are plenty of territorial and ideological tensions and jockeying for influence by the rising powers. It is, therefore, prudent for Australia to develop a capable high-technology force with which to defend itself and its vital interests. However, the cost of projecting and sustaining this sort of military power is increasing rapidly in the contemporary era and the range of Australia's national interests is expanding just as defence budgets are effectively declining. The ADF will have to deal simultaneously with increased sustainment costs for ageing equipment and a highly ambitious new acquisition program. This means priorities need to be set among competing military requirements much more rigorously than in the past.

It is obvious that fiscal constraint will endure until at least the government turns around the budget deficit. Under these circumstances, it will not be easy for any government to find large increases for defence spending. The Abbott government has committed itself to return the defence budget to 2 per cent of GDP within a decade.[15] According to the Australian Strategic Policy Institute (APSI), this will involve 5.3 per cent annual growth sustained over each of the next 10 years.[16] There is no precedent for such sustained growth, except in wartime or acute international crisis, and even then not for such an extended period. This goal, therefore, is simply not credible and there is the further challenge that Defence would face in responsibly ramping up expenditure levels at the rate envisaged.

A lack of publicly available information means that it is not possible to assess with accuracy the gap between the levels of funds likely to be available, and the costs of sustaining the current force and implementing the ambitious modernisation plan that was set out in the Defence Capability Program inherited from the previous Labor government. Suffice it to say that such analysis as has been attempted paints a persistently gloomy picture.[17]

Defence Policymaking in a New Era

The new Coalition government needs to come to terms with the challenge of reducing the gap between the cost of Australia's strategic ambitions and the funds available to achieve them. Given the size of this gap and the prospect of enduring austerity in the defence budget, this challenge will prove formidable. This will be particularly the case if the 2015 Defence White Paper reverts to the sort of strategic fantasies of the 2009 Defence White Paper, which talked about imposing substantial military costs on a major power adversary. This was widely interpreted as being China. One of the external advisers to the 2009 Defence White Paper process later proposed that Australia develop options that might include 'seriously damaging the capacities of China's strategic leadership to govern' and having the capability 'to stir serious internal disruptions and even revolts in the event that the Chinese leadership threatened Australia's vital interests'.[18]

It remains to be seen just how far the 2015 Defence White Paper will go with its assessments about China, but it is likely that the Abbott government will use words that are tougher than those in the 2013 document and perhaps even stronger than the wording in the 2009 Defence White Paper. It is worth recalling that the wording of the 2009 document drew the anger of Beijing in no uncertain terms. Moreover, a China retaliating to perceived insults is more likely. That should not prevent Australia from developing a high-tech defence force capable of defending itself and contributing to Allied operations in its region of primary strategic concern. However, it remains unlikely that Australia can develop a defence force capable of making a major contribution to high-intensity conflict in Northeast Asia. Instead, Australia's ambitions will have to be more modest than that and, as already suggested, there are other ways for Australia to contribute significantly to such scenarios.

It is likely that the Abbott government's Defence White Paper will seek to strengthen the defence of northern Australia and improve its military presence there. That would be a prudent step and is to be encouraged. It also seems likely that the government will give even more emphasis to the crucial strategic importance to us of Southeast Asia and especially Indonesia. A strong and stable Indonesia is very much in Australia's national interest. Indeed, Southeast Asia as a whole should be seen as a strategic shield to Australia's northern approaches and an important barrier to any future Chinese ambitions to establish spheres of influence in the neighbourhood.

It is important to make clear that over the longer term, situations developing in a manner adverse to Australia's interests should not be ruled out. Defence policy must ensure against such uncertainties and risks. Military capabilities and competence must continue to command respect. In this context, it has long been a fundamental priority of Australian defence policy to maintain a clear margin of regional technological superiority because its defence concerns focus on capabilities, rather than specific threats. This will become a much greater challenge as regional defence forces acquire more sophisticated weapons systems. Therefore, modernising the defence force so that it remains a highly competent high technological force is fundamental.

The other central issue is addressing the imbalance between the costs of the ambitions set out in the 2009 and 2013 Defence White Papers of the previous Labor governments and likely funding levels.[19] There are no easy solutions to the challenge of restoring the balance. If there are no large increases in the defence budget, this means government will need to be much more rigorous in setting priorities among competing military proposals than in the past. The current Defence Capability Plan[20] is far too ambitious and needs to be zero-based, such that future acquisitions can be afforded and are more demonstrably relevant to strategic circumstances.

As the new government considers particularly big capability proposals, it will be important for it to understand what the scale of investment means in terms of opportunity costs, that is, what other defence capabilities might need to be foregone. Three projects alone account for almost one-quarter of the currently planned Defence Capability Plan of $275 billion out to 2030. They are: twelve Future Submarines for $34 billion, 72 Joint Strike Fighters for at least $24 billion and Army's $19 billion replacement of its armoured and mechanised combat vehicles so that it can defeat 'a peer competitor' on the battlefield (whatever that means). These are projects that go well beyond the scale and risks in any previous big defence projects and they will crowd out what is required to restore current deficiencies in the ADF's emphasis on a maritime strategy. The huge cost of these programs needs to be reconsidered against economic circumstances and the fact that some of them simply do not have any plausible strategic justification.

In seeking to make efficiencies in the defence portfolio, the government will need to take a harsh look at the entire structure and functions of the Department of Defence and how it spends money. Too often, defence decisions have been dominated by the domestic politics of defence policy (see Chapter 1), parochial bureaucratic interests—both military and civilian—and sheer inertia in the cumbersome machinery that has been created in Canberra. The government has foreshadowed a 'first-principles review' of the Department of Defence's structure and major processes with a focus on minimising bureaucracy and maximising frontline resources. It also says it will reform the Defence Materiel Organisation[21] (whose annual running costs are about the same as those of the entire Department of Foreign Affairs) to make its procurements more cost-effective. That is something that needs to be implemented.

Another important observation must be made. The proportion of the defence budget that is now spent on investment has fallen to 22 per cent, when historically it has been about 33 per cent. In particular, personnel costs have risen dramatically and now account for 42 per cent of all defence spending. An option to consider is to cut ADF personnel numbers to find the additional $2.85 billion a year necessary to bring the investment share of the budget back up to 33 per cent—and even that might not be enough for the modernisation program currently envisaged. Even if the defence civilian workforce were cut by half (some 10 000), it would save only about $1.1 billion annually and still leave a shortfall of $1.8 billion in the historic share of capital investment. This would imply that cuts to the ADF—whose per capita costs are about 30 per cent higher than those of civilians—would also need to be made. To reduce ADF personnel costs by $1.8 billion would require ADF numbers to fall by some 12 500, or about 20 per cent of the ADF target strength of 59 000 full-time personnel.[22]

Such figures serve to show the magnitude of the problem, and neither of these options should be considered lightly, if at all. This is not to say that some reduction should not be made, provided the consequences have been thought through and the risks assessed. Indeed, in the likely absence of increased funding, some reductions would appear inevitable if a good balance is to be struck between the present force and the future force. But it would be a mistake to believe that radical and pain-free savings are easily available. Over recent decades, most easy savings have been made through the corporatisation and privatisation of defence factories and dockyards in the 1980s; the market testing of non-core functions in the early 1990s; the implementation of the Defence Reform Program in the late 1990s and the Strategic Reform Program of the 2000s.

Essentially, for the ADF the choices ahead will have to be between reductions to the preparedness—and therefore potentially also to the size—of the force in-being and to the modernisation program. In judging the best balance implied by this choice between the present and the future, it is important that expediency not cause undue weight to be given to preserving the force in-being at the expense of the future force. Australia's strategic circumstances are relatively benign at present but the longer term future, on which the more critical and costly parts of the modernisation program are focused, is likely to prove much more demanding. Giving priority to modernisation, however, does not imply that there is no scope to review the modernisation program and particularly the three very big projects that have been identified earlier with regard to the Future Submarine force, the numbers of Joint Strike Fighters to be acquired and expensive modernisation proposals for the Army. Were the funding situation to prove less dire than anticipated, there should be a strong preference for maritime capabilities and their modernisation.

This government faces some unpalatable facts because balancing capability with available money is the central challenge that its new Defence White Paper faces. There are no magic solutions to restoring this balance, only difficult compromises and painful trade-offs. On the one hand, cutting personnel numbers or planned capability has implications for the future force. On the other hand, continuing to allow huge personnel costs to distort the structure of Defence is no longer acceptable because of its impact on current war-fighting capabilities. Given the size of the gap between the cost of Australia's strategic ambitions and the prospect of austerity in the defence budget the challenge ahead is formidable. But the government must not fall into the trap of promising what is simply not doable economically, because if it does, Australia might have yet another defence train wreck on its hands.

Further Reading

Babbage, Ross, *Rethinking Australia's Defence*, University of Queensland Press, St. Lucia, 1980.

Ball, Desmond, *Maintaining the Strategic Edge: The Defence of Australia in 2015*, Strategic and Defence Studies Centre, Australian National University, Canberra, 1999.

Dibb, Paul, *Essays on Australian Defence*, Strategic and Defence Studies Centre, Australian National University, Canberra, 2006.

Dibb, Paul, *The Conceptual Basis of Australia's Defence Planning and Force Structure Development*, Strategic and Defence Studies Centre, Australian National University, Canberra, 1992.

Department of Defence, *Force Structure Review: Report to the Minister for Defence*, Commonwealth of Australia, Canberra, 1991. www.defence.gov.

au/oscdf/se/publications/ForceStructureReview1991_opt.pdf.

Frühling, Stephan, *A History of Australian Strategic Policy Since 1945*,
Commonwealth of Australia, Canberra, 2009.

Millar, Thomas Bruce, *Australia in Peace and War*, Australian National
University Press, Canberra, 1978.

Commonwealth of Australia, *The Defence of Australia*, Commonwealth of
Australia, Canberra, 1987.

Notes

1   TB Millar, *Australia's Defence*, Melbourne University Press, Carlton, 1965,
    p. 4.

2   See TB Millar, *Australia in Peace and War*, Australian National University
    Press, Canberra, 1978.

3   Commonwealth of Australia, *Australian Defence*, Commonwealth of
    Australia, Canberra, 1976, pp. 10–13. www.defence.gov.au/oscdf/se/
    publications/wpaper/1976.pdf (viewed January 2014).

4   Until October 1984, the position was known as Chief of Defence Force
    Staff.

5   P Dibb, *Review of Australia's Defence Capabilities: Report for the Minister
    of Defence*, Commonwealth of Australia, Canberra, 1986. www.defence.
    gov.au/oscdf/se/publications/defreview/1986/Review-of-Australias-
    Defence-Capabilities-1986_Part1.pdf (viewed January 2014).

6   The author of this chapter was the principal author of the 1987 Defence
    White Paper.

7   Department of Defence, *Force Structure Review 1991*, Commonwealth of
    Australia, Canberra, 1991, p. 3. www.defence.gov.au/oscdf/se/
    publications/ForceStructureReview1991_opt.pdf (viewed January 2014).

8   ibid., p. 43.

9   ibid.

10 M Thomson, *The Cost of Defence: ASPI Defence Budget Brief 2013–2014*,
    Australian Strategic Policy Institute, Canberra, 2013, p. 113. www.aspi.org.
    au/publications/the-cost-of-defence-aspi-defence-budget-
    brief-2013-2014/ASPI-CostDefence2013.pdf (viewed January 2014).

11 For a more extended discussion of these issues see P Dibb, *Managing
    Australia's Maritime Strategy in an Era of Austerity*, speech to the Chief of
    Navy's Sea Power Conference, Sydney, 9 October 2013 (to be published by
    the Royal Australian Navy's Sea Power Centre in 2014).

12 A Hawke and R Smith, *Australian Defence Force Posture Review*,
    Commonwealth of Australia, Canberra, 2012, p. 28. www.defence.gov.au/
    oscdf/adf-posture-review/docs/final/Report.pdf (viewed October 2013).

13 Commonwealth of Australia, *Defence White Paper 2013*, Commonwealth
    of Australia, Canberra, 2013, p. 25. www.defence.gov.au/whitepaper2013/
    (viewed December 2013).

14 For an expanded version of this discussion see P Dibb and R Brabin-
    Smith, 'Australian Defence: Challenges for the New Government', *Security
    Challenges*, vol. 9, no. 4, 2013. www.securitychallenges.org.au/

ArticlePDFs/SC9-4DibbandBrabin-Smith.pdf (viewed December 2013).

15 M Thomson, '2%—Can We, Should We, Will We?', *The Strategist*, Australian Strategic Policy Institute, 10 September 2013. www.aspistrategist.org. au/2-percent-can-we-should-we-will-we/ (viewed October 2013).

16 ibid.

17 See M Thomson, 'Defence Funding in 2013: Means, Ends and Make Believe', *Security Challenges*, vol. 9, no. 2, 2013, pp. 51–8. www. securitychallenges.org.au/ArticlePDFs/SC9-2Thomson.pdf (viewed January 2014); and M Thomson, *The Cost of Defence: ASPI Defence Budget Brief 2013–14*, 2013.

18 R Babbage, 'Australia's Strategic Edge in 2030', *Kokoda Paper*, no. 15, 2011, pp. 81 and 85. www.kokodafoundation.org/resources/documents/ kp15strategicedge.pdf (viewed January 2014).

19 The following paragraphs draw on P Dibb and R Brabin-Smith, 'Australian Defence: Challenges for the New Government', 2013, pp. 45–64.

20 Department of Defence, *Defence Capability Plan 2012*, Commonwealth of Australia, Canberra, 2012. www.defence.gov.au/publications/ CapabilityPlan2012.pdf (viewed January 2014).

21 B Nicholson, 'Abbott Government Plans a Review of Defence Deals', *The Australian*, 2 December 2013.

22 For the data on which these calculations are based see M Thomson, *The Cost of Defence: ASPI Defence Budget Brief 2013–2014*, pp. 37–48. www.aspi.org.au/publications/the-cost-of-defence-aspi-defence-budget- brief-2013-2014/ASPI-CostDefence2013.pdf (viewed January 2014).

8

Australian Strategy and Strategic Policy

Stephan Frühling

In his 1965 book, *Australia's Defence*, TB Millar wrote that '[a]ll defence thinking must be based on the answers to two questions. What is the nature of the threat, its direction, size and imminence? What resources can we draw upon to meet that threat?'[1] This chapter examines Australia's 'defence thinking' as the link between these two questions and discusses how Australia has used its limited resources to defend against threats to its territory, sovereignty, population and the nation's defence commitments overseas. The relationship between these ends, the means or resources to achieve them and the ways in which they are best employed, is commonly referred to as 'strategy'.

Strategy should relate the maintenance, threat and use of military force to the political objectives that a country seeks to achieve. Hence, strategy comprises the considerations that guide the use of the Australian Defence Force (ADF) on operations, but it should also link defence commitments to Australia's security, substantiate claims for defence 'requirements' and justify the way the defence budget is allocated to different capabilities. Strategy must provide the answers to the questions of how Australia's defence effort reduces risk to the country, how the ADF should be structured to best achieve Australia's security and how it is best used on operations.

Whereas these questions are simple and straightforward, an attempt at answering them is anything but—even if there is agreement on what Australia should seek to achieve through the use of the ADF, which often there is not. Strategy can be examined in relation to a particular conflict and Australia's contribution, or as the logical underpinning of Australia's long term defence effort writ large. (In the latter case, the term 'strategic policy' is often used.) Developing strategy and strategic policy is difficult not only because there are many influences out of any one country's control—not least the actions of a possible adversary—but also because there are different ways in which objectives and choices can be framed.

This is particularly the case for Australia, a country whose independence from Britain was a century-long process, lasting well into the second half of the twentieth century.[2] Australian strategy remained intricately linked to, if not indistinguishable from, that of the British Empire for several decades after Federation in 1901. The country was never thrown into a situation where suddenly it had to develop strategy for itself, or to confront serious threats on its own. There is no equivalent in Australia to the warnings by George Washington and Thomas Jefferson of 'entangling' alliances, which provided the basis for the foreign and defence policy of the young United States.[3] The bombing of Darwin and occupation of New Guinea by Japan in 1942 confirmed that Australia's security rested on support from larger, outside powers. In contrast, World War II sharply demonstrated the inadequacy of pre-war defence policies in almost all European countries and led them to seek security through new, collective defence arrangements after the war.

Hence, the development of Australia's strategy since Federation was a continuous evolution in which the two World Wars, while important, were not the great watersheds that they were for Australian society. Throughout this time, the core issue in Australia's 'defence thinking' has been how Australia's defence effort should relate to Imperial defence or the ANZUS alliance. For what aspects of defence could, or should, Australia rely on its alliances or assume its own responsibility? And how should it balance preparations for independent operations in its immediate neighbourhood against its contributions to a wider allied effort? Within that enduring framework, however, Australian strategy and strategic policy has evolved considerably over time. Indeed, this chapter argues that Australia is about to enter a new era that might bring a change in its strategy and strategic policy no less consequential than the change that TB Millar outlined in his 1965 book.

Australia's Contributions to the Defence of the Empire

Strategy as the use of force by organised groups and in pursuit of political objectives is intricately bound to questions of identity—in particular, what group participants identify with and for whose benefit they take up arms. The participation of Australia (and Australians) in war thus must be seen as part of the slow differentiation of Australian identity and of specifically Australian objectives from those of the larger British Empire and broader Anglosphere. But even if Australian governments became more discerning about the way they contributed to allied operations over time, shared values and historical links to allied nations remain a real and important factor in Australia's defence policy and national identity at large. As such, Australia's alliances with the United Kingdom and United States are not commitments that Australians approach in a purely transactional, utilitarian fashion, and neither have they done so when faced with the question of committing troops to conflicts overseas.

This is particularly true for the earliest Australian participation in the Empire's conflicts, beginning with Australian volunteers in the Maori Wars of the early 1860s. Australian colonies and the young Commonwealth contributed forces to British operations in the Sudan (1885), Boer War (1899–1902) and Boxer Rebellion (1900–1901). In all of these conflicts, it is difficult to see a distinct strategic concept that would link Australians' contribution—or the way Australian authorities sought to see it employed—to specific Australian strategic objectives. Rather, the contributions were made by colonies and a dominion that saw themselves as Australian, but still equally British. As part of the British Empire—whose foreign and defence policy was still largely set in London—Australians shared the same sense of outrage that supported these wars in Britain and identified the Empire's interests as their own.

The same is also true for Australia's participation in World Wars I and II. In 1914, then-opposition leader Andrew Fisher pledged that Australia would support Britain 'to the last man and last shilling'.[4] While earlier conflicts threatened little more than the Empire's prestige, the two wars with Germany were a threat to the Empire's power itself, on which Australia's security also depended. Australia's contribution to both wars was hence commensurately greater than that to earlier conflicts. World War I was the last time that the outbreak of war was seen as cause for celebrations in Australia. It remains Australia's most costly conflict by far, in relative as well as absolute terms. Nonetheless, when the Empire's existence was again threatened in 1939, prime minister Menzies informed Australians that 'Great Britain has declared war upon [Germany] and that as a result, Australia is also at war'.[5]

In terms of Australian strategy, the two world wars mark the first instances where Australia took a direct interest in the way its forces were used on operations. In World War I, the first task for Australia's forces was to clear German garrisons (and radio networks) from New Guinea, which an improvised Australian amphibious force achieved in September 1914. Removing the German threat in the Pacific protected the Empire's sea communications and freed Australian forces for service elsewhere. The New Guinea operation was small in scale and overshadowed by the subsequent service of the Australian Imperial Force (AIF) in the Middle East and France. Nonetheless it is notable because it was the first time that Australian forces conducted an operation, on their own, to achieve specifically Australian objectives—even though the strategic interest of Australia in this operation closely aligned with that of the Empire as a whole. In contrast, the use of the AIF was guided by Britain, as no specific Australian interests were involved.[6]

In World War II, there was a more pronounced and consistent, if not always more successful, effort by Australian governments to see Australian forces employed in a way that reflected the priority of strategic objectives as seen from Canberra. Australia gave more consideration to its requirement (and under Imperial arrangements, responsibility) for homeland defence against a possible Japanese threat than London did in light of the actual threat from Germany it was facing in 1940 and 1941. The difference in judgment should not be overstated, however, as Australia remained firmly committed to ensuring its own security through the defence of the Empire as a whole. While many Australian ships served under British command in the Pacific area (rather than in Europe), the expediency of organising Imperial air forces took priority over the generation of specifically Australian units. Until the Japanese attack on Britain's Asian colonies, Australia's main contribution to the Empire's air war was thus the provision of training and pilots for the European theatre.[7]

It was in the employment of its land forces that Australia's attempts at defining and advancing its own strategic judgments were most prominent. In essence, the continued existence of the Second AIF as an effective fighting force was a more important objective in its own right for Australia than it was for Britain. As concerns arose about British planning, the extent of consultation and the increasing dispersal of AIF units in the campaigns in Greece and Syria in 1941, Australia demanded the relief of the 9th Division in Tobruk. Upon outbreak of the war in the Pacific, Australia insisted on the AIF returning home rather than being used to defend other parts of the Empire in Asia.[8]

In Australia, the Curtin government accepted US General Douglas MacArthur as Supreme Commander for the Allied Powers in the Southwest Pacific Area. There was thus little high-level visibility of the Australian defence effort, or Australian input into strategy, even while Australia provided the majority of the forces under MacArthur's command. As the focus of operations moved out of the immediate Australian neighbourhood and into the Philippines, Australian units relieved US forces in New Guinea and Bougainville and conducted landings on Borneo in 1945. None of these operations influenced how or when the war ended, other than at a local level. Since the operations in New Guinea helped liberate Australian territory and populations, that was an understandable and specifically Australian objective in its own right. Another consideration also weighed heavily, however, and justified the Borneo landings in particular: as long as US forces were still conducting major operations against Japan, the Australian government wanted its Army to be seen as also fully engaged, to strengthen Australia's voice in postwar settlements.[9]

Forward Defence

The 1945 landings in Tarakan and Balikpapan in Borneo were thus the first instance of a new, distinctly Australian approach to strategy in a coalition context in which Australia contributed to achieve a specific Australian—as opposed to shared Empire—interest. Aimed primarily at influence on its allies—rather than the adversary—these operations represented a shift to a more directly utilitarian approach than the contributions to the common defence that had preceded them. From now on, Australia paid increasing attention to achieving its own, specifically Australian objectives when making contributions in a larger coalition context.

This change was accentuated after World War II as decolonisation in Southeast Asia transformed Australia's strategic circumstances. Australia's region had been controlled by the same powers that were also of immediate importance to Britain before the war—especially France and the Netherlands, the United States and Japan. Now, Australia increasingly found itself in a region of independent Asian countries. Concern about how its new neighbours perceived Australia was a significant factor behind its reluctance to accede to British requests for forces in Malaya in the late 1940s, and to a US push for allied military support to France in Indochina in 1954.[10] Although less prominent than later deployments to the region, these considerations highlight how Australia began to make decisions about the use of force in ways that more directly considered political costs and benefits for itself—in other words, in more strategic terms.

The first decision to commit Australian forces to combat after World War II followed the North Korean attack on the South in June 1950. Minister for External Affairs Percy Spender saw an opportunity to advance Australia's aim of a formal alliance treaty with the United States. On 17 July, he wrote to prime minister Menzies that '[f]rom Australia's long-term point of view any additional aid we can give to the US now, small though it may be, will repay us in the future one hundred fold'.[11] Once the Australian government learned that Britain would commit ground forces, it took advantage of time zones to decide and proclaim a similar contribution before London announced its own.[12] The way Australian forces were used in the theatre itself, however, had little bearing on the political considerations that caused them to be there in the first place.

By the end of the Korean War (1950–53), Australia had decided to focus its defence efforts on supporting and encouraging United Kingdom and United States efforts in Southeast Asia, rather than making contributions in accordance with global, Western priorities in the Middle East and beyond. This was the essence of the Forward Defence strategy, through which Australia tried to bind its major allies to the Southeast Asian region. In 1955, Australia committed a battalion to the Commonwealth Strategic Reserve in Malaya. While this force would also be used in the Malayan Emergency, Australia's immediate considerations were to gain insight and influence in the strategy of the United Kingdom and the United States in Asia. In the same vein, the Menzies government decided on three occasions during the Laos crises of 1959 and 1960–61 that Australia would commit forces to a possible intervention of the Southeast Asia Treaty Organisation (SEATO). Again, the objective was to encourage and influence United Kingdom and United States policy and military planning.[13]

From 1961, Britain faced increasing Indonesian provocations and incursions as part of Indonesia's policy of 'Confrontation' against Malaysia. Australia committed forces to support Britain in a gradual manner, mindful of regional perception and the danger of Indonesian retaliation against Australian-controlled Papua New Guinea. US support would have been important to Australia if conflict with Indonesia had escalated, but at the same time, the United States began more direct involvement in Vietnam. In this context, Australia's participation in the Vietnam War was then based on four related considerations that mirrored those of earlier commitments—to gain general political credit for Australia in the United States; to gain insight and influence into US policy and strategy discussions on Vietnam; to encourage US commitment to fight communism in Southeast Asia; and to increase the willingness of the United States to support Australia directly in a possible escalation of the Indonesian Confrontation. For these aims, Australia made a maximum contribution that was a quarter the size of that by the United States, relative to each country's overall population.[14]

Australian Strategic Policy, 'Defence of Australia' and 'Self-Reliance'

It is perhaps inevitable that the historical narrative of defence and strategy is dominated by the recollection of the wars a nation has fought. Yet although Australia's contribution to the Commonwealth Strategic Reserve in Malaya is mostly remembered for its involvement in the Malayan Emergency and Indonesian Confrontation, it was not specifically sent for those conflicts. Earlier, Australia had sent personnel to man two fighter squadrons (using British planes) in Malta in 1952–54, which participated in North Atlantic Treaty Organization (NATO) exercises throughout the Middle East and Europe. Between 1962–68, an Australian fighter squadron was forward-based in Thailand.

All three of these deployments—in Malaya, Malta and Thailand—marked another step in the evolution of Australia's approach to strategy, because Australian forces were not committed to fight along-side allies in ongoing conflicts. Rather, they were forward based to contribute to deterrence of possible aggression and to signal Australia's strategic commitment to the common defence. In each case the larger deterrence strategy was one that rested on the military capability of the allies rather than of Australia itself. However, Australia's defence relationships with Malaysia and Singapore through the Five Power Defence Arrangements—a holdover from the Forward Defence era—still include an element of forward-basing that is testament to this time. Mirage aircraft returned to Australia from Malaysia's Butterworth airbase in the 1980s, but an Australian rifle company and military staff in the Integrated Air Defence System remain there to this day.

Overall, however, forward deployment, standing international headquarters and the use of forces to signal political commitment are far more prominent in other US alliances—in NATO in particular—than they are for Australia. At a time that European countries increased their integration in NATO in the early 1970s, Australia's involvement in the Cold War was reduced to the joint facilities, and maritime surveillance of the Soviet Navy in Southeast Asia. The United Kingdom withdrew from Asia and looked to integrate with Europe rather than the Commonwealth. Domestically the Department of Defence and intelligence agencies moved from their colonial-era Melbourne settings and mind-sets to Canberra, and the election of the Whitlam government ended twenty-three years of conservative rule. Externally, US-Sino rapprochement and the fall of Sukarno made Australia's strategic environment far less threatening. This is the context in which Australia focused on the defence of the continent far more than it had done before—in particular, it sought to be able to do so self-reliantly without assistance by the combat forces of its allies.

A defence policy based on self-reliance in the Defence of Australia (DoA) posed new and difficult problems, both practically and conceptually. In practical terms, the topography, climate and expanse of Northern Australia are challenging for surveillance and response, and few ADF units or installations existed outside the Southeast of the continent. The expectation that the ADF should prepare to fight independently, rather than as part of a larger allied force, challenged longstanding service traditions. The consequence of Australia's relatively benign strategic environment was that force development focused on low-intensity threats and assumed years of warning of more significant adversaries. As a result, Australia's force structure and posture began to diverge significantly from those of the United Kingdom and United States, which focused on the Soviet threat to Europe.[15]

Yet, there were also significant continuities between the DoA era and earlier times. Australia did not end its alliances and it remained politically committed to the West. The policy of self-reliance did not equate to self-sufficiency and Australia continued to assume significant support from its allies in logistics, resupply and intelligence, as well as direct support in case of a threat from a large power. As such, Australia's turn to the defence of the continent after Vietnam can be understood in terms of the two enduring defence responsibilities that British dominions had carried since the late nineteenth century—to make contributions to the Empire's main effort globally and to defend themselves against attacks locally. Where to strike the balance between these two tasks had been contested in the Australian defence debates since Federation. In general,

Britain had consistently sought to emphasise wider Empire over specifically Australian concerns. In the 1969 Guam doctrine, however, the United States made explicit that it now expected (and accepted) that its Pacific allies would take greater responsibility for their own local defence.

Local defence had remained a strong Australian concern even during the Forward Defence era. It was the reason why Australia maintained the Citizen Military Forces, which were not available for service overseas. Even in the development of Australia's regular forces, considerations of local defence had become a prominent consideration from the early 1960s. The force structure of the modern ADF was largely created in the defence build-up during the Indonesian Confrontation, when Australia acquired Adams-class air warfare destroyers, F-111 and Mirage fighter aircraft.[16] All of these capabilities were of secondary importance to Australia's forward defence posture, but essential for defending Australia itself against Indonesia. In that sense, DoA was not a new preoccupation, but a continuing concern that had been overshadowed by the immediate operational commitments in Southeast Asia.

Australian strategic guidance documents during the late 1940s had pointed to logistic and efficiency reasons as the main justification for why Australia should assume responsibilities for local defence. From the late 1950s, however, the government's senior defence advisors had also begun to emphasise that Australia's allies might not be able to come to its assistance to the extent that Canberra would want them to, or may not be willing to do so, because of diverging strategic priorities. These considerations were reinforced by US equivocation in the West Papua dispute of the 1950s, and the prospect of the Indonesian Confrontation extending to Papua New Guinea in the 1960s. First voiced explicitly in the classified 1959 Strategic Basis document, classified guidance emphasised this consideration far more explicitly than public defence policy statements. The 1976 Strategic Basis in particular discussed in great detail why 'the general proposition about Australia's security from major military threat, and the assurance of US combat support, need qualification in respect of Indonesia'.[17]

What this should mean for Australian force structure, force posture and strategy, when there seemed little prospect of conflict with regional countries, remained the subject of acrimonious debate from the 1970s and into the 1990s. Only in the 1987 Defence White Paper did Australia express a military strategy of 'defence-in-depth' to underpin the self-reliant defence of the country. It was based on maritime interdiction by air and naval forces in the air-sea gap to Australia's north, and air and special forces to strike against enemy bases in the archipelago. Army's role was focused on the protection of the central Darwin-Katherine area and forward bases, and the defeat of such limited incursions on the mainland that could be expected.[18] The priorities that were set by the 1987 Defence White Paper guided the development of the ADF over the following decade, including in training and doctrine and the move of 1 Brigade to Darwin, the completion of the bare air base network across the North, the creation of the *Jindalee* over-the-horizon radar-network and the eventual acquisition of in-flight refuelling and airborne early warning and control aircraft.

The 'Concentric Circles' Synthesis of Australian Strategic Policy

The 1987 Defence White Paper was the high watermark of the DoA strategic policy, as it provided the detailed conceptual framework and capability development priorities that its predecessor of 1976 had not addressed. Yet, DoA was primarily a policy for the way the ADF was structured and postured, and not for the circumstances in which it was most likely to be used. The 1987 Defence White Paper itself mentioned that Australian forces might support US operations elsewhere.[19] Within months of this White Paper's release, the government approved sending mine clearance divers to protect shipping in the Persian Gulf (a plan that, in the end, was overtaken by events). Within a few years, Australia participated in United Nations peacekeeping operations in Namibia and Cambodia, the First Gulf War and humanitarian interventions in Somalia and Rwanda. Australia's objectives in making these contributions—which were all small, relative to those of other coalition partners and also relative to the size of the ADF—reflected those of earlier conflicts: to gain political credit from its allies,[20] and to support a system of collective security and liberal internationalism that echoed

Australian's value-based contributions to Imperial adventures before Federation.

The ADF did not have to defend Australia directly (although its contributions to border protection since 2004 reflect some of the elements of low-level conflict postulated in the 1970s and 1980s, and make use of facilities and systems acquired for that purpose). The need for self-reliance however did arise in the use of the ADF for regional stabilisation, which had not been foreseen by strategic policymakers in previous decades. The 1987 Operation *Morris Dance* to prepare for the evacuation of Australian citizens after the coup in Fiji highlighted that Australia's responsibility for local defence—to its own citizens and the wider international community—might require ADF operations beyond the continent. Australia's first longer operational commitment to regional security began in 1997, when it provided peace monitoring personnel on Bougainville.

The operation that most clearly demonstrated the importance of regional stabilisation for Australian strategy and strategic policy was the 1999 International Force for East Timor (INTERFET) mission.[21] After widespread communal violence following the independence vote in East Timor, Australia deployed more than 5 500 ADF personnel to bring order to the new nation. Association of Southeast Asian Nations (ASEAN) countries and others, including the United Kingdom, contributed forces but overall command and responsibility for the success of the operation rested with Australia. INTERFET was followed by the deployment of ADF and Australian Federal Police (AFP) in the Regional Assistance Mission to Solomon Islands (RAMSI) from 2003, as well as smaller deployments to help restore public order in East Timor, Solomon Islands and Tonga in 2006 (see Chapter 6).

It fell to the Howard government's 2000 Defence White Paper to balance the demands from stabilising the neighbourhood, with those of defending Australia itself and contributing to coalition operations further afield. The 2000 Defence White Paper established a strategic framework that was largely confirmed in the Coalition government's *Defence Update* in 2007 and also used by the Rudd and Gillard governments in their White Papers of 2009 and 2013. As such, it represents what might be called the current bi-partisan orthodoxy of Australian defence policy.[22] All three defence white papers since 2000 have aligned the discussion of Australian strategic interests, the objectives that the Australian government might want to achieve by using the ADF on operations and even the way the ADF should be structured with four or five particular geographic areas. For each area, they defined particular 'strategic' (2000) or 'principal' (in 2009 and 2013) 'tasks' for the ADF (the term 'quadrant' is also commonly used in the defence organisation since the 2009 White Paper). Although they are neither concentric nor circular, the term 'concentric circles' has become a popular shorthand for the overall approach.

Self-reliant DoA is the first task (or 'quadrant one'). The second task (or 'quadrant two') is support to the external and internal security of the Southwest Pacific and East Timor, where Australia wants to be able to have a lead role. Stabilisation missions in this region are thus a major force structure determinant for Army in particular since 2000. The next tasks relate to international stability in Asia—the 2000 Defence White Paper distinguished separate objectives for Southeast Asia and the Asia-Pacific as a whole; the 2009 Defence White Paper combined the two into one, while the 2013 Defence White Paper refers to the wider 'Indo-Pacific' (although all of them acknowledged the particular importance of Southeast Asia). While this task is not considered as a direct determinant of the structure of the ADF, the forces acquired and maintained for tasks one and two should be postured so they can make a 'substantial' contribution to coalition operations. The last task in all three White Papers was to contribute to operations in support of a functioning global security system.

Within this policy framework, Australia participated in the US-led coalitions in Afghanistan in 2001 and Iraq in 2003. Operations in the Middle East were politically prominent over the 2000s and strained parts of the ADF, which had to maintain them in parallel with commitments in the Southwest Pacific. But they did conform to the way Australia has made relatively small contributions to international operations for diplomatic reasons in the past, and were thus largely in accordance with the concentric circle framework.[23]

In Afghanistan, Australia's initial participation was driven by a shared sense of outrage over international terrorism. There and in Iraq two years later, however, Australian forces were largely withdrawn after the initial invasions. When ADF contingents returned in later years, it was largely for alliance and diplomatic reasons. Special operations forces redeployed to Afghanistan from 2005, followed by a provincial reconstruction team in Oruzgan province. (Unlike in Vietnam, Australia declined to take responsibility for command of international operations in the province until the withdrawal was decided.) In Iraq, Australia returned on a training and oversight mission when asked for assistance by Britain and Japan, which had an engineering unit deployed in the area. In both cases, Australia's main interest in the way its forces were employed was the desire— more successful in Iraq than in Afghanistan—to restrict them to regions and missions that minimised Australian casualties.

Insofar as distinct strategy underpinned Australian operations in the Southwest Pacific, it was that Australia consistently stuck to robust peacekeeping (rather than peace enforcement). The ADF was always deployed after invitation by the local government, as part of a regional coalition under the auspices of an international organisation—even if Australia was generally the de-facto leader. Initial stages of INTERFET and RAMSI had heavy ADF involvement to over-match possible adversaries, but generally Australian interventions were 'whole-of-government' efforts that included major contributions from the AFP.[24]

Australian Strategic Policy and Geostrategic Change in Asia

Recent history and strategic guidance thus reflect consistent Australian strategies for operations in support of the second (Southwest Pacific) and fourth (global stability) tasks. In contrast, there is much less to go on in relation to the first (DoA) and third (Indo-Pacific) tasks—both in terms of the role of armed force in Australia's international commitments and in the way the ADF should operate to support them. A combination of self-reliance and defence-in-depth was a credible strategy to defend Australia against Indonesia in the absence of direct US support. Like all strategic concerns, however, that particular one was also a product of its time, when the Asia-Pacific region was remarkably stable and peaceful, and the attention of great powers, including the United States, was focused elsewhere. This does not mean that the traditional, 1987 posture of self-reliance has lost its usefulness as a way of conceiving Australia's defence—but it is a posture of last resort, more useful for decisions about enduring force structure priorities than as a substitute for a strategy that explains how the ADF would be used to avoid that situation arising in the first place.

Australian strategic guidance over the last forty years has acknowledged that the emergence of a direct threat would result from a long development, which Australian governments would seek to influence beforehand, including through the use of armed force. Today, these developments are potentially in train. On the basis of its economic rise, China has been significantly and consistently increasing its military capabilities over the past two decades. It is acquiring air and maritime platforms, sensors and weapons that enable it to contest control of the seas at increasing distance from its coastline (see Figure 8.1). Moreover, it is becoming more assertive in the use of force in territorial disputes with US allies and partners. In response to regional concerns, the United States is re-focusing its military posture in the region to engage Southeast Asian countries far more closely than at any time since the Vietnam War, and to be better positioned for a Chinese attempt to deny the United States access to Asia in wartime.

Economic growth in Southeast Asia itself has not yet eliminated Australia's traditional military edge in the region, but the gap is shrinking and regional countries are becoming more self-confident at engaging outside powers on security issues. This does not mean that a specific direct threat to Australia is in prospect, let alone imminent or even particularly likely. However, uncertainty about the future shape of Australia's strategic environment is increasing and Australia has a strong interest in regional arrangements that reduce, rather than increase the risk of conflict in general, and to Australia in particular. The way the Australian government will use the ADF as part of a wider policy to support international stability in the Indo-Pacific—and especially in Southeast Asia—will shape the strategic environment from which direct threats to Australia might otherwise emerge, and within which Australia might have to defend itself directly in the future. As such, it is becoming more difficult to conceive of the first and third objectives in isolation. How Australia can influence, within its limited capabilities, geostrategic change in Asia is the most significant challenge for the way it thinks about the use of force in coming decades.

Figure 8.1: China's Anti-Access-Area Denial Ranges

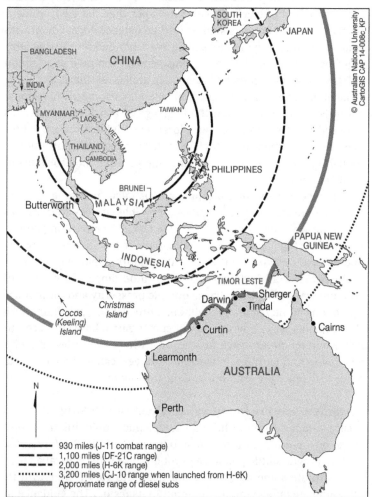

930 miles (J-11 combat range)
1,100 miles (DF-21C range)
2,000 miles (H-6K range)
3,200 miles (CJ-10 range when launched from H-6K)
Approximate range of diesel subs

Source: Map based on information from J Thomas, Z Cooper and I Rehman, Gateway to the Indo-Pacific: Australian Defense Strategy and the Future of the Australia-US Alliance', *Center for Strategic and Budgetary Assessments, Washington DC, 2013, p. 14.*

Today's Australian strategic policy however has little to offer in this regard. All three Defence white papers since 2000 have framed Australia's use of force in terms of 'contributions', emphasising the largely reactive way Australia has committed the ADF to operations in the past. In the 2013 Defence White Paper, the Gillard government placed increased emphasis on peacetime defence engagement with Asia, but ultimately failed to explain even in broad terms what strategic logic should underpin this engagement. It hinted at common defence to counter 'coercion' against Australia's 'partners', but also a more indirect and limited strategy of building the capacity of regional countries, and even evoked the language of common security (as opposed to common defence). Moreover, it is far from clear how defence engagement would relate to the 'substantial' contributions to high-intensity conflict in Asia that the government also wants to be able to make.[25]

In recent years, the concept of an Australian 'maritime strategy' has been advanced by the ADF as a possible strategy that bridges operations in support of the first three tasks.[26] The resulting debate has usefully highlighted Army's potential role beyond the continent and its relationship with the Navy, the enduring relevance of geography for Australia's defence and the importance of sea lines of communication for Australia's economic prosperity and for military operations in the region. Yet, without a broader strategic framework that explains what operational outcomes Australia would seek to achieve in relation to each task, against what adversaries and with what allies and partners, a 'maritime strategy' cannot be a practical guide to defence preparations and the use of force.

Towards a New Era in Australian 'Defence Thinking'

Australia today does not have a strategy that would link the use of force, or the threat of force, to stability in the Indo-Pacific region. History provides little guidance beyond the fact that Australia tends to contribute somewhat opportunistically, to gain favour with its allies and encourage them to commit to its region. The guidance in the 2013 Defence White Paper is essentially that the ADF could be used in any way that helps bring stability, peace and harmony to the region and that contributes to the general betterment of humankind. Neither is helpful as a guide to any practical decisions about priorities in force structure, posture, defence engagement and diplomacy, nor to the types of defence commitments Australia should be willing to enter (or avoid) in the region.

Developing such a strategy will be the main issue occupying Australia's 'defence thinking' in coming decades. Here, the concentric circle approach may be more hindrance than help because there are two assumptions embedded in it that are unlikely to be true in the future. The first assumption is that strategic interest, objective and ADF operations to achieve the related tasks could all be confined within the same geographic area. This is unlikely to be true as the reach of China's anti-access and area denial capability extends from the mainland. Already the United States is becoming seriously interested in strategies for conflict with China that include maritime interdiction campaigns in Southeast Asia and in operating from bases in Australia that would also need defending.

The second assumption is that balancing Australia's effort between the four tasks mainly relates to force structure priorities—hence the emphasis on graduated levels of contributions and focus on the roles of Army, Air Force and Navy in Australian strategic policy. In the future, however, that balance is likely to be more one of operational effort and immediate strategic priority, as it had been in the two World Wars and, to some extent, in Australia's strategic planning during the Indonesian Confrontation. As the current strategic framework treats each task in isolation, however, it is not well suited to examine the practical and political questions that Australia would face in such a conflict.

The last two Defence white papers have begun to acknowledge both developments, when they explicitly mentioned that Australia might have to keep forces in reserve for the defence of the continent as part of a regional conflict.[27] The political and strategic context of such operations would be very different to that envisaged during the DoA era. Australia would already be engaged alongside coalition partners, with US and ADF units likely to operate from Australian bases and conducting operations against an adversary across the wider area of operations in Southeast Asia. The concept of 'self-reliance' might even distract from consideration of the practical questions and their political implications that would be involved, especially regarding command and control of coalition forces operating from Australia—and possibly ADF units operating from regional countries to defend Australia itself. There will still be considerations about the extent to which Australia would want to become dependent on its allies—Australian concerns may well be about its priority for the resupply with scarce US war stocks and munitions, which had generally been assumed in the past as available for any major ADF operation.

Australian strategy will need to be developed in the context of US strategy for the region. That strategy is only slowly emerging and the speed and direction in which it will develop strongly depends on decisions that are yet to be taken in Washington, Beijing and other capitals in the region. However, increased interest in the US defence debate in possible Australian contributions is already clear.[28] Sooner or later, Australia will be confronted with the need or expectation to contribute forces to specific US commitments in the region, if it wants to gain and maintain influence, or even mere insight into the policy and operational planning of its major ally. That, at least, is a significant lesson from Australia's experience during the Forward Defence era.

Where Australia will place the emphasis among the tasks of the concentric circle framework will thus become a core question, with significant political implications for its relationship with its major ally. Political commitment and force structure priorities will be closely entwined, as they were when Australia had to balance preparations for local defence with contributions to the Empire's main effort until the late 1940s. The employment of land forces in the islands of Southeast Asia in future decades, for example, would likely call for high-end capabilities including amphibious forces, land-based anti-ship cruise missiles and organic air defence. The opportunity cost of focusing the Australian Army on stabilisation operations in the Southwest Pacific would thus significantly increase, especially as the United States makes arguments about alliance burden sharing in Southeast Asia. In that context, it might soon be able to point to a joint amphibious group, based on US marines in Darwin and contributions from the region, which could be used to collectively manage regional concerns in Southeast Asia and the Southwest Pacific.

Australian strategy will have to balance competing objectives as part of peacetime commitments and defence preparations, but also in light of Australia's influence on a possible postwar settlement. During World War II, this consideration saw Australian forces undertake the Borneo landings in 1945, with ultimately little military as opposed to political value. Today, the situation is different as Australia is already in a close alliance with the United States, which it could use to discuss a more meaningful role for Australia as part of the wider US posture and war plans in the region (see Chapter 9). Whether such war plans should assume that the ADF will operate as a joint force—with geographic responsibility in areas that are of particular importance to Australia, or whether Australia would have more influence if it allowed its forces to be subsumed into US operations as military expediency dictates—is yet another question that will shape Australian strategy in years to come.

In a way, none of these are strategic problems that are completely new for Australia. All of them relate to the core balance Australia has had to strike in its strategy and strategic policy since before Federation, between local defence and contributions to the wider allied war effort. But the last time Australia directly confronted them is effectively beyond the living memory of today's policymakers and politicians. Even if the themes and challenges that Australian strategy and strategic policy will confront in coming years and decades are historically familiar, Australia is still likely to enter a new era in its 'defence thinking'.

Further Reading

Evans, Michael, *The Tyranny of Dissonance: Australia's Strategic Culture and Way of War 1901–2005*, no. 306, *Land Warfare Studies Centre Study Paper*, Land Warfare Studies Centre, Canberra, 2005.

Frühling, Stephan, *A History of Australian Strategic Policy Since 1945*, Commonwealth of Australia, Canberra, 2009.

Grey, Jeffrey, *A Military History of Australia*, 3rd ed., Cambridge University Press, Melbourne, 2008.

White, Hugh, 'Strategic Interests in Australian Defence Policy: Some Historical and Methodological Reflections', *Security Challenges*, vol. 4, no. 2, 2008, pp. 63–79. www.securitychallenges.org.au/ArticlePDFs/vol4no2White.pdf.

Australian Defence White Papers and Defence Reviews, available at www. defence.gov.au/oscdf/se/publications.htm.

Notes

1   TB Millar, *Australia's Defence*, Melbourne University Press, Carlton, 1965, p. 5.
2   The *Australia Act 1986* severed the last legislative and judicial links between the United Kingdom and Australia.

3   D Fromkin, 'Entangling Alliances', *Foreign Affairs*, vol. 48, no. 4, July 1970, p. 688.

4   Quoted in J Grey, *A Military History of Australia*, 3rd edn., Cambridge University Press, Melbourne, 2008, p. 80.

5   Quoted in LC Key, 'Australia in Commonwealth and World Affairs, 1939–1944', *International Affairs*, vol. 21, no. 1, 1945, p. 67.

6   J Grey, *A Military History of Australia*, 2008, pp. 80–118.

7   ibid., pp. 140–59.

8   D Horner, *High Command*, Allen & Unwin, Sydney, 1992, pp. 65–128.

9   ibid., pp. 408–9.

10   P Edwards, *Crises and Commitments*, Allen & Unwin, Sydney, 1992, pp. 31–62, 120–38.

11   Quoted in R O'Neill, *Australia in the Korean War 1950–1953: Volume 1, Strategy and Diplomacy*, Australian War Memorial and Commonwealth of Australia, Canberra, 1981, p. 65.

12   After the North Korean attack and before committing ground forces, Australia committed a fighter squadron based in Japan to Korea and a bomber squadron to Malaya.

13   P Edwards, *Crises and Commitments*, 1992, pp. 160–81, 208–228.

14   F Frost, *Australia's War in Vietnam*, Allen & Unwin, Sydney, 1987, pp. 6–28; Edwards, *Crises and Commitments*, 1992, pp. 340–7, 361–2.

15   A Thompson, *Defence Down Under: Evolution and Revolution 1971–88*, no. 40, *Working Papers in Australia Studies*, Sir Robert Menzies Centre for Australian Studies, University of London, London, 1988.

16   The main exception is the aircraft carrier capability, which was not replaced in the 1980s.

17   Defence Committee, *Australian Strategic Analysis and Defence Policy Objectives*, 2 September 1976, para 86, reproduced in S Frühling (ed), *A History of Australian Strategic Policy Since 1945*, Commonwealth of Australia, Canberra, 2009, p. 565.

18   Commonwealth of Australia, *The Defence of Australia*, Commonwealth of Australia, Canberra, 1987, para. 3.44–3.50.

19   ibid., para 1.17.

20   The United States saw the Australian contribution to the Tanker War as a 'test' of its willingness to support its alliance partner. K Beazley, 'Operation Sandglass: Old History, Contemporary Lessons', *Security Challenges*, vol. 4, no. 3, 2008, pp. 23–43. www.securitychallenges.org.au/ ArticlePDFs/vol4no3Beazley.pdf (viewed January 2014).

21   For an overview on Australia's military operations in the neighbourhood up to and including INTERFET, see B Breen, *Struggling for Self Reliance*, Australian University Press, Canberra, 2008. www.press.anu.edu.au/sdsc/ sfsr/html/frames.php (viewed January 2014).

22   Commonwealth of Australia, *Defence 2000: Our Future Defence Force*, Commonwealth of Australia, Canberra, 2000, Chapters 4 and 6. www. defence.gov.au/publications/wpaper2000.pdf (viewed January 2014); Commonwealth of Australia, *Defending Australia in the Asia-Pacific Century: Force 2030*, Commonwealth of Australia, Canberra, 2009,

Chapter 3. www.defence.gov.au/whitepaper2009/docs/defence_white_paper_2009.pdf (viewed January 2014), www.defence.gov.au/publications/wpaper2000.pdf (viewed January 2014); Commonwealth of Australia, *Defence White Paper 2013*, Commonwealth of Australia, Canberra, 2013, Chapters 5–7. www.defence.gov.au/whitepaper2013/docs/WP_2013_web.pdf (viewed January 2014).

23 See A Palazzo, 'The Making of Strategy and the Junior Coalition Partner: Australia and the 2003 Iraq War', *Infinity Journal*, vol. 2, no. 4, 2012, pp. 27–30. www.infinityjournal.com/article/83/The_Making_of_Strategy_and_the_Junior_Coalition_Partner_Australia_and_the_2003_Iraq_War/ (viewed January 2014).

24 For RAMSI strategy, see R Glenn, *Counterinsurgency in a Test Tube: Analyzing the Success of the Regional Assistance Mission to Solomon Islands (RAMSI)*, RAND, Santa Monica, CA, 2007. www.rand.org/content/dam/rand/pubs/monographs/2007/RAND_MG551.pdf (viewed January 2014).

25 Commonwealth of Australia, *Defence White Paper 2013*, 2013, paras. 3.54, 3.56, 6.2, 6.5, 6.37.

26 See J Jones (ed), *A Maritime School of Strategic Thought for Australia: Perspectives*, Sea Power Centre, Canberra, 2013.

27 Commonwealth of Australia, *Defence White Paper 2013*, 2013, para 3.57; Commonwealth of Australia, *Force 2030: Defending Australia in the Asia-Pacific Century*, 2009, para. 7.18.

28 See for example J Thomas, Z Cooper and I Rehman, *Gateway to the Indo-Pacific: Australian Defense Strategy and the Future of the Australia-US Alliance*, Center for Strategic and Budgetary Assessments, Washington DC, 2013. www.csbaonline.org/publications/2013/11/gateway-to-the-indo-pacific-australian-defense-strategy-and-the-future-of-the-australia-u-s-alliance-2/ (viewed January 2014).

9

ANZUS: The 'Alliance' and its Future in Asia

Peter J Dean

On 16 January 2013, the United Kingdom and Australia signed a Defence and Security Co-operation Treaty. The parties announced that the treaty would give 'strategic direction' to the relationship and that there was potential for cooperation over the development of new capabilities. This new treaty would have fitted nicely with TB Millar's conception of Australia's alliance relationships. When he wrote *Australia's Defence* in 1965, Millar looked forward to an era, in the not too distant future, when the ANZUS Treaty between Australia, New Zealand and the United States would be extended to include Great Britain.[1] Despite Millar's wish, the tide had turned against him. It was clear by then that while there was still some intersection between Australia's two 'great and powerful friends,' the ties to the old ally Great Britain were held together more by common values and the vestiges of the past than shared strategic interests. Australia's strategic policy from this time onward was firmly centered on ANZUS and the Australia-United States (US) alliance.

It is important for any discussion of the Australia-US relationship to displace the ANZUS Treaty from the Australia-US 'Alliance' and the broader relationship. The Treaty sets out very specific terms and conditions that are unlikely to be revisited or changed into the future; whether or not its articles are reflective of the current state of the relationship. Despite its seemingly intractable nature, for over sixty years the Treaty has provided the foundation for the Alliance. The Alliance differs from the Treaty in that it includes all of the relationship building measures, engagement activities and shared history that has developed between Australia and the United States since the Treaty was signed in 1951. Beyond this security partnership is the broader 'relationship' between the two countries. This includes all of the other areas of engagement such as economic and cultural engagement. It must be noted here, that there is not always a direct correlation between the close nature of the security partnership and other areas of the relationship.[2]

Understanding Alliances

The defence relationship that Australia has with the United States is built on the back of a formal alliance. Alliances are commitments for security cooperation between two or more states that are usually formed in response to a major security threat. These can be formal commitments, like the North Atlantic Treaty, ANZUS, the US-Japan alliance and the US-South Korea alliance. Alternatively, they can also be informal (de facto) alliances like the relationship between the US-Taiwan and the US-Singapore; or they can take the form of a coalition, that is a temporary ad hoc arrangement between states for a specific purpose.

Alliances have various roles and functions. They can amass power by combining the forces of different states for the same strategic objective. They can be used to 'influence' partners within the alliance as well as being used to influence the behaviour of adversaries. They can enable conflict and they have also been seen to either promote stability through predictability in international affairs (the Cold War) or act as a destabilising influence (pre-World War I).

Alliances can be symmetrical, between states of a similar size, or as in the case of ANZUS asymmetrical—where there is a major power (the United States) and a smaller power (Australia). Another major factor in the consideration of alliances is that they may or may not come with a security guarantee; which is a commitment for the members of the alliance to give assistance to any act of aggression against treaty partners. This, for instance, is one of the major differences between an alliance like the North Atlantic Treaty (establishing NATO), which includes a specific security guarantee and ANZUS which does not.

Alliances come with a classic security dilemma: entrapment versus abandonment. In alliance relationships, especially asymmetrical ones, the smaller power often fears being abandoned in their hour of need. The major power, however, can be concerned about being entrapped in a confrontation or war in which they do not deemed to be in their strategic interests. Alternatively, the smaller power may well feel entrapped by the actions of their larger partner or a larger power may well be abandoned by a smaller power.

For instance Australia has long suffered from a fear of invasion as a result of its strategic circumstances and history. This has led it to contemplate the alliance abandonment dilemma. Australia faced such a position in early 1942 when Great Britain was unable to meet its obligations due to its decline as a major power and its concurrent commitments to the war in Europe and the Middle East. This episode was, as Rob Lyon has noted, a 'salutary warning about the dangers of a smaller power becoming too reliant on a great power to protect it'.[3]

At times abandonment issues have arisen in ANZUS due to the lack of a formal, written, security guarantee. For instance, during the early part of the Cold War Australia had major concerns over the extent to which ANZUS covered Australian troops fighting in Borneo during the Indonesian Confrontation. In addition there were questions as to the applicability of some sections of the ANZUS Treaty and its application in the event of an Indonesian attack on the Australian territory of Papua New Guinea.[4]

Alliance entrapment is also a significant issue. For instance the contemporary Asia-Pacific strategic landscape has seen a more assertive China in recent years and this has led to rising tensions between China and Japan in East Asia including over the disputed Senkaku/Diaoyu island chain. While the United States has endeavoured to support its Japanese ally it has made it clear that it wishes to see 'China and Japan resolve this matter peacefully through dialogue'.[5] The US intention is to not be entrapped by any rash Japanese actions in relation to China over the islands, while at the same time reassuring the Japanese that they will not be abandoned if attacked by China. For other US allies in the region, such as Australia, the question is then raised as to the extent of which US involvement in a conflict with China, sparked by a Sino-Japanese dispute, would involve countries like Australia as a result of their treaty obligations with the US?[6]

'Australia's Great and Powerful Friends'

Since British colonisation in 1788 Australia has only ever had Great Britain and the United States as its chief alliance partners. While Australia has maintained alliances with other states, such as New Zealand and Papua New Guinea, and alignments/security agreements with many more, these two major power relationships have dominated Australian strategic policy. This is, to a large extent, a result of Australia's enduring strategic geography and circumstances.

Being the sixth largest country in the world and the only one of the top six to be completely surrounded by water, Australia is a classic trade-dependent maritime state. It has a strong Western cultural identity, while its geography is Asian. The combination of its large land mass, location in Asia and Western cultural heritage, along with its small population and rich natural resources, means that Australians have always felt an acute sense of '(a tyranny of) distance' from the West. This means that, as former minister for Defence Kim Beazley has noted, 'we live in a large, sparsely populated, resource rich continent that is vulnerable to attack'.[7] All of these factors have meant that the 'popular fear—which still lingers in the collective consciousness—[is] that the country [is] indefensible'.[8]

As such it was to the British Empire, and specifically the Royal Navy, that Australia looked to guarantee Australian security in Asia up until 1941. While from 1942 it has been the United States Navy that has guaranteed it since. The only time that Australia did face the possibility of invasion was when this Anglo-Saxon maritime dominance of the Asia-Pacific became contested in the early phase of the war in the Pacific (1941–42).

Despite the grand rhetoric at the start of the Pacific War from Australia's Prime Minister, John Curtin, that 'without any inhibitions of any kind, I make it quite clear that Australia looks to America, free of any pangs as to our traditional links or kinship with the United

Kingdom'[9], this speech did not mark the beginning of an alliance between Australia and the United States. As the US Commander-in-Chief in Australian during the war, General Douglas MacArthur, made clear to Curtin in 1942:

> Australia was part of the British Empire and it was related to Britain and the other dominions by ties of blood, sentiment and allegiance to the Crown. *The United States* was an ally whose aim was to win the war, and it *has no sovereign interest in the integrity of Australia* ... In view of the strategical importance of Australia in a war with Japan, this course of military action would probably be followed *irrespective of the American relationship to the people who might be occupying Australia.*[10]

At the end of World War II, the path to ANZUS was not easy. In the post-war period it was soon apparent that the collective security system being developed through the United Nations (UN) was not adequate and that Australia was unable to defend herself unaided against a major power. Its security was, therefore, again intrinsically linked to the British Empire; for although it also saw US assistance as essential, it placed no reliance on this assistance being forthcoming, given the experience of relations with the United States in, and between, the two world wars.[11]

The dominant view of the formation of ANZUS is that Australian diplomats skilfully acquired the treaty in 1951 by exploiting the United States' desire to gain Australian and New Zealand acquiescence on a lenient peace treaty with Japan.[12] However there is an equally strong claim that the US treaties with Japan, Australia, New Zealand and the Philippines in 1951 were also desired by the United States as part of its policy of the containment of communism during the early phases of the Cold War. Thus it was not the major Australian diplomatic coup that it is often portrayed as.[13]

Despite the signing of ANZUS in 1951 it was not to become preeminent in Australian strategy and defence policy for another thirteen years. In the intervening period Australia made the most of its Commonwealth partnership in the British Commonwealth

Occupation Force (BCOF) in Japan, the Korean War, the Malayan Emergency and the Indonesian Confrontation. During this period Australia strategic policy had concentrated on a combination of collective security through: the British Commonwealth, ANZUS, the Southeast Asia Treaty Organisation (SEATO) and the UN.

In the post war period Australia came to realise that the UN had become deadlocked and largely ineffective in solving security problems, declining British power would lead to their withdrawal to behind the Suez Canal and that SEATO was highly ineffective. These measures and increasing cooperation with the United States meant that it was during the period 1963–65 that Australian strategic policy came to consider the relationship with the United States as Australia's most important strategic partnership.[14]

The Evolution of ANZUS

The formal Alliance was founded with the signing of the security treaty between Australia, New Zealand and the United States of America (ANZUS) in San Francisco on 1 September 1951 (see Appendix). It consists of eleven articles in order to coordinate the parties 'efforts for collective defense for the preservation of peace and security pending the development of a more comprehensive system of regional security in the Pacific Area'. The two critical articles of the Treaty are Articles I and IV which state:

Article IV
Each Party recognizes that an armed attack in the *Pacific Area* on any of the Parties would be dangerous to its own peace and safety and declares that it would act to meet the common danger *in accordance with its constitutional processes* ...

Article V
For the purpose of Article IV, an armed attack on any of the Parties is deemed to include an armed attack on the metropolitan territory of any of the Parties, or on the island territories under its jurisdiction *in the Pacific or on its armed forces, public vessels or aircraft in the Pacific.*

Two of the key elements of the Treaty are its geographic orientation to the Pacific and its lack of a security guarantee such as the one inherent in the North Atlantic Treaty. To many, including TB Millar, the restrictive language of the Treaty itself does not pose a significant problem. Millar argues that 'the degree of commitment under ANZUS is not in effect as vague as the letter of the treaty may indicate' as the United States could not, 'in the event of an overt attack... absolve themselves from action without a complete and public breach of faith'.[15]

The ANZUS Alliance has demonstrated that it has incredible resolve and the ability to adapt to the changing nature of strategic affairs. It can be said that over its sixty year history it has demonstrated the characteristics of an almost 'never ending' alliance; in that despite the changing strategic environment the Alliance has (and some would say unquestionably so) been able to redefine itself so as to maintain its central place in Australian strategic policy. This is because that since its inception, the ANZUS Alliance has continued to change its character to meet the challenges of the international environment. But while its character is ever changing, the underlying nature of the alliance—its support for the role of the 'west' in international affairs and for a world order buttressed by US power and international norms—has remained constant.

At its very beginning the Alliance was seen to perform two key roles: as a guarantee against a resurgence Japan in light of the events of the Pacific War (1941–1945) and a hedge against the rise of Communism. The latter soon became the dominate feature as Australia-Japan relations normalised and Japan was recognised as a key player in the United States' San Francisco alliance system.[16]

During the late 1950s and early 1960s ANZUS was of particular importance for two major reasons; post-colonial Indonesia's political leadership was oscillating between support for the Communist bloc and the west, and the spread of communist movements throughout Southeast Asia. This period of the Alliance also saw a dramatic increase in the sale of US military technology and weapon systems to Australia and the development of improved mechanisms to manage the security relationship and improve defence cooperation. However the key development was Australian participation in the war in South

Vietnam, the first time Australia had been involved in a conflict without the British.

Australian motivations for its involvement in the conflict were clear. As the Australian Minister-Counsellor in Washington, Alan Renouf, noted to the Menzies government:

> Our objective [in deciding to commit troops to South Vietnam] should be, it is suggested, to achieve such an habitual closeness of relations with the United States and sense of mutual alliance that in our time of need, after we have shown all reasonable restraint and good sense, the United States would have little option but to respond as we would want.
>
> The problem of Vietnam is one it seems where we could[,] without a disproportionate expenditure, pick up a lot of credit with the US[;] for this problem [Vietnam] is one to which the US is deeply committed and which it generally feels that it is carrying too much of the load, not so much the physical load, the bulk of which the US is prepared to bear, as the morale load.[17]

This approach was driven by Australia's desire to keep the United States heavily engaged in Southeast Asia. The major problem for the Menzies government was that it had a poor understanding of the nature of the war in South Vietnam and this meant that the political decision to commit Australian forces to the war did not translate into a coherent or an effective military role on the ground, although it did serve as an example of Australia's long term commitment to the Alliance. However the defeat in South Vietnam damaged the United States' regional and international standing, and in Australia, it also sparked some intense public criticism of the Alliance during the 1970's and into the 1980s.

The end of the Vietnam War was coupled with the Nixon (Guam) Doctrine, which emphasised that the Asia-Pacific allies of the US, like Australia, were required to provide for their own immediate security. In Australia these two factors spelled an end to the strategy of Forward Defence (1955–72) and a move to a focus on the 'self-reliant' Defence of Australia (DoA) (1973–97) within the Alliance framework. The basis of Australian security also moved to regional networks of cooperation and engagement; in particular post-Vietnam was a time when Australia began to seek security with, rather than from, Asia (see Chapter 7).

It must, however, be noted that 'self-reliance' is not self-sufficiency and Australian remained heavily reliant on the United States for military technology, logistics and training support. Intelligence cooperation had also increased dramatically from the 1960s which included the establishment of facilitates at Pine Gap, North West Cape and Narrunga. Of particular note is that since the 1980s these signals stations have been joint facilitates, rather than US bases. They are jointly staffed with US and Australian personnel and Australia has 'full knowledge and concurrency' of their operations.[18]

With the end of the Cold War it might well have been expected that the role of ANZUS would have declined in importance to Australian strategic policy. With the fall of communism and the decline of a direct 'threat' to Australia and 'the west', neorealist literature on alliances would argue that ANZUS should have drawn to an end or that it would be downgraded; however while the treaty commitment became a lot less important, the broader Alliance grew in stature.

While the post-Cold War era would deliver some 'peace dividends' to the US and its allies, this era would soon be characterised by destabilisation, failing/failed states and an increase in peacekeeping and military operations. Australia participated in a number of United Nations operations in conflict areas such as Somalia, Namibia, Afghanistan, Pakistan, Cambodia and Rwanda, amongst many others. These operations, in coalition with other nations, were part of Australia's long standing approach to exercising influence through international organisations and its commitment to liberal internationalism and to being a 'good international citizen'.[19]

However the most significant military involvement of Australians in the immediate post-Cold War era was the commitment to the US-led operations to free Kuwait after the Iraqi invasion, which included the RAN's role in the Maritime Interception Force in the Persian Gulf.[20] The major regional Australian operation at the end of this decade was the International Force for East Timor (INTERFET) mission to East Timor in 1999. US backing for this Australia-led action was critical in terms of diplomatic, intelligence and logistic support. While the US did not provide large numbers of 'boots on the ground' for INTERFET, this was not a necessary precondition for the success of the operation. Broader US support was, however, absolutely critical to the accomplishment of this mission.

The period after the end of the Cold War brought closer cooperation in the Alliance and an increase in the military-to-military collaboration and the strengthening of the formal structures around the management of the Alliance. However the real acceleration of military-to-military engagement occurred after the 11 September 2001 terrorist attacks. Australia's participation in the War on Terror (WoT), especially its contribution of military forces to Iraq and Afghanistan, would result in levels of combined military operations with the United States not seen since Vietnam. Thus the 2000s would see a broadening and deepening of the Alliance. Significantly, despite the actual ANZUS Treaty focusing the relationship in the Pacific, the post-Cold War and WoT periods would see the alliance 'go global' and the strategic and military links between the two countries would rise to their strongest point in thirty years.[21]

The continued belief in the value of US global leadership to Australian strategic interests means that despite the changing character of the Alliance over this period, the underlying premise has not changed. Of equal significance has been the fact that over the last forty years, US primacy in the Asia-Pacific region has remained uncontested. As we enter a new era characterised by the increasing importance of the Asia-Pacific to global strategic affairs, the rise of China and challenges to US primacy the question becomes not only about the changing character of the ANZUS alliance, but also the viability of its underlying nature.

Risks and Costs of ANZUS to Australia

Despite the longevity and success of ANZUS, no alliance is without risks and costs. The greatest criticism in regard to Australia's attachment to having 'great and powerful friends' is the persistent argument that this means that Australia has fought 'other people's wars'. This argument is, however, much overplayed and does not stand up to considered analysis.

In both World War I and World War II Australia fought for both country and Empire. While it is hard for Australians to conceive today during the nineteenth century and the early twentieth century there was no delineation between identity as an Australian and as member of the British Empire. Beyond issues of identity there was also a clear Australian strategic interest in the preservation of the Empire and British maritime supremacy in the Asia-Pacific, during both world wars.

In the Korea War (1950–53), Australia fought as part of the United Nations in defence of collective security against an invasion by communist North Korea. As noted above, Australia approached Vietnam in a hawkish manner, actively encouraging US participation and proactively lobbying for its involvement. Australia's contribution to the 1991 Gulf War was, like Korea, made within a UN collective security action as well as complementing the alliance with the United States.

The Alliance played a central role in Australia's wars of the early twenty-first century. As Al Palazzo has argued, in Iraq in 2003 the Australian government never 'adopted the US plan for regime change'; instead the Howard government prescribed to a secondary goal, the 'reinvigoration of Australia's bilateral security relationship with the United States'.[22] This was the primary focus of the Australia commitment and the Howard government was remarkably successful in this endeavour through providing political support for the US-led coalition backed up by a minimal commitment of military force, under restricted rules of engagement, in limited areas of operations. While Australia's Iraq War was principally about the US alliance, it was a decision and a strategy enacted by the Australia government. As Lloyd Cox and Brendan O'Connor have noted, in Iraq, as in Vietnam, Australia was a 'hound dog' not a 'lapdog' when it came to its involvement in these conflicts and its relationship with the United States.[23]

Australia's commitment of troops to the US-led operation in Afghanistan is somewhat more complicated. The only time the ANZUS Treaty has been invoked was by John Howard on 12 September 2001, after the attacks on the east coast of the United States at the World Trade Centre in New York City and the Pentagon in Washington DC the day before. While ANZUS is a Pacific security agreement, Howard was able to utilise Article Five, which states that 'an armed attack on the metropolitan territory of any of the Parties' constitutes a trigger for the Treaty. Australia's stance in relation to the WoT was heavily influenced by both this event and the Bali bombings in 2002. The other major reason that facilitated Australia's involvement in these 'wars of choice' in the Middle East after September 11 is that Australia's great power ally was guaranteeing its security in the Asia-Pacific by remaining the uncontested hegemonic maritime power in that region.

It is important to note that whatever the rationale for Australia's involvement in these conflicts; be they self-evident, contested, flawed or otherwise, they have been Australia's own. They were made to achieve policy objectives, as they were perceived and understood by Australian government at that time. As Craig Stockings has noted while there 'remains a powerful temptation to believe in our enduring historic innocence ... [and it] eases our collective conscience to suggest that we were somehow tricked or pressured into doing someone else's dirty work ... in each and every case ... the historical trail leads elsewhere'.[24]

While Australia's wars have been her own, there are legitimate questions to be asked as to the level of its involvement, the strategic rationale behind some of these decisions and the cost-in lives, resources and Australia's diplomatic relations. For Iraq (2003) and Afghanistan, there are valid questions to be asked as to the extent in which these actions may have increased the risk to Australia of a terrorist attack? A similar question can also be raised as to the potential for Australia to become a target in a nuclear war as a result of the establishment of the joint facilities from the 1960s onwards. Furthermore there is the question as to the extent to which the Alliance has meant that Australia feels the pressure to share in US conflicts, and the extent to which Australian participation has become expected in Washington DC?

Strong support for US actions also carries the risk of Australia being seen to be simply doing the bidding of the US. Lines such as Australia being a 'deputy sheriff' of the US and the inference that Australia is 'prepared to back US global posture without reservation' has aroused criticism of Australia in regions such as Southeast Asia.[25] The 'deputy sheriff' tag and incidents such as prime minister

Howard's channelling the Bush Doctrine in relation to regional 'pre-emptive strikes' to thwart possible terrorist attacks have caused diplomatic problems for Australia. These particular episodes brought into question both the autonomy of Australia's foreign and defence policy and its ability to develop regional bilateral relationships.[26]

The Benefits of the Alliance

While every alliance carries risks and costs, there are also a number of major benefits that Australia accrues from the US Alliance. As the 2013 Defence White Paper states, it is crucial to Australia's 'access to capabilities, intelligence and capacity that we could not generate on our own'.[27] To many, the 'jewel in the crown' of Australia's major bene-fits from the Alliance is the intelligence relationship. On a day-to-day interaction, this is where Australia gets the most for the least and it is this aspect of the relationship that is often regarded as the 'strategic essence' of the Alliance.[28] This intelligence sharing partnership, however, predates the ANZUS Treaty. Since World War II the 'five eyes' nations of the US, UK, Canada, Australia and New Zealand have been heavily involved in collecting and sharing signals intelligence (SIGNIT). This relationship was formalised through the United Kingdom-United States of America Agreement (UKUSA) (1947–48), which is considered 'quite likely the most secret agreement ever entered into by the English-speaking world'.[29]

This agreement formally lays out the cooperation and exchange with respect to SIGINT activities—an undertaking which is an indus-trial size enterprise. The Australian element of this arrangement is the Defence Signals Bureau (DSB), renamed the Defence Signals Directorate (DSD) in October 1977 and then the Australian Signals Directorate (ASD) in 2013. Australia's area of responsibility in this global intelligence network covers the eastern Indian Ocean, parts of Southeast Asia, and the South West Pacific. Australia is an immense beneficiary of this relationship and it simply can't undertake such extensive intelligence operations on its own. This access is critical at the strategic, operational and tactical levels for defence policy and military operations.

Other key areas of the intelligence sharing network are in foreign intelligence collection, imagery and analysis. These are less significant than the SIGNIT material but are still exceptionally important and Australia is a major net recipient in this information sharing arrangement. The big question in relation to the Alliance and intelligence collection is what would and could Australia do if it lost this privileged access? How critical is it to our security if we lost it? And how much would we be willing to spend to try and replace it?[30]

Another crucial benefit from the relationship is in technology transfers. A critical element of the Australian Defence Force's posture is its ability to maintain a regional 'capability edge'. This is underpinned by Australia's access to US defence technology. While this technology edge is declining, relative to the rise in capabilities of Australia's neighbours, its maintenance is critical and is becoming ever more dependent on the United States. This is because there are few producers at the cutting edge of high end military capabilities and technology. The numbers of players in this field has steadily decreased and few countries are proficient in building capabilities such as fifth generation aircraft. Australia does not have the capacity to build military hardware such the F-35 Joint Strike Fighter (JSF) on its own and Australia will never again independently build a frontline fighter, strike aircraft or similar high technology platforms for air, sea or land warfare. Those platforms that we do build are heavily dependent on input from the United States, such as the combat system and weapons on the *Collins*-class submarines and the Air Warfare Destroyers.

In some ways, our access to US technology rivals or surpasses the intelligence sharing access. The ADF operates US technology in its aircraft, combat systems, surface vessels, missile systems, torpedoes, tanks, armoured personnel carriers, and precision guided munitions. The most critical of these systems being JSF, *Growler* electronic warfare aircraft and the AEGIS naval weapons system, technology that which cannot be procured from other any other source. These are just some of the vast array of military technology, some of it exceptionally privileged, that Australia benefits from in its relationship with the United States. These systems and capabilities are also supported by ongoing upgrades, maintenance and access to logistics and resupply.

Crucially, it cannot be overlooked that in the contemporary context, the Alliance means that Australia falls under the umbrella of

US extended conventional and nuclear deterrence. Any aggressor would have to contemplate the likelihood and extent of US support in its planning for operations against Australia, while many believe that despite the vagueness of the text in the ANZUS Treaty that the United States would come to Australia's aid in the event of it being directly attacked.[31] In addition to this 'implied' security guarantee the Alliance continues to provide Australia with access to the corridors of power in Washington DC. While this should not be overstated—as traditionally Australia has struggled hard to get more access than it has received—it is nonetheless a major advantage to Australia's security.

The Alliance also allows Australia to reduce its expenditure on defence—or as some would say, it allows for 'defence on the cheap' or 'free riding' on the US. Since the time of the Menzies Administration the Australian government has been consciously able to reduce defence outlays as a result of the Alliance. This funding minimalisation strategy has meant that billions of dollars have been able to be redirected to other programs such as education, health, welfare and infrastructure rather than defence. Conversely, as noted above, Australia does meet its expectations in comparison to some other US allies and has maintained a degree of defence spending that is roughly commensurate with international comparisons and its economic capacity. Given Australia's strategic circumstances, there is no doubt that the Alliance has allowed Australia, over the last fifty years or more, to reduce its defence spending. A major question for the future is how far can Australia sustain this stance, especially in light of increasing strategic competition to US primacy in Asia, the deteriorating US military edge in the Asia-Pacific and its reducing global economic power?[32]

Underlying all of these benefits is the fact the Alliance continues to see Australia aligned with *the* major global military power. The United States has maintained uncontested primacy in the Asia-Pacific region for close to four decades and its interests are generally aligned with those of Australia. While not as important as interests, shared values such as democracy and Western culture also continue to help with Australia's understanding and acceptance of the Alliance. This has also been a critical factor in ensuring the long-standing public support for the Alliance. Overall though, the key benefit of the

Alliance is that it continues to underwrite Australia's security and as academic Harry Gelber has noted, while this continues to be the case the continuation of the Alliance 'is the merest common sense'.[33]

Limits

The ANZUS alliance is not, however, an open cheque book. It does not involve unrestrained commitments from either power. For instance while Australia has received almost unparalleled access to US technology, there are limits to cooperation in this and other areas. As the former Defence official Alan Behm has noted; 'when it comes to Australian access to US source codes ... the relationship has been less forthcoming.'[34]

There have also been limits to the security commitment and the defence cooperation that Australia has received from the United States—in particular these have been related to our nearest neighbour, Indonesia. The issue first came to prominence in relation to Australian forces involved in the Indonesian Confrontation. As the 1964 Strategic Basis of Australian Defence Policy noted, while the Barwick/Kennedy conversation of 1963 in relation to ANZUS covered Australia armed forces in Malaysia, it was only in relation to an 'overt attack and not subversion, guerrilla warfare or indirect aggression'.[35] More recently John Howard was taken aback when President Clinton rejected his request for US 'boots on the ground' for the INTERFET mission to East Timor in 1999.[36]

Limits also work both ways. As Mark Thompson has noted, 'the disproportionately small scale of Australian contributions to operations in Iraq and Afghanistan follows the pattern set earlier in the Vietnam and Korean conflicts'.[37] The reason that Australia manages to 'get away with such small contributions is because other US Allies do similarly'.[38] Al Palazzo has also noted that there is a perennial myth that the Australia 'punches above its weight' in the Alliance, but a rather a more realistic appraisal recognises that Australia's contribution lies in the bottom half of the 'middle power' countries for spending on defence and portion of population in the military. In addition, its commitments to overseas conflicts in support of the Alliance have been very carefully managed. In the end, we do our share and we are not 'shirking our responsibilities' but we also don't 'punch above our weight'.[39]

In the end limitations on the Alliance are a reflection of the fact that the strategic interests of each partner in a relationship, even one as close as the US-Australian alliance, do not always go hand in hand. As Viscount Lord Palmerston has noted, nations, have 'no eternal allies and no perpetual enemies, only interest that are eternal and perpetual'.[40]

ANZUS: Towards a New Era

As noted earlier the Australia-US alliance has proven remarkably adaptable. At key moments in time—its creation in 1951; the Vietnam War; the Nixon doctrine and DoA; the end of the Cold War; and September 11—it has been able to recast itself and change its character to meet the needs of the contemporary strategic landscape. Today, once again, ANZUS is at one of these turning points.

ANZUS had initially been conceived as a response to the rise of communism in the Asia-Pacific and in particular the communist takeover of China in 1949. This threat dominated the Alliance until the announcement of the Guam Doctrine and Nixon's visit to China to normalise relations in 1972. Nixon's visit ushered in a period of uncontested US primacy in the Asia-Pacific that had allowed the Alliance to take on a much more global posture, especially in the post-Cold War and WoT eras.[41]

With the end of the September 2001 decade it has been evident that a major strategic shift has been underway in the Asia-Pacific region. The announcement of the US 'pivot' or 'rebalance' to the Asia-Pacific region and increasing Chinese assertiveness in areas such as the East and South China Seas has seen the focus of the Alliance move away from operations in the Middle East to focus (once again) on Asia and China. Thus the role of the Middle East and the global focus that the Alliance developed over the preceding two decades has been slowly replaced by its original Asia-Pacific geographic focus. This means that, once again, the character of the Alliance has been redefined and is in the process of evolution.

This new era is reflective of a number of strategic issues; the movement of the global economic centre of gravity to the Asia-Pacific; the relatively decline of US power in comparison to rising states such as India and China; the end of American unilateralism in global affairs; the rise of a world with multiple centres of power or influence;[42] and a resurgent China which is contesting US primacy in the Asia-Pacific. These significant shifts mean that the ANZUS Alliance, as we have known it, will change and be recast in relation to its role in both Australian and US strategic thinking.

But as long as Australia maintains a belief in, and a commitment to, US primacy and the preservation of the current rules based international order under US leadership, Australia will see the Alliance as in its long term strategic interest. As the National Security Strategy of 2012 noted 'the Alliance' is 'as strong as ever' and it will remain 'our most important security relationship' and a 'pillar' of Australia's national security.[43]

However shifts are ongoing in the way in which the Alliance is understood and these changes have already started to be reflected in Australian policy. The 2009 Defence White Paper 'hinted at a hedging posture for Australia's future' against China, and in 2011 the prime minister Julia Gillard reiterated Australia's firm support as an ally of the United States 'for all the years to come'.[44] These moves have been reflected in the 2013 Defence White Paper's language that was indicative of 'a phase of re-orientation in the Alliance: away from operations further afield towards the increasing security dynamics in Australia's own region'.[45]

While the regional reorientation of the Alliance is one important policy move in the 2013 Defence White Paper, the other significant shift was the redefinition of the notion of 'self-reliance'—a concept that has been key to Australia's interpretation of ANZUS since 1972. In the 2013 White Paper 'self-reliance' was interpreted in a new way, it has moved beyond being situated just in relation to ANZUS and now works within the context of our 'Alliance with the United States *and our cooperation with regional partners*'.[46] This framework indicates a new approach to both the Alliance and Australia's broader security relationships in the Asia-Pacific region.

The most visible manifestation of the emergence of a new era in the Alliance has come through the drawdown of Australian and US commitments to operations in the Middle East, and the US 'pivot' or 'rebalance' to the Asia-Pacific. The announcement of this move by President Barack Obama—in the Australian Parliament in November 2011—was the critical moment in the recasting of the Alliance and in ushering in a new era in its evolution.

This Asia-Pacific reorientation is significant. As one of Australia's most important strategic thinkers, Coral Bell, noted back in 1988: 'it was clearly an omen of the future that the first American interest in Australia [in 1941] …was a by-product of [US] interests in Asia.'[47] The greater the US interests in Asia, the greater their interest in Australia.

In 2013 a US think tank report on Australian defence strategy and the future of the US alliance noted that Australia had moved from 'down under' to 'top centre in terms of geographical import' and that its geographic position makes it a 'gate keeper' for the Indian Ocean. While analogies such 'down under to top centre' are prone to over exaggeration, there is an underlying veracity to this claim. As the Centre for Strategic and Budgetary Assessments notes, 'we are now in *the* most significant time in the relationship in terms of the overlapping of US and Australian strategic interest in the region since the end of the Pacific War'.[48] One of the major consequences of this change in US strategic interest in Australia is that its geography, once a source of anxiety manifested in Geoffrey Blainey's notion of a 'tyranny of distance', [49] has now become a source of strength and opportunity.

Australia's geography is critical to the US in a number of ways. In an age of increasing long-range anti-access weaponry, especially in China, Australia can provide US forces in the region with strategic depth, forward operating bases, a logistical hub, and training facilities. This recognition has been evident in the commencement of an annual rotation of US Marines and US Air Force units through Darwin. The Australian naval base in Western Australia, HMAS *Stirling*, has also long been acknowledged for its ability to provide a safe and secure port facility for visiting US naval ships operating in the Indian Ocean and Southeast Asia, while Australia's off shore assets such as the Cocos Islands provide an excellent location for future increased reconnaissance and surveillance operations in the Indian Ocean.[50]

As a recent US think tank report noted:

[T]he distance between the base at Her Majesty's Australian Ship (HMAS) Stirling (near Perth) and the South China Sea is roughly the same as the distance between Guam and the South China Sea, HMAS *Stirling*'s use as a forward operating location for US nuclear-powered submarines would help to diversify port options in theater, while also increasing the operational availability of US submarines in the Indian Ocean and the Persian Gulf. Unlike Guam, all of these locations are outside the reach of the PLA's existing conventional missile forces, as well as those known to be in development. As the United States intensifies its focus on the South China Sea, Australia's northern airbases and Fleet Base West near Perth will become even more attractive as safe bastions for US forces.[51]

There have also been some significant increases in Australia-US military relations in recent years. 2013 saw an Australian serving as Deputy Commanding General (Operations) US Army Pacific and HMAS *Sydney* operating out of Japan as part of the US Seventh Fleet. In 2012, for the first time ever, an Australian naval officer commanded a significant portion of the combined fleet in the United States run Rim of the Pacific (RIMPAC) naval exercises. Developments such as this have seen a deepening of engagement between the ADF and the US military in the region. In addition, Australia has provided stronger political and diplomatic support for the United States and its allies over maritime and territorial disputes with China. The strong statement from the Australia United States Ministerial (AUSMIN) Meeting in 2013 and Australian support for United States and Japanese concerns over the Chinese declaration of Air Defence Identification Zone (ADIZ) in the East China Sea provides evidence of the Abbott government's determination to provide stronger diplomatic and strategic support to the US and its allies in the region.

Despite this strong support for the United States, the changing dynamics in the region—most prominently the rise of China—has led to debates over the ongoing viability of Australia's security attachment to the US and the difficulty of Australia having to face up to the fact that for the one of the first times in its history its 'great and powerful friend' is no long is major trading partner.[52] This has provoked some to question the possibility of Australia having to face a choice between its alliance partner, the US and its major trading partner, China.

Irrespective of this debate, the evolution of the character of the Alliance in recent years has reiterated the fact that Australia has already made its 'China choice'. Australia is a friend of both countries, but an ally of only one. However Australia's ability to 'thread the needle' between its close economic partnership with China and its security partnership with the United States will become even more difficult to manage in the future. An indication of the difficulties arising from this complex set of relationships came with Prime Minister Tony Abbott's statement on 28 November 2013, that Australia's stance on the ADIZ would not affect the timeline to negotiate the free trade deal with China. Positions such as these may well prove difficult to maintain in the future.

The economic relationship with China is exceptionally important but its potential to influence Australian actions on security issues in the future needs to be contextualised. It should also not be overlooked that the China-Australian trade relationship is rather shallow.[53] While China is Australia's number one trading partner, the United States and Japan are Australia's number two and three partners and their combined economic weight in terms of trade outweighs that of China. In terms of direct foreign investment in Australia, the United States spends ten times (and Japan five times) more than the Chinese. Chinese foreign investment in Australia is only equal to that of Switzerland, meanwhile Australia invests at five times the rate in the United States as it does in China, four times more in the United Kingdom, and twice as much in New Zealand and Canada.

More broadly the continued belief in the importance of the US Alliance is a reflection of Australia's traditional approach to the rules based international order, democracy, capitalism, human rights and free markets. That is, liberal western democratic values. Support amongst the political and policy elites and the general populace for the US Alliance is also exceptionally high. The Alliance holds bipartisan political support in the major parties, while the 2012 Lowy Institute poll indicated that support amongst Australians for the Alliance remains as high as 82 per cent, and the basing of US forces in Australia is an increasingly popular policy, favoured by 61 per cent of the population[54] (see Chapter 3). All of these factors combine to make the Australia-US alliance an embedded part of Australian strategic culture.

In recent year's successive Australian governments have drawn the country closer to the United States. This is based on concerns over the security impact of China's rise, recent instability in the region, a rational calculation of cost and benefits to Australia's interests, the solid framework of domestic support for the Alliance and the increasing geographical and political significance of Australia to the United States. Yet the move to a closer relationship does not automatically mean that Australia should, or has to, be acquiescent to any US request. Australian politicians and policymakers must be careful of incrementalism in the Alliance. Rather, a clear strategy must be articulated and key questions around the deepening of any alliance must be asked, such as; where are the limits? And where does it end? As Bill Tow has stated: 'a greater determination by Australia to cultivate a more balanced approach to alliance politics will under write national security interests more effectively than a sustained and rigid adherence to alliance loyalty under any circumstances.'[55]

The New Era

The increasing importance of Australia in relation to US strategic priorities does carry risks and costs. The relative decline in US global hegemony and the rise of a more multi-polar world will most likely mean increased demands by the United States from its allies.[56] 'Burden sharing', especially in the Asia-Pacific, will becomes less of a call based on rhetoric and more of one based on realistic appraisals by the US of its allies abilities to contribution to combined military operations. With increased tension in the region, especially in relation to China, the cost of the US Alliance has the potential to be much higher. Australia will find it much more difficult to commit small, niche and largely single service military forces to any potential US-led operation in Southeast Asia or the eastern Indian Ocean. Rather than simply doing our reasonable share, as we have done for the past sixty years, it is likely the United States will ask Australia to actually 'punch above its weight' in the future.

As noted one major and ongoing complication is the extent to which Australia can continue to limit defence spending due to the Alliance. This is particularly poignant area for discussion in an era of fiscal austerity and where there is an increasing gulf between the type of defence force that the Australian government wants and its ability to pay for it. There has already been some extensive criticism from US commentators and politicians[57] about recent cuts to Australia's defence budget and as US expectations of its allies rise so too will the costs to meet them. This means that the gap is currently growing between increasing US expectations of its alliance partners and Canberra's declining commitment to fund Australia's share. As ANU Professor and former secretary of the Department of Foreign Affairs and Trade Michael L'Estrange has noted '[t]his means that Australia's capacity for burden sharing and value adding with the US is [actually] diminishing not expanding'.[58]

This reiterates how critical it is to understand the 'limits of Australia's capacity' especially given the priority of its range of strategic interests and objectives. This means that Australia will have to focus much more on the South Pacific, Southeast Asia and its immediate region and it needs to clearly articulate to the US what is it they can expect from Australia in these regions as well as in East Asia—an area were Australia will have little strategic impact on the outcome of any major conflict.

Finally the changing dynamics of the Asia-Pacific region and the rise of greater multi-polarity means there is likely to be changes to the US San Francisco alliance system. The old hubs and spokes model where the United States could control the spokes independently is declining, as countries such as Japan, South Korea, the Philippines, Singapore, Thailand and Australia interact more with each other and some become less constrained by US power. Australia needs to undertake a rational cost benefit analysis of any increased cooperation, especially in relation to abandonment and entrapment concerns with both the US and other security partners in Asia. In addition Australia must consider the impact of deepening of relations with the United States or its allies in relation to its developing bilateral defence relations with other countries such as Indonesia. While at present the view is that our alliance with the US is generally seen as an asset for our regional engagement activities Australia must balance the demands of its bi-lateral relationship with the US against the needs and interests of Australia's other partners. In addition Australia needs to be cognisant of its role, place and importance within the US' security interests in the Asia-Pacific and its needs to be exceptionally careful to not over or understate its role.

As it stands by far and away, the current benefits of the alliance outstrip the costs. This is more than likely to remain the case into the near future. However, managing the Alliance in a clear and coherent manner without falling prey to the costs and limits of the partnership will continue to be difficult. At all times Australia should constantly assess the cost and benefits of the Alliance and its expectations/commitments to our national interest and never fall into complacency about Australia's strategic position or the capacity of the United States to continue to play a role that helps to ensure Australia's security. Taking ANZUS for granted or lapsing in due diligence as to character, role and nature of the alliance can be fatal. No alliance relationship should ever be taken for granted, otherwise as Harvard Professor Stephan Walt warns, 'the [A]lliance may be dead long before anyone notices, and the discovery of the corpse may come at a very inconvenient time'.[59]

Further Reading

Bell, Coral, *Dependent Ally*, Oxford University Press, Melbourne, 1987.

Edwards, Peter, *Permanent Friends? Historical Reflections on the Australian-American Alliance*, no. 8, *Lowy Institute Paper*, Lowy Institute for International Policy, Canberra, 2005. www.lowyinstitute.org/files/pubfiles/Edwards%2C_Permanent_friends.pdf.

Hubbard, Christopher, *Australian and US Military Cooperation: Fighting Common Enemies*, Ashgate, Aldershot, 2005.

Kelton, Maryanne, *'More than an Ally'?: Contemporary Australia-US Relations*, Ashgate, Aldershot, 2008.

Lyon, Rod and Tow, William T, *The Future of the Australian US-Security Relationship*, US Army War College, Strategic Studies Institute, Carlisle, PA, 2003. www.strategicstudiesinstitute.army.mil/pdffiles/pub50.pdf.

McClausland, Jeffrey, Stuart, Douglas, Tow, William T, Wesley, Michael, *The Other Special Relationship: The United States and Australia at the Start of the 21st Century*, US Army War College, Strategic Studies Institute, Carlisle, PA, 2007. www.strategicstudiesinstitute.army.mil/pubs/display.cfm?pubID=760.

Notes

1   ANZUS will be dealt with in this chapter as the bilateral relationship between Australia and the United States.

2   See M Kelton, *'More than an Ally'?: Contemporary Australia-US Relations*, Ashgate, Aldershot, 2008.

3   R Lyon, 'Do Alliances Work?', *The Strategist*, Australian Strategic Policy Institute, 19 December 2012. www.aspistrategist.org.au/do-alliances-work/ (viewed February 2014).

4   In May 1963, Australia obtained a specific US assurance that ANZUS would apply to New Guinea in the events of an attack by Indonesia. See TB Millar, *Australia's Defence*, Melbourne University Press, Carlton, 1965, p. 75.

5   AFP, 'Clinton Stands by Japan on China Island Row', *SBS News*, 26 August 2013. www.sbs.com.au/news/article/2013/01/19/clinton-stands-japan-china-island-row (viewed February 2014).

6   For a discussion of detailed discussion of this alliance dilemma see GH Snyder, 'The Security Dilemma in Alliance Politics', *World Politics*, vol. 36, no. 4, 1984, pp. 461–495. For an overview of the role and function of alliances see SM Walt, 'Why Alliances Endure or Collapse', *Survival: Global Politics and Strategy*, vol. 39, no. 1, Spring 1997, pp. 156–79; and WT Tow, 'Alliances and Alignments in the Twenty-First Century', in Brendan Taylor, (ed), *Australia as an Asia-Pacific Regional Power: Friends in Flux?*, Routledge, London, 2007.

7   Kim Beazley as quoted in P FitzSimons, *Beazley: A Biography*, Harper Collins, Sydney, 1998, pp. 227–8.

8   P Dibb, 'Is Strategic Geography Relevant to Australia's Current Defence Policy?', *Australian Journal of International Affairs*, vol. 60, no. 2, June 2006, p. 248.

9   John Curtin, 'The Task Ahead', *The Herald* (Melbourne), 27 December 1941. http://john.curtin.edu.au/pmportal/text/00468.html (viewed April 2014).

10   Prime Minister's War Conference (PWC), *Minutes of Melbourne, 1 June 1942*, National Archives of Australia, no. 1 of 8/4/42 to no. 69 14/1/43, and no. 78 and 79 of 17/3/43, A5954 1/1. (Emphasis added).

11   'An Appreciation of the Strategical Position of Australia, February 1946', in S Frühling, (ed), *A History of Australian Strategic Policy Since 1945*, Commonwealth of Australia, Canberra, 2009, p. 58.

12   See R O'Neill, *Australia in the Korean War 1950–53: Volume 1, Strategy and Diplomacy*, Commonwealth of Australia, Canberra, 1981, pp. 185–200.

13   For a summary of this debate see D Mclean, 'ANZUS Historiography', American History for Australasian Schools, University of Sydney. www.anzasa.arts.usyd.edu.au/ahas/anzus_historiography.html (viewed February 2014).

14   'Strategic Basis of Australian Defence Policy, 1964', in S Frühling (ed), *A History of Australian Strategic Policy Since 1945*, p. 58. Up to 1962 the Strategic Basis of Australian Defence policy saw SEATO 'for the time being, reduc[ing] the need for planning under ANZUS. At this stage ANZUS was 'potentially' the most valuable treaty to which Australia is a partner', p. 287.

15   Millar, *Australia's Defence*, 1965, p. 78.

16   The United States' San Francisco alliance system is used here to mean the

process of 'engaging the United States in the security of the western Pacific through a variety of commitments and alliances that began with the San Francisco Conference' in 1951. This is represented by the hub and spokes alliance model that consists of the US bilateral security treaties signed with Japan (1951); Australia and New Zealand (1951); Philippines (1951); South Korea (1953); and Thailand (1954). The name derives from the peace treaty with Japan that was signed on 8 September 1951 in San Francisco and is known as the Treaty of San Francisco. A security treaty signed with Japan that same day, is said to mark the beginning of the 'San Francisco System'. See L Buszynski, 'The San Francisco System: Contemporary Meaning and Challenges', *Asian Perspective*, vol. 35, 2011, pp. 315–335.

17 Alan Renouf as quoted in F Frost, *Australia's War in Vietnam*, Allen & Unwin, Sydney, 1987, p. 16.

18 See D Ball, *A Suitable Piece of Real Estate: American Installations in Australia*, Hale & Iremonger, Sydney, 1980.

19 D Horner and J Connor, *The Good International Citizen: Australian Peacekeeping in Asia, Africa and Europe*, vol. 3, *The Official History of Australian Peacekeeping, Humanitarian and Post-Cold War Operations*, Cambridge University Press, Melbourne, (forthcoming, 2014).

20 D Horner, *Australia and the New World Order: From Peacekeeping to Peace Enforcement: 1988–1991*, vol. 2, *The Official History of Australian Peacekeeping, Humanitarian and Post-Cold War Operations*, Cambridge University Press, Melbourne, 2011.

21 M Thomson, 'Australia's Future Defence Spending and its Alliance with the United States', Alliance 21 Meeting, Washington DC, 28 February 2013. www.aspi.org.au/events/alliance-21-australias-future-defence-spending-and-its-alliance-with-the-united-states (viewed February 2013).

22 A Palazzo, 'The Making of Strategy and the Junior Coalition Partner: Australia and the 2003 Iraq War', *Infinity Journal*, vol. 2, no. 4, 2012, p. 27. www.infinityjournal.com/article/83/The_Making_of_Strategy_and_the_Junior_Coalition_Partner_Australia_and_the_2003_Iraq_War/ (viewed February 2014).

23 L Cox and B O'Connor, 'Australia, the US, and the Vietnam and Iraq Wars: "Hound Dog" Not "Lapdog"', *Australian Journal of Political Science*, vol. 47, no. 3, June 2012, pp. 173–187.

24 C Stockings, 'Other People's Wars', in Craig Stockings (ed), *Anzac's Dirty Dozen: 12 Myths of Australian Military History*, NewSouth Publishing, Sydney, 2012, p. 97.

25 WT Tow, 'Deputy Sheriff or Independent Ally? Evolving Australian-American Ties in an Ambiguous World Order', *The Pacific Review*, vol. 17, no. 2, June 2004, p. 272.

26 N Bisley, '"An Ally for All the Years to Come"; Why Australia is Not a Conflicted US Ally', *Australian Journal of International Affairs*, vol. 67, no. 4, 2013, pp. 403–418.

27 Commonwealth of Australia, *Defence White Paper 2013*, Commonwealth of Australia, Canberra, 2013, para 6.8.

28 D Ball, 'The Strategic Essence', *Australian Journal of International Affairs*, vol. 55, no. 2, 2001, pp. 235–248.

29 J Bamford, *The Puzzle Palace: A Report on NSA, America's Most Secret Agency*, Houghton Mifflin, Boston, 1982, p. 309.

30 The intelligence relationship does not come without potential costs. These costs have been highlighted through both Julian Assange and the *Wikileaks* cables and more significantly the Edward Snowden revelations and the recent diplomatic row over Australian intelligence operations in Indonesia.

31 Although as Australia discovered in 1942, it is critical to analyse the ability of Australia's allies to meet its Alliance agreements, especially if it is preoccupied elsewhere.

32 Thomson, 'Australia's Future Defence Spending and its Alliance with the United States', 2013.

33 HG Gelber, *Australian-American Relations After the Fall of Communism*, no. 304, *Strategic and Defence Studies Centre Working Paper*, Strategic and Defence Studies Centre, Australian National University, Canberra, 1996, p. 5.

34 A Behm, 'Strategic Tides: Positioning Australia's Security Policy to 2050', *Kokoda Paper*, no. 6, November 2007, p. 77. www.kokodafoundation. memberlodge.com/Resources/Files/Kokoda%20Paper%206%20 Strategic%20Tides_Final.pdf (viewed February 2014).

35 Frühling (ed), *A History of Australian Strategic Policy Since 1945*, 2009, p. 326.

36 J Howard, 'Reflections on the Australia-United States Alliance', speech to the United States Study Centre, University of Sydney, Sydney, 15 February 2011, pp. 4–5.

37 M Thomson, *Punching Above Our Weight: Australia as a Middle Power*, no. 18, *APSI Strategic Insights*, Australian Strategic Policy Institute, 2005, p. 2. www.aspi.org.au/publications/strategic-insights-18-punching-above-our-weight-australia-as-a-middle-power/SI_Strategic_weight.pdf (viewed February 2014).

38 Thomson, 'Australia's Future Defence Spending and its Alliance with the United States', 2013.

39 A Palazzo, 'The Myth that Australia "Punches Above its Weight"', in C Stockings (ed), *Anzacs Dirty Dozen*, 2012, p. 212.

40 Henry John Temple Viscount Lord Palmerston, quoted in D Brown, *Palmerston and the Politics of Foreign Policy, 1846–1855*, Manchester University Press, Manchester, 2002, pp. 82–83.

41 This is evident in the 2010 US Quadrennial Defence Review which states that 'our partnership with Australia, [is] an alliance that stretches beyond Asia to provide essential cooperation on a wide range of global security challenges', Department of Defense, *Quadrenniel Defense Review Report*, United States of America Department of Defense, Washington DC, 2010, p. 59. www.defense.gov/qdr/qdr%20as%20of%2029jan10%201600.pdf (viewed February 2014).

42   This is opposed to the bi-polar era of the Cold War or the unipolar era dominated by the United States after the collapse of the Soviet Union.

43   Prime Minister and Cabinet, *Strong and Secure: A Strategy for Australia's National Security*, Commonwealth of Australia, Canberra, 2013, pp. 22–23.

44   Bisley, '"An Ally for All the Years to Come"; Why Australia is Not a Conflicted US Ally', 2013.

45   B Schreer, 'Business as Usual? The 2013 Defence White Paper and the US Alliance', *Security Challenges*, vol. 9, no. 2, 2013, p. 42. www.securitychallenges.org.au/ArticlePDFs/SC9-2Schreer.pdf (viewed February 2014).

46   Commonwealth of Australia, *Defence White Paper 2013*, 2013, para 3.36 (Emphasis added). See S Frühling, 'The 2013 Defence White Paper: Strategic Guidance Without Strategy', *Security Challenges*, vol. 9, no. 2, 2013, pp. 43–50. www.securitychallenges.org.au/ArticlePDFs/SC9-2Fruehling.pdf (viewed February 2013).

47   C Bell, *Dependent Ally*, Oxford University Press, Melbourne, 1987, p. 7.

48   See J Thomas, Z Cooper, and I Rehman, *Gateway to the Indo-Pacific: Australian Defense Strategy and the Future of the Australia-US Alliance*, Center for Strategic and Budgetary Assessments, Washington DC, 2013. www.csbaonline.org/publications/2013/11/gateway-to-the-indo-pacific-australian-defense-strategy-and-the-future-of-the-australia-u-s-alliance-2/ (viewed February 2014).

49   G Blainey, *The Tyranny of Distance: How Distance Shaped Australia's History*, Macmillan, Sydney, 2001.

50   See B Schreer, *Planning the Unthinkable War: 'AirSea Battle' and its Implications for Australia*, Australian Strategic Policy Institute, Canberra, 2013. www.aspi.org.au/publications/planning-the-unthinkable-war-airsea-battle-and-its-implications-for-australia/Strategy_AirSea.pdf (viewed February 2013).

51   Thomas et al., *Gateway to the Indo-Pacific: Australian Defense Strategy and the Future of the Australia-US Alliance*, 2013, p. 17.

52   As noted in Chapter 4, Australian trade with Japan overtook that with the United States during a period in the 1980s. The difference today being that China is not part of the San Francisco System.

53   Bisley, '"An Ally for All the Years to Come"', 2013, p. 413.

54   F Hanson, *Australia in the World: Public Opinion and Foreign Policy*, Lowy Institute for International Policy, Sydney, 2012. www.lowyinstitute.org/files/lowy_poll_2012_web3.pdf (viewed February 2014).

55   Tow, 'Deputy Sheriff or Independent Ally? Evolving Australian-American Ties in an Ambiguous World Order', 2004, p. 271.

56   See Department of Defense, *2014 Quadrennial Defense Review*, 2014, pp. 9, III.

57   For details see A Carr and PJ Dean, 'The Funding Illusion: The 2% of GDP Furphy in Australia's Defence Debate', *Security Challenges*, vol. 9, no. 4, 2013, pp. 65–86. www.securitychallenges.org.au/ArticlePDFs/SC9-4CarrandDean.pdf (viewed February 2014).

58 See 'Defence White Paper 2013: Special Edition', *Security Challenges*, vol. 9, no. 2, 2013. www.securitychallenges.org.au/TOCs/vol9no2.html (viewed February 2014).

59 SM Walt, 'Why Alliances Endure or Collapse', *Survival: Global Politics and Strategy*, vol. 39, no.1, 1997, p. 167. www.polsci.colorado.edu/sites/default/files/6B_Walt.pdf (viewed February 2014).

Part IV:
Size and State of Our Defences

10

The Evolution of the ADF into a Joint Force

James Goldrick

The opening years of the twenty-first century have seen considerable development of the Australian Defence Forces (ADF) as a Joint force. 'Joint' are those 'activities, operations and organisations in which elements of at least two Services participate'.[1] Even before 2000 there had been profound changes from the very basic arrangements described by TB Millar in 1965, in which the Chairman of the Chiefs of Staff Committee had practically no executive powers and the Joint staff was little more than embryonic. Nevertheless, while many of the recommendations that Millar made[2] for improved Joint arrangements had been implemented by 2000, the advances of the last fourteen years have been even greater.

The Evolution Towards a More Joint ADF

Compared to earlier years, 'Jointery' today involves all of the 'fundamental inputs to capability',[3] including 'people, collective training, major systems, supplies, facilities and support', whereas just 'organisation' and 'command and management' had been the focus of earlier integration. Yet, as David Horner has remarked, 'command structures are about power relationships'.[4] The 'command and management' reforms in the ADF (as well as within the Department of Defence as a whole) had to come first and be continued to create the conditions under which other reforms could be achieved.

In recent years, the Vice Chief of Defence Force (VCDF) has become a much more significant player and increasingly *primus inter pares*, relative to the Service Chiefs and the Chief of Joint Operations (CJOPS). There has been a steady movement of previously semi-autonomous (but bureaucratically vulnerable) Joint organisations from other parts of the organisation into the VCDF group. In addition, new organisations such as the Joint Capability Coordination (JCC) Division have been created under the Vice Chief to fulfil roles that were either previously neglected, or the need for which had not been identified until the true imperatives of complex Joint operations became apparent.

Events also mattered. At least until 2010, improved funding allowed many initiatives that could not have been achieved in the 1980s or 1990s. In particular, a series of contingencies within the nearer region, as well as in the Middle East, served to highlight the requirement for a modern combatant force to be effectively integrated across the environments. They provided laboratories for testing theory and doctrine in different scenarios, as well as much hard-won experience for those involved. Technology played another part. The invention of the Global Positioning System (GPS) (first experienced operationally during the Gulf War of 1991) did more practically for Joint operations, as well as the working of coalitions, than any other factor because it allowed units and headquarters to operate in the same geographic frame of reference, no matter what their environment. The fundamental importance of this development should not be under-estimated, since it has simplified or removed so many problems at both the tactical and the operational level.[5]

Reconciling Jointery with Enduring Differences of Maritime, Land and Air Environments

The Australian journey to a fully integrated Joint force is not complete (if it ever will be), nor has it been entirely straightforward.[6] A central problem for the ADF is not that of conflict between the Services, but the lack of expert human resources to manage both Joint and Service issues effectively. Australia's move to an increased level of 'Jointness' occurred at the same time the Department of Defence (Defence), as a whole, has had to cope with the demands of 'self-reliant' national defence. These have created overheads of development, training and support which did not exist before. Finding solutions has not been helped by the Anglo-American paradigm of military organisation, where much larger armed forces have the ability to generate sufficient expert personnel to man their Joint staffs, as well as meet their single Service requirements. In other words, the ADF is not capable of organising and managing multiple headquarters and staffs in a way other, larger defence forces are.

In these circumstances, the Australian Joint ideal has often had to give way to the Service reality, since it is axiomatic that effective Joint operations remain dependent upon single Service expertise and capability. To be fair, careful identification of compatible activities has allowed some outright integration of activities, notably in Joint Logistics and Joint Health, as well as the use of a 'lead' Service, of which Air Force's responsibility for airworthiness and the concentration of many types of specialist training within particular Service schools are good examples. This effort can and should continue, but it requires clarity as to the work that has to be done and a readiness to recognise when fundamental environmental differences do exist. One size does not fit all, and there is always the danger in a Joint training effort that there are inefficiencies when developing and teaching the curriculum. Conversely, by going for a broad-brush Joint approach too early, it is equally possible to produce personnel who lack the basic skills that their environments require.

The Jointery devil is always in the detail and this analysis involves diving into the organisation of the ADF and the Department of Defence in order to create a picture of the situation. Given the constraints of space, the assessment is inevitably highly selective and there are many other areas of innovation in Joint capability and operations that cannot be detailed in this chapter.

Early Steps: Command of Joint Operations

By the mid-1990s, Joint operations were the responsibility of the two-star Commander Australian Theatre working on a component command arrangement. In 1996, Headquarters Australian Theatre (HQAST) was assigned an 'interim' headquarters building at Potts

Point in Sydney, adjacent to Maritime Command Headquarters, to take advantage of its communications and intelligence facilities. The three environmental headquarters (Maritime, Land and Air) continued operating, with the intent that each force assigned the required units to Australian Theatre (AST) for operations, but actually still controlled them operationally as a component command under AST. From the start, this was only intended as an interim arrangement, with the idea that a permanent headquarters be built in the future.

The increased operational tempo from 1999 created further pressure for development in Joint command and control. The simultaneous management of Australian-led regional interventions and high intensity coalition operations in the first years of the twenty-first century placed a spotlight on both the effectiveness of the existing ADF command and control arrangements, and their efficiency. Reviews were conducted in 2003 and 2005. These suggested that there were problems due to different Service concepts of command and control, as well as duplication and ambiguity in the command relationships between the Services and within the Joint arrangements themselves. In the case of East Timor, the Chief of the Defence Force (CDF) removed the Commander of the AST from the reporting chain and had the Commander of the International Force for East Timor (INTERFET) report directly to him. During the Iraq War, arrangements were more complex—the deployed Australian National Commander designated as Commander Joint Task Force 633 had a direct line to the CDF for strategic and national issues, and also reported to the Commander Australian Theatre. Neither arrangement was entirely satisfactory. There were recurrent tensions between the staff elements working to the CDF in Canberra—designated at various times 'Strategic Operations Division' or 'Strategic Command'— and those working to the Commander AST in Sydney.

Some changes were made in 2004, with the Commander AST being replaced by the CJOPS. Although this was a three-star appointment—with the old two-star billet being allocated to the Deputy Commander—it was initially the existing VCDF who also served as CJOPS. Given VCDF's inevitably close relationship with the CDF, this removed many of the difficulties of the previous arrangement and certainly made management of the continuing operations in both the Middle East and the region more straightforward.

A further review conducted by Major General Richard Wilson in 2005 recommended that an integrated headquarters be established with the associated implication that the three individual environmental commands be restricted to the raising, training and sustaining of forces, and not be involved directly in operations. The timing of this change was to be aligned with the transition to the new purpose built headquarters for the Joint Operations Command (JOC) at Bungendore, Canberra, which had been announced in 2001 and was due for completion in 2008. A separate three star position for the CJOPS was established in September 2007, with Lieutenant General David Hurley the first CJOPS. Occupation of the General John Baker Complex in Bungendore began towards the end of 2008. Although there was deep and justified cynicism within the ADF regarding the politics behind the geographical location of the new headquarters, unnecessarily far from Canberra, the building itself was designed to purpose, and provided a secure facility with excellent communications.

The first decade of the century saw the ADF make complex, significant and sustained contributions to coalition operations.[7] The nature of these contributions was initially similar to that of the past, in that they consisted of (generally single Service) 'packages of forces', which served as niche contributions to the coalition effort.[8] The role of deployed national commanders was therefore one of managing the ADF contribution, monitoring its employment and ensuring that operations were conducted within the parameters of national guidance. This task was clearly simplified by the evolution of the JOC providing for a clear link between the Joint Task Force (JTF) Commander and CJOPS and a single information flow. The growing sophistication of the Australian communications networks has also proved important, since one of the greatest problems that commanders experienced in the past involved attaining timely situational awareness of the activities of units in theatre that were under their command, but not their operational control. In the Middle East, this was provided by the Joint-manned Force Communications Unit. Arguably, the concept of the deployed Task Force and the arrangements associated with it is now one of the most mature elements of the ADF's Joint construct.

Figure 10.1: Headquarters Joint Command Structure

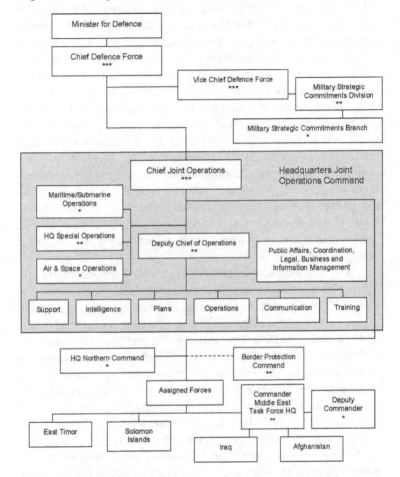

Source: Adapted from Raspal Khosa, Australian Defence Almanac: 2011–2012, Australian Strategic Policy Institute, Canberra, 2011, p. 15. www.aspi.org.au/publications/australian-defence-almanac-2011-2012/12_53_35_PM_ASPI_defence_almanac_2011_12.pdf.

Challenges to Jointery in Joint Operations Command (JOC)

The establishment of JOC was not without problems in balancing the desire for a Joint headquarters, with the particular needs of operating in the land, air and maritime environments. As an organisation, the

JOC Headquarters (HQJOC), inevitably, was a compromise between a theoretical command and control model largely derived from land force concepts, the needs of maritime and air operations and the realities of ADF resources. The theoretical model would suggest that HQJOC functions at the strategic and operational levels, with JTFs subordinate to it. This worked well with overseas deployments and, to a degree, with specific national tasks such as the Defence contribution to civil maritime security within Border Protection Command (JTF 639). It was also effective for land forces, which would undergo force preparation, be provided to JOC, assigned to a JTF for deployment and then returned to the Army for reconstitution.

However, this model could not work properly for either ships or aircraft. Both operate in the 'real world', with a less clear distinction between periods of operational availability and reconstitution than is the case for land forces.[9] While this problem would ideally have been solved by the Fleet and Air Commands maintaining their own operations centres, there were too few personnel to perform these functions and meet the needs of HQJOC.

There was a lively debate over this issue, as there was over the total numbers of staff required for the new construct. The staffing levels proposed by the Wilson Review were also progressively reduced, as it became clear that personnel numbers were oversubscribed. The eventual compromise was that the Maritime Operations, Submarine Operations and Air Operations organisations would be incorporated into JOC with dual responsibilities, working to CJOPS for operations and to their Chief of Service for activities related to the raising, training and sustainment of forces. Similarly, Special Operations Command—despite itself having a very wide range of raise, train and sustain responsibilities—was also physically incorporated within JOC.

The new arrangements took some time to bed down and were probably not fully settled until the former incumbents of the Maritime and Air Commands had moved to other duties.[10] Moreover, junior commanders and staff officers also had to understand how to operate under the new arrangements. The nexus between the Joint headquarters with air and sea operations and their sustainment will always need management, which is best achieved by encouraging open reporting of issues and close liaison between all concerned.

Deployable Joint Force Headquarters: Unfinished Business
This maturity has not been achieved with the Deployable Joint Force Headquarters (DJFHQ), based on Army's Headquarters of First Division in order to provide a deployable command element capable of controlling a complex land-based Joint operation and the supporting sea and air elements. Although it provided many personnel to man various JTF headquarters during the period of remote and regional contingences, the headquarters itself did not deploy after the first East Timor intervention and for a long time remained as an Army formation with a handful of other service personnel as liaison officers. This situation changed to a degree with the need to prepare for the new amphibious capability, because DJFHQ has a force preparation as well as an operational command role in this area. This brought about the establishment of an Amphibious section in the Plans (J5) Branch, as well as a specific amphibious element in the Logistics (J4) Branch within DJFHQ. The Navy also recognised that the headquarters required a much stronger naval presence if it was to be an effective Joint organisation. Thus, a component of the Fleet Battle Staff (FBS), the navy's core seagoing command and control staff, was moved to DJFHQ.

The relationship between the DJFHQ and the FBS will need to evolve further. Arguably, the FBS is of itself too small to take on the command and control of a complex maritime operation, but the DJFHQ is still organised primarily for the conduct of land operations and thus not particularly suited to acting as a maritime command entity. The issue here is not simply the changes necessary to be effective in amphibious warfare, but those required to provide a deployable command and control organisation adequate for operations with a primarily maritime focus. There are many potential contingencies in which the land role will not be the dominant or a 'supported' element. Given that the integration of air operations also needs to be considered, this is an area for further development.

Civil Maritime Security and the Inter-Agency Effort: What Relationship Between BPC and JOC?
The increased demands of civil maritime security led to a series of reviews of the civil maritime surveillance and response program and the Defence role within it. The 2004 Taskforce on Offshore Maritime

Security had a particular focus on the protection of Australia's fast developing offshore resources industry and its vulnerability to terrorist action. It identified that considerable improvements were needed in the coordination of the national effort. In 2005, the creation of a new inter-agency Joint Offshore Protection Command (JOPC) organisation was nested within Customs—the lead department for civil maritime surveillance and response. JOPC was led by a Navy Rear Admiral, who had formerly been seconded to Customs as the Director General of Coastwatch. He retained this role but also took on that of Commander Joint Task Force 639—the Defence contribution to civil maritime security—with the Commander of Northern Command responsible to him for the tactical control of ADF assets as Deputy Commander JTF 639. In 2006, because of some confusion over the title (use of the word 'Joint' in particular did not reflect the inter-agency nature of the organisation in the eyes of those not in the military), JOPC was renamed Border Protection Command (BPC). In the same year, the various Defence operations involved in civil maritime security were brought together under the designation of Operation *Resolute*.

As of 2014, BPC continues to operate with two separate operations rooms in Canberra and in Darwin. As the headquarters of JTF 639, Northern Command in Darwin has tactical control of the Defence assets, while the Australian Maritime Security Operations Centre in Canberra directs those of the Customs and Border Protection Service. This arrangement requires considerable good will to work effectively, and often leads to duplication of effort. There have been proposals to combine the two operations rooms, but as the result of local political pressure, successive governments have been unwilling to allow the relatively small number of personnel involved to move out of Darwin.[11]

Combining the two would also provide the foundation for the further development of BPC as the national 'Sea Frontier Command' in a conflict. Given that this function would only be required in the event of a direct threat to Australia, there is the potential for the development of a Reserve headquarters, activated in a contingency and subject to a regular programme of exercises. This has already started on the small scale with the embedding of the Navy's Reserve manned Maritime Trade operations activity within BPC.

On the civil side, co-location of the Rescue Coordination Centre run by the Australian Maritime Safety Authority (AMSA) with BPC would simplify some of the tasking of surface and air assets in search and rescue operations. This would, however raise the question of the relationship with JOC, its Directorate of Domestic Regional Operations, its Joint Control Centre and the Maritime and Air Operations directorates, which currently work with AMSA to coordinate the tasking of Defence assets for both maritime and land Search and Rescue (SAR).

If the Defence coordination of SAR as a whole (including overland SAR) were to move to BPC, it is possible that the 'Sea Frontier Command' concept could be extended even further, possibly on the model of the 'Canada Command' of the Canadian Armed Forces. In peacetime, such a headquarters could coordinate domestic disaster relief and community assistance.[12] Whether this model would be a better solution than the current one depends largely upon which division of responsibilities between JOC and BPC is more efficient in the number of staff required. But the 'less staff' question needs to be asked in the right context, which is not that of managing routine peace operations or 'one off' emergencies, but of multiple contingencies—domestic and international—and of varying intensity and complexity.

Capability Development

Controversies over particular projects have tended to disguise the extent to which Defence capabilities have developed through a more integrated approach under the Defence Capability Plan (DCP). An examination of the latest public version of the 2012 DCP and a comparison with equivalent information from the 1980s and 1990s shows that operating across or providing services within multiple environments has become a fundamental requirement for new capability. The designation of Joint Capability Authorities (JCA)—with responsibility for management across environments of a particular capability—has been in recognition of this reality. Although individual Service Chiefs are the designated JCAs for a number of other activities, it was significant that in 2011 the VCDF was designated as the JCA for the amphibious capability.

The amphibious force is a focus of this effort, under the designation of Joint Project (JP) 2048. Centred on the two Landing Helicopter Dock ships (LHDs) that will enter service in coming years, this also includes other ships and systems to meet the full requirement for conducting amphibious operations. The amphibious concept itself provides for an on-call Amphibious Ready Element—a single major amphibious ship with an embarked company group—and an ability to generate, at longer notice, an Amphibious Ready Group (comprised of the entire amphibious fleet) with the ability to deploy a battalion battle group.[13]

As noted, the VCDF became the amphibious Joint Capability Authority in 2011. The Joint Amphibious Capability Implementation Team (JACIT) was already working on bringing JP 2048 to fruition, but it was apparent that additional expertise and resources were needed within both Navy and Army. Experts from the British Ministry of Defence (MOD) and the US Marine Corps assisted with the transition to the new force, while the British MOD also cooperated with an ADF recruiting program for its redundant personnel. This allowed the creation of an Amphibious Force Generation cell within the Fleet Battle Staff to support the Commander Amphibious Task Group as the LHDs are brought into service.

There are other Joint implications of JP 2048. A key one was the Army's recognition of the challenge that moving from the existing level of land force expertise represented. The fundamental question was whether the requirement could be met by a rotating allocation of battalions to the amphibious role or whether it was better to designate a single permanent unit. Wisely, Army decided in 2013 to designate the Townsville based 2nd Battalion to be the core of the land force capability within the 3rd Brigade. As the amphibious forces approach their required levels of operational capability over the next few years, the Chief of Army's comments indicate what will follow: 'Then we're going to make some decisions about how we spread that capability across more than just 3 [Brigade], but we're going to learn that as we go.'[14]

The arrival of the *Wedgetail* Aerial Early Warning and Control (AEWC) (Project Air 5077) aircraft is another important Joint development. The *Wedgetail* aircraft will provide battlespace management in the airspace above an Australian force to a level which has never before been possible for the ADF, which hitherto had to rely largely upon the United States for an equivalent capability. Compatible data links and computer systems already mean that there is a high degree of integration between the *Wedgetail* and the Navy's major surface combatants. This will improve even more with the arrival of the Air Warfare Destroyers (AWD). In the future, it is likely that the *Wedgetail* will be capable of remotely firing the long-range anti-air missiles carried by the AWD at targets that are over the visual and radar horizons of the ships. Even now, the quality of the data exchange is such that the effective range of the missiles carried by the FFG class frigates is significantly extended by the *Wedgetail's* presence. Given the combination of the capacities of the LHDs, the AWDs and the *Wedgetail*, the ADF is acquiring the elements of a coherent Joint command and control organisation for the maritime domain. In both its sea-focused and amphibious aspects, this capability will be important both for national operations and regional contingencies, particularly in coalition.

Two other areas of activity deserve mention because they intend to provide the ADF with a better ability to integrate its sensors, information networks and command systems, and communicate effectively. JP 2030 is a progressive project to provide the ADF with a single Joint Command Support Environment, effectively an operating picture common to all units and commanders. This is dependent upon networks that allow the participants to share data and the communication systems that allow the data to be exchanged in a timely and secure way. It is part of wider developments aimed towards having a single Defence information environment. Other initiatives include the Joint Intelligence Support System (Project DEF 7013) and the increasing priority being given to cyber security.

While work continues in areas such as terrestrial High Frequency radio, satellite capacity has become a vital element of communications. There has been a series of decisions to create a system that provides access in and around Australia and on remote operations under JP 2008. In 2007, Defence committed to the US-led Wideband Global Satellite (WGS) program through the funding of a sixth WGS satellite to add to the constellation. In addition to fixed and mobile ground stations, later stages of the project include the development of a whole of ADF wideband network management system.

There are many more projects in train or planned within the DCP. All require resources and the very severe budget cuts (see Chapter 11) within Defence threaten to halt or even reverse the progress that has been made. Sustained investment will be essential if the ADF is to operate effectively, whether on national or coalition operations.

Logistics

The stresses created by the East Timor intervention in 1999 confirmed the view that the logistics elements of all the services were under-resourced, but that there was also considerable inefficiency. The creation of the Defence Materiel Organisation (DMO) in 2000 and the disestablishment of Support Command Australia saw many support functions pass from direct military control. Yet the requirement for logistic support of operations represented a separate problem, which could not be delegated. The Joint Logistics Group (JLG) was set up— among its key roles being the planning, coordination and delivery of logistics support for both operations and exercises. Initially an independent group within Defence, headed by a two star officer, JLG was moved under the command of the VCDF and redesignated the Joint Logistics Command (JLC). As with Joint education, this gave Joint logistics a three star champion. The chronic under-resourcing of logistics in all three Services in previous decades meant that there was a considerable backlog of work for JLC, one which will take further effort, well beyond 2014, to remedy because it involves not only the acquisition of adequate supply stocks but the provision and maintenance of modern supporting infrastructure, such as fuel storage systems. The slowing and potential reversal of the gains made within JLC is another key concern associated with the reduction in Defence funding in recent years. If the ADF is to meet the likely challenges of the next decade, it will be vital that the development of JLC and the acquisition of improved stockholdings continue.

Joint Education

A key development for Joint education was the movement in 2007 of Joint training and education from a semi-autonomous place within the Defence Personnel Executive to the command of the VCDF. This considerably strengthened the position of those responsible for the conduct of Joint education and training, since it gave them a three-star champion who could work as an equal with the Chiefs of Service. The new organisation was initially called the Joint Education, Training and Warfare Command (JETWC), but later developments— which brought responsibilities for Australian Public Service training within Defence—made this title inappropriate. Instead, the Australian Defence College (ADC) umbrella was extended to cover the entire command.

The ADC itself remains an evolving construct. It was originally formed in 1999 as a result of the plan to replace the Joint Services Staff College (JSSC) and higher level Australian College of Defence and Strategic Studies with a single organisation. It incorporated the replacements for these activities, as well as the Australian Defence Force Academy (ADFA), as a 'cradle to grave' Joint education institution. ADC progressively came to incorporate the Australian Defence Force Warfare Centre (ADFWC) and a number of other Defence training units (including the School of Languages) in 2011, as well as the Defence Learning Branch, when it took responsibility for Department of Defence training activities.

Despite repeated embroilment in public controversy, ADFA has developed significantly since it began operations in 1986. The relationship between ADFA and the University of New South Wales has matured, which has seen agreements renegotiated in 2003 and 2009. At the time of writing, the first officers to undertake the full program of ADFA have reached one-star rank.[15] The connections that exist between the graduates in the three Services are a noticeable and wholly beneficial element in the conduct of Joint operations. This effect was the result of the personal connections between the officers concerned, rather than any detailed knowledge of Joint operations that had been gained from the ADFA military curriculum. In other words, ADFA has been successful in producing what a Commander ADC once termed 'Joint Mates'.

One profound change to the initial concept of complete Jointery at ADFA was introduced by Navy in 2000 with the insertion of a first, single service year before arrival at ADFA,[16] followed by further training in ships and bases. This was in response to Navy's perception that ADFA graduates were not well prepared for their full time service with Navy. The scheme has proved successful, but equivalent arrangements have yet to be adopted by Army or Air Force, despite the favourable judgement of the Sex Discrimination Commissioner's 2011 review into the Academy's culture. The author can provide a personal reflection on this issue from the perspective of more than three years as Commandant and a further three years as Commander of the ADC. Young officers who arrive at the Academy with the benefit of immersion in their own Service are generally more confident and perform better academically and in military training than those straight from school. They have a much better basis to understand the nexus between what is required for the individual Service and that needed for the Joint environment. As the Army Warrant Officer First Class (in his first Joint appointment in a forty-plus year career serving as Academy Sergeant Major in 2004) remarked of the Navy's midshipmen, 'they're officers. The others aren't yet, but they are—not that I'll give them an inch'. Extension of pre-ADFA programs tailored to the Army and Air Force's needs for their own cadets would not only make ADFA a more adult environment, but also allow the Joint agenda to be pursued much more comprehensively during the military training that runs alongside the degree programs that are the central activity of the Academy.

However, ADFA itself provides no more than about a third of the ADF's junior officers. Although many mature age students undertake bachelor degrees at the Academy as part of their commissioning programs, there must be a question as to whether the routine Joint exposure of non-ADFA graduates at the junior commissioned ranks is sufficient, particularly as the tempo of operations eases and the opportunities for inter-Service interaction diminish.

This question also applies to staff training. In 2001 the Australian Command and Staff College (ACSC) began operations in Canberra, replacing the three single Service staff colleges with a year-long program that attempted to meet both Joint and essential single Service requirements. The curriculum of the College has evolved substantially since the first course, with a steady increase in the Joint elements. The tension which exists between the three Services' unique professional requirements and those within the Joint domain has been largely managed through the development of much more comprehensive single Service curricula within the junior officer career continuum. This is something to which Army gave a priority from the time that the ACSC was first proposed and which Air Force eventually followed.

Nevertheless, the ACSC is not without its limitations. First, its curriculum is largely for operational planners. Second, the number of enrolled students is limited to 180—a proportion of whom are overseas students. As with ADFA, this equates to something like one third of a particular cohort of officers across the ADF.[17] The College manages both Navy and Army Reserve staff training, but, although some regular officers participate, these are fundamentally single Service activities. There has been consideration of an external Joint staff course to provide additional officers with an educational experience modelled on the ACSC, but the staff resources required are such that this has not yet been pursued.[18] There remains, however, a view within the ADF that not enough officers have access to Joint staff training and that this not only constitutes too great a restriction on the potential pool for promotion to the highest ranks, but also limits the effectiveness of the ADF's staff organisations at the working level.

Part of the requirement for a wider approach to ADF staff training was recognised by the transfer of the Army Technical Staff Officers Course to the ADC in 2008 and its redesignation as the Capability and Technology Management Course (CTMC). Since the transfer, not only have the other Services put officers onto the CTMC staff, but also the number of Navy and Air Force students has increased progressively. As the CTMC focuses on capability development, it effectively provides a parallel career track to the operationally focused ACSC.

There have been other educational initiatives that have improved Joint understanding. Amongst these is the inclusion of selected warrant officers in elements of the ACSC and annual Joint conferences for selected other ranks, many of who have never had exposure to the Joint environment.

The senior course of the ADC, the Defence and Strategic Studies Course, has also evolved significantly. It has up to fifty course members, some half of whom are overseas students. This means that only a limited cadre of officers at O6 rank can undertake the course (approximately one-third more undertake overseas defence college programs), but there has been a reasonably high correlation with graduates being promoted by at least one rank. The course itself has undergone many changes since the first Australian attempt at this level of defence education in 1994. Its current form largely derives from an extensive review conducted in 2004 and the subsequent guidance of the CDF and Chiefs of Service, although evolution continues. A key part of its development was to increase the emphasis on the exercise of military command in applying 'military power to achieve strategic objectives' in order to prepare officers for complex command, particularly at the operational level. By 2011, the first officers who were both graduates of ADFA and of the ACSC were undertaking the Defence and Strategic Studies course.

Practical Realities: A Case Study

The development and teaching of Joint doctrine illustrates the resource limitations in Australia. Early efforts to capitalise on the lessons of World War II and meet future threats resulted in the establishment of the School of Land Air Warfare by the Air Force in 1947 and the Australian Joint Anti-Submarine School (AJASS) by the Navy and Air Force in 1951. Both were focused largely on tactics and procedures. In time, the School of Land Air Warfare was reborn as the Australian Joint Warfare Establishment (AJWE)—operating in the land and air domain—and AJASS evolved into the Australian Joint Maritime Warfare Centre (AJMWC)—operating in the sea and air domain. AJWE operated very effectively in the land/air domain, AJMWC in that of sea/air. In 1990, the ADFWC was formed by amalgamating the two existing centres. In 1993, a Peacekeeping Training Centre was established within ADFWC.

It has been argued that the combination of AJWE and AJMWC freed sufficient teaching staff to allow the formation of a dedicated element for doctrine development and writing. This was true enough, but not the whole story. The problem was that ADFWC was not capable of maintaining a focus on tactical development and innovation at the same time as it managed the entire gamut of ADF doctrine writing, teaching and, from 1997, joint and combined exercise planning. At the higher level, it met its tasking very effectively, including the production of an increasingly comprehensive suite of Joint doctrine. However, the courses that were run, valuable as they were, focused much more on the mechanics of Joint operations and their command and control than on tactics and tactical development. Even with the injection of personnel from the old Joint Exercise Planning Staff, a result was the slow degradation of both close air support (CAS) and Joint anti-submarine warfare (ASW) expertise at the tactical level in the ADF as AJWE and AJMWC resources had been reallocated to meet the new requirements.

With the demands of Middle East operations, the urgent need for improved land/air procedures was recognised. Subsequently, the Forward Air Control Development Unit was formed in 2002 from elements of No. 76 Squadron. The unit became No. 4 Squadron in 2009. In addition, in the last few years both Navy and Air Force have attempted to marshal resources to improve ASW, identified as a priority in the 2009 and 2013 Defence White Papers.

In fact, the Warfare Centre paradigm was still itself unstable within these limits. ADFWC suffered as a result of the increased operational demands on the ADF from 1999 onwards, with unfilled appointments and concerns about the operational currency of some of its staff. These problems became more apparent after 2003. As efforts were focused on the development of HQJOC, operational demands continued. An abortive attempt to commercialise many of the functions of ADFWC followed, but the effort was abandoned in 2008 when it became apparent that the solution was not cost-effective. In the difficult discussions that followed, the ADFWC surrendered its exercise planning and analysis role with a handful of billets to HQJOC, reshaped its military establishment to align with the actual numbers of military staff available and reallocated the funding intended for commercialisation to acquiring permanent APS staff—notably as its doctrine writers and editors within the new Joint Doctrine Centre. The result is inevitably something of a compromise, but it is a manageable one. The lesson for the ADF is that new organisations can only be stood up at a price. That price needs to be clearly understood and, where possible, compensated for.

Conclusion

A 'Joint' ADF, by its nature, will always be a 'work in progress' and one subject to controversy and conflict. Some features of the Australian experience are worth noting. The first is that the deeper the collective understanding of Joint, the more consciousness there is of the key differences between the Services and of the relationship between their individual cultures and the unique requirements of their environments. The second is that the international experience of Joint operations and Joint organisation can provide valuable insights, but not necessarily solutions for the Australian condition.

However, pragmatism will not provide the answer if the resources are fundamentally inadequate. The achievements of recent years could be threatened by a failure to provide sufficient funds to continue the improvement of the ADF's Joint capabilities. Many of these improvements are particularly vulnerable because they involve aspects of Defence that are unglamorous, invisible and often difficult to understand. But they matter, and must continue if the ADF is to enter a new era of Joint endeavour.

Further Reading

Horner, David, *Making the Australian Defence Force*, vol. 4, *The Australian Centenary History of Defence*, Oxford University Press, Melbourne, 2001.

Horner, David, 'The Higher Command Structure for Joint Operations', in Huisken, Ron and Thatcher, Margaret (eds), *History as Policy: Framing the Debate on the Future of Australia's Defence Policy*, Australian National University Press, Canberra, 2007.

Notes

1   See 'Glossary' in Department of Defence, *Defence Annual Report 2009–10*, Commonwealth of Australia, Canberra, 2010. www.defence.gov.au/ Budget/09-10/dar/dar_0910_v1_full.pdf (viewed January 2014).

2   TB Millar, *Australia's Defence*, Melbourne University Press, Carlton, 1965, especially Chapter 7, pp. 160–167.

3   Department of Defence, *Defence Capability Development Handbook 2012*, Commonwealth of Australia, Canberra, 2012, p. 2. www.defence.gov.au/ publications/DefenceCapabilityDevelopmentHandbook2012.pdf (viewed March 2014).

4   D Horner, 'The Higher Command Structure for Joint Operations', in R Huisken and M Thatcher (eds), *History as Policy: Framing the Debate on the Future of Australia's Defence Policy*, Australian National University Press, Canberra, 2007, p. 160. www.press.anu.edu.au/sdsc/hap/html/ frames.php (viewed January 2014).

5   It has also created a potential vulnerability.

6   For a comprehensive history of Australia's earlier Joint efforts, see D Horner, *Making the Australian Defence Force*, vol. 4, *The Australian Centenary History of Defence*, Oxford University Press, Melbourne, 2001.

Other volumes of *The Australian Centenary History of Defence* provide the Single Service context.

7   This was the case in Vietnam.

8   Although the commitment to Afghanistan became much more complex in its later stages.

9   Land forces need to be within an operational command and control environment even when at the most basic stages of trials and training.

10 Maritime has since been renamed 'Fleet'.

11 Northern Command itself remains something of an anomaly in other regards, with regional command and mounting base responsibilities, which are not mirrored by any equivalent Joint organisation elsewhere in Australia.

12 In addition to having responsibility for search and rescue.

13 One early acquisition was the British dock landing ship RFA *Largs Bay*, renamed HMAS *Choules* in Royal Australian Navy (RAN) service. HMAS *Choules* was intended primarily to cover the shortfall in the ADF's intervention capability that developed when the elderly HMAS *Manoora* and *Kanimbla* were taken out of service, but it soon became clear that the ship also met the long term major unit sea transport requirements of the amphibious project.

14 Lieutenant General D Morrison, *Army News*, 2 February 2012, p. 18.

15 As of 2014, there is one two-star officer who had a year under the pre-ADFA naval degree program before joining the Academy from the beginning.

16 This incorporated initial entry officer training at the Royal Australian Naval College, HMAS *Creswell* and, just as important, time with operational units to see the 'real' Navy rather than the 'initial training' Navy.

17 Although there are other officers who undertake similar programs in equivalent overseas institutions.

18 Successful external courses of this nature require as many staff as residential programmes. There is no 'free lunch' in distance education from the provider's perspective.

11

Funding Australian Defence

Mark Thomson

Although Millar's 1965 book, *Australia's Defence*, devoted a mere three pages to the question of defence spending and manpower, it was a rich discussion nonetheless. Consistent with the thinking of the day, it not only stressed the need to 'carefully manage' defence spending to preserve a favourable balance of payments but also highlighted the role of immigration in sustaining a civil workforce depleted by national service. More congruent with today's concerns, Millar also examined the capacity of the Australian economy to sustain higher levels of defence spending and even touched on the question of our free-riding on allies in terms of 'paying as little as we could without forfeiting their goodwill and their readiness to protect us'.[1]

Millar knew there was a lot more to be said about the resourcing of Australia's defence. In fact, he said that a book could, and probably should, be written on the topic. No doubt he understood that then, as now, Australia's military strength was constrained by two factors: the scale of human and financial resources it devotes to the task and the efficiency with which it uses those resources to generate military capability. This chapter explores these factors in turn.

Historical Perspective on Australian Defence Spending

Twice in the first half of the twentieth century, Australia mobilised its economy and population to prosecute war on a massive scale. World War I saw 417 000 Australians serve from a population of 5 million, while World War II saw 993 000 serve from a population of around 7 million. But even these forbiddingly high figures beguile the true extent of national effort. An informative picture of historical defence spending arises from looking at the share of gross domestic product (GDP) allocated to defence over time (see Figure 11.1).[2]

Figure 11.1: Australian Defence Spending as a Share of GDP, 1901–2013

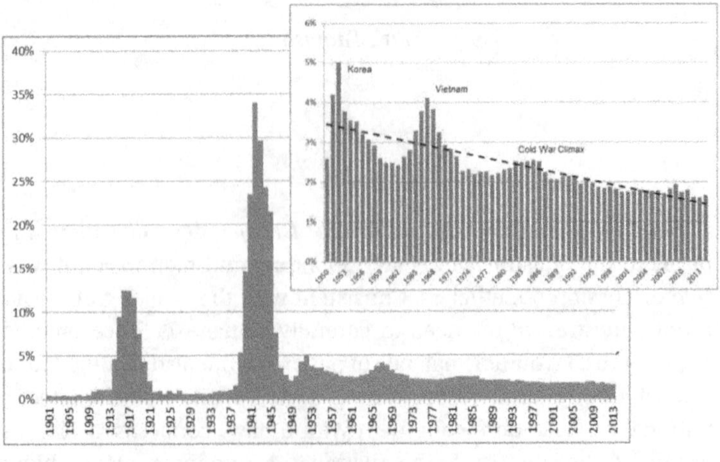

Source: Department of Defence, 2001–02 Defence Budget Brief and subsequent Defence Annual Reports, Commonwealth of Australia, Canberra.

Unsurprisingly, defence spending as a share of GDP peaked massively during each of the world wars from a remarkably low peacetime base. In the second half of the twentieth century, however, the pattern of defence spending in Australia changed fundamentally in tandem with the rest of the Western world. In both economic and human terms, wars became less costly while peacetime became more costly. The former reflects the practical inhibition against war between great powers following the advent of nuclear weapons; the latter reflects the transition to expensive well-equipped permanent armed forces during the Cold War.

The essential features of Australia's defence efforts since World War II are mirrored in the expanded panel in Figure 1. The onset of the Cold War in 1947 and the ongoing occupation of Japan put a halt to what might have otherwise been a more complete demobilisation after World War II. Following a surge due to the Korean conflict from 1950–53, spending fell steadily for almost a decade until the Menzies government initiated a major expansion and modernisation of the defence force, culminating in Australia's involvement in the Vietnam conflict from 1965.

Defence spending fell rapidly after Vietnam and then settled at around 2.25 per cent of GDP during the late 1970s. The 1979 Soviet invasion of Afghanistan then led to surge in US defence spending in the first half of 1980s under the Reagan Administration, which was echoed in Australia. As a result, defence spending grew to around 2.5 per cent of GDP and stayed there from 1982–86 before falling rapidly to a bit over 2 per cent in the closing years of the decade.

From the late 1980s through to 1999, defence funding was more or less kept constant in real terms, resulting in a slow decline in GDP share as economic growth outpaced inflation. But because the real cost of maintaining modern military capabilities comfortably outpaces inflation, the Australian Defence Force (ADF) declined in size, preparedness and technical sophistication. Assets replacements were deferred; platforms were built 'fitted for but not with' weapons and sensors, and the Army lost front-line battalions and supporting elements.

Motivated by the Australian-led intervention into East Timor in 1999, the Howard Government's 2000 Defence White Paper ended the austerity of the late 1980s and 1990s by promising a decade of 3 per cent real growth in funding. While this was generous compared with the preceding fifteen years, in reality the new funding did little more than make a start on clearing the accumulated backlog of delayed investment. Had additional funding not been forthcoming in 2000, substantive cuts to the scale and scope of the ADF would have been inevitable.

As it happened, the terrorist attacks of 11 September 2001 led to still further funding for deployments to Afghanistan and Iraq, then East Timor and Solomon Islands in the ensuing years. More funding was then provided in the mid-2000s to expand the Army and re-equip the Air Force. Strong economic growth around this time both enabled higher defence spending and caused the defence share of GDP to stabilise at around 1.75 per cent until the onset of the Global Financial Crisis (GFC) in 2008.

A complementary view of Australia's defence effort since 1950 is provided by the evolution of personnel numbers over the period. Figure 11.2 plots the number of permanent and part-time reserve force members along with the number of civilian employees in the Department of Defence (including the Department of Defence Supply where applicable) by year.

Figure 11.2: Australian Defence Personnel Numbers, 1950–2013

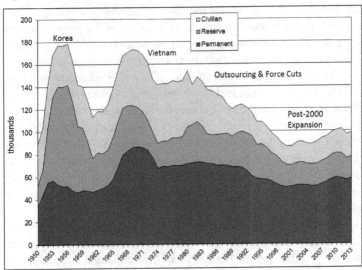

Source: Department of Defence, 2001–02 Defence Budget Brief and subsequent Defence Annual Reports, Commonwealth of Australia, Canberra.

Several points are noteworthy. The aggregate peaks around the times of the Korean and Vietnam conflicts are bolstered by national service and the flow-on effect of national service into the reserve force. The decline in civilian numbers from the 1980 onwards reflects the sale of government-owned munitions plants, shipyards and air-craft factories and subsequently the transfer of other support activities to the private sector. Similarly, the decline in permanent

ADF numbers from 1990 onwards reflects the outsourcing of non-core functions, coupled with some cuts to the combat force.

After 2000, the expansion of the permanent uniformed and civilian workforce is apparent, although growth in military numbers was less than planned during the middle years of the decade, as buoyant economic conditions impeded recruitment and retention. Things had changed by the end of the decade when uniformed numbers grew beyond budgeted levels due to higher than usual retention—again, arguably a consequence of economic circumstances.

Recent Developments and Current Challenges in Australian Defence Spending

Despite the steady growth in defence spending from 2000 onwards, the incoming Rudd Government faced a funding dilemma upon entering office in 2007. While the budget had grown, so too had plans for expanding and equipping the ADF. In a practical sense, the Rudd Government faced the same choice as its predecessor in 2000; provide more money or scale back on existing plans for the ADF.

To resolve the gap between means and ends, work began on a new Defence White Paper in early 2008. But before the document could be completed, global financial markets were rocked by the collapse of Lehman Brothers in September 2008, leading to the Global Financial Crisis (GFC). When the White Paper was finally released in April 2009, great uncertainty prevailed over the how the world economy would fare—with the prospect of a second great depression considered a real possibility.

It was therefore surprising that the 2009 Defence White Paper set out an expanded vision for the future ADF. Not only were all the initiatives of the Howard Government retained, but an ambitious program to strengthen the Navy was also laid out. Key elements included a doubling in size of the submarine fleet from six to twelve boats, a larger than expected replacement for existing frigates and the replacement of today's patrol boats with larger and more capable offshore combat vessels. Perhaps even more surprising, a twenty-one year funding commitment was made; 3 per cent real growth to 2017 followed by 2.2 per cent real growth to 2030.

The affordability of the overall program was far from assured; although there was more money promised, there was also a lot more equipment to be delivered, crewed and maintained. In any case, the question quickly became moot when the 2009 federal budget deferred $8.8 billion of promised funding to beyond 2016. There followed a series of further cuts and deferrals which saw around $20 billion of promised funding taken away as part of the Rudd and Gillard Government's attempt to return the Commonwealth to surplus prior to the 2013 election.

By 2012, the gap between ambitions and funding had grown to the point that the plans of 2009 were no longer plausible in the short to medium term. To redress this situation, the Gillard Government promised to produce a new Defence White Paper in 2013. The document was duly delivered in May of that year with an explicit funding commitment out to 2022 disclosed in the budget that followed soon after. Regrettably, it did nothing to resolve the situation; the scale and scope of plans for the ADF were retained with only marginal changes, yet funding remained well below what was promised in 2009. An opportunity to put some reality back into Australian defence planning was lost.

Meanwhile, on the personnel front, challenges continued. Over the first couple of years of the new decade, the maintenance of personnel numbers again became a problem for the ADF with a spike in separations and a shortfall in recruiting. To some extent, the unfavourable outcomes were probably the natural consequence of the end to a decade of operational deployments coupled with improved economic prospects. Around the same time, however, the ADF was also encountering personnel problems of a quite different nature.

In March 2011, the 'Skype incident' at the Australian Defence Force Academy highlighted problems with personal conduct and attitudes to women in the ADF.[3] There followed a series of external reviews and subsequent reforms to ensure that the defence force provides a safe and supportive workplace for all employees, regardless of gender. However, as recently as mid-2013, serious issues of contemporary misconduct were still coming to light. While it is hard to judge the impact of such events on recruitment and retention, it cannot be positive, and with women accounting for only 13 per cent of the permanent ADF, there is still a long way to go.

As a result of the cuts to defence funding between 2009 and 2012, defence spending fell to just under 1.6 per cent of GDP in 2012 and remained there in 2013. As this represented the smallest proportion of GDP allocated to defence in the post World War II era, the question of GDP share became central to the political debate. The observation that defence spending had fallen to the 'lowest level since the Nuremberg rallies' was just too powerful a sound bite to pass by.

Pretty soon, both the Labor Government and Coalition opposition were talking about their 'aspiration' to return defence spending to 2 per cent of GDP—albeit carefully caveated with reference to the economic and fiscal situation.[4] This was not the first time that discussions of defence spending had been reduced to catchphrases; throughout the 2000s the notion of '3 per cent real growth' had displaced serious discussion of defence spending in many quarters.

The choice of 2 per cent as a target remains somewhat obscure, but two factors probably played a role.[5] First, 2 per cent of GDP corresponds to the North Atlantic Treaty Organization (NATO) burden sharing benchmark from the Cold War, and although only three of twenty-six NATO members met the standard as at 2011,[6] several visiting US commentators admonished Australia for failing to do so in the early 2010s. Second, 2 per cent of GDP is probably in a vicinity of what is required to deliver the capability aspirations set out in the 2009 Defence White Paper in the medium term.

Whatever the reasons, the soon to be prime minister Tony Abbott surprised many on the eve of the 2013 election by promising to increase defence spending to 2 per cent of GDP 'within a decade'. To put this in context, the funding promised in the Rudd Government's 2009 Defence White Paper would have taken defence spending to around 1.8 per cent of GDP in 2023, while the Gillard Government's 2013 commitment would have delivered only around 1.65 per cent by the same date. Recent and projected defence spending are shown in Figure 11.3.

From a political perspective, the promise to spend 2 per cent of GDP on defence allows the Abbott Government to claim the mantle of being 'stronger on defence' than the Labor opposition—especially after four years of broken promises under the Rudd and Gillard Governments. But from a public policy perspective, it makes the cardinal error of putting financial inputs above policy goals. With a new Defence White Paper planned for 2015, it would have made more sense to examine the relative merits of larger and smaller defence forces in light of their cost and capacity to secure Australia's interests.

Figure 11.3: Recent and Prospective Defence Spending

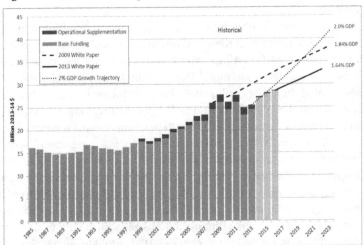

Source: Department of Defence, Defence Annual Reports and Budget Papers; and Australian Strategic Policy Institute analysis based on 2010 Treasury Intergenerational Report.

There is surely nothing magical about 2 per cent of GDP. A reasoned analysis might well conclude that either a higher or lower level share of national output is appropriate to the strategic challenges the nation faces. By setting the funding envelope *a priori*, there is a very real risk that the military will simply go on a shopping spree up to the constraint set by the 2 per cent target.

Irrespective of its merits, the Abbott Government's 2 per cent of GDP promise is likely to be a hard one to keep. The government faces a difficult fiscal outlook. It is now appreciated that Australia rode a revenue boom in the 2000s which concealed a deep structural deficit—an excess of expenditure over revenues when the economic cycle is factored out. With Australia's terms of trade falling from the anomalously high levels gained around 2010, the outlook for government revenues is far from encouraging. To make matters worse, the Abbott Government has also promised to reduce the size

Figure 11.4: Average US Navy Cost per Active Duty Vessel, 1951–2011

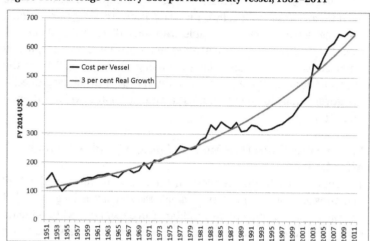

Source: US Pentagon FY2014 Budget Green Book and US Naval History and Heritage Command.

of government as a share of GDP and to deliver a surplus equal to 1 per cent of GDP in a decade's time. And before they get there, they have to pay down the accumulated debts of the past five years while accommodating growing costs in health, aged care, disability assistance and education.

Thus, even with the best intentions, it will be difficult for the 2 per cent promise to be met. It is also far from clear that the Department of Defence (Defence) can absorb the additional spending within the timeframe envisaged. During the 2000s, when defence spending was rising by 3 per cent a year in real terms, around $4.4 billion of funding has either handed back unspent or deferred in anticipation of not being able to be spent. To reach 2 per cent of GDP by 2023 will require steady real growth of around 5 per cent a year over the next decade.

Perhaps the biggest impediment to growing defence spending to 2 per cent of GDP in a decade's time is the declining priority of defence and security in the public eye. The distant strategic concerns of the post-September 11 2001 decade have been replaced by the more immediate and intimate worries of economic security after the

GFC. To achieve all that it has promised, the Abbott Government will need to take some politically difficult decisions to reallocate national resources towards defence. Simple arithmetic dictates that if defence spending is 2 per cent of GDP and the government is in surplus by 1 per cent of GDP while taking a smaller share of GDP from the economy than today, a reduced share of GDP will be available for the government to spend on health, education and welfare than at present.

Future Directions: How Much Is Enough? And is 'Enough' Affordable?

To properly reach a judgement on the size and shape of the ADF demands an assessment of the strategic risks Australia faces, coupled with an understanding of how military force can be used to mitigate those risks in the context of a strategy. But cost must also be taken into account—as in any other area of public policy, the benefits from defence spending should outweigh the costs incurred. On this there is no doubt; if costs outweigh benefits, resources are squandered, pure and simple.

The benefit of a defence force is that it can both reduce the likelihoods (though defence engagement or deterrence) and reduce the consequences (by prevailing in combat) of adverse strategic developments. Of course, it is very difficult to quantify the likelihood and consequence of the strategic events that Australia might face in the future. Thus, in practice, unquantified judgements lead to the allocation of human and financial resources to the nation's defence.

It is well beyond the scope of this chapter to try and produce such an analysis for Australia. However, it is open to readers of this volume to draw their own conclusion about how much Australia should be spending on its defence. To assist in doing so, the following analysis of defence costs will likely be useful because it allows the scale of Australia's defence effort to be calibrated against its economic capacity.

Defence Inflation: The Rising Cost of Maintaining the ADF

An important factor in defence budgeting is that the cost of maintaining military capability outpaces the inflation of prices in the economy overall. Estimates vary, but studies tend to reveal that the cost of maintaining an up to date defence force exceeds inflation by 2 to 3 per cent a year. For example, Figure 11.4 shows that the average real cost per active duty-US Navy vessel from 1951–2011 is growing at an underlying rate of 3 per cent a year. To keep the fleet running, this figure includes the cost of personnel, recapitalisation, maintenance, consumable items and administrative overheads.

At least two factors contribute to military costs growing at a rate exceeding inflation. First, despite technological innovation, defence forces remain stubbornly labour intensive. Elsewhere in the economy, innovation has reduced the demand for labour in many sectors, thereby increasing the productivity and wages of the remaining workers. Thus, rising productivity in the broader economy causes wages to grow in real terms (typically 1 to 2 per cent above inflation). But the wage gains in the broader economy then spill over into the defence sector, where the labour component has remained largely fixed, with the result that military personnel costs grow more quickly than inflation.

Second, when it comes to military equipment, the technological gains that reduce the cost of production of consumer goods are instead directed towards performance improvement. By its very nature, military equipment is designed to outperform that of potential adversaries rather than meet a performance standard that is static, or set by what the market is willing to pay. The resulting cycle of measure and countermeasure between potential adversaries' modernisation drives costs steadily upwards. Moreover, competition between producers of military equipment is less than for most private sector goods—and less in today's consolidated global defence industry than it was during the Cold War. Historical studies show the real rate of growth in the unit price of military platforms such as air-craft, ships and submarines running at 3 to 4 per cent a year.

A bottom up analysis of trends in the cost of personnel, equip-ment and other inputs to Australia's defence effort in 2008 concluded that to maintain a defence force of the size and shape then in exist-ence, it would require average real growth of around 2.6 per cent a year.[7] But since that time, plans for the ADF have grown more ambi-tious, at the same time as substantial cuts have been imposed on the budget. It follows therefore that even if 2.6 per cent growth would be adequate in the long run to 'tread water', a higher rate of growth will be required in the medium term to make up for lost progress and to fund the planned expansion of the force.

The long term economic cost to Australia of maintaining a modern defence force on any given scale is thus readily estimated as follows. Medium to long-term economic growth is expected to moderate from 3 to 2.5 per cent in the decades ahead, mainly due to slower growth in the size of the workforce. Thus, the cost of maintaining a defence force at a particular scale will grow at a rate more-or-less commensurate with the anticipated growth of the economy. To a rough approximation, therefore, the scale and sophistication of the ADF can probably be maintained in the long term by keeping defence spending at a more-or-less constant share of GDP. Taking account of recent cuts and current plans to expand the force, this means that defence spending will need to rise in the medium term as a share of GDP but should level out in the long term. What exactly the required long term share of GDP will have to be is a matter for detailed analysis—we will know a lot more after the 2015 Defence White Paper—but something in the vicinity of 2 per cent of GDP looks plausible on the basis of what we know today.

How Much Can Australia Spend on Defence?

The preceding analysis contains many assumptions and uncertainties: the historical trend in costs could moderate, GDP growth could fall into a malaise and the cost of fulfilling today's plans for the ADF could exceed our estimates. Or it might be that the 2015 Defence White Paper concludes that we need an even larger defence force than currently planned. Taking all these factors into account, it is still probably safe to assume that defence will command no more than 2.5 per cent and certainly less than 3 per cent of GDP out to mid-century. Indeed, figures below 2 per cent of GDP are at least as credible. Be that as it may, the question, in a worst-case sense, is whether Australia can afford to devote 2 or 3 per cent of its national output to defence in the decades ahead.

From a purely economic perspective, the answer is unambiguously yes. In the second half of the twentieth century Australia's defence spending exceeded 2 per cent of GDP in forty-three years, and 3 per cent of GDP in twelve years. What is more, this occurred at a time when Australia was much less prosperous than today, so that the absolute material opportunity cost was more acute. Today the United States spends more than 4 per cent of GDP and Israel spends more than 5 per cent without compromising their prosperity. The point is this: defence employs people and firms to do things in exactly the same way as the production of consumer goods or delivery of social services does. People are employed, money is invested and economic output ensues.

Of course, there are no free lunches. There is more to the world than aggregate economic output; every dollar spent on defence is a dollar that cannot be spent on private consumption or social services (such as health, education and welfare). Economic growth might be largely insensitive on how much we decide to spend on defence, but our access to competing private and public goods is not. It is explicitly a zero-sum game.

Absent of a clear and present strategic imperative, it is politically difficult to reallocate national resources to defence. In fact, the tendency has been to do exactly the opposite. As Figure 11.1 demonstrates, there has been a steady decline in the defence share of GDP after World War II, interrupted only by conflicts such as Korea and Vietnam. This century, the downward decline was only arrested by the onset of a series of operational deployments which have now ended.

Burden Sharing

No discussion of Australian defence spending would be complete without mention of burden sharing in the context of the ANZUS alliance (see Chapter 9). The carefully nurtured narrative of plucky Australia 'punching above its weight' stands in stark contrast to the facts. For the past sixty years, the unspoken reality has been that we have 'free ridden' on the efforts of the United States.

Since the late 1970s, it has all but been written into our defence policy: Australia has designed a defence force to defend its territory and explicitly relegated regional security under ANZUS to an afterthought. More important than Australia's declared position have been actions. In peace and war Australia has consistently made disproportionally small contributions to the common defence relative to the United States. The numbers tell the story; as a share of GDP, Australia has tended to spend around half or less than the United States on defence and has sent smaller proportions of its population than the United States to every coalition conflict since World War II.

Our free riding on the United States has rested on two things. First, as shown in Figure 11.5, Australia has closely mirrored the ebb and flow of US strategic concerns in both deployments and defence spending. So while absolute contributions have been disproportionately small, support has been responsive and visible. This is hardly a secret devised for Australia's interest; the vast majority of US allies have adopted the same approach over the past six decades. If Australia has been more successful than others—as reflected in privileged access to technology and intelligence—it is because of Australia's willingness to free ride just a little bit less than others. Given the habitual reluctance of some US allies in continental Europe and elsewhere to look beyond their own parochial concerns, it has been easy to look good.

Figure 11.5: Comparative Australian and United States Defence Spending, 1950–2012

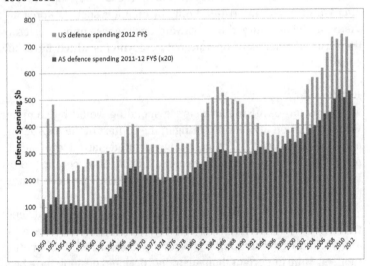

Note: Australian data has been multiplied by twenty to allow a visible comparison of the relative real increases and decrease in defence spending.

Source: US Pentagon, FY2014 Budget Green Book; Department of Defence, 2001–02 Defence Budget Brief and subsequent Defence Annual Reports, Department of Defence, Canberra.

The second reason that Australia has been able to free ride is that the United States contributes to regional and global security for its own good reasons, in pursuit of its own interests, and will do so irrespective of what Australia does. Just as importantly, Australia's contribution to the common defence is unlikely to make a difference in anything other than very special circumstances. Consequently, doing more than the minimum necessary to keep the alliance alive would increase the costs we incur without making any difference to our security. We do not do more because we know there is no reward to be had.

Free riding is central to Australian strategy. Since the 1970s we have maintained a defence force capable of unilaterally dealing with problems close to home—especially those where the United States has few intrinsic interests (such as the stability of our near region) or potentially divided interests (such as an Australia-Indonesia conflict). Beyond these limited goals we have relied on the United States to maintain regional and global security, making only carefully circumscribed contributions where necessary.

A key question for Australian policymakers is how much longer we can continue to rely on the United States to keep the peace, especially as the power dynamics in our part of the world change. The scale of our defence spending has long been calibrated by a regional security order underpinned by a strong and largely unchallenged US role. If it were to be judged that the United States might play a lesser, or less certain role in regional security, we would then have to choose between spending more on our own defence or accepting elevated risks.

Defending Australia with an Aging Population

As the post-war baby boom works its way through Australia's demographic profile, the proportion of persons in the prime-recruiting cohort for the ADF (18–26 year olds) will change. Whereas in 2012, around 12.7 per cent of the population fell into the cohort, by 2050 the proportion will have fallen to between 10.2 per cent and 11.3 per cent. While the decline is far from alarming, the aging of the population has prompted predictions of a looming crisis in defence force recruiting, with some commentators going so far as to argue the need to reinstitute national service.[8] However, closer examination reveals that the demographic trends are hardly an issue for defence, and challenges should be manageable without conscription.

To start with, it is important to put the size of the ADF into context. With around 60 000 permanent members, the ADF accounts for only around 0.5 per cent of Australia's 11.6 million strong workforce. Given anticipated trends in Australia's population and workforce participation, the percentage will decline further in the years ahead. With more than 200 civilian workers in the economy to every uniformed member of the ADF, it is hard to see how demographics could lead to a military personnel shortage now or in the future.

The situation looks even more favourable if we look at what's likely to happen in absolute terms to the youth cohort from which the ADF traditionally draws its initial recruits. Figure 11.6 shows the Australian Bureau of Statistics (ABS) projections for the number of persons in the 18–26 year old age group. As is apparent from the projections, even under the most pessimistic of projections the ADF will have more people to draw upon in the future than it does today. Once again, to put things into perspective, there will be more than 3 million young Australians from which the defence force will recruit around 6 000 people each year, or around 0.2 per cent of the available cohort.

Even if the *proportion* of younger people in the population and workforce declined this would not necessarily be a problem. Mechanisation of industry and agriculture long ago all but did away with the backbreaking human labour that put a priority on young bodies. So while the military has retained the need for large numbers of young workers, the corresponding demand in the civil economy has declined.

Thus, to the extent that the defence force finds it difficult to recruit young people in the years ahead, it will not be demographics that are to blame. There will be plenty of young people available; the question is whether the defence force can make them a good enough offer—and herein lies a problem. As recently as twenty years ago, the defence force could offer young people opportunities for travel, adventure and career development that were relatively difficult to access in the civilian world. But prosperity has gradually eroded the gap between what the military can offer and what a motivated person can achieve alone. Australians make more than 8 million overseas trips each year,[9] adventure sports are commonplace and the cutting edge of technology is firmly is in civil rather than military hands. What is more, structural changes to the Australian economy have increased the proportion of well-paid high-productivity jobs.

Figure 11.6: Projected Number of Australians Aged 18–26 Years

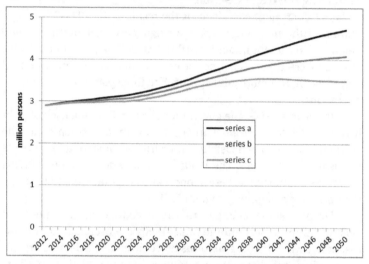

Source: Australian Bureau of Statistics, ABS Series 3222.0, released November 2012.

Young people will increasingly have the opportunity to pursue interesting and rewarding jobs in the civil economy without the strictures and hardships inherent in military service. This can only make it more difficult for the defence force to recruit and retain personnel, or more accurately it can make it more expensive to do so. The young people will be there, the challenge for the ADF will be to meet their expectations.

The defence force is well aware of the challenges and the past decade has seen encouraging innovation in both recruiting and retention. A few minutes on the ADF recruiting website is sufficient to show how sophisticated and youth-focused ADF recruiting has become, including the extensive use of social media. And there is more planned, including a revamp of part-time service to provide greater career flexibility more attune to modern expectations.[10] The challenge of maintaining a competitive employment package will be ongoing. As the range of opportunities open to young Australians expands in the future, the defence force will have to continue to innovate or it will find itself left behind.

Managing Australia's Defence

Today's Department of Defence is the result of the 1973–74 amalgamation of the previously separate single service departments and defence department under Sir Arthur Tange. The goals of the Tange reforms were to establish better-coordinated government control and to facilitate a more joint approach to force planning and military operations.

In the late 1980s, the government began divesting itself of publicly owned defence production facilities, with the last remnant—the corporatised Australian Defence Industries—transferred into private hands in the late 1990s. The 1990s also saw widespread outsourcing of various maintenance, base support and corporate functions under the Commercial Support Program (CSP).

Despite some changes to the executive arrangements in Defence in the 1980s, until the mid-1990s the overall structure was essentially what the Tange reforms had delivered: a federated organisation where the three services managed many of their own affairs but with centralised delivery of intelligence, force development and equipment acquisition along with key aspects of finance, personnel and facilities. All that changed with the Defence Reform Program (DRP) in 1997.[11]

The DRP was an attempt to free up money to address the then growing gap between tightly constrained funding and the demands of block obsolescence of significant components of the ADF asset base. Key initiatives included the rationalisation of the defence estate (leading to property sales) and the removal of duplication both between the services and between the civilian and military components of the organisation. As a result, many activities previously undertaken separately by the three services were consolidated into common 'shared services' programs. At the same time, the previously separate civilian and military areas of the organisation that developed policy advice were melded together. While this eliminated duplication, it also reduced civilian oversight and put control of force planning firmly into uniformed hands.

The DRP planned to deliver recurrent savings of around $1 billion a year representing roughly 10 per cent of the then budget. By the time the dust settled it was impossible to tell what had really been achieved financially, though within a couple of years a major cash injection was required to cover urgent budget pressures. During the 2000s, reform continued with the consolidation of materiel support activities and equipment acquisition to form the Defence Materiel Organisation (DMO) in 2000. A subsequent review of defence procurement in 2003 led to the reconstitution of the DMO as a quasi-independent agency in an attempt to make it more 'commercially orientated'. Also during the 2000s, a 600-strong Joint Operations Command was created and given a purpose-built headquarters adjacent to Bungendore—in a marginal electorate—near Canberra. Although previous joint operational commands existed under different names, the new headquarters provides a much higher level of connectivity to deployed forces and greater capacity to direct and oversight operations (see Chapter 10).

As part of the funding arrangements for the 2009 Defence White Paper, the Rudd Government initiated the Strategic Reform Program (SRP) with the aim of improving Defence planning, governance and efficiency.[12] Central to the SRP was the goal of achieving more than $20 billion in savings over a decade for redirection to priority areas within Defence. Unlike its predecessor (the DRP) the SRP program was modest in the range and depth of what it sought to accomplish organisationally. Rather than wholesale consolidations and rationalisations, the SRP was about incremental improvements to existing arrangements. As such, the notion of extracting savings of around $2 billion a year from a budget of $24 billion was simply implausible. Consistent with this, the initial savings reported by the program were reported relative to grossly inflated and unsubstantiated estimates of business-as-usual costs.

In 2012, the SRP was effectively abandoned after successive reductions in defence funding undermined the planning basis of the program. Funding had been cut so deeply that it made little sense to pretend that productivity was somehow increasing, rather than that austerity was being accommodated under duress. Nonetheless, the SRP did help to finally bed down the shared services model that the DRP had introduced more than a decade earlier. In fact, there is evidence that real and worthwhile efficiencies were delivered in the areas of materiel sustainment and non-materiel support—though not on the exaggerated scales claimed.

Structure and Accountability

The current organisational structure of Defence appears in Chapter 10 of the book. To the uninitiated eye it probably reveals little other than that the organisation is complicated, even at a high level of aggregation. Figure 11.7 attempts to capture the essential features of the structure by grouping the various components of the organisation into three categories: administration and policy, shared services and capability outputs.

Figure 11.7: The Defence Organisation

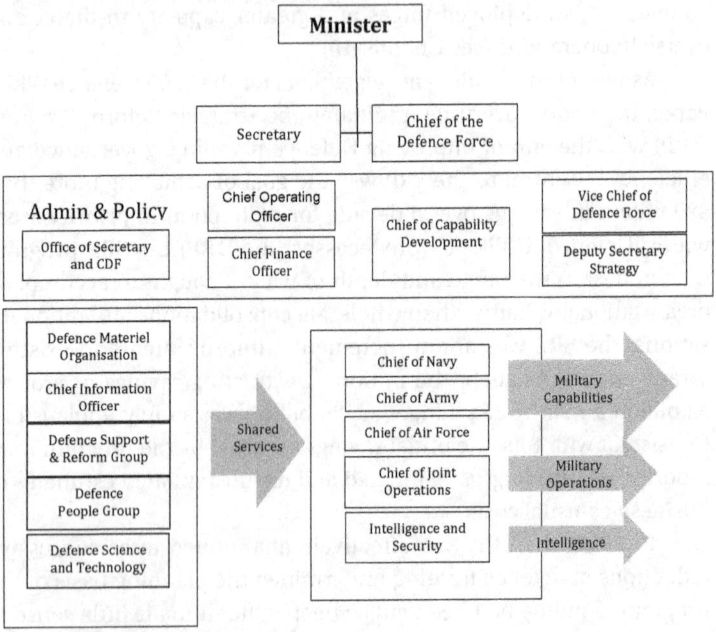

Source: Adapted from Department of Defence, Defence Annual Report 2012–13, Commonwealth of Australia, 2013.

Defence is jointly led by a diarchy comprising the Secretary and the Chief of the Defence Force. While this arrangement has attracted adverse commentary over the years, it appears to work surprisingly well in practice. Below the diarchy are fourteen 'groups', including the quasi-independent DMO. The substantive outputs of the organisation (setting aside policy advice) are the responsibility of the three services, along with the head of the intelligence group, and for military operations, the Chief of Joint Operations.

These five 'capability output' groups depend upon inputs provided by the 'shared service' groups, which include the DMO, the Defence Science and Technology Organisation (DSTO) and the Defence Support Group. The Defence Support Group is responsible for base support, facilities acquisition and maintenance, personnel policy and services, non-materiel procurement, legal services and health. The remaining groups in Defence comprise an overlay of administrative and policy overhead. The Vice Chief of the Defence Force group somewhat defies categorisation because it includes a host of support, policy and administrative functions that would otherwise fall through the gaps.

The central issue surrounding Defence's organisational structure is the extent to which those nominally responsible for delivering outputs—and in particular the service chiefs—can be held to account when they rely on others to provide critical inputs. In this regard, there is an inherent tension between maintaining clear lines of accountability and exploiting the efficiencies available through shared service delivery.

The issue came to a head in early 2011, when the Navy's entire amphibious lift capability was found to be unavailable for service on the eve of a cyclone impact in north Queensland. The ensuring inquiry revealed a number of shortcomings, including the failure of both DMO and Navy to properly manage the material state of the assets in question. A subsequent review of submarine maintenance reached similar conclusions. Although a number of factors contributed in each case—including inadequate technical expertise, insufficient maintenance funding and sub-optimal contracting—the question of accountability and control of resources was clearly a critical factor.

A number of changes were implemented following the problems encountered with the amphibious and submarine fleets, including a clearer and more intimate role for the service chiefs in oversighting the maintenance of platforms. But this is unlikely to put an end to changes. A 'first principles' review of Defence is planned for 2014 in tandem with the development of the 2015 Defence White Paper. Although the review's terms of reference had not been disclosed at the time of writing, it would be surprising if the shared services model and the role of the service chiefs were not central issues.

However, while the question of accountability cannot be divorced from Defence's structure, it would be a mistake to think that billions of dollars of strategic assets were lying moribund because of the lines on the department's organisational chart. Irrespective of the extent that accountability for the maintenance and support of the submarines and amphibious vessels was unclear, it took a serious case of learned helplessness within the organisation to allow the situation to emerge and persist—especially in the case of submarines, where the malaise had been publicly visible for years.

Governance

Central to the smooth administration of Defence is the relationship between the Department and its minister. Unfortunately, a long series of scandals, mishaps and debacles engendered growing distrust between Defence and its ministers through the 2000s, culminating in the rocky tenure of Stephen Smith between 2010 and 2013. With growing distrust has come a tendency to refer ever more minor matters upwards for ministerial approval. Apart from slowing down administrative activities, distrust misdirects ministerial attention away from strategic matters onto the minutiae of the day-to-day affairs of a sprawling organisation. It remains to be seen how the new minister will decide to delegate authority under his tenure.

Within Defence, major decisions (or more accurately advice to the minister regarding major decisions) tend to emerge from the organisation's labyrinthine committee system. To some extent this is unavoidable, as the cross dependencies inherent in current organisational arrangements make intra-departmental consultation necessary. That said, the habitual recourse to consultation reduces clarity about who is responsible for decisions. While success is hard to judge, an attempt was made in 2011 to rationalise the number of committees, working groups and other internal fora.

Procurement and Sustainment Reform

Reviews of defence procurement and sustainment in 2003 and 2008 led to a host of changes to how acquisitions are planned and executed, including most importantly the 2005 re-establishment of DMO as a quasi-independent agency. Eight years on, the question is whether to move DMO further away from Defence by making it either an executive agency or perhaps even a privately-managed government-owned corporation, or to reabsorb it back into Defence proper. The latter seems most likely because of the risks associated with a more independent arrangement. While a more independent status would facilitate greater flexibility in personnel management and more commercially orientated practices, the additional transaction costs inherent in an arms-length relationship would be substantial. Even if the benefits of the former outweighed the cost of the latter, the apportionment of responsibility and risk between Defence and a corporate acquisition/sustainment agency would be problematic to say the least.

Irrespective of the organisational arrangements under which DMO operates, the new Coalition Government appears eager to change how procurement and sustainment are executed. On the procurements side, the aim will be to reduce the extended time it takes to plan, initiate and deliver projects. On the sustainment side, the goal will be to transfer more responsibility (and workforce) to industry through the introduction of performance-based contracts which specify the availability of assets rather than mandate specific maintenance activities. In each case, progress should be possible and will be worthwhile if accomplished.

Efficiency

The constant flow of additional money into Defence during the 2000s resulted in substantial growth in management and command overheads within the organisation. Without doubt the most visible sign has been the disproportionate growth in the number of civilian and military senior officers and executives over the period (see table 11.1).

Table 11.1: Growth in Command and Management Overheads in Defence

Category	2000	2013	Increase %
Senior Executive Service	103	168	63.1
Senior Officers (EL1 &EL2)	3 317	6 767	104.0
Total Civilian Workforce	16 295	21 217	30.2
Star-ranks Officers	120	190	58.3
Senior Officers (O5 & O6)	1 415	2 042	44.3
Total Military Workforce	50 355	58 253	15.7

Source: Department of Defence, Defence Annual Reports and Budget Papers, Commonwealth of Australia.

Given the relatively tight fiscal outlook, the new government is understandably looking to harvest efficiency gains—and the first principles review mentioned earlier is the vehicle through which they hope to do so. Given the alarming growth in senior and middle management numbers, that is an obvious place to start. There are also likely to be opportunities for further efficiency within Defence's shared service providers—either through outsourcing, process improvement or greater use of information technology to reduce costs and personnel numbers. In the final analysis, however, the long-running process of defence reform has reached the point diminishing returns with most of the low-lying fruit having been harvested. What remains is worthwhile but hardly substantial on the scale of defence spending.

A sizable gap exists between the existing plans for the ADF and currently available funding. It will be the job of the 2015 Defence White Paper to close the gap by either delivering the promised boost of defence spending to 2 per cent of GDP or revising downwards the planned scale and sophistication of the ADF. There is no credible third option; whatever efficiency measures are adopted within Defence will be far short of what is needed to make ends meet. As has been the case on many previous occasions, the government will either have to dig deep and find more money, or else moderate its ambitions.

Irrespective of how much the government decides to spend on defence, some level of at least medium term reliability is needed to allow for sensible and efficient defence planning. The recent years of bold plans and systemic underfunding have led to a cycle of wasteful spending and damaging thrift. To continue with such an approach would squander public money and compromise Australia's defence capability.

Further Reading

For insight into economics of defence capability see, Thomson, Mark, *Trends in US Defence Spending: Implications for Australia*, no. 56, *APSI Policy Analysis*, Australian Strategic Policy Institute, Canberra, 2010. www.aspi. org.au/publications/trends-in-us-defence-spending-implications-for-australia-by-mark-thomson; and Davies, Andrew and Thomson, Mark, *Strategic Choices: Defending Australia in the 21st Century*, no. 45, *APSI Strategic Insights*, Australian Strategic Policy Institute, Canberra, 2008. www.aspi.org.au/publications/strategic-insights-45-strategic-choices-defending-australia-in-the-21st-century.

For an analysis of recent Australian defence funding, see Thomson, Mark, *The Cost of Defence: ASPI Defence Budget Brief 2013–14*, Australian Strategic Policy Institute, Canberra, 2013. www.aspi.org.au/publications/the-cost-of-defence-aspi-defence-budget-brief-2013-2014. See especially Chapter 3, 'White Papers and Money', pp. 113–136. A more detailed analysis of earlier years is available in prior editions going back to 2002–3.

For a thorough examination on defence efficiency, see Ergas, Henry and Thomson, Mark, 'More Guns Without Less Butter: Improving Australian Defence Efficiency', in W Coleman (ed), *Agenda: A Journal of Policy Analysis and Reform*, vol. 18, no. 3, 2011, pp. 31–52. www.press.anu. edu.au/titles/agenda-a-journal-of-policy-analysis-and-reform-2/volume-18-number-3-2011/pdf-download/.

For Defence business model and related issues, see Thomson, Mark, *Serving Australia: Control and Administration of the Department of Defence*, no. 41, *APSI Special Report*, Australian Strategic Policy Institute, Canberra, 2011. www.aspi.org.au/publications/special-report-issue-41-serving-australia-control-and-administration-of-the-department-of-defence/5_28_33_PM_SR41_Serving-Australia.pdf.

An overview of recent reviews of Defence appears in Ergas, Henry, 'Australia's Defence: A Review of the "Reviews"', in Coleman, William, (ed), *Agenda—A Journal of Policy and Reform*, vol. 19, no. 1, 2012, (viewed 17 December 2013), www.epress.anu.edu.au/apps/bookworm/view/Agenda,+Volume+19,+Number+1,+2012/9601/Ergas.html.

Recent major external reviews of Defence relevant to efficiency include:

Department of Defence, *2008 Audit of the Defence Budget*, Commonwealth of Australia, Canberra, 2009. www.defence.gov.au/publications/DefenceBudgetAudit.pdf.

Rizzo, Paul J, *Plan to Reform Support Ship Repair and Management Practices*, Commonwealth of Australia, Canberra, 2011. www.defence.gov.au/oscdf/rizzo-review/Review.pdf.

Black, Rufus, *Review of the Defence Accountability Framework*,
Commonwealth of Australia, Canberra, 2011. www.defence.gov.au/oscdf/
BlackReview/black_review.pdf.

Coles, John, *Study into the Business of Sustaining Australia's Strategic Collins
Class Submarine Capability*, Commonwealth of Australia, Canberra, 2012.
www.defence.gov.au/dmo/publications/Coles_Report_Final_22Nov12.pdf.

Notes

1   TB Millar, *Australia's Defence*, Melbourne University Press, Carlton, 1965,
    p. 143.

2   Aside from directly measuring the proportion of national output
    allocated to defence, GDP share has the advantage of being unaffected by
    inflation.

3   S Smith, 'Minister for Defence—Outcomes of the Kirkham Inquiry',
    Defence Media Release, Commonwealth of Australia, Canberra, 7 March
    2012. www.minister.defence.gov.au/2012/03/07/minister-for-defence-
    outcomes-of-the-kirkham-inquiry/ (viewed December 2013).

4   M Thomson, 'Second Chance: Will They Deliver?', Defence Special
    Report, *The Australian*, 25 May 2013.

5   A Carr and P Dean, 'The Funding Illusion: The 2% of GDP Furphy in
    Australia's Defence Debate', *Security Challenges*, vol. 9, no. 4, 2013, pp.
    65–86. www.securitychallenges.org.au/ArticlePDFs/SC9-4CarrandDean.
    pdf (viewed January 2014).

6   North Atlantic Treaty Organisation, *Information on Defence Expenditures*,
    www.nato.int/cps/en/natolive/topics_49198.htm (viewed January 2014).

7   A Davies and M Thomson, *Strategic Choices: Defending Australia in the
    21st Century*, no. 45, *APSI Strategic Insights*, Australian Strategic Policy
    Institute, Canberra, 2008. www.aspi.org.au/publications/strategic-
    insights-45-strategic-choices-defending-australia-in-the-21st-century
    (viewed December 2013).

8   C Barrie, 'We Need to Debate Conscription', *Sydney Morning Herald*, 4
    October 2009.

9   Australian Bureau of Statistics, 'ABS Series 3401—Overseas Arrivals and
    Departures, Australia, October 2013', Australian Bureau of Statistics.
    www.abs.gov.au (viewed January 2014).

10 S Robert, 'Assistant Minister for Defence—ADF launches Enhanced
    Workforce Model', Defence Media Release, Commonwealth of Australia,
    Canberra, 26 November 2013. www.minister.defence.gov.au/2013/11/26/
    assistant-minister-for-defence-adf-launches-enhanced-workforce-
    model/ (viewed January 2014).

11 Department of Defence, *Future Directions for the Management of
    Australia's Defence: Report of the Defence Efficiency Review*,
    Commonwealth of Australia, Canberra, 1997. www.defence.gov.au/
    minister/der/report.pdf (viewed January 2014).

12 Department of Defence, *The Strategic Reform Program 2009: Delivering
    Force 2030*, Commonwealth of Australia, Canberra, 2009. www.defence.
    gov.au/publications/reformbooklet.pdf (viewed December 2013).

12

Developing ADF Force Structure and Posture

Richard Brabin-Smith

The end-point of the government's defence policies is an Australian Defence Force (ADF) that is able to deter or to conduct operations. But there is a penultimate stage in the process that gets to this point. This is the set of decisions that the government makes on the level of resources to be allocated to Defence (that is, the Department of Defence), on their allocation within Defence and on where and when it expects the ADF to be used. These decisions result in a force structure, comprising the ADF's various force elements (such as submarines, battalions and fighter aircraft), plans for modernisation and the ADF's posture (that is, where the force elements are based and the levels of preparedness at which they are held). In effect, the structure and posture are the culmination of the government's response to the challenges of Australia's strategic environment discussed earlier in this book.

This decision-making relies heavily on judgement. It reflects choices made about the factors that should have a strong influence, and those that should have less influence, in working out what Australia's defence priorities should be. Judgements are needed in striking the balance between levels of expenditure and levels of strategic risk, and between the shorter and the long term. And

judgements need to take into account the length of the time-scales—
often decades—that can be associated with the acquisition of
defence equipment and the development of operational doctrine
and expertise. The potential for change over such time-scales needs
to be taken into account, such as changes in strategic circumstances,
technology and prospective levels of funding. Because of this extensive reliance on judgement, decisions can often be highly contested
within government, Defence itself and the public sphere.

Dominating the judgements and decision-making processes is
the notion of 'priorities' and how they are derived. There is no simple
formula that can be applied to determine what these priorities are.
Defence is too multi-dimensioned and complex for that. Rather,
what is needed is a top-down approach to decision-making that is
intellectually robust and which fosters an internally consistent
approach to the difficult questions that need to be addressed. The
term 'conceptual framework' is a useful expression for referring to
such an approach. This framework has to be accepted not only
within Defence itself (at least by the principal players such as
the Secretary and the Chief of the Defence Force) but also by other
senior Defence-interested actors within the machinery of government: the Departments of Prime Minister and Cabinet, Foreign
Affairs and Trade, Treasury and Finance and the Office of National
Assessments.

Above all, the conceptual framework needs to be owned by the
government, for it is ministers who make the decisions, not their
public service or defence force advisors. It is therefore government-
endorsed documents, in particular defence white papers, to which
we turn to find out what guides ministers' thinking. To date there
have been six defence white papers, the first in 1976 and the most
recent in 2013. A close reading of these documents shows that some
important themes have persisted over this period. In particular there
have been four policy principles which together have provided the
conceptual framework that has been the foundation for much of the
subsequent assessment and decision-making.

A Conceptual Framework for Defence Priorities

The first of these policy principles is self-reliance in the defence of
Australia. In terms of priorities for the force structure, this leads to an

immediate focus on the direct needs of Australia itself, as the 1987 Defence White Paper illustrates:

> Australians have a right to expect that their nation is able to defend itself. That is at the core of nationhood, and has long been an Australian aspiration. The exercise of authority over our continent and off-shore territories, our territorial sea and resource zones, and airspace, and the ability to protect our maritime and air approaches, is fundamental to our sovereignty and security.[1]

The second policy principle is that there are limits to Australia's military resources and influence. Perhaps the central point here is one of expectation management. While Australia's military tradition is built, in many respects, on a proud history of supporting and fighting along side the United Kingdom and the United States—the global leaders of their day—in much of the twentieth century, it has few if any major-power attributes itself. This observation can sit uncomfortably with those who seek a significantly wide or global role for Australia and its defence effort. The consequence for force structure and posture is that it is important to avoid excessive, costly and ultimately unattainable levels of ambition and overreach. As the 2000 Defence White Paper reminds us:

> [W]e must be realistic about the scope of our power and influence and the limits to our resources. We need to allocate our effort carefully and prioritise our strategic interests and objectives.[2]

The third policy principle is the strong priority for operations closer to home over more-distant operations. There are two particular consequences of this principle. The first is expressed in the *priority* of tasks for the ADF. The 2013 Defence White Paper makes this clear. It spells out that these 'Principal Tasks', in priority order, are: first, to deter and defeat armed attacks on Australia; second, to contribute to stability and security in the South Pacific and Timor-Leste; third, to contribute to military contingencies in the Indo-Pacific region; and fourth, to contribute to military contingencies in support of global security.[3] The second consequence is the critical judgement that some tasks (those relating to the defence of Australia and to operations in our neighbourhood) should determine the capabilities of the force structure and others should not:

> The Government recognises that we need clear priorities for building the ADF's capabilities so that Defence's resources are focused effectively. We therefore structure our forces around the first two Principal Tasks, on the understanding that the resulting force structure provides capabilities that can meet other needs.[4]

A specific point is worth emphasising, not least because it is often misunderstood in much public commentary and sometimes even within Defence itself. The policy framework differentiates between the contingencies for which the ADF is structured and those for which it may be used. The former are the contingencies in which Australia would be obliged to be involved. The latter are those where involvement would be more discretionary and these do not affect decisions on the force structure, except conceivably at the margins of capability. They would however affect the preparedness of elements of the ADF if the government decided that Australia should get involved in a specific contingency.

The fourth policy principle brings together the issues of level of contingency, warning time, and force expansion. This core subject is often strongly contested: what are the contingencies that the government wants the ADF to be able to handle, and within what timescales? Judgements about warning time and types of contingency have a determining influence on decisions about the size and shape of the defence force and the levels of preparedness at which its various elements are held. These judgements include assessments of what is needed as a basis of equipment, expertise, doctrine and industry support from which to expand in the event of serious deterioration in Australia's strategic circumstances.[5]

Although it is often neglected in much defence planning, time is an important parameter in a government's approach to defence policy, risk management and resource allocation. Two examples illustrate the importance of this principle. First, preparedness can be expensive, so not all elements of a defence force are kept at short notice for operations. There will usually be a spectrum of preparedness. At one end are counter-terrorist forces ready to move within hours and at the other end, Defence Reserve forces mostly able to become operational only after months, if not years. Second is the idea of reconstitution or mobilisation. When threats emerge, a defence force will be expanded, and when threats go away—as at the end of the World Wars and the Cold War—forces will be reduced.[6]

In Australia's case, the end of the war in Vietnam called for fresh thinking about defence policy. The emerging ideas in *Defence of Australia*[7] (DoA) filled some of the gaps, but there was a need also for an analytical basis from which to argue for levels of defence funding—else the prospective budget cuts at a time of evident 'low threat' would have been harsh. This led Defence to develop the concept of the core force and expansion base. In brief, a force-in-being would evolve which would both meet the demands of those important lesser contingencies that might arise in the shorter term and be the base from which expansion would occur in the event of major strategic deterioration. Intelligence would be critical in assessing warning time and ensuring that expansion would be timely.[8]

Two points from this principle should be noted. First, contingencies of importance to Australia that might arise at short notice might be critical to national survival or sovereignty. Second, the threat of major attack on Australia is something that could arise only in the long term, after a period of considerable warning, during which the government would expand the ADF and more generally increase preparedness.

These ideas, which emerged in the early 1970s and which were first formally set out in the 1976 Defence White Paper, attracted incredulous and hostile comment. Yet the concepts have endured and have become embedded in the conceptual framework that continues to guide Defence planning. Perhaps to rebut any continuing criticism, the 1987 White Paper took the effort to reinforce why these judgements were sound. It spelt out how Australia was different from 'its traditional friends and allies in the northern hemisphere'. Not only was there an absence of motive and intent for major conventional assault on Australia, but it would take many years for any plausible adversary to develop the necessary levels of capability and expertise.[9] The latter observation was the key point: no credible adversary had the capability, experience or doctrine necessary to mount and sustain a major amphibious assault—least of all one which Australia would oppose with great tenacity. It would take years and great expense to develop such a capability, and an adversary's preparation could not escape detection by Australia's advanced intelligence capabilities.

In more contemporary times, the 2013 Defence White Paper continued with essentially the same approach, using familiar language and ideas. With respect to the prospect of major power attack, 'we would require an even stronger ADF than is currently planned', and 'we would still expect substantial warning time ... including dramatic deterioration in political relationships'. Further, 'Defence will continue to balance its finite ... resources to meet current and short term requirements while retaining a baseline of skills, knowledge and capability as the foundation for force expansion should strategic circumstances deteriorate'.[10]

There is also the argument that even contingencies that might arise in the shorter term would not occur without at least some warning. The 1976 Defence White Paper observed that '[u]se of military force is not a course adopted lightly by one nation against another ... The conjunction of [the necessary] conditions is infrequent among the nations of the world and takes time to develop'.[11] The 2013 Defence White Paper appears to go further than this, where it states that 'adjustments to preparedness levels ... can take effect relatively quickly compared to long term basing and force structure decisions'.[12] Such observations have consequences for judgements about priorities for preparedness even for the force-in-being: many of the contingencies to which the government would require the ADF to be able to respond would not arise without a degree of warning (they would not just come out of the blue), and preparedness levels across the ADF need to reflect this.

Taken together, the preceding four policy principles do much to guide the priorities for the size and shape of the ADF, the basing that is required to support it and the levels of preparedness at which its various elements should be held. They also allow some further principles to be deduced, built around the idea of 'Australia's strategic geography'. Two points stand out. The first is that the capabilities required for the defence of Australia and for operations in the region will have a strong maritime focus (see Chapter 6). A glance at the charts will make this obvious: Australia itself surrounded by vast oceans on three sides and with a significant air-sea gap to the north (see Figure 8.1), the Indonesian and Philippine archipelagos and maritime southeast Asia to the northwest and north (see Figure 5.1) and the island states of the southwest Pacific (see Figure 6.1). It follows that maritime capabilities—both Navy and Air Force—will command a high level of priority in planning for all levels of contingency.

This does not mean that Army is without a role. The need to protect the bases from which Australia would be projecting maritime power or to conduct a variety of peacemaking or peacekeeping operations in the region are just two of the more obvious examples of where Australia has a need for Army capabilities. But it does mean that it is difficult to develop the case for a more-conventional Army structure that gives priority to intense, multi-divisional operations, especially when compared to the more obvious priority for high levels of maritime capability. By the mid-1980s, this general conclusion had become highly contested and the civilian policy areas of the Department of Defence (Defence, who were proponents of this conclusion) and the ADF Headquarters (who opposed it) proved unable to resolve their differences. This impasse led the then minister for Defence to appoint a consultant to conduct an independent *Review of Australia's Defence Capabilities*.[13] In brief, this Review confirmed the priority for maritime capabilities but did not accept the arguments that the ADF Headquarters made for priorities for the development of the Army.[14] The Review's judgements and conclusions formed the basis of the subsequent 1987 Defence White Paper.

The second point flowing from Australia's strategic geography is that the high priority for maritime effectiveness needs to be reflected in the levels of capability of individual platforms and how they work together. On the one hand, this means that weapons and sensors need to be capable and to take advantage of advances in technology. And because the distances involved in operations in the defence of Australia are large, there is also a priority for equipment with significant operational range and endurance. Further, because the lead-times to acquire, learn how to operate and maintain, and develop doctrine[15] for high-technology equipment can be long, equipment numbers in service should be sufficient to facilitate force expansion in the event of strategic deterioration.

On the other hand, Australia's strategic circumstances have not, in general, required the acquisition of the most capable equipment developed by nations subject to higher levels of threat than Australia. Instead, and in the absence of an evident and specific 'threat' against which to benchmark ADF capabilities, a guiding principle has been that Australia should seek to maintain a capability or technology edge against trends in Australia's wider (but unspecified) region. For example, the 2000 Defence White Paper says that 'Australia's defence planning should aim to provide our forces with a clear margin of superiority against any credible adversary'.[16] This principle has had wide application in Australian defence planning, especially when deciding levels of naval and air capability.

By and large, the principles set out above have been reflected in the development of the ADF over the past forty years or so, as the following examples illustrate:

- An increasingly well-integrated and capable Australian Intelligence Community and a capable Defence Science and Technology Organisation (DSTO) that focuses its work on Australian priorities.
- The evolution of Australian Joint-force command arrangements and the associated advanced communications and command-support systems.
- The introduction into service and continued development of the *Jindalee* over-the-horizon radar network.
- Selection of the characteristics of the *Collins*-class submarines to match the demands of Australia's strategic geography (notwithstanding the difficulties that Australia has had in keeping the *Collins*-class operational).
- A destroyer force, which has had range and endurance capabilities increasingly matched to the demands of Australia's geography and combat capabilities which have kept pace with the likely demands of regional contingencies.
- An Army which has built on the success of its light infantry

traditions, including flexibility and mobility, and which has avoided a distracting focus on the heavier forms of land warfare.

- Air Force combat capabilities characterised by high-end platforms, sensors and weapons and good range and endurance, amplified in recent years by more-capable in-flight refuelling, state-of-the-art Airborne Warning and Control aircraft, and the decision to acquire the specialised electronic warfare (EW) *Growler* version of the F/A-18 Super Hornet.[17]

- A spectrum of preparedness across the ADF which, when combined with intelligence assessments, has allowed the deployment of suitable ADF elements on operations, including in support of the Australia-US alliance. (This preparedness profile has allowed the government to make a good number of decisions to deploy the ADF, notwithstanding the large element of discretion in Australia's involvement in many of them (that is, whether to get involved and how to get involved). Examples include Kuwait, Iraq and Afghanistan, and a variety of United Nations peacekeeping operations. In contrast, Australia's involvement in Bougainville, Timor-Leste and the Solomon Islands was much less discretionary. Also, the ADF has been frequently involved in humanitarian assistance and disaster relief.)

- The development of bases across the north of Australia, from west to east, and in Fremantle. (Some of these bases are bare-base airfields, that is, bases for which the long-lead-time infrastructure such as heavy-duty military runways has been put in place, where ADF elements are not home-based but which, with some preparation, could be used for exercises and contingencies.)

It would be wrong to conclude that this decision-making has all been plain sailing. As befits matters that were complex, important and costly, issues were hammered out step by step, with a range of options for numbers, levels of capability and timing being considered. And there were some casualties along the way, such as the decision not to continue with a fixed-wing aircraft carrier, the arguments over the direction for the development of the Army (mentioned earlier in this chapter), and the decision not to replace the RAAF's obsolete ground-based long-range air defence missile system.

Further, it is important not to overlook current problems with defence force capabilities. Examples here are to be found in the areas of mine-countermeasures, anti-submarine warfare (ASW), and the maintenance of the *Collins*-class submarines (mentioned above), and the preparedness of the ADF is at best opaque as far as the public is concerned. Nevertheless, the overall direction of development of the ADF has been consistent with the policy principles set out in the first part of this chapter.

Issues for the Immediate Future

In the short term, there are several important issues relating to the force structure and its posture that need to be addressed. The most important of these is that the cost of the extensive modernisation program set out in the 2009 and 2013 Defence White Papers is much greater than the level of funding that might realistically become available, as discussed at greater length in Chapter 11.[18] This kind of situation is nothing new in defence planning, but the problems seem particularly severe at present. These pressures imply the need for difficult decisions both to reduce the scope of the ambitions for modernisation and the preparedness and size of elements in the ADF and other areas of Defence.[19]

In the case of the Royal Australian Navy (RAN), the biggest current modernisation challenge is to decide the way ahead for the future submarines. To a first approximation, this is a trade-off between capability on the one hand, and cost and technical risk on the other. This can be seen in the public debate: the government could reduce the projects costs and risks by buying boats to a more-or-less proven European design, and by having them built in Europe not Australia. Critics of this approach respond that there is no off-the-shelf design of a conventionally-powered submarine that would even come close to meeting the needs for range and endurance (and other characteristics) demanded by Australia's strategic geography and operating environment. Such considerations determined the basic characteristics of what became today's *Collins*-class submarines, and which in many respects have led to the current maintenance difficulties of the *Collins* fleet, for example with the propulsion system.

There are two other important issues concerning the future

submarines. First is the numbers of new boats to be acquired. There has been no public justification of the decision to double the size of the fleet from six boats to twelve, least of all in a situation where no other ADF element is being expanded in such a way. At a time of acute pressure on the modernisation program and no articulated strategic argument for twelve boats, there is *prima facie* a compelling reason to review the numbers to be acquired. Second is the timing issue. The more that decisions on the new boats are delayed, the more difficult the transition will be from the *Collins*-class to the new boats, leading to a gap in capability—similar to that which occurred in the transition from the previous *Oberon*-class to the *Collins*.

There are no clear answers to the best way ahead for the future submarines. Rather, the issues are a good illustration of the dilemmas that governments can face in getting a good balance between cost, capability and risk—not just technical and cost risk but also strategic risk. In this particular case, the judgement will need to be applied to a component of the ADF which has consistently commanded a high priority for the force structure.

The biggest force structure challenge for the Army in the immediate future is to adjust to Australia's strategic situation following the withdrawal from Afghanistan. There are some parallels here with the adjustments that the ADF needed to make following the withdrawal from Vietnam in the early 1970s (Army in particular). The challenge that Army faces is to ensure that its ambitions for its current and future capabilities are demonstrably consistent with the priorities of the 2013 Defence White Paper (and of the eventual successor document), at a time when Defence could face austere budgets for an indefinite period. The need to make difficult choices seems unavoidable.

An issue to be addressed is the size of the Regular Army: whether Australia's strategic circumstances over the next few years really demand three full brigades, especially given the relatively short expansion times for some Army capabilities and the policy, at least of the previous government, that makes it clear that the structure of the ADF will be determined only by the first two of the Priority Tasks, 'deter and defeat armed attacks on Australia,'[20] and 'contribute to stability and security in the South Pacific and Timor-Leste'.[21] This is not to argue that the Army should be reduced in size. Rather, at the present time, the focus needs to be freeing up funds sufficient to sustain and modernise the ADF as a whole.

A similar argument applies to the Army's ambition to shift from a light infantry army to a light mechanised army, deployable by sea. The Chief of Army argues that this would lead to an Army capable of surviving against a peer competitor or a potent irregular enemy.[22] At the present time, it is difficult to see how this is consistent with strategic priorities and why the associated and significant equipment costs should be given priority in Defence's forward equipment program. There is a related concern with respect to Australia's amphibious capability, based on the two new Landing Helicopter Docks (LHDs) planned to be commissioned in 2014 and 2015. The 2013 Defence White Paper made it clear that the initial focus of this will be on 'security, stabilisation, humanitarian assistance and disaster relief tasks', but it is tempting to infer that there will be a need to resist pressures to move more quickly to 'a robust amphibious capability able to respond across the spectrum of contingencies' than strategic circumstances would justify.[23]

Government-endorsed strategic guidance has been consistent over many decades in giving priority to Australia's air combat capabilities. There are, however, some current uncertainties over the way ahead, because of technical, timing and cost issues with the Joint Strike Fighter (JSF). This aircraft has, in principle, been chosen to follow on from the F/A-18 Hornet fleet when it reaches the end of its operational life. The 2000 Defence White Paper announced that up to 100 new combat aircraft would replace both the F/A-18 and F-111 fleets, with the first aircraft entering service in 2012.[24] Clearly, this has not happened. A further complication relates to Australia's acquisition, at least as an interim measure, of twenty-four F/A-18F Super Hornets, and decision to acquire twelve specialist electronic warfare aircraft, the EA-18G *Growler* version of the Hornet.

Many advanced-capability combat aircraft encounter difficulties in their development phase, and the JSF has proved no exception. Only when the technical and cost uncertainties have been sufficiently clarified should the Australian government have made its final commitment to the JSF and the numbers to be acquired. It will be for consideration whether the costs of replacing the twenty-four

Super Hornets would be compensated by the savings resulting from the operation of only one type of advanced combat aircraft. But the decision to acquire the F/A-18-based EW *Growler* aircraft implies an expectation that both the Growlers and Super Hornets will be kept in service, and with only 72 JSFs to be acquired, at least until the Super Hornets reach the end of their time in service, in say 2030.[25]

An important observation of the 2012 Defence Force Posture Review was that Australia's changing strategic environment does not necessitate widespread changes in the location of the ADF's bases.[26] It did find, however, that there are some significant weaknesses, mostly relating to the capacity of ADF bases, facilities and training areas to support current and future capabilities, particularly in Australia's north and west, and the ADF's ability to sustain high tempo operations in northern Australia and beyond. Implementing many of the Review's recommendations would require significant investment in bases and facilities. The need to make this investment will add to the pressures on an already-stretched defence modernisation program, leading to questions about the timescales in which the upgrades will prove feasible.

Future Challenges

The biggest challenge for Defence in the long term, as also for the short term, is to ensure that there is consistency between the government's strategic ambitions and the level of defence funding that is likely to be made available. The main discussion of funding issues is discussed in Chapter 11 of this book, but the issue is sufficiently serious to be reinforced here. In the absence of significant strategic deterioration, there are compelling grounds for believing that Defence faces austere levels of funding for the indefinite future. In brief, the national economy faces years of only modest growth, there are sharp pressures on the federal budget (made more acute by the government's determination to balance the budget) and the cost of defence is rising in real terms at a rate far higher than ordinary inflation. Even without these pressures it seems that likely funding levels will not be enough to sustain the current force and simultaneously to modernise it. In brief, in the likely absence of higher levels of funding, there will have to be hard decisions to reduce the size of the ADF and its preparedness, to reduce the scope of the modernisation program (leading to a smaller and less capable ADF in the future), or to do both.

Another long-term challenge will come from the economic growth and military modernisation that can be expected from many of the countries in Australia's broader region. On the one hand, this will mean that, over time, Australia's comfortable assumptions about being able to maintain a capability edge will become increasingly challenged. It will mean that Australia will have to work harder to ensure success in operations in defence of the homeland, and that operations further afield, even within the region, will become more hazardous. On the other hand, military modernisation in the region will also give opportunities for more substance in the defence relationships that these countries have with Australia, should they want to pursue them. There could be implications here for the attention that will need to be given to interoperability and secure communications, for example. Regional developments will also mean that the operational (as opposed to political) value of potential Australian contributions to regional contingencies will diminish, as more players move towards comparable levels of capability, operated with similar levels of competence.

Technology will continue to change the nature of warfare, as it has done over countless previous generations. Science and technology at a basic level will continue to advance on a broad front, often rapidly, and often driven more by potential civil than military application: stronger, lighter and more innovative materials; faster and smaller highly-integrated electronic devices; solid-state devices that integrate a range of phenomenologies, such as electronic, optical, mechanical and biological effects; software, including advanced intelligence-like functionality; human and biological sciences; energetic materials (with application to batteries, propellants and explosives). This is not an exhaustive list but merely some of the areas in which significant advances can be expected.

It is simply not possible to give a comprehensive listing of the consequences for war-fighting, as new ways not yet thought of will be found to exploit the many opportunities that new science and technology will bring. However there are already some good indications of what might change. These areas include cyber activities (both offensive and defensive); autonomous systems (in the air, on ground, and on and under the sea); electronic warfare (which will in some respects come to resemble cyber); human performance (cognitive, physical and medical); cryptography (especially if and when quantum computing becomes operationally useful); stealth technologies (and countermeasures to them); and greater precision. Some degree of speculation is necessary here but the general thrust is clear: as always, there will be significant advances in military technology, bringing both opportunity and threat. Australia will need to know which of the advances will be the most consequential for its national security. In particular, there will likely be areas where Australia will need to develop its own capabilities to overcome the problems that arise when, for reasons of their own national security, even close allies will not make available to us the levels of capability that our strategic circumstances require. (Examples of this over recent decades have included aspects of electronic warfare, signature management and stealth technologies.)

To the extent that Australia's strategic circumstances do become more demanding—either because of a general trend or from a sharp strategic deterioration—it will become more important for Australia's defence capabilities to be closer to the leading edge, and be amenable to regular in-service updates to keep them there. This would be in contrast to the present situation where Australia's strategic circumstances often allow the country to be behind the leading edge and to acquire equipment only once many of the technical problems have been solved at the expense of the original customer. This will bring a need to review current assumptions about the best balance between procurement risk and operational risk. As always, acquiring the tried and true would bring fewer problems in the acquisition phase but would increase the risk of defeat on the battlefield. The need will be to manage procurement risk, rather than automatically to be averse to it—with the latter seeming to have been governments' preferred position over recent years.

Australia's response to more-demanding strategic circumstances would also benefit from the wider and more comprehensive application of operational research. The benefits of this would include insights which not only would lead to the more-effective development of the ADF and the conduct of operations—especially where new technologies were involved—but which would also indicate more clearly where the level of operational risk would exceed the benefits that the operations under analysis were hoped to bring. It is reassuring to see that DSTO is moving to improve the quality and relevance of its work in this area.[27]

There is also the question of independence in the review of defence capabilities. For most government portfolios, the Department of Finance (Finance) provides assessments to ministers of the costs and benefits of new policy proposals. These assessments are independent of the departments that are putting the proposals forward. Finance's capacity to do this for Defence proposals is quite limited and Defence's capacity for independent internal review has waned considerably. Given the importance of defence and its costs, there is a strong argument that proposals for defence expenditures should be subject to more independent review, not less. It is a concern that governments have not already drawn this conclusion. Further, as any increased funding that Defence might get seems unlikely to meet current ambitions, let alone any increasing demands as strategic circumstances change, the need for independent review will itself become greater, as there will be less room to accommodate poor decisions. It would be reassuring to see wider recognition of this.[28]

So far, this chapter has taken an orthodox approach to the force structure and the factors which determine its size, shape and posture. To recapitulate, there are sound reasons for taking this line: defence policy has in effect been bipartisan for the past four decades; there are good if informal indications that the new Coalition government is broadly happy with the policy content of the previous Labor government's 2013 Defence White Paper;[29] there appears to be no compelling reasons to change the *status quo*; and the financial pressures on the government and therefore on the Defence budget are so severe that arguments to spend significantly more on defence would have to be very strong for them to carry the day in a hostile cabinet room.

On this basis, we should expect a force structure and posture which are not radically different from those of today. Modernisation of the ADF will take advantage of new technologies, where the benefits and costs are consistent with the priorities of Australia's strategic circumstances. Likely examples here include long-range autonomous vehicles, greater use of stealth technologies and the ever-more-pervasive use of advanced electronics in, for example, surveillance, cooperative engagement and command support systems. There is a real prospect of a scaling back in both the size of the ADF and the scope of the modernisation program, leading to a future force smaller than currently planned and perhaps smaller than today's ADF. Preparedness levels will be constrained, but not to dangerously low levels, and no radical changes to basing will occur. All this is much more evolutionary than revolutionary.

So if there is to be a new era in Australian defence and security, its effect on the force structure is likely to be muted for some years. Yet some modest speculation is appropriate. Easiest to conjecture is that the planned rotations of US forces through Australia will lead to an increase in the preparedness of some elements of the ADF, as there will be increased opportunities and pressures for combined training. This could in turn lead to higher levels of interoperability, and to increased expectations that Australia would take part in US-led contingencies in the region and would be integrally involved in planning for them. Such contingencies could well include operations in which the antagonist was China, especially if that country were to become more aggressive in its foreign and security policies. Other chapters in this book have discussed this possibility, and the challenges it would pose for Australia's own independent foreign and security policies. Suffice it to say here that such circumstances, if sufficiently severe, would lead to pressures to increase defence spending in Australia—both to increase preparedness and to expand the ADF and other defence elements, such as intelligence. Such a turn of events would expose the lack of preparation for force expansion, especially the part that Australia's industry base would play.

In contrast to the often-overplayed prospect of strategic deterioration, Australia's strategic circumstances could well continue to be benign, with the challenge being more to manage the peace than to prepare for war. Perhaps Australia will move more quickly than seems to be the case at present towards finding 'our security in and with Asia, not against Asia'[30] (see Chapters 4 and 5). If this turns out to be so, the case for spending more on defence will be that much harder to argue, leading more assuredly to a smaller ADF at lower levels of preparedness than we have now.

Two points in conclusion. First, it is difficult to imagine

circumstances within the timescales addressed in this book in which Australia would move away from a force structure that gives priority to high-technology maritime capabilities. These reflect the realities of our strategic geography and are, at least for now, an area in which we can claim to have some kind of natural advantage. Second, it would be good if the government were to be more open with the Australian people about defence: its costs, the realities of funding and how ambitions for the force structure will have to be wound back. Perhaps a good start would be for it to treat defence more like the instrument of state policy that it is, and less like a constituency that has to be flattered and cajoled.

Further reading

Betts, Richard K, *Military Readiness*, The Brookings Institution, Washington DC, 1995.

Brabin-Smith, Richard, 'Defence and the Need for Independent Policy Analysis', *Security Challenges*, vol. 6, no. 2, 2010, pp. 9–17. www.securitychallenges.org.au/ArticlePDFs/vol6no2BrabinSmith.pdf.

Commonwealth of Australia, *Defence White Paper 2013*, Commonwealth of Australia, Canberra, 2013. www.defence.gov.au/whitepaper2013/docs/WP_2013_web.pdf.

Commonwealth of Australia, *Defence 2000: Our Future Defence Force*, Commonwealth of Australia, Canberra, 2000. www.defence.gov.au/publications/wpaper2000.pdf.

Commonwealth of Australia, *Defending Australia*, Commonwealth of Australia, Canberra, 1994. www.defence.gov.au/OSCDF/se/publications/wpaper/1994.pdf.

Commonwealth of Australia, *The Defence of Australia*, Commonwealth of Australia, Canberra, 1987. www.defence.gov.au/oscdf/se/publications/wpaper/1987.pdf.

Commonwealth of Australia, *Australian Defence*, Commonwealth of Australia, Canberra, 1976. www.defence.gov.au/oscdf/se/publications/wpaper/1976.pdf.

Dibb, Paul and Brabin-Smith, Richard, 'Australian Defence: Challenges for the New Government', *Security Challenges*, vol. 9, no. 4, 2013. www.securitychallenges.org.au/ArticlePDFs/SC9-4DibbandBrabin-Smith.pdf.

Dibb, Paul, *Review of Australia's Defence Capabilities: Report for the Minister of Defence*, Commonwealth of Australia, Canberra, 1986. www.defence.gov.au/oscdf/se/publications/defreview/1986/Review-of-Australias-Defence-Capabilities-1986_Part1.pdf.

Frühling, Stephan (ed), *A History of Australian Strategic Policy Since 1945*, Commonwealth of Australia, Canberra, 2009.

Frühling, Stephan, *Defence Planning and Uncertainty: Preparing for the Next*

Asia-Pacific War, Routledge, Abington, 2013.

Hawke, Allan and Smith, Ric, *Australian Defence Force Posture Review*, Commonwealth of Australia, Canberra, 2012. www.defence.gov.au/oscdf/adf-posture-review/docs/final/Report.pdf.

Prime Minister Hawke, Robert, 'Australia's Security in Asia', the Asia Lecture, The Asia-Australia Institute, University of New South Wales, Sydney, 24 May 1991.

Notes

1   Commonwealth of Australia, *Defence of Australia*, Commonwealth of Australia, Canberra, 1987, p 1. www.defence.gov.au/oscdf/se/publications/wpaper/1987.pdf (viewed February 2014).

2   Commonwealth of Australia, *Defence 2000: Our Future Defence Force*, Commonwealth of Australia, Canberra, 2000, p. 29. www.defence.gov.au/publications/wpaper2000.pdf (viewed February 2014).

3   Commonwealth of Australia, *Defence White Paper 2013*, Commonwealth of Australia, Canberra, 2013, p. 28. www.defence.gov.au/whitepaper2013/docs/WP_2013_web.pdf (viewed February 2014).

4   ibid., p. 28.

5   This section draws on the author's paper: R Brabin-Smith, 'Force Expansion and Warning Time', *Security Challenges*, vol. 8, no. 2, 2012, pp. 33–47. www.securitychallenges.org.au/ArticlePDFs/vol8no2BrabinSmith.pdf (viewed February 2014).

6   A useful discussion of the challenges of preparedness management will be found in R Betts, *Military Readiness*, The Brookings Institution, Washington DC, 1995. Although this book focuses on the United States, a good many of its observations are also relevant to middle powers like Australia. See Chapter 2 of this book for a detailed discussion of Australia as a middle power.

7   Commonwealth of Australia, *Defence of Australia*, 1987.

8   The phrase 'force-in-being' is notable for being useful in defence policy analysis. The term embraces whatever the current force ('today's ADF') is and future versions of the ADF towards which the current force will or might evolve. It can imply an expectation that deficiencies or excesses in the current force (that is, differences between what the current force is and what for preference it ought to be) will have become remedied.

9   Commonwealth of Australia, *Defence of Australia*, 1987, p. 30.

10 Commonwealth of Australia, *Defence White Paper 2013*, 2013, pp. 30, 44, 45.

11 Commonwealth of Australia, *Australian Defence*, Commonwealth of Australia, Canberra, 1976, p. 2. www.defence.gov.au/oscdf/se/publications/wpaper/1976.pdf (viewed February 2014).

12 Commonwealth of Australia, *Defence White Paper 2013*, 2013, p. 43.

13 P Dibb, *Review of Australian Defence Capabilities: Report for the Minister of Defence*, Commonwealth of Australia, Canberra, 1986. www.defence.gov.au/oscdf/se/publications/defreview/1986/Review-of-Australias-

Defence-Capabilities-1986_Part1.pdf (viewed February 2014).

14   ibid. See for example p. 89: 'This Review does not support more than a limited allocation of defence resources to the development of ground skills related principally to the somewhat remote prospect of large-scale land conflict in the defence of Australia.'

15   Including for joint operations.

16   Commonwealth of Australia, *Defence 2000: Our Future Defence Force*, 2000, p. 55.

17   The impressive range and payload of the F-111 aircraft, now retired from service, were also well matched to the demands of Australia's strategic geography.

18   While the 2009 and 2013 Defence White Papers were the product of the previous Labor government, it is widely understood that the new Coalition government has similar ambitions for ADF modernisation.

19   These issues are explored at greater length in P Dibb and R Brabin-Smith, 'Australian Defence: Challenges for the New Government', *Security Challenges*, vol. 9, no. 4, 2013, pp. 45–64. www.securitychallenges.org.au/ ArticlePDFs/SC9-4DibbandBrabin-Smith.pdf (viewed February 2014).

20   Commonwealth of Australia, *Defence White Paper 2013*, 2013, p. 28.

21   ibid., p. 31.

22   Lieutenant General David Morrison, Chief of Army's address to the Chief of Navy's Sea Power Conference, Sydney, 7 October 2013.

23   Commonwealth of Australia, *Defence White Paper 2013*, 2013, p. 77.

24   Commonwealth of Australia, *Defence 2000: Our Future Defence Force*, 2000, p. 87. At that time, the F-111s were expected to remain in service to between 2015 and 2020 (ibid. p. 93), but had left service by December 2010. The first Australian JSF is now expected to be delivered to the Royal Australian Air Force in the summer of 2014.

25   For a more extended discussion of air combat aircraft, see J Blackburn, 'The Future for Aerospace Forces', *Security Challenges*, vol. 9, no. 2, 2013, pp. 67–74. www.securitychallenges.org.au/ArticlePDFs/SC9-2Blackburn. pdf (viewed February 2014).

26   A Hawke and R Smith, *Australian Defence Force Posture Review*, Commonwealth of Australia, Canberra, 2012. www.defence.gov.au/oscdf/ adf-posture-review/docs/final/Report.pdf (viewed February 2014).

27   Defence Science and Technology Organisation, *Strategic Plan 2013–2018*, Commonwealth of Australia, Canberra, 2013. www.dsto.defence.gov.au/ attachments/DSTO-Strategic-Plan.pdf (viewed February 2014).

28   This topic is explored further in R Brabin-Smith, 'Defence and the Need for Independent Policy Analysis', *Security Challenges*, vol. 6, no. 2, 2010, pp. 9–17. www.securitychallenges.org.au/ArticlePDFs/ vol6no2BrabinSmith.pdf (viewed February 2014). For a more recent critique (and criticism) of Defence's processes for capability development, see: Australian National Audit Office, *Capability Development Reform*, The Auditor General, Performance Report, Audit Report no. 6, 2013–14, Performance Audit, Commonwealth of Australia, Canberra, 2013. www.anao.gov.au/~/media/Files/Audit%20

Reports/2013%202014/Audit%20Report%206/AuditReport-2013-2014_06.
pdf (viewed February 2014).

29 The informal view expressed around Canberra is that the new Coalition
    government is 'happy with the first six chapters' of the Labor
    government's 2013 Defence White Paper.

30 R Hawke, 'Australia's Security in Asia', the Asia Lecture, The Asia-Australia
    Institute, University of New South Wales, Sydney, 24 May 1991.

Appendix: ANZUS Treaty

Security Treaty between Australia, New Zealand and the United States of America [ANZUS]

(San Francisco, 1 September 1951)

Entry into force generally: 29 April 1952

THE PARTIES TO THIS TREATY,

REAFFIRMING their faith in the purposes and principles of the Charter of the United Nations and their desire to live in peace with all peoples and all Governments, and desiring to strengthen the fabric of peace in the Pacific Area, NOTING that the United States already has arrangements pursuant to which its armed forces are stationed in the Philippines, and has armed forces and administrative responsibilities in the Ryukyus, and upon the coming into force of the Japanese Peace Treaty may also station armed forces in and about Japan to assist in the preservation of peace and security in the Japan Area.

RECOGNIZING that Australia and New Zealand as members of the British Commonwealth of Nations have military obligations outside as well as within the Pacific Area, DESIRING to declare publicly and formally their sense of unity, so that no potential aggressor could be under the illusion that any of them stand alone in the Pacific Area, and DESIRING further to coordinate their efforts for collective defense for the preservation of peace and security pending the development of a more comprehensive system of regional security in the Pacific Area,

THEREFORE DECLARE AND AGREE as follows:

Article I
The Parties undertake, as set forth in the Charter of the United Nations, to settle any international disputes in which they may be involved by peaceful means in such a manner that international peace and security and justice are not endangered and to refrain in their international relations from the threat or use of force in any manner inconsistent with the purposes of the United Nations.

Article II
In order more effectively to achieve the objective of this Treaty the Parties separately and jointly by means of continuous and effective self-help and mutual aid will maintain and develop their individual and collective capacity to resist armed attack.

Article III
The Parties will consult together whenever in the opinion of any of them the territorial integrity, political independence or security of any of the Parties is threatened in the Pacific.

Article IV
Each Party recognizes that an armed attack in the Pacific Area on any of the Parties would be dangerous to its own peace and safety and declares that it would act to meet the common danger in accordance with its constitutional processes. Any such armed attack and all measures taken as a result thereof shall be immediately reported to the Security Council of the United Nations. Such measures shall be terminated when the Security Council has taken the measures necessary to restore and maintain international peace and security.

Article V

For the purpose of Article IV, an armed attack on any of the Parties is deemed to include an armed attack on the metropolitan territory of any of the Parties, or on the island territories under its jurisdiction in the Pacific or on its armed forces, public vessels or aircraft in the Pacific.

Article VI

This Treaty does not affect and shall not be interpreted as affecting in any way the rights and obligations of the Parties under the Charter of the United Nations or the responsibility of the United Nations for the maintenance of international peace and security.

Article VII

The Parties hereby establish a Council, consisting of their Foreign Ministers or their Deputies, to consider matters concerning the implementation of this Treaty. The Council should be so organized as to be able to meet at any time.

Article VIII

Pending the development of a more comprehensive system of regional security in the Pacific Area and the development by the United Nations of more effective means to maintain international peace and security, the Council, established by Article VII, is authorized to maintain a consultative relationship with States, Regional Organizations, Associations of States or other authorities in the Pacific Area in a position to further the purposes of this Treaty and to contribute to the security of that Area.

Article IX

This Treaty shall be ratified by the Parties in accordance with their respective constitutional processes. The instruments of ratification shall be deposited as soon as possible with the Government of Australia, which will notify each of the other signatories of such deposit. The Treaty shall enter into force as soon as the ratifications of the signatories have been deposited.

Article X

This Treaty shall remain in force indefinitely. Any Party may cease to be a member of the Council established by Article VII one year after notice has been given to the Government of Australia, which will inform the Governments of the other Parties of the deposit of such notice.

Article XI

This Treaty in the English language shall be deposited in the archives of the Government of Australia. Duly certified copies thereof will be transmitted by that Government to the Governments of each of the other signatories.

IN WITNESS WHEREOF the undersigned Plenipotentiaries have signed this Treaty.

DONE at the city of San Francisco this first day of September, 1951.

FOR AUSTRALIA:
[Signed:]
Percy C Spender

FOR NEW ZEALAND:
[Signed:]
CA Berendsen

FOR THE UNITED STATES OF AMERICA:
[Signed:]
Dean Acheson
John Foster Dulles
Alexander Wiley
John J Sparkman

Bibliography

AAP, 'Tony Abbott reaches out to Australia's 'best friend in Asia', Japan', *The Australian*, 10 October 2013. www.theaustralian.com.au/national-affairs/policy/tony-abbott-reaches-out-to-australias-best-friend-in-asia-japan/story-fn59nm2j-1226736508726 (viewed March 2014).

AFP, 'Clinton Stands by Japan on China Island Row', *SBS News*, 26 August 2013. www.sbs.com.au/news/article/2013/01/19/clinton-stands-japan-china-island-row.

Attorney Generals Department, *2010 Treasury Intergenerational Report*, Commonwealth of Australia, Canberra, 2010. www.archive.treasury.gov.au/igr/igr2010/report/pdf/IGR_2010.pdf.

Australian Bureau of Statistics, '3222.0—Population Projections, Australia, 2012 (base) to 2101', Australian Bureau of Statistics, Canberra, 2012. www.abs.gov.au

Australian Bureau of Statistics, 'ABS Series 3401—Overseas Arrivals and Departures, Australia, October 2013', Australian Bureau of Statistics, Canberra, 2013. www.abs.gov.au.

Australian National Audit Office, *Capability Development Reform*, The Auditor General, Performance Report, Audit Report No. 6, 2013–14, Performance Audit, Commonwealth of Australia, Canberra, 2013. www.anao.gov.au/~/media/Files/Audit%20Reports/2013%202014/Audit%20Report%206/AuditReport-2013-2014_06.pdf.

Australian Trade Commission, 'The ASEAN-Australia-New Zealand Free Trade Agreement (AANZFTA)', Commonwealth of Australia, Canberra, 2009. www.austrade.gov.au/AANZFTA.

Babbage, Ross, 'Australia Strategic Edge in 2030', *Kokoda Paper*, no. 15, 2011. www.kokodafoundation.org/resources/documents/kp15strategicedge.pdf.

Babbage, Ross, *A Coast Too Long: Defending Australia Beyond the 1990s*, Allen & Unwin, Sydney, 1990.

Babbage, Ross, *Rethinking Australia's Defence*, University of Queensland Press, St Lucia, 1980.

Ball, Desmond, 'The Strategic Essence', *Australian Journal of International Affairs*, vol. 55, no. 2, 2001, pp. 235–248.

Ball, Desmond, *A Suitable Piece of Real Estate: American Installations in Australia*, Hale & Iremonger, Sydney, 1980.

Bamford, James, *The Puzzle Palace: A Report on NSA, America's Most Secret Agency*, Houghton Mifflin, Boston, 1982.

Barker, Geoffrey, 'Turmoil as Defence Chief Exits', *Australian Financial Review*, 17 September 2012.

Barrie, Chris, 'We Need to Debate Conscription', *Sydney Morning Herald*, 4 October 2009.

Beazley, Kim, 'Operation Sandglass: Old History, Contemporary Lessons', *Security Challenges*, vol. 4, no. 3, 2008. www.securitychallenges.org.au/ArticlePDFs/vol4no3Beazley.pdf.

Behm, Allan, 'Strategic Tides: Positioning Australia's Security Policy to 2050', *Kokoda Paper*, no. 6, November 2007. www.kokodafoundation.memberlodge.com/Resources/Files/Kokoda%20Paper%206%20Strategic%20Tides_Final.pdf.

Bell, Coral, *Dependent Ally: A Study in Australian Foreign Policy*, 3rd edn., Allen & Unwin, Sydney 1993.

Bell, Coral, *Dependent Ally*, Oxford University Press, Melbourne, 1987.

Bell, Coral, (ed), *Agenda for the Eighties: Contexts of Australian Choices in Foreign and Defence Policy*, Australian National University Press, Canberra, 1980.

Bentley, Scott, 'Implications of Recent Incidents for China's Claims and Strategic Intent in the South China Sea (Part 2)', *The Strategist*, Australian Strategic Policy Institute, Canberra, 28 November 2013. www.aspistrategist.org.au/implications-of-recent-incidents-for-chinas-claims-and-strategic-intent-in-the-south-china-sea-part-2/.

Berinsky, Adam, 'Assuming the Costs of War: Events, Elites and American Public Support for Military Conflict', *The Journal of Politics*, vol. 69, no. 4, 2007, pp. 975–997.

Betts, Richard K, *Military Readiness*, The Brookings Institution, Washington DC, 1995.

Bishop, Julie, Minister for Foreign Affairs, 'China's Announcement of an Air-Defence Identification Zone over the East China Sea', Minister for Foreign Affairs, Media Release, Department of Foreign Affairs and Trade, Commonwealth of Australia, 26 November 2013. www.foreignminister.gov.au/releases/2013/jb_mr_131126a.html.

Bisley, Nick, '"An Ally for All the Years to Come"; Why Australia is Not a Conflicted US Ally', *Australian Journal of International Affairs*, vol. 67, no. 4, 2013, pp. 403–418.

Blackburn, John, 'The Future for Aerospace Forces', *Security Challenges*, vol. 9, no. 2, 2013, pp. 67–74. www.securitychallenges.org.au/ArticlePDFs/SC9-2Blackburn.pdf.

Blainey, Geoffrey, *The Tyranny of Distance: How Distance Shaped Australia's History*, Macmillan, Sydney, 2001.

Blaxland, John, *The Australian Army from Whitlam to Howard*, Cambridge University Press, Melbourne, 2013.

Blaxland, John, 'Beef, Boats and Spies: Australia's Brash Treatment of Indonesia', Australian Broadcasting Corporation, 21 November 2013. www.abc.net.au/news/2013-11-21/beef-boats-and-spies-australias-brash-treatment-of/5109520.

Blaxland, John, 'All Aboard: ADF and Regional Defence Diplomacy', in Taylor, Brendan, *A New Flank: Fresh Perspectives for the Next Defence White Paper*, no. 6, *Centre of Gravity Series*, Strategic and Defence Studies Centre, Australian National University, Canberra, April 2013. www.ips.cap.anu.edu.au/sdsc/cog/COG6_NewFlank_WEB.pdf.

Blaxland, John, 'Game-Changer in the Pacific: Surprising Options Open Up With The New Multi-Purpose Maritime Capability', *Security Challenges*, vol. 9, no. 3, 2013, pp. 31–41. www.securitychallenges.org.au/ArticlePDFs/SC9-3Blaxland.pdf.

Blaxland, John, 'Refocusing the Australian Army', *Security Challenges*, vol. 7, no. 2, 2011 pp. 47–54. www.securitychallenges.org.au/ArticlePages/vol7no2Blaxland.html.

Brabin-Smith, Richard, 'Force Expansion and Warning Time', *Security Challenges*, vol. 8, no. 2, 2012. www.securitychallenges.org.au/ArticlePDFs/vol8no2BrabinSmith.pdf.

Brabin-Smith, Richard, 'Defence and the Need for Independent Policy Analysis', *Security Challenges*, vol. 6, no. 2, 2010, pp. 9–17. www.securitychallenges.org.au/ArticlePDFs/vol6no2BrabinSmith.pdf.

Breen, Bob, *Struggling for Self Reliance*, Australian National University Press, Canberra, 2008. www.press.anu.edu.au/sdsc/sfsr/html/frames.php.

Brown, David, *Palmerston and the Politics of Foreign Policy, 1846–1855*, Manchester University Press, Manchester, 2002.

Brown, Gary; Frost, Frank; and Sherlock, Stephen, 'The Australian-Indonesian Security Agreement—Issues and Implications', *Research Paper 25 1995–1996*, Commonwealth of Australia, 1995.

Buszynski, Leszek, 'The San Francisco System: Contemporary Meaning and Challenges', *Asian Perspective*, vol. 35, 2011, pp. 315–335.

Carr, Andrew, 'Is Australia a Middle Power? A Systemic Impact Approach', *Australian Journal of International Affairs*, vol. 68, no. 1, 2014, pp. 1–15.

Carr, Andrew and Dean, Peter, 'The Funding Illusion: The 2% of GDP Furphy in Australia's Defence Debate', *Security Challenges*, vol. 9, no. 4, 2013, pp. 65–86. www.securitychallenges.org.au/ArticlePDFs/SC9-4CarrandDean.pdf.

Carr, Bob, 'Australia Indonesia Inaugural 2+2 Dialogue', Australian Government, Department of Foreign Affairs and Trade, Commonwealth of Australia, Canberra, 15 March 2012. www.foreignminister.gov.au/releases/2012/bc_mr_120315.html.

Cha, Victor D, 'Powerplay: Origins of the US Alliance System in Asia', *International Security*, vol. 34, no. 3, 2009/2010, pp. 158–196.

Cheeseman, Graeme, 'Australia: The White Experience of Fear and Dependence', in Booth, Ken and Trood, Russell (eds), *Strategic Culture in the Asia-Pacific Region*, Macmillan Press, London, 1999.

Clark, Christopher, *The Sleepwalkers: How Europe Went to War in 1914*, Penguin Books, London, 2013.

Commonwealth of Australia, *Defence White Paper 2013*, Commonwealth of Australia, Canberra, 2013. www.defence.gov.au/whitepaper2013/docs/WP_2013_web.pdf.

Commonwealth of Australia, *Strong and Secure: A Strategy for Australia's National Security*, Commonwealth of Australia, Canberra, 2013. www.dpmc.gov.au/national_security/docs/national_security_strategy.pdf.

Commonwealth of Australia, *Australia in the Asian Century*, Commonwealth of Australia, Canberra, 2012. www.asiaeducation.edu.au/verve/_resources/australia-in-the-asian-century-white-paper.pdf.

Commonwealth of Australia, *Defending Australia in the Asia Pacific Century: Force 2030*, Commonwealth of Australia, Canberra, 2009. www.defence.gov.au/whitepaper2009/docs/defence_white_paper_2009.pdf.

Commonwealth of Australia, *Inquiry into Australia's Relations with ASEAN*, Joint Standing Committee on Foreign Affairs, Commonwealth of Australia, Canberra, 2009.

Commonwealth of Australia, *Defence 2000: Our Future Defence Force*, Commonwealth of Australia, Canberra, 2000. www.defence.gov.au/publications/wpaper2000.pdf.

Commonwealth of Australia, *Defending Australia*, Commonwealth of Australia, Canberra, 1994. www.defence.gov.au/oscdf/se/publications/wpaper/1994.pdf.

Commonwealth of Australia, *Strategic Review 1993*, Commonwealth of Australia, Canberra, 1993. www.defence.gov.au/oscdf/se/publications/stratreview/1993/1993.pdf.

Commonwealth of Australia, *The Defence of Australia*, Commonwealth of Australia, Canberra, 1987. www.defence.gov.au/oscdf/se/publications/wpaper/1987.pdf.

Commonwealth of Australia, *Australian Defence*, Commonwealth of Australia, Canberra, November 1976. www.defence.gov.au/oscdf/se/publications/wpaper/1976.pdf.

Commonwealth of Australia, *The Commonwealth of Australia Constitution Act*, Commonwealth of Australia, 1900. www.austlii.edu.au/au/legis/cth/consol_act/coaca430/.

Cook, Ivan, *Australia, Indonesia and the World: Public Opinion and Foreign Policy*, Lowy Institute for International Policy, Sydney, 2006. www.lowyinstitute.org/files/pubfiles/Lowy_Institute_Poll_2006.pdf.

Cox, Lloyd and O'Connor, Brendan, 'Australia, the US, and the Vietnam and Iraq Wars: "Hound Dog" Not "Lapdog"', *Australian Journal of Political Science*, vol. 47, no. 3, June 2012, pp. 173–187.

Curran, James, *Curtin's Empire*, Cambridge University Press, New York, 2011.

Davies, Andrew and Thomson, Mark, *Strategic Choices: Defending Australia in the 21st Century*, no. 45, *APSI Strategic Insights*, Australian Strategic Policy Institute, 2008. www.aspi.org.au/publications/strategic-insights-45-strategic-choices-defending-australia-in-the-21st-century (viewed December 2013).

Dean, Peter J (ed), *Australia 1943: The Liberation of New Guinea*, Cambridge University Press, Port Melbourne, 2013.

Dean, Peter J, 'Amphibious Warfare and the Australian Defence Force', McMullen Naval History Symposium, United States Naval Academy, Annapolis, 20 September 2013.

Defence Science and Technology Organisation, *Strategic Plan 2013–2018*, Commonwealth of Australia, Canberra, 2013. http://www.dsto.defence.gov.au/attachments/DSTO-Strategic-Plan.pdf.

'Defence White Paper 2013: Special Edition', *Security Challenges*, vol. 9, no. 2, 2013. www.securitychallenges.org.au/TOCs/vol9no2.html.

Department of Defence, 'South Pacific Defence Ministers Meeting Joint Communique', Commonwealth of Australia, Canberra, 2 May 2013. http://www.minister.defence.gov.au/files/2013/05/South-Pacific-Defence-Ministers-Meeting-Joint-Communique2.pdf.

Department of Defence, *Defence Capability Plan 2012*, Commonwealth of Australia, Canberra, 2012. www.defence.gov.au/publications/CapabilityPlan2012.pdf.

Department of Defence, 'Exercise Bersama Shield 2012—Partners In Peace Enhance Regional Security', Defence Media Release, Commonwealth of Australia, Canberra, 24 April 2012. www.news.defence.gov.au/2012/04/24/exercise-bersama-shield-2012-partners-in-peace-enhance-regional-security/.

Department of Defence, *Defence Annual Report 2009–10*, Commonwealth of Australia, Canberra, 2010. www.defence.gov.au/Budget/09-10/dar/dar_0910_v1_full.pdf.

Department of Defence, *The Strategic Reform Program 2009: Delivering Force 2030*, Commonwealth of Australia, Canberra, 2009. www.defence.gov.au/publications/reformbooklet.pdf.

Department of Defence, *Defence Capability Plan 2004–2014*, Commonwealth of Australia, Canberra, 2004.

Department of Defence, *Defence Capability Review: Statement of Findings*, Defence Media Release, Commonwealth of Australia, Canberra, 142/01, 7 November 2003. www.defence.gov.au/minister/13tpl.cfm?CurrentId=3252.

Department of Defence, *Australia's Strategic Policy*, Commonwealth of Australia, Canberra, 1997. www.defence.gov.au/minister/sr97/SR97.pdf.

Department of Defence, *Future Directions for the Management of Australia's Defence: Report of the Defence Efficiency Review*, Commonwealth of Australia, Canberra, 1997. www.defence.gov.au/minister/der/report.pdf.

Department of Defence, *Force Structure Review 1991*, Commonwealth of Australia, Canberra, 1991. www.defence.gov.au/oscdf/se/publications/ForceStructureReview1991_opt.pdf

Department of Defence, *Australia's Strategic Planning in the 1990s*,

Commonwealth of Australia, Canberra, 1989. www.defence.gov.au/OSCDF/se/publications/Australias-Strategic-Planning-1990s.pdf.

Department of Defence, *Australian Defence Review*, Commonwealth of Australia, Canberra, 1972. www.defence.gov.au/oscdf/se/publications/defreview/1972/Australian-Defence-Review-1972.pdf.

Department of Defense, *National Defense Budget Estimates for FY 2014*, United States of America Department of Defense, Washington, 2013. www.comptroller.defense.gov/defbudget/fy2014/FY14_Green_Book.pdf.

Department of Defense, *Quadrenniel Defense Review Report*, United States of America Department of Defense, Washington DC, 2010. www.defense.gov/qdr/qdr%20as%20of%2029jan10%201600.pdf.

Department of External Affairs, 'No. 2 Security Treaty Between Australia, New Zealand and the USA [ANZUS]', Commonwealth of Australia, Canberra, 1997. www.dfat.gov.au/geo/new_zealand/anzus.pdf.

Department of Foreign Affairs and Trade, 'Port Moresby Declaration', 2013. www.aid.dfat.gov.au/countries/pacific/Pages/Port-Moresby-Declaration.aspx.

Department of Foreign Affairs and Trade, 'Joint Statement of Strategic Partnership Between Australia and France', 2012. www.dfat.gov.au/geo/france/joint_statement.html.

Department of Foreign Affairs and Trade, 'Pacific Partnerships for Development', 2008. www.aid.dfat.gov.au/countries/pacific/partnership/Pages/default.aspx.

Department of Foreign Affairs and Trade, 'Agreement Between the Republic of Indonesia and Australia on the Framework for Security Cooperation', 2006. www.dfat.gov.au/geo/indonesia/ind-aus-sec06.html.

Department of Foreign Affairs and Trade, 'Joint Declaration of Principles Guiding Relations Between Australia and Papua New Guinea', 1987, as amended by exchange of letters in 1992, Commonwealth of Australia, Canberra. www.dfat.gov.au/geo/png/jdpgr_aust_png.html.

Department of Foreign Affairs and Trade, '222 Agreement on Commerce Between the Commonwealth of Australia and Japan: Published Letters and Agree Minutes', Historical Publications, Commonwealth of Australia, Canberra, 1957. www.info.dfat.gov.au/info/historical/HistDocs.nsf/(LookupVolNoNumber)/20~222.

Department of Foreign Affairs and Trade, 'Regional Comprehensive Economic Partnership Negotiations'. www.dfat.gov.au/fta/rcep/.

Department of Foreign Affairs and Trade, 'Thailand Australia Free Trade Agreement', www.dfat.gov.au/fta/tafta/.

Department of Foreign Affairs and Trade, 'ASEAN Regional Forum (ARF)'. www.dfat.gov.au/arf/.

Department of Foreign Affairs and Trade, 'Agreement Between the Republic of Indonesia and Australia in the Framework for Security Cooperation', Commonwealth of Australia. www.dfat.gov.au/geo/indonesia/ind-aus-sec06.html.

Department of Foreign Affairs and Trade, 'Thailand: Smart Traveller', www.smartraveller.gov.au/zw-cgi/view/Advice/Thailand.

Department of Foreign Affairs and Trade, 'The East Asia Summit'. www.dfat. gov.au/asean/eas/.

Department of Foreign Affairs and Trade, 'Trans-Pacific Partnership Agreement Negotiations'. www.dfat.gov.au/fta/tpp/.

Department of Foreign Affairs and Trade, 'Vietnam Country Brief'. www.dfat. gov.au/geo/vietnam/vietnam_brief.html.

Dibb, Paul, 'Is Strategic Geography Relevant to Australia's Current Defence Policy?', *Australian Journal of International Affairs*, vol. 60, no. 2, June 2006, pp. 247–264.

Dibb, Paul, 'The Importance of the Inner Arc to Australian Defence Policy and Planning', *Security Challenges*, vol. 8, no. 4, 2012, pp. 13–31. www. securitychallenges.org.au/ArticlePDFs/Vol8No4Dibb.pdf.

Dibb, Paul and Brabin-Smith, Richard, 'Australian Defence: Challenges for the New Government', *Security Challenges*, vol. 9, no. 4, 2013, pp. 45–64. www. securitychallenges.org.au/ArticlePDFs/SC9-4DibbandBrabin-Smith.pdf.

Dibb, Paul, 'Why I Disagree with Hugh White on China's Rise', *The Australian*, 13 August 2012.

Dibb, Paul, 'Managing Australia's Maritime Strategy in an Era of Austerity', speech to the Chief of Navy's Sea Power Conference, Sydney, 9 October 2013.

Dibb, Paul, *Review of Australia's Defence Capabilities: Report for the Minister of Defence*, Commonwealth of Australia, Canberra, 1986. www.defence.gov. au/oscdf/se/publications/defreview/1986/Review-of-Australias-Defence-Capabilities-1986_Part1.pdf.

Dibb, Paul; Hale, David; and Prince, Peter, 'Asia's Insecurity', *Survival*, vol. 41, no. 3, 1999, pp. 5–20.

Dinnen, Sinclair, 'The Trouble with Melanesia', in Molloy, Ivan (ed), *In the Eye of the Cyclone—Issues in Pacific Security*, University of the Sunshine Coast, Sippy Downs, 2004, pp. 67–75.

Dinnen, Sinclair, *Lending a Fist? Australia's New Interventionism in the South Pacific*, State, Society and Governance in Melanesia Discussion Paper 2004/5, State, Society and Governance in Melanesia conference, Australian National University, Canberra, 2004. www.digitalcollections.anu.edu.au/ bitstream/1885/42136/2/04_05_dp_dinnen.pdf.

Dinnen, Sinclair; May, R; and Regan, AJ, *Challenging the State: The Sandline Affair in Papua New Guinea*, Research School of Pacific and Asian Studies, Australian National University, Canberra, 1997.

Dobell, Graeme, 'Labor Loses Defence, and a Secretary', *The Interpreter*, Lowy Institute for International Policy, 17 September 2012. www.lowyinterpreter. org/post/2012/09/17/Labor-loses-Defence-as-well-as-a-Secretary.aspx.

Dobell, Graeme, 'The "Arc of Instability": History of an Idea', in Huisken, Ron and Thatcher, Meredith (eds), *History as Policy: Framing the Debate on the Future of Australia's Defence Policy*, Australian National University Press, Canberra, 2004.

Dorney, Sean, *The Sandline Affair*, ABC Books, Sydney, 1998.

Downer, Alexander, 'Australia and China—Partners for Progress', speech by the Minister for Foreign Affairs and Trade, China Oration of the

Australia-China Business Council, Sydney, 1999. www.foreignminister.gov.au/speeches/1999/991125_aust_china.html.

Downer, Alexander, 'Much More Than a Middle Power', speech to the Young Liberals Convention, Liberal Party of Australia, Canberra, 8 January, 1996.

Doyle, Michael W, 'Kant, Liberal Legacies, and Foreign Affairs', *Philosophy and Public Affairs*, vol. 12, no. 3, 1983, pp. 205–235.

Drysdale, Peter, 'Australia and Japan in the Pacific and World Economy', in Drysdale, Peter and Kitaoji, Hironobu (eds), *Japan and Australia: Two Societies and their Interaction*, Australian National University Press, Canberra, 1981.

Dupont, Alan, *Australia's Security Interests in Northeast Asia*, Strategic and Defence Studies Centre, Australian National University, Canberra, 1991.

Edwards, Peter, *Crises and Commitments*, Allen & Unwin, Sydney, 1992.

Evans, Gareth and Grant, Bruce, *Australia's Foreign Relations: In the World of the 1990s*, Melbourne University Press, Carlton, 1995.

Evans, Michael, *The Tyranny of Dissonance: Australia's Strategic Culture and Way of War 1901–2005*, no. 306, *Land Warfare Studies Centre Study Paper*, Land Warfare Studies Centre, Canberra, February 2005.

Farhi, Paul, 'Elephants Are Red, Donkeys Are Blue', *Washington Post*, 2 November 2004.

Feigenbaum, Evan A and Manning, Robert A, 'A Tale of Two Asias', *Foreign Policy*, 31 October 2012. www.foreignpolicy.com/articles/2012/10/30/a_tale_of_two_asias.

FitzSimons, Peter, *Beazley: A Biography*, Harper Collins, Sydney, 1998.

Flitton, Daniel, 'Clinton Stresses US Role in Pacific Security', *Sydney Morning Herald*, 1 September 2012. www.smh.com.au/world/clinton-stresses-us-role-in-pacific-security-20120901-256sh.html.

Freedman, Lawrence, *Strategy: A History*, Oxford University Press, New York, 2013.

Fromkin, David, 'Entangling Alliances', *Foreign Affairs*, vol. 48, no. 4, July 1970.

Frost, Frank, *Australia's War in Vietnam*, Allen & Unwin, Sydney, 1987.

Frühling, Stephan, 'The 2013 Defence White Paper: Strategic Guidance Without Strategy', *Security Challenges*, vol. 9, no. 2, 2013, pp. 43–50. www.securitychallenges.org.au/ArticlePDFs/SC9-2Fruehling.pdf.

Frühling, Stephan (ed), *A History of Australian Strategic Policy Since 1945*, Commonwealth of Australia, Canberra, 2009.

Frühling, Stephan, 'Golden Window of Opportunity: A New Maritime Strategy and Force Structure for the Australian Navy', *Security Challenges*, vol. 4, no. 2, 2008. www.securitychallenges.org.au/ArticlePDFs/vol4no2Fruehling.pdf.

Fry, Greg, and Kabutaulaka, Tarcisius Tara, *Intervention and State-Building in the Pacific: The Legitimacy of 'Cooperative Intervention'*, Manchester University Press, Manchester, 2008.

Garnaut, Ross, *Dog Days: Australia After the Boom*, Redback, Melbourne, 2013.

Garnaut, Ross, 'Australia and the Northeast Asian Ascendancy: Report to the Prime Minister and the Minister for Foreign Affairs and Trade', Commonwealth of Australia, Canberra, 1989.

Gelber, Harry G, *Australian-American Relations after the Fall of Communism*, no. 304, *Strategic and Defence Studies Centre Working Paper*, Strategic and Defence Studies Centre, Australian National University, Canberra, 1996.

Glenn, Russell, *Counterinsurgency in a Test Tube: Analyzing the Success of the Regional Assistance Mission to Solomon Islands (RAMSI)*, RAND, Santa Monica, CA, 2007. www.rand.org/content/dam/rand/pubs/monographs/2007/RAND_MG551.pdf.

Goh, Evelyn, 'Institutions and the Great Power Bargain in East Asia: ASEAN's Limited "Brokerage" Role', *International Relations of the Asia Pacific*, vol. 11, 2011, pp. 373–401.

Grey, Jeffrey, *A Military History of Australia*, 3rd edn., Cambridge University Press, Melbourne, 2008.

Gyngell, Allan, *Australia and the World: Public Opinion and Foreign Policy*, Lowy Institute for International Policy, Sydney, 2007. www.lowyinstitute.org/files/pubfiles/Lowy_Poll_2007_LR.pdf.

Hanson, Fergus, *Australia in the World: Public Opinion and Foreign Policy*, Lowy Institute for International Policy, Sydney, 2012. www.lowyinstitute.org/files/lowy_poll_2012_web3.pdf.

Hanson, Fergus, *Australia and the World: Public Opinion and Foreign Policy*, Lowy Institute for International Policy, Sydney, 2011. www.lowyinstitute.org/files/pubfiles/Lowy_Poll_2011_WEB.pdf.

Hanson, Fergus, *Australia and the World: Public Opinion and Foreign Policy*, Lowy Institute for International Policy, Sydney, 2010. www.lowyinstitute.cachefly.net/files/pubfiles/LowyPoll_2010_LR_Final.pdf.

Hanson, Fergus, *Australia and the World: Public Opinion and Foreign Policy*, Lowy Institute for International Policy, Sydney, 2009. www.lowyinstitute.org/files/pubfiles/Lowy_Poll_09.pdf.

Hanson, Fergus, *Australia and the World: Public Opinion and Foreign Policy*, Lowy Institute of International Policy, Sydney, 2008. www.lowyinstitute.org/files/pubfiles/Lowy_Poll08_Web1.pdf.

Hartcher, Peter, 'China Vents its Anger at Australia's Stand on Airspace Rights', *Sydney Morning Herald*, 3 December 2013.

Hawke, Allan and Smith, Ric, *Australian Defence Force Posture Review*, Commonwealth of Australia, Canberra, 2012. www.defence.gov.au/oscdf/adf-posture-review/docs/final/Report.pdf.

Hawke, Robert, 'Australia's Security in Asia', the Asia Lecture, The Asia-Australia Institute, University of New South Wales, Sydney, 24 May 1991.

Hegarty, David and Powles, Anna, 'South Pacific Security', in Ayson, Robert and Desmond Ball (eds), *Strategy and Security in the Asia-Pacific*, Allen & Unwin, Sydney, 2007.

Henry, Iain, 'Playing Second Fiddle on the Road to INTERFET: Australia's East Timor Policy Throughout 1999', *Security Challenges*, vol. 9, no. 1, 2013, pp. 87–111. www.securitychallenges.org.au/ArticlePDFs/SC9-1Henry.pdf.

Hogan, Gary, 'Indonesia: Signs of New Thinking on Papua', *The Interpreter*, Lowy Institute for International Policy, Sydney, 1 March 2013. www.lowyinterpreter.org/post/2013/03/01/Indonesia-Signs-of-new-thinking-on-Papua.aspx.

Hogan, Gary, 'Is Papua the Next East Timor? Part II', *The Strategist*, Australian Strategic Policy Institute, 13 May 2013. www.aspistrategist.org.au/is-papua-the-next-east-timor-part-ii/.

Horner, David and Connor, John, *The Good International Citizen: Australian Peacekeeping in Asia, Africa and Europe*, vol. 3, *The Official History of Australian Peacekeeping, Humanitarian and Post-Cold War Operations*, Cambridge University Press, Melbourne, (forthcoming, 2014).

Horner, David, *Australia and the New World Order: From Peacekeeping to Peace Enforcement: 1988–1991*, vol. 2, *The Official History of Australian Peacekeeping, Humanitarian and Post-Cold War Operations*, Cambridge University Press, Melbourne, 2011.

Horner, David, 'The Higher Command Structure for Joint Operations', in Huisken, Ron and Thatcher, Meredith (eds), *History as Policy: Framing the Debate on the Future of Australia's Defence Policy*, Australian National University Press, Canberra, 2007, pp. 143–161. www.press.anu.edu.au/sdsc/hap/html/frames.php.

Horner, David, *Making the Australian Defence Force*, vol. 4, *The Australian Centenary History of Defence*, Oxford University Press, Melbourne, 2001.

Horner, David, *High Command*, Allen & Unwin, Sydney, 1992.

Howard, John, 'Reflections on the Australia-United States Alliance', speech to the United States Study Centre, University of Sydney, Sydney, 15 February 2011. www.aph.gov.au/About_Parliament/Parliamentary_Departments/Parliamentary_Library/pubs/rp/RP9596/96rp25.

iCasualties, 'Coalition Casualties: Operation Enduring Freedom'. www.icasualties.org/OEF/index.aspx.

Ignatieff, Michael, *The Warrior's Honor: Ethnic War and the Modern Conscience*, Chatto & Windus, London, 1998.

International Crisis Group, 'Stirring up the South China Sea (I)', no. 223, *Asia Report*, International Crisis Group, 2012, pp. 8–19. www.crisisgroup.org/~/media/Files/asia/north-east-asia/223-stirring-up-the-south-china-sea-i.pdf.

International Commission on Intervention and State Sovereignty, *The Responsibility to Protect: Report of the International Commission on Intervention and State Sovereignty*, International Commission on Intervention and State Sovereignty, New York, 2001. www.responsibilitytoprotect.org/ICISS%20Report.pdf.

International Institute for Strategic Studies, *The Military Balance 2013*, vol. 113, no.1, *The Military Balance*, International Institute for Strategic Studies, London, 2013.

International Monetary Fund, 'Direction of Trade Statistics'. www.elibrary-data.imf.org/.

Issenberg, Sacha, *The Victory Lab: The Secret Science of Winning Campaigns*, Crown, New York, 2012.

Jakarta Globe, 'Indonesia's Military Flexes Muscle as S. China Sea Dispute Looms', *Jakarta Globe*, 13 March 2014. http://www.thejakartaglobe.com/news/indonesia-military-flexes-muscle-s-china-sea-dispute-looms/.

Jakobson, Linda, 'China's Foreign Policy Dilemma', *Lowy Institute Analysis*,

Lowy Institute for International Policy, Sydney, February 2013. www.
lowyinstitute.org/files/jakobson_chinas_foreign_policy_dilemma_web3_
use_this.pdf.

Jakobson, Linda and Knox, Dean, *New Foreign Policy Actors in China*, no.
26, *SIPRI Policy Paper*, Stockholm International Peace Research Institute,
Stockholm, 2010. www.books.sipri.org/files/PP/SIPRIPP26.pdf.

Jentleson, Bruce W, 'The Pretty Prudent Public: Post-Vietnam American
Opinion on the Use of Force', *International Studies Quarterly*, vol. 36, no. 1,
1994, pp. 49–74.

Johnson, Chalmers, *MITI and the Japanese Miracle: The Growth of Industrial
Policy, 1925–1975*, Stanford University Press, Stanford, 1982.

Johnston, David, 'Minister for Defence: Kokoda Foundation Annual Dinner—
Rydges Hotel Canberra', speech to the Kokoda Foundation Annual Dinner,
Canberra, 31 October 2013. www.minister.defence.gov.au/2013/10/31/
minister-for-defence-kokoda-foundation-annual-dinner-rydges-hotel-
canberra/.

Joint Standing Committee on Foreign Affairs, Defence and Trade, *Inquiry Into
Australia's Relations with ASEAN*, Commonwealth of Australia, Canberra,
2009.

Jones, Justin (ed), *A Maritime School of Strategic Thought for Australia:
Perspectives*, Sea Power Centre, Canberra, 2013.

Jordaan, Eduard, 'The Concept of a Middle Power in International Relations:
Distinguishing Between Emerging and Traditional Middle Powers',
Politikon: South African Journal of Political Studies, vol. 30, no. 1, 2003, pp.
165–181.

Joye, Christopher, 'NBN Ban on Huawei Stays: Brandis', *Australian Financial
Review*, 29 October 2013.

Kaempf, Sebastian, 'US Warfare in Somalia and the Trade-Off Between
Casualty Aversion and Civilian Protection', *Small Wars and Insurgencies*,
vol. 23, no. 3, 2013, pp. 388–413.

Kagan, Robert, *Paradise and Power*, Atlantic, London, 2005.

Katz, Richard, 'Mutual Assured Production: Why Trade Will Limit
Conflict Between China and Japan', *Foreign Affairs*, July/August
2013. www.foreignaffairs.com/articles/139451/richard-katz/
mutual-assured-production.

Katz, Richard, 'Chinese-Based Assemblers Need Japanese Parts', *The Oriental
Economist*, 19 February 2013.

Katz, Richard, 'Limits to Chinese Economic Leverage, Economic Fallout from
Senkakus, Part 2', *The Oriental Economist*, 11 February 2013.

Keating, Paul, 'Asia-Australia Institute Address', Sydney, 7 April 1992, in
Ryan, Mark (ed), *Advancing Australia: The Speeches of Paul Keating, Prime
Minister*, Big Picture Publications, Sydney, 1995, pp. 187–196.

Kelly, Paul, *The March of Patriots: The Struggle for Modern Australia*,
Melbourne University Press, Carlton, 2009.

Kelton, Maryanne, *More Than An Ally? Contemporary Australia-US Relations*,
Aldershot, Ashgate, 2008.

Key, LC, 'Australia in Commonwealth and World Affairs, 1939–1944',

International Affairs, vol. 21, no. 1, 1945, pp. 60–73. www.jstor.org/ stable/3018993.

Khosa, Raspal, *Australian Defence Almanac: 2011–2012*, Australian Strategic Policy Institute, Canberra, 2011. www.aspi.org.au/publications/ australian-defence-almanac-2011-2012/12_53_35_PM_ASPI_defence_ almanac_2011_12.pdf.

Kilcullen, David J, 'Australian Statecraft: The Challenge of Aligning Policy with Strategic Culture', *Security Challenges*, vol. 3, no. 4, 2007, pp. 45–65. www. securitychallenges.org.au/ArticlePDFs/vol3no4Kilcullen.pdf.

King, Amy, *Resignation of Japanese Defence Minister Fumio Kyuma: Implications for Australia*, no. 10, *ASPI Policy Analysis*, Australian Strategic Policy Institute, Canberra, 23 July 2007. www.aspi.org.au/publications/ resignation-of-japanese-defence-minister,-fumio-kyuma-implications-for- australia-by-amy-king/Policy_analysis10.pdf.

King, Peter (ed), *Australia's Vietnam: Australia in the Second Indo-China War*, Allen & Unwin, Sydney.

Kull, Stephen and Destler, IM, *Misreading the Public: The Myth of a New Isolationism*, The Brookings Institution, Washington DC, 1999

Luttwak, Edward, 'Toward Post-Heroic Warfare', *Foreign Affairs*, May/ June 1995. www.foreignaffairs.com/articles/50977/edward-n-luttwak/ toward-post-heroic-warfare.

Lyon, Rod, 'Do Alliances Work?', *The Strategist*, Australian Strategic Policy Institute, Canberra, 19 December 2012. www.aspistrategist.org.au/ do-alliances-work/.

Mabon, David W, 'Elusive Agreements: The Pacific Pact Proposals of 1949– 1951', *Pacific Historical Review*, vol. 57, no. 2, 1988, p. 147–177.

Macmillan, Alan; Booth, Ken; and Trood, Russell, 'Strategic Culture', in Booth, Ken and Trood, Russell (eds), *Strategic Culture in the Asia-Pacific Region*, Macmillan Press, London, 1999.

Matthews, Trevor and Reid, GS, 'The Australian Bureaucracy and the Making of Foreign Policy', in Drysdale, Peter and Kitaoji, Hironobu (eds), *Japan and Australia: Two Societies and Their Interaction*, Australian National University Press, Canberra, 1981.

McAllister, Ian and Clark, Juliet, *Trends in Australian Political Opinion: Results from the Australian Election Study 1987–2007*, Australian Election Study, 2008. www.assda.anu.edu.au/aestrends.pdf.

McAllister, Ian, *Public Opinion in Australia Towards Defence, Security and Terrorism*, no. 16, *APSI Special Report*, Australian Strategic Policy Institute, Canberra 2008. www.aspi.org.au/publications/special-report-issue-16- public-opinion-in-australia-towards-defence,-security-and-terrorism/ SR16_Public_opinion.pdf.

McLean, David, 'ANZUS Historiography', American History for Australasian Schools, University of Sydney. www.anzasa.arts.usyd.edu.au/ahas/anzus_ historiography.html.

McLean, David, 'From British Colony to American Satellite? Australia and the USA During the Cold War', *Australian Journal of Politics and History*, vol. 52, no. 1, 2006, pp. 64–79.

Megalogenis, George, 'The Book of Paul: Lessons in Leadership and Paul Keating', *The Monthly*, Sydney, 2011.

Millar, Thomas Bruce, 'Strategic Studies in a Changing World', in Thatcher, Meredith and Ball, Desmond (eds), *A National Asset: Essays Commemorating the 40th Anniversary of the Strategic and Defence Studies Centre (SDSC)*, no. 165, *Canberra Papers on Strategy and Defence*, Strategic and Defence Studies Centre, Australian National University, Canberra, 2006.

Millar, Thomas Bruce, *Australia in Peace and War*, 2nd edn., Maxwell Macmillan Publishing, Sydney, 1991.

Millar, Thomas Bruce, *Australia in Peace and War*, Australian National University Press, Canberra, 1978.

Millar, Thomas Bruce, *Australia's Defence*, Melbourne University Press, Carlton, 1965.

Miller, Charles, 'Post-Heroic or Defeat Phobic? Re-Examining the Australian Public's Attitude to Military Casualties', *Australian Journal of International Affairs*, (forthcoming, 2014).

Miller, Charles, 'Endgame for the West in Afghanistan? Explaining the Decline in Support for the War in Afghanistan in the United States, Great Britain, Canada, Australia, France and Germany', PhD thesis, Strategic Studies Institute, Carlisle, PA, 2010. www.strategicstudiesinstitute.army.mil/pdffiles/pub994.pdf.

Ministry of Foreign Affairs, Republic of Korea, 'Launch of MIKTA: A Mechanism for Cooperation Between Key Middle-Power Countries', Ministry of Foreign Affairs, Republic of Korea, Seoul, 2013. www.mofa.go.kr/webmodule/htsboard/template/read/engreadboard.jsp?boardid=302&typeID=12&tableName=TYPE_ENGLISH&seqno=312809.

Ministry of Foreign Affairs of Japan, 'Japan-Australia Joint Declaration on Security Cooperation', Ministry of Foreign Affairs of Japan, Tokyo, 13 March 2007. www.mofa.go.jp/region/asia-paci/australia/joint0703.html.

Ministry of Foreign Affairs of Japan, 'The Guidelines for Japan-US Defense Cooperation', Ministry of Foreign Affairs of Japan, Tokyo, 1997. www.mofa.go.jp/mofaj/area/usa/hosho/kyoryoku.html

Morrison, Lieutenant General David, *Army News*, 2 February 2012.

Morrison, Lieutenant General David, Chief of Army's address to the Chief of Navy's Sea Power Conference, Sydney, 7 October 2013.

Mueller, John, 'Trends in Popular Support for the Wars in Korea and Vietnam', *American Political Science Review*, vol. 65, 1981, pp. 358–375.

National Nine News, 'Opposition's Military-Led Refugee Plan Slammed', National Nine News, 25 July 2013. www.news.ninemsn.com.au/national/2013/07/25/05/56/coalition-boat-policy-to-involve-military.

'Naval History and Heritage Command'. www.history.navy.mil/.

Nicholson, Brendan, 'Abbott Government Plans a Review of Defence Deals', *The Australian*, 2 December 2013.

Nelson, Brendan, 'Australia and Philippines Strengthen Defence Ties', Defence Media Release, Commonwealth of Australia, Canberra, 31 May 2007. www.defence.gov.au/minister/49tpl.cfm?CurrentId=6724.

North Atlantic Treaty Organisation, *Information on Defence Expenditures*, North Atlantic Treaty Organisation. www.nato.int/cps/en/natolive/topics_49198.htm.

O'Neill, Robert (ed), *The Defence of Australia: Fundamental New Aspects*, Strategic and Defence Studies Centre, Australian National University, Canberra, 1976.

O'Neill, Robert, *Australia in the Korean War 1950–1953: Volume 1, Strategy and Diplomacy*, Australian War Memorial and Commonwealth of Australia, Canberra, 1981.

Oliver, Alex, *Australia in the World: Public Opinion and Foreign Policy*, Lowy Institute for International Policy, Sydney, 2013. www.lowyinstitute.org/files/lowypoll2013_web_1.pdf.

Olson, Mancur and Zeckhauser, Richard, *An Economic Theory of Alliances*, RAND, Santa Monica, CA, 1966.

Palazzo, Albert, 'The Making of Strategy and the Junior Coalition Partner: Australia and the 2003 Iraq War', *Infinity Journal*, vol. 2, no. 4, 2012, pp. 27–30. www.infinityjournal.com/article/83/The_Making_of_Strategy_and_the_Junior_Coalition_Partner_Australia_and_the_2003_Iraq_War/.

Palazzo, Albert, 'The Myth that Australia "Punches Above its Weight"', in Stockings, Craig (ed), *Anzacs Dirty Dozen: 12 Myths of Australian Military History*, NewSouth Publishing, Sydney, 2012.

Palazzo, Albert, 'No Casualties Please, We're Soldiers', *Australian Army Journal*, vol. 5, no. 3, 2008, pp. 65–79.

Pemberton, Gregory, *All The Way: Australia's Road to Vietnam*, Allen & Unwin, Sydney, 1987.

Pitsuwan, Surin, opening address of the Australian National University's Southeast Asia Institute, Australian National University, Canberra, 24 October 2012.

Prime Minister's Science, Engineering and Innovation Council, *Australia and Food Security in a Changing World*, Commonwealth of Australia, Canberra, 2010. www.chiefscientist.gov.au/wp-content/uploads/FoodSecurity_web.pdf.

Prime Minister's War Conference (PWC), *Minutes of Melbourne, 1 June 1942*, National Archives of Australia, no. 1 of 8/4/42, no. (69) 14/1/43, and (no. 78 and 79 of 17/3/43), A5954 1/1, 1 June 1942.

Quinn, Andrew, 'Clinton Says China Seeks to Outflank Exxon in Papua New Guinea', Reuters, 2 March 2011. www.reuters.com/article/2011/03/02/us-china-usa-clinton-idUSTRE7215UV20110302.

Regional Assistance Mission to Solomon Islands, *People's Survey*, ANU Edge and University of The South Pacific. www.ramsi.org/solomon-islands/peoples-survey.html.

Reilly, James, 'China's Economic Statecraft: Turning Wealth Into Power', Lowy Institute for International Policy, Sydney, November 2013. www.lowyinstitute.org/files/reilly_chinas_economic_statecraft_web.pdf.

Robert, Stuart, 'Assistant Minister for Defence—ADF Launches Enhanced Workforce Model', Defence Media Release, Commonwealth of Australia, Canberra, 26 November 2013. www.minister.defence.gov.au/2013/11/26/

assistant-minister-for-defence-adf-launches-enhanced-workforce-model/.

Roberts, Chris, *ASEAN Regionalism: Co-operation, Values and Institutionalisation*, Routledge, Oxford, 2012.

Robertson, Geoffrey, *The Statute of Liberty: How Australians Can Take Back Their Rights*, Vintage, Sydney, 2009.

Rudd, Kevin, 'The Rise of the Asia Pacific and the Role of Creative Middle Power Diplomacy', speech to the Professor Bernt Seminar Series, Oslo University, Oslo, 19 May 2011. www.foreignminister.gov.au/speeches/2011/kr_sp_110519.html.

Sato, Yochiro, 'Japan-Australia Security Cooperation: Jointly Cultivating the Trust of the Community', *Asian Affairs: An American Review*, vol. 35, no. 3, 2008, pp. 152–172.

Schreer, Benjamin, 'Business as Usual? The 2013 Defence White Paper and the US Alliance', *Security Challenges*, vol. 9, no. 2, 2013, pp. 35–42. www.securitychallenges.org.au/ArticlePDFs/SC9-2Schreer.pdf.

Schreer, *Moving Beyond Ambitions? Indonesia's Military Modernisation*, APSI Strategy Paper, Australian Strategic Policy Institute, Canberra, November 2013.

Schreer, Benjamin, *Planning the Unthinkable War: 'AirSea Battle' and its Implications for Australia*, APSI Strategy Paper, Australian Strategic Policy Institute, Canberra, 2013. www.aspi.org.au/publications/planning-the-unthinkable-war-airsea-battle-and-its-implications-for-australia/Strategy_AirSea.pdf.

Shambaugh, David, 'China Engages Asia: Reshaping the Regional Order', *International Security*, vol. 29, no. 3, 2004/2005, pp. 64–99.

Shearer, Andrew and Oliver, Alex, *Diplomatic Disrepair: Rebuilding Australia's International Policy Infrastructure*, Lowy Institute for International Policy, Sydney, 2011. www.lowyinstitute.org/files/pubfiles/Oliver_and_Shearer%2C_Diplomatic_disrepair_Web.pdf.

Sheridan, Greg, 'Tokyo Rejects Security Treaty', *The Australian*, 12 March 2007. www.news.com.au/national/tokyo-rejects-security-treaty/story-e6frfkp9-1111113136781.

Smith, Stephen, 'Minister for Defence—Minister For Defence Attends Second ASEAN Defence Minister's Meeting-Plus in Brunei', Defence Media Release, Commonwealth of Australia, Canberra, 29 August 2013. www.minister.defence.gov.au/2013/08/29/minister-for-defence-minister-for-defence-attends-second-asean-defence-ministers-meeting-plus-in-brunei/.

Smith, Stephen, 'Minister for Defence—Inaugural Australia-Vietnam Defence Ministers Meeting', Defence Media Release, Commonwealth of Australia, Canberra, 19 March 2013. www.minister.defence.gov.au/2013/03/19/minister-for-defence-inaugural-australia-vietnam-defence-ministers-meeting/.

Smith, Stephen, 'Minister for Defence Stephen Smith—Minister for Defence Completes Visit to Vietnam', Defence Media Release, Commonwealth of Australia, Canberra, 31 August 2012. www.minister.defence.gov.au/2012/08/31/minister-for-defence-stephen-smith-minister-for-defence-completes-visit-to-vietnam/.

Smith, Stephen, 'Minister for Defence—Outcomes of the Kirkham Inquiry', Defence Media Release, Commonwealth of Australia, Canberra, 7 March 2012. www.minister.defence.gov.au/2012/03/07/minister-for-defence-outcomes-of-the-kirkham-inquiry/.

Smith, Stephen, 'Australia and Vietnam Deepen Defence Cooperation', Defence Media Release, Commonwealth of Australia, Canberra, 11 October 2010. www.defence.gov.au/minister/105tpl.cfm?CurrentId=10924.

Snyder, Glenn H, 'The Security Dilemma in Alliance Politics', *World Politics*, vol. 36, no. 4, 1984, pp. 461–495.

Stewart, Cameron, 'Defence White Paper Goes Down in Flames', *The Australian*, 4 May 2013.

Stockings, Craig, 'Other People's Wars', in Stockings, Craig (ed), *Anzac's Dirty Dozen: 12 Myths of Australian Military History*, NewSouth Publishing, Sydney, 2012.

Stuart, Nicholas, *Rudd's Way: November 2007–June 2010*, Scribe Publications, Melbourne, 2010.

Tange, Arthur, in P Edwards (ed), *Defence Policy-Making: A Close Up View 1950–1980—A Personal Memoir*, no. 169, *Canberra Papers on Strategy and Defence*, Australian National University Press, 2006.

Thayer, Carlyle A, 'The Five Power Defence Arrangements: The Quiet Achiever', *Security Challenges*, vol. 3, no. 1, 2007, pp. 79–96. www.securitychallenges.org.au/ArticlePDFs/vol3no1Thayer.pdf.

Thomas, Jim; Cooper, Zack and Rehman, Iskander, *Gateway to the Indo-Pacific: Australian Defense Strategy and the Future of the Australia-US Alliance*, Center for Strategic and Budgetary Assessments, Washington DC, 2013. www.csbaonline.org/publications/2013/11/gateway-to-the-indo-pacific-australian-defense-strategy-and-the-future-of-the-australia-u-s-alliance-2/.

Thompson, Alan, *Defence Down Under: Evolution and Revolution 1971–88*, no. 40, *Working Papers in Australia Studies*, Sir Robert Menzies Centre for Australian Studies, University of London, London, 1988.

Thomson, Mark, '2%—Can We, Should We, Will We?', *The Strategist*, Australian Strategic Policy Institute, Canberra, 10 September 2013. www.aspistrategist.org.au/2-percent-can-we-should-we-will-we/.

Thomson, Mark and Davies, Andrew, 'Defence', in Jennings, Peter; Thomson, Mark; Davies, Andrew; Bergin, Anthony, Bryden, Kristy; Trood, Russell; Stokes, Ryan, *Agenda for Change: Strategic Choices for the Next Government*, Australia Strategic Policy Institute, Canberra, August 2013, pp. 17–30. www.aspi.org.au/publications/agenda-for-change-strategic-choices-for-the-next-government/3_55_03_PM_Strategy_agenda_for_change.pdf.

Thomson, Mark, 'Economists and Strategists', *The Strategist*, Australian Strategic Policy Institute, Canberra, 29 April 2013. www.aspistrategist.org.au/economists-and-strategists/.

Thomson, Mark, 'Second Chance: Will They Deliver?', Defence Special Report, *The Australian*, 25 May 2013.

Thomson, Mark, 'Australia's Future Defence Spending and its Alliance with the United States', Alliance 21 Meeting, Washington DC, 28 February 2013.

www.aspi.org.au/events/alliance-21-australias-future-defence-spending-and-its-alliance-with-the-united-states.

Thomson, Mark, *The Cost of Defence: ASPI Defence Budget Brief 2013–2014*, Australian Strategic Policy Institute, Canberra, 2013. www.aspi.org.au/publications/the-cost-of-defence-aspi-defence-budget-brief-2013-2014/ASPI-CostDefence2013.pdf.

Thomson, Mark, 'Defence Funding in 2013: Means, Ends and Make Believe', *Security Challenges*, vol. 9, no. 2, 2013. www.securitychallenges.org.au/ArticlePDFs/SC9-2Thomson.pdf.

Thomson, Mark, *Trade, Investment and Australia's National Security ... Or How I Learned to Stop Worrying and Love Chinese Money*, no. 56, *ASPI Strategic Insights*, Australian Strategic Policy Institute, Canberra, 18 April 2012. www.aspi.org.au/publications/strategic-insights-56-trade,-investment-and-australias-national-security...or-how-i-learned-to-stop-worrying-and-love-chinese-money/SI56_Trade_investment_security.pdf.

Thomson, Mark, *Serving Australia: Control and Administration of the Department of Defence*, no. 41, *APSI Special Report*, Australian Strategic Policy Institute, Canberra, June 2011. www.aspi.org.au/publications/special-report-issue-41-serving-australia-control-and-administration-of-the-department-of-defence/5_28_33_PM_SR41_Serving-Australia.pdf.

Thomson, Mark, *Punching Above Our Weight: Australia as a Middle Power*, no. 18, *APSI Strategic Insights*, Australian Strategic Policy Institute, Canberra, 2005. www.aspi.org.au/publications/strategic-insights-18-punching-above-our-weight-australia-as-a-middle-power/SI_Strategic_weight.pdf.

Tow, William T, 'Alliances and Alignments in the Twenty-First Century', in Brendan Taylor, (ed), *Australia as an Asia-Pacific Regional Power: Friends in Flux?*, Routledge London, 2007.

Tow, William T, 'Deputy Sheriff or Independent Ally? Evolving Australian-American Ties in an Ambiguous World Order', *The Pacific Review*, vol. 17, no. 2, June 2004, pp. 271–290.

Trood, Russell, 'Kevin Rudd's Foreign Policy Overshoot', *Quadrant*, vol. LIV, no. 11, November 2010. www.quadrant.org.au/magazine/2010/11/kevin-rudd-s-foreign-policy-overshoot/.

Turnbull, Malcolm, Minister for Communications, speech launching *Dog Days: Australia After the Boom* by Ross Garnaut, National Press Club, Canberra, 15 November 2013. www.malcolmturnbull.com.au/media/breathing-life-back-into-australias-reform-era-launch-of-ross-garnauts-dog.

United Nations General Assembly, *A More Secure World: Our Shared Responsibility*, Report of the High-Level Panel on Threats, Challenges and Change, UN Doc. A/59/565; *In Larger Freedom: Towards Development, Security and Human Rights For All*, Report of the Secretary-General, UNGA 59th session, 21 March 2005, UN Doc. A/59/2005. www.un.org/en/peacebuilding/pdf/historical/hlp_more_secure_world.pdf.

Valentino, B, 'Poll Responses by Party ID', YouGov, Dartmouth College. www.dartmouth.edu/~benv/files/poll%20responses%20by%20party%20ID.pdf.

Vogel, Ezra, *Japan as Number One: Lessons for America*, Harvard University Press, Cambridge, MA, 1979.

Wainwright, Elsina, *Our Failing Neighbour: Australia and the Future of the Solomon Islands*, Australian Strategic Policy Institute, Canberra, 2003. www.digitalcollections.anu.edu.au/bitstream/1885/41686/3/solomons.pdf.

Wallis, Joanne, 'The Pacific: From "Arc of Instability" to "Arc of Responsibility" and Then to "Arc of Opportunity?"', *Security Challenges*, vol. 8, no. 4, 2012, pp. 1–12. www.securitychallenges.org.au/ArticlePDFs/Vol8No4Wallis.pdf.

Walt, Stephen M, 'Why Alliances Endure or Collapse', *Survival: Global Politics and Strategy*, vol. 39, no. 1, 1997, pp. 156–79. www.polsci.colorado.edu/sites/default/files/6B_Walt.pdf.

Welfield, John B, 'Australia and Japan in the Cold War', in Drysdale, Peter and Kitaoji, Hironobu (eds), *Japan and Australia: Two Societies and Their Interaction*, Australian National University Press, Canberra, 1981.

Wesley, Michael, *The Howard Paradox: Australian Diplomacy in Asia 1996–2006*, ABC Books, Sydney, 2007.

Wesley, Michael, *There Goes the Neighbourhood: Australia and the Rise of Asia*, University of New South Wales Press, Sydney, 2011.

White, Hugh, 'What Indonesia's Rise Means for Australia', *The Monthly*, June 2013. www.themonthly.com.au/issue/2013/june/1370181600/hugh-white/what-indonesia-s-rise-means-australia.

White, Hugh, *The China Choice: Why America Should Share Power*, Black Inc., Collingwood, 2012.

White, Hugh, *An Australia-Japan Alliance?*, Centre of Gravity Series, Strategic and Defence Studies Centre, Australian National University, Canberra, 2012. www.ips.cap.anu.edu.au/sites/default/files/COG4_White.pdf.

White, Hugh, 'Australia-South Pacific', in Brendan Taylor (ed), *Australia as an Asia Pacific Regional Power: Friendship in Flux?*, Routledge, Abingdon, 2007.

White, Hugh, 'Power Shift: Australia's Future Between Washington and Beijing', *Quarterly Essay*, vol. 39, September 2010.

White, Hugh, *A Focused Force: Australia's Defence Priorities in the Asian Century*, Lowy Institute for International Policy, Sydney, 2009.

Wit, Joel W; Poneman, Daniel B; Gallucci and Robert L, *Going Critical: The First North Korean Nuclear Crisis*, Brookings Institution Press, Washington DC, 2004.

World Values Survey, '1981–2008 Official Aggregate', World Values Survey Association, 2009. www.worldvaluessurvey.org.

Wuthnow, Joel, 'Decoding China's New "National Security Commission"', Center for Naval Analyses, Alexandria, 2013. www.cna.org/sites/default/files/research/CPP-2013-U-006465-Final.pdf.

Index

2nd Battalion AIF 247

3 Brigade AIF 247

11 September 2001 terrorist attacks
ANZUS Treaty invoked after 216
effects on public opinion 66, 68
engagement with US increased
after 215
Japanese response to 92
view of weak states changed by
147–148

28th Commonwealth Brigade 123

A Coast Too Long 2

abandonment issues in alliances
208

Abbott, Tony 70, 226, 263–264

Abbott Coalition government
abolishes NSA 32
border security policies 23–24
defence funding pledges 263–264
defence policies 173, 279, 298
Defence portfolios in 16
military spending by 176–177
relations with China 99–101
relations with Japan 97–98
supports US policies 225

Abe, Shinzo 97

accountability of Department of
Defence 33–34, 276–278

Aceh Province, Indonesia 113

acronyms ix–xi

Aerial Early Warning and Control
aircraft 247–248

Afghanistan, invasions of
Australia's contributions to 45,
196–197, 216–217
by Russia 67
casualties in 70–72, 74

defence spending during 259

distracts attention from maritime
strategy 172

public opinion opposed to 61

under Howard, Rudd and Gillard
23–24

age factors, support for US Alliance
and 69

aging population, implications of for
defence 271–272

Air Defence Identification Zones
99, 225

Air Operations 243, 246

Air Warfare Destroyers 248

Airborne Warning and Control
aircraft 291

alliances, understanding 207

allies, public opinions on 67–70

amphibious capabilities 244,
246–247, 294

Amphibious Force Generation cell
247

Amphibious Readiness Group 149,
247

Annual Defence Ministers'
Dialogues 127

Annual Defence Report, scrutiny
of 25

Anti-Access-Area denial ranges
(China) 199

ANZUS Treaty 206–234 *see also*
Australia–United States Alliance
perceived importance of 68
provisions of activated 18, 216–217
signing of 83
text of 304–307

Argentina, middle power status of
49–50

Armed Forces of the Philippines 125–126

Army Technical Staff Officers Course 252

ASEAN *see* Association of Southeast Asian Nations

ASEAN Defence Ministers Meeting-Plus 108–110, 130

ASEAN Institutes of Strategic and International Studies 130

ASEAN Regional Forum 89, 108, 129–130

ASEAN–Australia–New Zealand Free Trade Agreement 133

Asia *see also* Asia–Pacific; East Asia; Southeast Asia
economic dependence on 57
geostrategic change in 197–200

Asia Pacific Community project 46–47

Asia–Europe Meeting 130–131

Asian Financial Crisis 51, 112

Asia–Pacific *see also* South Pacific
defence policy regarding 196
Indo-Pacific strategic system 4
US dominance in 37–38
US reorients towards 223–224

Asia–Pacific Economic Cooperation Forum 44, 89, 110, 128–129

Association of Southeast Asian Nations (ASEAN) *see also* ASEAN…
Australian links with 108–110
bilateral ties with members of 124–131
Indonesia 'constrained' by 51
intervention in East Timor by 195
map of members 109
relations with China 131–132
support for East Timorese independence 113

asymmetrical alliances 207

Australia and the Northeast Asian Ascendancy 86

'Australia and the World' poll 62

Australia in Peace and War 38

Australia in the Asian Century White Paper 47, 94–95

Australia United States Ministerial Meeting 225

Australian Army
capabilities required 290
combat vehicles to be replaced 179, 181
expeditionary operations 6
future role 289, 293–294
size of increased under Howard 149
training priorities 252

Australian College of Defence and Strategic Studies 250

Australian Command and Staff College 251–252

Australian Constitution, defence powers and obligations in 15–16

Australian Defence 168

Australian Defence Association 23–24, 27, 34

Australian Defence College 250–253

Australian Defence Force
concentrated in southeastern Australia 192
control of 16
evolution of 5, 237–256
expanded under Howard 45
factors in shaping 5–6
financial demands on 176–177
force structure and posture 184–185, 193, 283–303
funding for 257–282, 295–296
geographical structure of 166, 196
in World Wars 187–188
inter-service rivalries 30
lacks joint force experience 168
lacks maritime strategy 172–173
officers of commanding multinational forces 225
Pacific contingents drawn down 150
personnel numbers over time 243, 260, 262, 293–294
public attitudes to 72–73
recruitment for 271–273

rising costs per unit 180–181, 266–269

rivalry with Department of Defence 169, 289

technological modernisation of 298–299

technology obtained from US 218

Australian Defence Force Academy 28, 250–251

Australian Defence Force Warfare Centre 250, 253–254

Australian Defence Industries 274

Australian Defence Review 1972: 83

Australian Election Survey 63–66

Australian Federal Police 195

Australian government *see* Commonwealth government

Australian Imperial Force 187–188

Australian Intelligence Community 290

Australian Joint Anti-Submarine School 253

Australian Joint Maritime Warfare Centre 253

Australian Joint Warfare Establishment 253

Australian Labor Party, defence policies under 22 *see also names of Labor administrations*

Australian Maritime Safety Authority 246

Australian Maritime Security Operations Centre 245

Australian Military Court 24

Australian National Commander 240

Australian National University 63, 108

Australian Signals Directorate 25, 218

Australian Strategic Policy Institute (ASPI)

  as interest group 26

  establishment of 2

  on planned growth 177

  on policymaking 95

  on public opinion 66

Australia–Philippines Defence Cooperation Program 125

Australia's Defence (Millar) *see also* Millar, TB

  as pioneering work 1

  on defence funding 257

  on defence thinking 184

  on Northeast Asia 81

  on public discussion 61

Australia's Strategic Planning in the 1990s 144–145

Australia–United States Alliance 206–234

  adaptability of 5

  changing expectations in 53

  'free-riding' on 71–72, 269–271

  implications for future conflicts 203

  obligations under 93

  potential for conflict with China 299

  provides 'capability edge' 40

  public attitudes to 67–70

  under Howard 44–46

Australia–Vietnam Defence Cooperation Senior Officials' talks 127

Babbage, Ross 2

Bali bombings 30, 66, 113, 217

Bali Process 45

Balibo, journalists killed in 112

Balikpapan landing 189

Ball, Des 27

Barratt, Paul 30

Barrie, Chris 27

Barwick, Garfield 221

Bavadra, Timoci 144

Bay Class Landing Ship Docks 154

Beazley, Kim

  as Minister for Defence 17, 44, 168–169

  on Australian vulnerability 209

Behm, Alan 221

Bell, Coral 87, 224

'Bersama Shield' exercise 123

Biketawa Declaration 148

Blainey, Geoffrey 224
Blaxland, John xiii, 4
Boer War 14, 186
border security
    ADF involvement in 194–195
    Border Protection Command
        244–245
    command structure in 23–24
    joint operations and 243
Borneo, Australian troops in
    188–189, 208
Bougainville 144–145, 152, 291
Boxer Rebellion, Australian troops
    sent to 186
Brabin-Smith, Richard xiii, 5–6
Brandis, George 101
Brazil, middle power status of 49–50
Britain *see* United Kingdom
British Commonwealth Far Eastern
    Strategic Reserve 123
Brunei, Australian military ties with
    128
'burden sharing' 227, 269–271
Burma (Myanmar) 128, 134
Bush, George W. 69, 73, 92
Bush Doctrine 217–218
Butterworth base 123, 191

Cambodia 89, 126, 194
Canada
    attitudes to military forces in 72
    Australian public feels warm
        towards 70
    'Canada Command' 246
    middle power status of 49–50
Canberra, Defence departments
    moved to 192
Cantwell, John 27
Capability and Technology
    Management Course 252
capability development 179,
    246–249
'capability edge' 40
capability output groups 277
Carr, Andrew xiii, 3
casualties, public tolerance for
    70–72, 74

Centre for Strategic and Budgetary
    Assessments 224
Changi Command and Control
    Centre 124
Cheeseman, Graeme 13
Cheonan 93
Chief of Army 294
Chief of Joint Operations 238, 277
Chief of the Defence Force
    role of 29, 277
    takes direct control of INTERFET
        240
    unable to achieve compromise
        with Defence 169
Chifley Labor government, on
    middle power status 41–42
China *see also* Northeast Asia
    Anti-Access-Area denial ranges
        198
    Australian relations with 69, 92,
        96–97, 225–226
    Australian trade with 85, 94
    changing military assessments
        of 89
    disputes with the Philippines 126
    disputes with Vietnam 88
    harasses US surveillance ship 93
    in Defence White Papers 177–178
    increased involvement in regional
        affairs 93, 96–97, 155–156,
        222–223
    Indonesian relations with 118
    influence on Cambodia 126
    military spending in 40
    potential for threat from 64–65,
        198
    potential for US conflict with 201
    relations with ASEAN nations
        131–132
    relations with Japan 98–100,
        208–209
    role in military exercises 135
    Taiwan Straits Crisis 88–89
    'wars of liberation' supported by
        81–83
Choules, HMAS 154
Citizen Military Forces 193

civil maritime security *see* maritime security

climate change, effects of 156

Clinton, Bill 128–129, 221

Clinton, Hillary 155

Coalition parties, defence policies under 22 *see also names of Coalition administrations*

Coast Too Long, A 2

Cocos Islands 224

Cold War

ANZUS Treaty motivated by 210

Australian response to 42–43, 191–192

changes after end of 86, 214–215

demobilisation halted by 259

Indonesian response to 111

public perceptions of threats during 63–66

Southeast Asian operations during 123

Collins-class submarines 290–293

colonial Australia, defence issues in 14–15

combat vehicles, replacement of 179, 181

command structure, joint services 242

Commander Australian Theatre 239–240

Commander Joint Task Force 639 245

Commander of Northern Command 245

Commander of the AST 240

Commercial Support Program 170, 274

Commonwealth government *see also* Department of Defence; *names of administrations*; Parliament

Defence portfolios in 15–19

inter-departmental committee on Japan 84

regional achievements by 40

South Pacific policies 148

Commonwealth Occupation Force 210–211

Commonwealth Strategic Reserve 190–191

communications, technological improvements in 248–249

communism *see also* Cold War

in Indonesia 111

seen as threat 42, 167, 212, 222

'concentric circles' synthesis 194, 201–202

Conference on Security and Cooperation for Asia proposals 90

conflicts of necessity 158

'Confrontation' (Indonesia/ Malaysia)

Australian involvement in 167

directed at UK 190–191

fighting in Borneo during 208

threat of expansion 193

US policy towards 221

conscription debate 20

Constitution, defence powers and obligations in 15–16

contingencies, planning for 286–287

core force concept 287

corporations, interest groups composed of 27

Cosgrove, Peter 113

Council for Security Cooperation in the Asia Pacific 130

Cox, Lloyd 216

Cui Tiankai 155

Curtin, John 209–210

Curtin Labor government 41–42, 188

Customs Department 245

Darwin, US Marines to be rotated through 118–119, 224, 299

Davies, Andrew 66

Dean, Peter J xiii–xiv, 5, 154

Defence Act 1903: 16, 24

Defence and Security Co-operation Treaty 206

Defence and Strategic Studies Course 252–253

Defence Attachés 127–128

Defence Capability Plan 179, 246–249

Defence Capability Program 177
Defence Capability Reviews 147
defence contractors, as interest
    group 27
Defence Cooperation and Status of
    Forces Agreement 153
Defence Cooperation Program 113,
    127, 143
Defence Cooperation Scholarship
    Program 125
Defence Force Posture Review 21,
    295
Defence Imagery and Geospatial
    Organisation 25
defence in depth strategy 169, 194
Defence Intelligence Organisation
    25
Defence Learning Branch 250
Defence Materiel Organisation
    as 'shared service' group 277
    establishment of 249, 275
    reform planned for 179–180, 279
Defence of Australia policy 55,
    190–194, 196–197, 213–214
Defence Procurement, review of 21
Defence Reform Program 180,
    274–275
Defence Reserve forces 287
Defence Science and Technology
    Organisation 277, 290, 298
Defence Signals Bureau 218
Defence Support Group 277
Defence Update 195
Defence White Papers see also below
    increasing frequency of 20–21
    policy principles in 284
Defence White Paper 1976
    core force concept 287–288
    on domestic defence 168
    on Japan 83
    on South Pacific 143
Defence White Paper 1987
    core force concept 287–289
    defence-in-depth policy 194
    follows Dibb Review 168–169
    on self-reliance 285
    on South Pacific 144

Defence White Paper 1994
    on domestic defence 88–89
    on Papua New Guinea 145
    on South Pacific 148
Defence White Paper 2000
    on combat aircraft 294
    on funding 259
    on margin of superiority 290
    on maritime strategy 172
    on middle power status 285
    on South Pacific 147–148
    strategic framework in 195
Defence White Paper 2008
    (Indonesia) 118
Defence White Paper 2009
    on China 19
    on domestic defence 195–196
    on funding 261, 263
    on 'hedging' strategy 223
    on modernisation 292
    on national security 40
    on Northeast Asia 94
    on South Pacific 149
    Rudd involved in 47, 195
    'strategic fantasies' 177
Defence White Paper 2013
    Abbott government adopts 298
    core force concept 287–288
    Gillard involved in 195
    launch of 24
    modernisation program 291
    on amphibious capabilities 154,
        294
    on Asia–Pacific policy 94–95
    on attitudes to Australia 155
    on balancing security and
        prosperity 95
    on funding 262
    on Indo-Pacific contingencies 54
    on maritime defence 175
    on middle power status 39
    on peacetime defence 200–201
    on PMSP 157
    on South Pacific 150
    on US Alliance 218, 223
Defence White Paper 2015 3,
    177–178, 263–264

Defending Australia 88–89
demographic trends 271–273
Department of Defence
  accountability in 33–34
  budgeting for 39–40, 66–67, 176, 179, 227–228
  civilian vs military employees 30, 279–281
  cost estimates from 298
  funding for 170–171, 257–282, 295–296
  organisational reform required in 32–33
  personnel numbers over time 260
  policy and decision making in 29–32, 165–183
  policy debates regarding 19–21
  responsible for ADMM-Plus arrangements 130
  reviews of 21
  rivalry with ADF 169, 289
  'self-reliance' goals 239
  spending patterns 179–180
  structure of 274–276
Department of Finance 284, 298
Department of Foreign Affairs and Trade 129, 284
Department of Prime Minister and Cabinet 284
Department of Trade, on Japan 84
Deployable Joint Force Headquarters 244
destroyer force 290
Dibb, Paul
  as contributor xiv, 4–5
  as defence specialist 27
  on conflicts of necessity 158
  on geography 140
  visits Japan 89
Dibb Review 90, 143–144, 168, 169
Dili harbour, secured by ADF 146–147
Dinnen, Sinclair 146
Directorate of Domestic Regional Operations 246
disaster relief, planning for 134

domestic defence, priority given to 285–286
domino theory 167
Downer, Alexander 55–56, 93
Dupont, Alan 88

EA-18G *Growler* aircraft 291, 294–295
East Asia *see also* Asia–Pacific; Northeast Asia; Southeast Asia
  military spending in 50
  trade relations with 83–84
East Asian Summit 108, 129
East China Sea 93, 99, 225
East Timor
  ADF contingent in reduced 150
  as Melanesian state 142
  ASEAN nations contribute to UN mission in 125
  Australia heads intervention force 195, 214–215, 291
  chain of command in 240
  defence policy regarding 196
  defence spending prompted by 259
  fragility of 151
  Indonesia and 110–113
  International Stabilisation Force 149
  military intervention in 22, 44–45, 68
  US policy towards 221
'Economic Asia' and 'Security Asia' 94
Economist, The 41
education and training 249–256
educational links with Southeast Asia 108
efficiency of Defence organisations 279–281
energy disruptions, as threat to Australia 65
Enhanced Cooperation Program 148–150
entrapment issues in alliances 208
European Union
  economic crises in 175

involvement in NATO 191–192
relations with Asian nations
130–131
Evans, Gareth, as Foreign Minister
44, 126
Evans, Michael 13
Evatt, Herbert 'Doc', as Foreign
Minister 42
exclusive economic zones 157

F/A-18 Super Hornets 291, 294–295
Federal Government *see*
Commonwealth government
Federation of Australia, defence
policy resulting from 14–15
Feigenbaum, Evan 94
Fiji
Australia's relations with 154–155
coups in 144, 149, 195
elections scheduled for 153–154
sanctions against 150
First Gulf War 194, 214, 216
Fisher, Andrew 187
fishing licence agreements, breaches
of 157
Fitzgibbon, Joel, as Minister for
Defence 26
Five Power Defence Arrangements
119–121, 191
Fleet Battle Staff 244
Force Communications Unit 241
Force Posture Review 173
Force Structure Review 1991:
144–145, 170
Foreign Affairs, Defence and Trade
Committee 25
foreign policy, perceived as less
important than domestic 62
'fortress Australia' mentality 43
Forum Fisheries Agency 157
Forward Air Control Development
Unit 254
forward defence policy 42, 167,
189–191, 213
France
Australian public feels warm
towards 70

focus on Polynesia 142
military commitment to New
Caledonia 153
perceived threat to Australia from
167
France, Australia and New Zealand
Agreement 153
Fraser Coalition government,
defence policies 43
Freedman, Lawrence 4
'free-riding' on US military
capabilities 71–72, 220, 269–271
Frühling, Stephan xiv, 4–5
Future Submarines program 179,
181

Gallipoli landing, special resonance
of 15
Garnaut, Ross 86
Gelber, Harry 221
General John Baker Complex 241
geography, importance of 166, 172
Germany 70, 167, 187
Gillard, Julia 223
Gillard Labor government
Defence budget cut by 47–48, 262
defence policies 19, 195, 200
Defence portfolios in 16
Defence White Paper 2013: 21,
94–95
fails to identify strategic policy 46
military interventions by 23
National Security Strategy (2013)
150
on middle power status 39
relations with Japan 97
Global Financial Crisis 67, 93,
260–261
Global Positioning System 238
global warming, as a threat to
Australia 65
Goldrick, James xv, 5
governance of defence
administration 278–279
Governor General, as nominal head
of armed forces 16
Gration, Peter 89

Growler aircraft *see* F/A-18 Super
  Hornets
Guam (Nixon) doctrine 168, 193,
  213–214, 222
Guam, US military presence in 155,
  224–225
Gulf Wars *see* First Gulf War; Second
  Gulf War

Habibie, BJ 112, 129
Hawke Labor government
  defence policies 44
  East Asian policies 86–90
  relations with Japan 89–90
Hayden, Bill 44
Headquarters Australian Theatre
  239–240
Hogan, Gary 127
Holt Coalition government, defence
  policies 43
Horner, David 237
Howard, John
  defence policies under 18
  discussions on Indonesia 129
  free trade agreement with
    Thailand 133
  increases size of army 149
  invokes ANZUS Treaty 216
  requests US support in East Timor
    221
  supports Bush Doctrine 217–218
Howard Coalition government
  Army increased in size by 149
  defence policies 44–45, 195,
    260–261
  East Timor policy 112
  military interventions by 22–23,
    216
  Northeast Asian policies 90–93
  refuses to intervene in Fiji 149
  relations with Japan 97
Hu Jintao 92
Huawei company 101
humanitarian interventions
  147–148, 154, 194
Hun Sen 126
Hurley, David 241

Impeccable, USNS 93
India, Chinese relations with 82–83,
  93
Indian Ocean, maritime security
  in 173
Indian Ocean tsunami, relations
  with Indonesia improve after 113
Indochina *see* Southeast Asia;
  Vietnam
Indonesia *see also* 'Confrontation'
  ARF field exercise in 130
  Australia's relations with 107–139
  disputes with China 131–132
  interests in Papua New Guinea
    143, 151–152
  middle power status of 49–51,
    53
  need for stability in 178
  potential role in Australian
    defence policy 54–55
  preparations for defence against
    193
  public perceives as threat 64
  US policy towards 221
Indonesian National Armed Forces
  118
Indo-Pacific strategic system 4
Integrated Area Defence System 123
intelligence services, co-operation
  with US agencies 214, 218–219,
  221
interest groups, role in Defence
  policy 26–28
International Commission
  for Non-Proliferation and
  Disarmament 46–47
international comparisons
  attitudes to military forces 72–73
  Australian attitudes to other
    countries 70
  levels of Australian investment
    226
  levels of Australian trade 85
  'middle powers' 49–52
International Force for East Timor
  (INTERFET)
  Australia leads 146

chain of command for 240
humanitarian intervention by 195
partners in 113
US backing for 214–215
International Peace Monitoring
  Team 146
International Stabilisation Force
  149
inter-service rivalries 30
investment, declining proportion of
  in budget 180
Iraq *see* First Gulf War; Second Gulf
  War
Irian Jaya *see* Papua New Guinea
Islamic nations 64–65
Israel 49–51, 269

Jaggabatra, Songkitti 113
Jakobson, Linda 97
Japan *see also* Northeast Asia
  ANZUS Treaty and 212
  Australian public feels warm
    towards 70, 74
  Australian relations with 89–91,
    97–98
  Australian trade with 82–84, 85, 94
  military spending in 40
  New Guinea and Darwin attacked
    by 185
  perceived threat to Australia from
    65, 167
  post-war security concerns over
    83
  relations with China 93, 96,
    98–100, 208–209
  South Pacific invaded by 142–143
  Southeast Asia occupied by 110
Japanese Self-Defence Forces 89, 92
Jennings, Peter 27
Jentleson, Bruce 73
Jervis Bay, HMAS 144, 145
Jindalee over-the-horizon radar 290
Johnston, David, as Minister for
  Defence 98
Joint Amphibious Capability
  Implementation Team 247
Joint Capability Authorities 246–247

Joint Capability Coordination
  Division 238
Joint Command Support
  Environment project 248
Joint Control Centre 246
Joint Declaration of Principles 145,
  147, 152
Joint Doctrine Centre 254
Joint Education, Training and
  Warfare Command 249–256
Joint Exercise Planning Staff 254
joint force, evolution of 237–256, 290
Joint Foreign Affairs/Defence
  Australia–Vietnam Strategic
  Dialogue 127
Joint Health 239
Joint Intelligence Support System
  248
Joint Logistics Group/Command
  239, 249
Joint Offshore Protection Command
  245
Joint Operations Command
  241–246, 275
Joint Project 2048: 247
Joint Services Staff College 250
Joint Standing Committee on Foreign
  Affairs Defence and Trade 25
Joint Strike Fighter program
  costs of 179
  need to source from overseas 219
  numbers of fighters 181
  questions surrounding 6, 294–295
Joint Task Force Commander 241
Jordaan, Eduand 48

Kanimbla, HMAS 145, 147, 149, 154
Keating, Paul 44, 87
Keating Labor government
  defence policies 44
  East Asian policies 86–90
  relations with Indonesia 112
  relations with Japan 90
Kelly, Paul 27
Kennedy, John F. 221
Kerdphol, Saiyud 124
Kerin, John 27

Khmer Rouge 126
Kilcullen, David 13
King, Amy xv, 4
Koike, Yuriko 98
Koizumi, Junichiro 98
Kokoda Foundation 27, 98
'Konfrontasi' see 'Confrontation'
Korean War
  as forward defence policy 167
  Australia commits to 189–190
  defence spending during 258–260
  North Korea invades south 216
  reasons for participation 216
Kuwait 194, 214 see also First Gulf
  War

Labor Party see Australian Labor
  Party, defence policies under;
  names of Labor administrations
Landing Helicopter Dock ships 147,
  174, 247, 294
Laos 127, 190
Lasswell, Harold 14
Law Enforcement Liaison Offices
  127
'lead' Services 239
Leahy, Peter 27
legislation relating to Defence 24
L'Estrange, Michael 228
Lewis, Duncan 30
Liberal Party, defence policies under
  22 see also names of Coalition
  administrations
logistics 244, 249
Lombok Treaty 113–116, 152
Lon Nol, General 126
Lowy Institute for International
  Policy 2, 26–27
Lowy Polls
  Australian warmth of feeling
    towards countries 70
  on Australia-US Alliance 68–69
  on defence spending 66
  on perceived threats to Australia
    64–66
  polls by 62–63
  support for US Alliance 226

Lyon, Rob 208

MacArthur, Douglas 188, 210
Malayan Emergency 167, 189–191
Malaysia, Australian military ties
  with 119–124, 191 see also
  'Confrontation'
Malaysian Airlines, missing plane
  from 134–135
Malta, Australian pilots sent to 191
MANIS nations 134–135
Manning, Robert 94
Manoora, HMAS 145, 147, 149, 154
Maori Wars 186
Maritime Interception Force 214
Maritime Operations 243, 246
maritime security
  importance of 168, 171–172, 200,
    289
  in South Pacific 156–157
  joint operations and 244
McAllister, Ian 73
McEwen, John 'Black Jack', as
  Minister for Trade 84
McMahon, William 84
media outlets, defence specialists
  employed by 27
Megalogenis, George 41
Melanesia 140–141, 146, 151
Melanesian Spearhead Group
  154–155
Menzies, Robert 187
Menzies Coalition government 190,
  213
Mexico, middle power status of
  49–50
MH370 aircraft lost 134–135
Micronesia 142
Middle East see Afghanistan; First
  Gulf War; Israel; Second Gulf War
middle power status 37–58, 285
migration to Australia from
  Southeast Asia 108
MIKTA power bloc 52
Millar, TB see also Australia's
  Defence
  Australia in Peace and War 38

on ANZUS Treaty 206, 212
on Australian experience of war
    11
on defence funding 257
on defence thinking 184
on joint operations 237
on Northeast Asia 81
on Papua New Guinea 140, 158
on public discussion 61
on Tange reforms 29
on the Australian people 41
Miller, Charles xv, 3–4, 28
Miller, JDB 1
Ministers for Defence portfolios
    see also Department of Defence;
    names of ministers
    legislated powers of 16
    Minister for Defence Materiel 16
    Minister for Defence Science and
        Personnel 16
    relations with Department 30
    relations with Prime Ministers
        17–18
    time spent in job by 16–17
modernisation program 181
Molan, Jim 27
Moore, John, as Minister for Defence
    30
Morris Dance operation 195
Moslem nations 64–65
multilateralism, as a 'band aid'
    solution 39
Myanmar 128, 134

Namibia, peacekeeping in 194
Natalegawa, Marty 119
National Broadband Network 101
National Party see Coalition parties,
    defence policies under
National Security Adviser 32
National Security Commission
    (China) 97
National Security Committee of
    Cabinet 18, 20
national security community,
    defence policy in 32
National Security Statements 32

National Security Strategy (2012) 223
National Security Strategy (2013) 5,
    150
Natuna Islands 118, 131–132
Ne Win, General 128
Nelson, Brendan 17
New Caledonia, independence
    referendum due in 152–153
New Guinea see Papua New Guinea
'new interventionism' policy
    147–148, 149
New Zealand see also ANZUS Treaty
    attitudes to military forces in 73
    Australian investment in 226
    Australian public feels warm
        towards 70, 74
    drastically cuts defence forces 56
    facilitates peace talks between
        PNG and Bougainville 145
    Five Power Defence Arrangements
        119
    focus on Polynesia 142
    free trade agreement with 133
    Maori Wars 186
    resumes diplomatic relations with
        Fiji 150
Nicholson, Brendan 27
Nixon (Guam) doctrine 168, 193,
    213–214, 222
No. 4 Squadron RAAF 254
No. 76 Squadron RAAF 254
'non-traditional' security threats
    65–66
North Atlantic Treaty Organization
    as central organising body 131
    Australian pilots participate in
        191
    budget allocation levels for 263
    public opposes Afghanistan
        invasion by 61
    security guarantees given by 208
North Korea see also Korean War
    attacks South Korean vessels 93
    middle power status of 51
    public perceives as threat 65
    withdraws from Nuclear
        Non-Proliferation Treaty 88

Northeast Asia 4, 81–102, 175 *see also* East Asia
northern Australia
  improving military capabilities in 178, 291, 295
  maritime strategy for 194
  surveillance and response difficult in 192
  under-resourced bases in 173
nuclear deterrence, Australia under US umbrella of 219
nuclear proliferation, perceived as a threat to Australia 65
Nuclear Security Summit 47
Nye report 91

Obama, Barack
  election of increases trust in US 69
  on Asia-Pacific policy 223
  opposes war in Iraq 62
  organises Nuclear Security Summit 47
O'Connor, Brendan 216
Office of National Assessments 284
Operation Gateway 123
operational research, need for 297–298
Oruzgan province, Afghanistan 197

Pacific Islands Forum 148, 155
Pacific Maritime Security Program 157
Pacific Partnerships for Development 150
Pacific Patrol Boat Program 157
Palazzo, Al 216, 221
Palmerston, Lord 222
Panguna mine 145
Papua New Guinea
  as Australian protectorate 142
  Australia vulnerable to attacks from 140
  Australian interests in 142–143
  commitments to 147
  Enhanced Cooperation Program 148–149
  involvement in Pacific region 154
  lost to Germany in WWI 187
  Millar's concerns over 158
  potential for instability 117, 151–152, 173–174
  self-determination movements in 144–145
  Strongim Gavman Program 150
  US policy towards 193
  Western section becomes Irian Jaya 111
Papua New Guinea Defence Force 145
Paracel Islands 93
Parliament
  addressed by foreign leaders 92, 223
  approval of not required for military intervention 24
  committee system in 25–26
  role in Defence policy 21–26
Parliamentary Joint Committee on Intelligence and Security 25
Parliamentary Secretaries for Defence 16–17
Peacekeeping Training Centre 253
People's Liberation Army (China) 135
Philippines 93, 125, 130
Pitsuwan, Surin 108
politics, defence and 11–36
Polynesia 142
Port Moresby Declaration 149–150
preparedness, spectrum of 287–288, 291
'pretty prudent public' 73–74
Prime Minister's Office, security centralised within 32
Prime Ministers, relations with Defence ministers 17–19
Principal Tasks 285–286
priorities, determining 284–285
privatisation of defence production 274
procurement procedures, reform of 279

public opinion
  attitudes to defence 32–33, 47,
    61–78
  interest groups aid in forming 28
  role in Defence policy 28–29
  support for US Alliance 226

Qarase, Laisenia 149
Quadrilateral Defence Coordinating
  Group 157
quantitative analysis 165

Ray, Robert, as Minister for Defence
  17, 170
'ready reserves' 170
refugee policy, Indonesian response
  to 115–116
Regional Assistance Mission to
  Solomon Islands
  as humanitarian intervention
    22–23
  Australian responsibility for 195
  difficulties faced by 153–154
  forces involved in 148
  remains active 151
  under Howard 45
Regional Comprehensive Economic
  Partnership 101–102, 133
Regional Security Dialogues 127
regional stabilisation activities
  195–196
Reilly, James 101
Reith, Peter, as Minister for Defence
  17
Renouf, Alan 213
Rescue Coordination Centre 246
Resolute Operation 244–245
Returned and Services League 27
*Review of Australia's Defence
  Capabilities* 90, 143–144, 168–171
Rim of the Pacific naval exercises
  225
Robb, Andrew 101
Robertson, Geoffrey 42
Romney, Mitt 69
Royal Air Force, Australia provides
  pilots for 188

Royal Australian Air Force
  air defence missile system 292
  Butterworth base 123
  capabilities required for 291
  commitment to training 253–254
  training priorities 252
Royal Australian Navy
  amphibious capabilities 149, 277
  capabilities required for 290
  commitment to training 253–254
  lobbies for replacement aircraft
    carrier 30
  South Pacific capabilities 147
  submarine fleet 292–293
  Sydney centenary of 11
  training by 250–251
Royal Brunei Armed Forces 128
Royal Malaysian Air Force 123
Royal Thai Air Force 124
Royal Thai Armed Forces 124
Rudd, Kevin
  foreign policy ambitions 46–47
  Port Moresby Declaration 150
  supports 'big Australia' 56
Rudd Labor government
  centralises national security 32
  defence policies 18–19, 195
  Defence White Paper 21, 94–95
  dysfunctional policy process 20,
    46–48
  funding issues 261
  military interventions by 23
  on middle power status 39
  relations with Japan 97
  Strategic Reform Program
    275–276
Russia *see also* Northeast Asia
  Afghanistan invaded by 67
  influence on Indonesia 111
  perceived threat to Australia from
    64–65, 167
Rwanda, humanitarian
  interventions in 194

San Francisco Alliance System 228
Sanderson, John 126
Sandline crisis 145

Santo Rebellion 144
satellite capacity 248–249
Scarborough Shoal 126
School of Land Air Warfare 253
School of Languages 250
'Sea Frontier Command' 245–246
Search and Rescue operations 246
Second AIF *see* Australian Imperial
 Force
Second Gulf War
 Australian casualties in 70–71
 Australian troops in 45, 196–197,
  216–217
 chain of command in 240
 distracts attention from maritime
  strategy 172
 Japan sends engineers to 92
 Labor opposes intervention in 22
Secretaries for Defence 17
'Security Asia' and 'Economic Asia'
 94
'self-reliance' goals 223, 239,
 284–285
Senate Estimates process 25
Senate Foreign Affairs Defence and
 Trade Committee 25–26
Senkaku/Diaoyu territorial dispute
 96, 99–100, 208–209
September 11 2001 terrorist attacks
 see 11 September 2001 terrorist
 attacks
Service Chiefs 238
Sex Discrimination Commissioner
 251
sexual harassment charges 28, 262
shared service groups 277
Sheridan, Greg 27
Shinawatra, Thaksin 133
signals intelligence, sharing 218–219
Sihanouk, Prince Norodom 126
Singapore 49–50, 70, 119–124
'Singapore Strategy' 122
Sino-Indian border war 82–83, 93
'Skype incident' 262
Smith, Stephen, as Minister for
 Defence 278
Solomon Islands *see also* Regional

Assistance Mission to Solomon
 Islands
 ADF contingent in reduced 150
 Australian involvement in 291
 conflicts in 146, 149, 153–154
 contingent remaining in 151
 military intervention in 22–23
Somalia, humanitarian
 interventions in 194
South African (Boer) War 14, 186
South Australia, defence industries
 in 27
South China Sea 118, 126, 131–132,
 174
South Korea *see also* Korean War;
 Northeast Asia
 Australian trade with 85, 94
 middle power status of 49–52
 vessels attacked by North Korea 93
South Pacific *see also* Asia–Pacific
 Australian engagement with 4,
  140–162
 defence policy regarding 196
 in ANZUS Treaty 211–212
 map of 141
 military spending in 50
 need for readiness in 173
South Pacific Community Secretariat
 157
South Pacific Defence Ministers
 meeting 158
Southeast Asia
 Allied operations against Japan
  in 188
 Australian role in security of
  54–55
 Australia's relations with 4,
  107–139
 growth and development in 198
 independent states emerge in 43,
  189
 need for readiness in 173–174
 potential for conflicts in 202
 terrorism in 45
Southeast Asia Institute 108
Southeast Asia Treaty Organisation
 113, 190, 211

Southwest Pacific *see* South Pacific

Soviet Union *see* Russia

Special Operations Command, incorporated into JOC 243

Spender, Percy, as Minister for External Affairs 83, 189

Spratly Islands 93

State governments, as interest group 27

State Oceanic Administration (China) 96

Status of Forces Agreements 119, 125

status quo, maintaining 53–54

Stewart, Cameron 27

Stirling, HMAS 224–225

Stockings, Craig 217

Strategic and Defence Studies Centre ANU 1, 27

Strategic Basis of Australian Defence Policy
   1959: on Papua New Guinea 143, 193
   1964: on US alliance 221
   1973: on South Pacific 143
   1975: on Papua New Guinea 143
   1976: on East Timor 143
   1976: on Indonesia 193

strategic culture 12–15

'strategic denial' policy 143

Strategic Operations Division/ Command 240

Strategic Partnership Agreements 153

Strategic Policy Reports 148

Strategic Reform Program 180, 275–276

Strategic Review 1993, on Northeast Asia 87–89

strategy issues 4–5, 37, 184–205

Strongim Gavman Program 150

submarine fleet 277, 290–293

Submarine Operations, incorporated into JOC 243

Submariners Association 27

Sudan War, Australian troops in 14, 186

Suharto, President 111–112

Sukarno, President 110–111

'Suman Protector' exercise 123–124

Support Command Australia 249

sustainment, reform of 279

Sydney, HMAS 225

Sydney, RAN centenary in 11

symmetrical alliances 207

Taiwan, Australian trade with 85, 94

Taiwan Straits Crisis 88–89

Tange, Arthur 166

Tange reforms 29, 274

Tarakan landing 189

Taskforce on Offshore Maritime Security 244–245

Taylor, Brendan xv–xvi, 27

technology
   increasing costs of 267
   keeping up with 296–299
   need for use of 289–290

Tentara Nasional Indonesia 118

terrorism
   perceived threat from to Australia 65
   'war' on 45, 215, 259

Thailand
   ARF field exercise in 130
   Australian links with 108
   Free Trade Agreement with 125, 133
   in UN East Timor mission 113
   military ties with 124–125, 191

The Economist 41

think tanks 26–27

Thomson, Mark xvi, 5, 101, 221 *see also* Australian Strategic Policy Institute (ASPI)

threats to Australia, public perceptions of 63–66

time factor in defence planning 286–288

Timor-Leste *see* East Timor

Tobruk, HMAS 144, 147, 149

Tonga, mission to 195

Tow, Bill 227

Townsville Peace Agreement 146

Trans-Pacific Partnership 101, 133
Treasury Department 284
Trilateral Security Dialogues 91
Trood, Russell xvi, 3
Turkey, middle power status of
    49–50
Turnbull, Malcolm 101

Ubon air base 124
United Kingdom
    assists with amphibious capacity
        247
    attitudes to military forces in 72
    Australia relies on for defence
        167, 209
    Australian contributions to
        defence of 186–188
    Australian investment in 226
    Australian public feels warm
        towards 70, 74
    commitment to Korean War
        189–190
    fails to meet alliance obligations
        208
    Five Power Defence Arrangements
        119
    in Malaya, 'Confrontation' with
        190
    military links to 185, 206
    shares signals intelligence with
        US 218
    'Singapore Strategy' 122
    switches focus to Europe 192
    withdraws military support from
        Australia 41–43
United Nations
    Act of Free Choice in Papua 111
    Assistance Mission to East Timor
        112–113
    Cambodian mission 89, 126
    East Timor mission 44–45, 146
    Evatt's influence on 42
    in Korean War 216
    peacekeeping operations
        194–195, 214
    perceived ineffectiveness of 210
    Security Council membership 89

    trust in military actions led by 74
United States see also Australia–
    United States Alliance; Guam
    (Nixon) doctrine; US Marine
    Corps
    attitudes to military forces in 72
    Australia relies on for defence
        167, 209
    Australian investment in 226
    Australian levels of trust in 73–74
    Australian opinions of 65
    Australian policy towards 53
    Australian public feels warm
        towards 70
    Australian troops provide support
        for 194
    co-operation with intelligence
        agencies of 214
    cost per active vessel 267
    defence spending in 259, 269–270
    direct investment in Australia
        226
    domestic crises in 43
    dominance in Asia 37–38, 42–43
    early defence policies 185
    East Asia policies 91, 102
    economic crises in 175
    forward defence strategy and 190
    'free-riding' allies of 71–72,
        269–271
    impact of potential withdrawal
        from Asia 54
    levels of trade with 85, 87
    Micronesian bases 142
    'middle powers' and 48
    military technology sold by 212
    nuclear deterrence policies
        219–220
    on Senkaku/Diaoyu territorial
        dispute 208–209
    perceived influence on Australian
        policy 69
    perceptions of security threats 66
    potential for conflict with China
        201
    public opinion research in 62–63
    'rebalancing' of dominance 135

re-engagement with Southeast Asia 198, 201–202, 222–224
relations with Indonesia 111–112, 118, 119
relations with North Korea 88
risks of unqualified support for 217–218
South Pacific policies 155–156
support for INTERFET 215
Taiwan Straits Crisis 88–89
technological edge held by 219
treaties with Japan 83
trust in to act responsibly 69–70
views of Australian strategic importance 224
West Papua policies 193
University of New South Wales 250
US Marine Corps
assists with amphibious capacity 247
rotation through Darwin base 118–119, 224, 299
USSR *see* Russia

Vajiralonkorn, Crown Prince 124
Vanuatu, rebellion in 144
veterans' associations, as interest group 27
Vice Chief of the Defence Force group 238, 277
Vietnam
Australian military ties with 127
Cambodia invaded by 126
Chinese disputes with 88
disputes with China 93
Vietnam Veterans Association 27
Vietnam War
as election issue 20
as forward defence policy 42, 167
Australia participates in 190–191, 212–213
defence policy after 287
defence spending during 258–260
growing public opposition to 62
perceived mandate for participation 22
reasons for participation 216

Wallis, Joanne xvi, 4
Walt, Stephan 229
War on Terror 45, 215, 259
Wedgetail aircraft 247–248
'Wellington route' 56–57
Wesley, Michael 90–92
Westminster system 16 *see also* Commonwealth government; Parliament
White, Hugh 27, 98, 147
'White Australia' policy 107
Whitlam Labor government 43, 112, 168
Wideband Global Satellite program 248–249
Wilson Review 241, 243
women, ADF attitudes to 262
Woolcott, Richard 46
World Trade Center attacks *see* 11 September 2001 terrorist attacks
World War I
Australian participation in 187
conscription debate 20
defence spending during 258
Gallipoli landing 15
reasons for participation 216
World War II
Australian participation in 187–188
defence spending during 258
Japanese advance through Pacific 142–143
Japanese occupation of Southeast Asia 110
lessons learnt from 185, 208, 253
reasons for participation 216

Xi Jinping, Chinese defence policy under 96–97

Yasukuni Shrine 98
Yeongpeong Island 93
Yudhoyono, Susilo Bambang 119